P9-BYB-823

The FACILITATOR'S FIELDBOOK

The

FACILITATOR'S FIELDBOOK

- **Step-by Step Procedures**
- **Checklists and Guidelines**
- **Samples and Templates**

Thomas Justice
David W. Jamieson, Ph.D.

AMACOM
American Management Association

New York • Atlanta • Boston • Chicago • Kansas City • San Francisco • Washington D.C.
Brussels • Mexico City • Tokyo • Toronto

This book is available at a special
discount when ordered in bulk quantities.
For information, contact Special Sales Department,
AMACOM, an imprint of AMA Publications, a division of
American Management Association,
1601 Broadway, New York, NY 10019.

This publication is designed to provide accurate and authoritative information in regard to the subject matter covered. It is sold with the understanding that the publisher is not engaged in rendering legal, accounting, or other professional service. If legal advice or other expert assistance is required, the services of a competent professional person should be sought.

Library of Congress Cataloging-in-Publication Data

Justice, Thomas.
The facilitator's fieldbook : step-by-step procedures, checklists
and guidelines, samples and templates / Thomas Justice, David
Jamieson.
p.   cm.
Includes biographical references and index.
ISBN 0-8144-7038-6
1. Teams in the workplace. 2. Group facilitation. 3. Group
relations training. 4. Group problem solving. 5. Consensus (Social
sciences) I. Jamieson, David II. Title
HD66.J87 1999
658.4'036—dc21   98–56110
                                                            CIP

© 1999 HRD Press, Inc.
All rights reserved.
Printed in the United States of America.

This publication may not be reproduced,
stored in a retrieval system,
or transmitted in whole or in part,
in any form or by any means, electronic,
mechanical, photocopying, recording, or otherwise,
without the prior written permission of AMACOM,
an imprint of AMA Publications, a division of
American Management Association,
1601 Broadway, New York, NY 10019.

Printing number

10 9 8 7

THE FACILITATOR'S FIELDBOOK
TABLE OF CONTENTS

SECTION I—PHASE I: PREPARATION

SECTION III—PHASE III: FOLLOW-UP

FACILITATOR RESOURCES

SECTION IV—SPECIAL MEETINGS

FACILITATOR RESOURCES

SECTION V—FACILITATING WITH TECHNOLOGY

PREFACE

The use of groups and teams in most aspects of organizational life has steadily risen over the past decade. The normal ups and downs of working in groups have brought elation and frustration to many, prompting an interest in learning how to help groups and teams operate effectively. Consequently, publications and workshops on teams, team development, and team facilitation have proliferated, offering an abundance of definitions and theories to choose from. The result? While some resources out there do offer solid guidance, in numerous cases this proliferation has led to oversimplifications, too many models, and unnecessary confusion.

We have written this book to clear up any confusion about one highly important topic in this age of participation: facilitation. As the domain of facilitation is helping people successfully work together in groups and teams, its art and science are not only critical to future achievements in organizations, but also integral to advancements in the societies that support those organizations. The more businesses and communities use participation, involving groups of people to plan, manage, and problem-solve, the more facilitation will play a role in their success.

CONTENTS AND ORGANIZATION

In this Fieldbook, you will discover what facilitation is and what facilitators need to do. You will find a selection of resources—procedures, guides, and samples—designed for facilitators at all levels of experience, as well as a concluding section, with an overview contributed by Eric Olson, devoted to facilitating in the "electronic age" via audio, video, and the Internet.

To keep the book's contents as user-friendly as possible, we have organized the work of facilitation into three phases, with primary tasks and outcomes for each. This three-phase model frames the scope of what facilitators need to think about and do and what skills they must develop to be effective; it also creates an organizing structure for the many facilitation resources we have included. We have tried to be fairly comprehensive in our selection of resources, supplementing the basic facilitation material with more sophisticated methods for special situations and nontraditional facilitation challenges.

We hope that by bringing clarity to the task of facilitation and providing resources for immediate use, we will expand and improve the practice of facilitation. The word *facilitate* is derived from the Latin word *facilitas,* which means easiness. While working with groups has never been, and probably will never be, completely easy, we trust that *The Facilitator's Fieldbook* will lend some quality of ease to facilitators and groups alike.

☞ **Using The Facilitator's Fieldbook**

If you are a beginner, this book will provide you with an introduction and a framework for what you need to know and do, as well as a comprehensive set of basic how-to procedures and guides that will give you the extra boost you need to begin facilitating. Variations of, and alternatives to, these basics are also included as a convenient resource for expanding your repertoire and improving your facilitation skills.

If you are a more experienced facilitator, this book will give you a conceptual framework that you can use to identify paths for continuing development. It will also equip you with procedures and guides for more challenging facilitation situations, such as new models for facilitating large and small groups and comprehensive chartering of new teams and groups.

ACKNOWLEDGMENTS

We'd like to thank:

Mike Doyle, Bill Daniels, and Warren Schmidt for igniting our interest in the subject of facilitation and "modeling the way."

Dianna Old, Dave Hetrick, Barbara Hoskins, and Scott Wimer for sharing insights from their own practices and providing helpful inputs along the way as the manuscript progressed.

Abby Deschapelles for believing in the value of process facilitation strongly enough to sponsor the development of some of our first tools.

Eric Olson for his excellent contribution to our section on facilitating with technology.

Ken Olsen, Dave Hetrick, Dathan Rush, Scott Wimer, Bill Daniels, Kathleen Swanson, and Pete Zajac for their detailed reviews and feedback on our first draft, which greatly improved subsequent versions.

We'd also like to thank the many clients and colleagues who provided us with facilitation challenges and opportunities to continually "learn by doing" and shared their leadership talent and process skills as we worked together on important matters over the years. After nearly 50 years of facilitation work, we know there are too many to mention in this space. However, we'd especially like to acknowledge:

John Corpolongo, Cathy Perri, Margaret Bergeant, Emiko Banfield, Liz Brekke, Julie Groshens, Tim McNulty, Victoria Medina, Mary Higgins, Pat Del Monico, Dave Foggerty, Milt LaPointe, Jill Gray, Gene Lenz, Jeanne Hartley, Ira Blatt, Dawn Hunter, Penny Bryan, Curt Plott, Bill Bradley, Tim Kelly, Dick Zeller, Caroline Moore, Anita

Pierce, Glenn Latham, John Copenhaver, Ed O'Leary, Cheryl Liles, Dick Kropp, Marty Martinson, Bob Sterrett, Linda Brekken, Pat Dougan, Karl Murray, Damon Dickinson, Marie Roane, Nancy Safer, Carol Valdevieso, Alysia Vanitzian, Dick Stephens, Lee McGehee, Mary Beth Pridgeon, Marianne Mathis, Larry Dyer, Lynn Baroff, Jerry Gullo, Doug Thomas, Jan Duke, Rus Kinderman, Bob Thomas, Woody Williams, Irv Margol, Walt Ross, Bob Canady, Dick Williams, and numerous ASTD leaders.

And a special thanks to Chris Hunter at HRD Press for his encouragement, support, and patience, Mary George for her outstanding editorial assistance, and Michele Anctil for her typesetting assistance.

ABOUT THE AUTHORS

Tom Justice is President of Justice & Associates in Santa Monica, California. He has been operating his own consulting firm since 1981. An organizational development practitioner who focuses his practice on process facilitation, building high performance teams, and the management of organizational change projects, Tom has served as process facilitator for more than 30 different organizations in 16 states.

He has 13 years of management experience, having served as a project director at the University of Southern California, as an educational administrator in Marin County and Santa Barbara, California, and as a training developer for the California State Department of Education. He has also conducted numerous workshops on meetings management, process facilitation, team building, effective training, and the management of organizational change. In his consulting and facilitation work, he specializes in in-depth interventions that bolster the capacity of the organization.

Tom holds an A.B. in international studies from Miami University of Ohio, a lifetime California Secondary Teaching Credential from California State University at San Francisco, an M.A. in education from California State University at Long Beach, and an Administrative Services Credential from the California State Department of Education.

Today, Tom is focusing on working with organizations to implement a model of process facilitation training that builds a long-lasting capacity within organizations for enabling groups to succeed.

David W. Jamieson, Ph.D., is President of the Jamieson Consulting Group. For nearly 30 years, he has assisted organizations on strategy, design, change, and human resource issues. He has consulted with organizations of all sizes, across varying industries and in both public and private sectors, combining his in-depth knowledge base with practical expertise in many crucial organizational areas: form-ulating strategies; designing organizations; evolving desired cultures; creating and facilitating change strategies; managing for high performance, quality, and service; creating diversity-friendly organizations; building effective teams; and developing leaders for the future.

David is highly respected as well for his work as author, speaker, leader, and educator. He co-authored the best-selling book *Managing Workforce 2000: Gaining the Diversity Advantage* (Jossey-Bass, 1991) and has published works on such organizational issues as managing workforce diversity, developing teams and team-based organizations, and organizational alignment. He is currently a member of the editorial boards for *Journal of Organizational Change Management* and *Organization Development Practitioner.* Previously, Dave served in leadership roles for many professional groups. He has served as president of the American Society for Training and Development (1984), president of the International Federation of Training and Development Organizations (1985–86), and chair of the Managerial Consultation Division of the Academy of Management (1995–96).

Dr. Jamieson received a Ph.D. in management from UCLA. He is an adjunct professor of management in the Graziadio School of Business and Management and is a visiting professor for the Graduate School of Education and Psychology at Pepperdine University where he serves as Academic Director for the doctoral program in organizational change and as a faculty member in the Master of Science in Organization Development (MSOD) program.

At present, David is focused on advancing our understanding of organization change and consultation. He divides his time between consulting in organization change, educating executives and practitioners of change, and writing to bridge knowledge and practice.

INTRODUCTION

➥ **Facilitation Overview**

➥ **Primers:**

   A. Understanding Adult Learning

   B. Understanding Group Dynamics
      and Decision Making

   C. Understanding Process
      Consultation

FACILITATION OVERVIEW

The Content

Organizations are rapidly changing and everyone's getting involved! People in organizations of all types and sizes are responding to the need for significant transformations in organizational nature and functioning. Both internal and external pressures have made such efforts a necessity. These pressures come from inside in the form of work-related values, employee dissatisfaction, workforce diversity, evolving structures, and new technology, and from the outside in the form of economic realities, competitive dynamics, regulatory influences, and market demands. They have driven a flurry of change activity in the past decade and will certainly continue to drive more change through the next.

Change efforts today are guided and shaped by lessons learned over the past 30 years of trial and error in planned organization change. Judging from the practices in most organizations today, three lessons in particular have taken hold:

1. Participation is important.
2. Teams generally perform better than individuals.
3. Process (how something is done) affects outcome (what is accomplished).

Various combinations of these three lessons have greatly influenced the entire spectrum of change methodologies, from quality circles to Total Quality Management (TQM), from work redesign to reengineering, from task forces to large system change. Today virtually all methodologies, whether tightly or loosely structured, use greater degrees of involvement up, down, and across the organization; they employ more team-based structures (both temporary and permanent); and they focus more keenly on the design of change processes.

The result? An unprecedented use of groups and teams in all shapes and sizes, structured for a variety of purposes. Generally, people work in groups to:

- Coordinate interdependent work
- Share information
- Make decisions
- Integrate multi-functional or multi-disciplined expertise
- Solve problems
- Plan for something

The groups may be temporary or permanent, large or small, intra- or inter-unit, old or new; their members may communicate face to face or via electronic networking such as the Internet. They may be called committees or task forces, councils or steering groups, project teams, cross-functional work teams, management teams, quality teams, design groups, planning groups, or department staff. Yet, no matter what a group is called or why it's been formed, *any group that has a task to accomplish can benefit from facilitation.*

With the increased use of groups, there has been an exponential growth in the need for facilitative help. Thus more and more people from all organizational levels and functions, as well as numerous external resources, are now in, or need to be in, facilitator roles. For some individuals, this will be their primary role; but for most, serving as a facilitator will be a part-time role or a new way of working with groups while remaining in their current roles.

The facilitation role is often separated from the participant and leadership roles for an important reason: Facilitation involves managing group processes and dynamics—influencing how members work together—and the nature of that responsibility calls for a high degree of neutrality about content issues and a focus on group needs. Participation and leadership require quite the opposite: an active engagement in content issues (e.g., expressing opinions, presenting arguments) and a focus on matters of the moment. A facilitator who crosses roles and engages in content issues will lose neutral ground; his or her "power" to manage and influence the group—a power given to the facilitator by members—will thus be diminished. Conversely, any participant or leader who crosses roles and tries to manage group processes will find it difficult to become fully immersed in content issues and group interaction.

Does this mean it is impossible for groups to become self-facilitative? No. With maturity and skill development, a group can balance facilitation and participation, carrying out the roles in shared or integrative ways and clarifying responsibilities should the lines get blurred. However, it takes a lot of time and effort to reach this level of functioning; most groups have a long way to go and benefit from a separate facilitator role.

The Importance of Facilitation

First, the use of groups and teams is increasingly prominent in business strategies and change efforts. ***Now we have to enable groups to succeed.*** As more and more work is done in a variety of team settings, the cost of ineffective group work soars.

Second, people working in groups have common, even natural, problems to overcome.

Everyone has experienced problems such as drifting focus, misunderstood communications, uneven participation, conflict, struggles for power and control, difficulties reaching consensus, and frustrations with obtaining commitment to follow-up action.

Finally, facilitation focuses on the design and management of processes that enable groups to succeed in their missions. Facilitation helps ensure the following:

— The right resources are in hand and are being used.
— Useful information is generated, shared, and used.
— Quality decisions are made.

— Quality decisions are implemented.

— Desired outcomes are realized.

What It Is

We define facilitation as ***enabling groups to succeed***. More specifically:

> ☞ **Facilitation is . . .**
>
> the design and management of structures and processes that help a group do its work and minimize the common problems people have working together.

Facilitation is therefore a neutral process (with respect to the content and participants) that focuses on:

- What needs to be accomplished
- Who needs to be involved
- Design, flow, and sequence of tasks
- Communication patterns, effectiveness, and completeness
- Appropriate levels of participation and the use of resources
- Group energy, momentum, and capability
- The physical and psychological environment

The work of facilitation can be framed in three phases: Preparation, Working With the Group, and Follow-Up. Each phase has intended outcomes and primary tasks as depicted in Figure 1. The work of each phase is further elaborated in the first three sections of this book through text and resources (procedures, guides, and samples.)

What Facilitators Do

Facilitators are neutral guides who take an active role in process management. It is difficult to find and develop good facilitators, for many people—particularly those in organizations—are more accustomed to being players or to being in charge. Good facilitators have a number of essential capabilities. They can:

— Effectively carry out the **core processes** of facilitation.

— Draw on certain **knowledge bases** useful to facilitation.

— Develop and exercise **fundamental skills** to better meet their responsibilities as facilitators.

— Employ **personal characteristics** that are helpful to the facilitator role.

Let's take a closer look.

FIGURE 1: Facilitation Phases

PREPARATION	GROUP WORK	FOLLOW-UP
Outcomes	**Outcomes**	**Outcomes**
1. Group organized 2. Membership determined 3. Purposes made clear 4. Roles clarified 5. Logistics planned 6. Facilitation work contract clear 7. Group, work, participants, and context understood 8. Agenda determined and communicated	1. Meeting purposes and outcomes achieved 2. Participants worked well together 3. Participants satisfied with progress 4. Meeting design effectively implemented 5. Facilitation capacity of group enhanced 6. Next steps clear 7. Effective group task and maintenance behaviors observed	1. Meeting record/outputs produced and distributed 2. Results of group work communicated to members, sponsors, and stakeholders 3. Approvals of results obtained and announced 4. Next steps carried out 5. Need for further group work determined
Primary Tasks	**Primary Tasks**	**Primary Tasks**
1. Establishing the contract for facilitation 2. Collecting information on context, work, and participants 3. Clarifying the group charter 4. Analyzing stakeholders 5. Selecting group members and group leader 6. Building agendas for meetings 7. Publishing agenda and disseminating information 8. Attending to meeting logistics	1. Creating a foundation for working together 2. Managing data generation 3. Managing analysis and interpretation of the data 4. Managing decision making 5. Managing group dynamics 6. Evaluating group process and progress 7. Closing group sessions	1. Preparing the meeting record/outputs 2. Informing and communicating with others 3. Obtaining approvals of group work 4. Monitoring interim/ implementation work 5. Identifying further needs for group work

Core Processes

Facilitators work in a variety of capacities across the phases of facilitation. However, most facilitation revolves around nine primary core processes:

1. **Analyzing information** about purposes, desired outcomes, work context, and participants to determine the best approach.

2. *Designing meetings* to enable the group to succeed at its purposes using appropriate structures, processes, and sequences.

3. *Establishing group climate, norms, and roles* with the group to help members do their work.

4. *Creating and implementing structures and processes* to accomplish tasks and meet objectives.

5. *Intervening to manage group dynamics,* to enforce norms, and to influence what members are doing or how they are doing it.

6. *Coaching/training group leaders and members* in effective behaviors.

7. *Evaluating meeting and facilitation effectiveness* to make adaptations and enhance the group's learning.

8. *Navigating decision processes* through the established organizational hierarchy or decision structure.

9. *Ensuring follow-up action* related to production and distribution of the meeting record, results, communication with stakeholders, and implementation of decisions.

Knowledge Bases

There are three basic areas of knowledge that are useful for facilitation: principles of adult learning, group dynamics and decision making, and process consultation. Basic information about these knowledge areas is included later in the Introduction, and additional resources for more in-depth understanding are provided in the "Facilitator Resources" sections of the book.

Fundamental Skills

To be effective, facilitators need certain fundamental skills, including:

- Contracting
- Designing structured activities and processes
- Listening, paraphrasing, observing, clarifying, elaborating
- Interpreting verbal and nonverbal behavior
- Confronting others
- Managing differences
- Collaborating with others
- Project management
- Meeting management
- Logistics management

In one sense, these can be seen as pre-qualifications for effective facilitation. The more specific facilitation tools presented in this book require competent execution using these basic skills.

Personal Characteristics

Finally, personal characteristics play a role in being facilitative. The characteristics that seem most effective are:

- Steadiness (Serenity—calm and centered)
- Confidence
- Assertiveness
- Openness
- Flexibility
- Authenticity
- Humility
- Optimism
- Results-oriented disposition

Being willing and able to detach oneself from, and to relinquish control of, the results of the group's work is perhaps the most significant personal challenge faced by the facilitator.

Though the process work, knowledge, skills, and personal characteristics required of the successful facilitator represent a formidable challenge, the person learning to be a facilitator should not be disheartened. Fully competent professional facilitators are continually working on all of these areas, and even the best facilitator knows there is always room for improvement. That is one reason why this book was created as a resource for both **new** and **experienced** facilitators. All of us can benefit from more clearly understanding what facilitation is; what facilitators need to do; why each phase, task, or outcome is important; and how (through procedures, guides, and samples) we can do the work of facilitation.

ABOUT THE PRIMERS

In the second half of the Introduction, we have included more information on the three areas of knowledge essential to facilitation. We refer to these as "primers" and regard them as critical corollaries to effective group facilitation. We use the word *primer* in the sense of a critical domain, the understanding of which is a prerequisite to effective facilitation. The primers are analogous to the paint an automotive body shop applies first so that the later coats of paint will properly adhere; in a similar manner, these facilitation primers are the key underpinnings of effective facilitation. Primer A covers the principles of adult learning; Primer B focuses on managing group dynamics and decision making; and Primer C discusses process consultation and how facilitators might intervene to enable groups to succeed.

PRIMER A

Understanding Adult Learning

IT IS IMPORTANT for facilitators to know how people learn because such knowledge influences the quality of facilitation, especially in these areas:

- The presentation of information
- The generation and processing of data
- The use of participant resources
- The use of different media and ways of working on group tasks

All learning involves taking in information, processing information, gaining understanding or insight, and retaining what has been learned.

In group work we are regularly generating, organizing, and analyzing data; creating solutions, alternatives, and explanations; enhancing understanding among group members; moving toward consensus; establishing commitment. For this work to be effective, learning must occur continuously. Understanding principles of adult learning helps the facilitator fulfill the critical role of designing and conducting group sessions in which learning occurs.

It is most important to remember:

➤ People learn in **different** ways.
➤ Different methods **facilitate learning** for different people.
➤ Learning in any group **will depend on the design** of the session.

LEARNING MODALITIES AND INFORMATION PROCESSING

Learning theory and brain research are more complex than can be discussed here, but there are a few basics that will help the facilitator. We begin with an old Chinese proverb, shown at the right, that is particularly relevant to understanding the differences in how people learn.

> **Chinese Proverb**
>
> *I hear and I forget.*
> *I see and I remember.*
> *I do and I understand.*

In adults there are three learning modes: **auditory**, **visual**, and **kinesthetic**. In general, people learn through all three modes; but individuals differ in their preferences for, or strengths in, each mode. You probably know some people who cannot seem to grasp a concept until they can be shown a visual representation of it and others who must try something before they can understand it. To account for these differences and to maximize the learning in your group work, it is best to involve all the modalities. That is, it is best to do the following:

- Tell members what they must learn, so they can **hear** it.
- Show members what they must learn, so they can **see** it.
- Let members try out what they must learn, so they can **do** it.

People also differ in how they **process information**. Some people need to work with the data, engage in conversation about it, and discuss what it means; others need to think about the data, listen to discussions about it, and put the pieces together in their mind. This dimension of processing information is often associated with the popular theory of personality that distinguishes between the internal (introvert) and the external (extrovert) processor.

Groups of people can differ widely in learning-mode and information-processing preferences. It is therefore helpful to learn as much about the group members as you can. However, even if you know little about your group's composition, you can assume there will be a mix of personalities and preferences, and so you should design the session using a variety of methods, with alternatives available at key points. For example, you could have small groups discuss and analyze a selection of data and, later, have members work alone on a question that prompts further data generation or interpretation.

Key Considerations When Designing or Redesigning Sessions

Always keep the following in mind when designing your sessions initially, or when redesigning as you are facilitating a session:

1. For adults, learning occurs best when it's **motivated,** not coerced or forced. **The participant's motivation comes from the context, relevance, and involvement level of the work.** The work's context needs to be clear, understood, and agreed with. Why is the work being undertaken? Does the rationale make sense? How does the work fit into the organization's bigger picture? How does it fit into participants' personal interests and jobs? The relevance to the participants thus involves a number of factors:

   - The problem-centeredness of the work
   - The need to do the work
   - Participants' judgment about the appropriateness of the tasks
   - Participants' value of the usefulness of the tasks
   - The timeliness of the work

   For participants, it's important that a task (or whatever they are doing) be guided by their needs, objectives, and preferences. Their involvement is essential if they are to direct, or at least influence, the what and the how of the work.

2. For adults, learning occurs best when it is conducted as a **partnership.** The facilitator's work with the group, and participants' work with one another, must be a partnership to which each party brings resources and expectations. There is give and take. Direction, approach, and methods are negotiable. There needs to be an ongoing "contracting" concerning what, how, and why.

3. For adults, learning occurs best when it involves their **primary learning mode and is interactive and experiential.** They need to stay engaged, use their senses, and utilize their knowledge and skills. They need to be listening, talking, doing, watching, moving, or reading. Some may need to "try" or "apply" what is being worked on, or they may need a smaller group to interact with or question.

4. For adults, learning occurs best when there is **an understandable structure and reinforcement.** It helps most people to see the whole and the parts, to know where they are going and where they have been. New ideas, new ways of thinking, and new skills all need continuous and consistent reinforcement both within and outside the learning environment.

5. Learning occurs best when people's **attention and energy stay engaged and focused,** and that is usually impossible if people feel uncomfortable in their surroundings. Even if they are motivated to learn and the learning mode, level of interaction, and reinforcements are right, adults will not learn well unless their physical surroundings are pleasant and their psychological environment feels safe. The rule is: Discomfort is distracting and saps energy.

   Thus to keep participants' attention and energy focused on the task at hand, you must ensure that there is a high measure of physical comfort—surroundings with enough space, moderate temperature, good lighting, and so forth—as well as psychological comfort—an open environment in which people feel they can contribute ideas and express their feelings freely, without worry of disapproval and personal attacks. This comfort and freedom furthers everyone's learning; energy levels stay high as people focus on the work rather than wane as people struggle with discomforts and psychological barriers.

These five considerations for adult learning are crucial not only because they help facilitators design sessions but also because they can be useful for diagnosing what is wrong in a flat or hostile group.

Putting Your Understanding of Adult Learning Into Practice

You can use your knowledge of adult learning in many ways, for many facilitation purposes. Keep these suggestions in mind:

- Know what you are trying to accomplish and the group you are trying to accomplish it with. Consider the various options for designing their work, and choose the path (learning mode) that will enable them to succeed.

- Discuss the context and charter up front. Have people talk about what it means for the organization and for them.

- Try to use all learning modes when groups are together for more than a few hours.

- Be sure all of the logistics and physical environmental needs are taken care of.

- Review and discuss the agenda, get participant input, and ask for agreement.

- Talk about the group's work in macro and micro terms. For example, mention how their work fits into the bigger organizational picture; also talk about the smaller, specific tasks they are currently undertaking. Try to keep both views open to the group at all times.

- As you work with the group, clarify what you are doing or will be doing next. Ask for their input or questions, and ask for their acceptance and agreement ("contract").

- Design with optional methods in mind for certain parts of session; then, when facilitating, give the group members a choice when you come to those parts.

- Watch the amount of time between breaks, how breaks are used, and the length of time participants remain in any one learning mode. Try to create periodic movement. Suggest ways to use breaks to refresh and renew.

- Attend to the psychological environment if people are flat, cautious, or holding back. Ask why.

- Build in ways for group members to share what they know, to interact with each other, and to utilize their skills.

- Build reinforcement into the design by using progress reviews, summaries of key data or decisions, follow-up steps, and repetition of key ideas, words, or phrases.

- Use a group memory to visually capture key information that is provided verbally.

PRIMER B

Understanding Group Dynamics and Decision Making

ONE KEY ROLE of the facilitator is to identify the dynamics that develop when people interact with one another and to help groups manage those dynamics. The comprehensive study of group dynamics is a complex, scholarly undertaking; yet it is not necessary to become a social psychologist to get a handle on the types of group dynamics that are relevant to facilitation. Those types, which we will cover in Primer B, include the following:

1. Stages of group development
2. Development of group roles
3. Psychosocial issues (individual and interpersonal needs)
4. Task progress
5. Leadership
6. Communication patterns
7. Participation
8. Conflict management
9. Decision-making processes

When you are working with groups, your understanding of such dynamics becomes a crucial element in your ability to facilitate effectively.

Group dynamics are important because they drive the group processes and, in turn, the task work. Dysfunctional dynamics have a negative impact on group members, hindering their ability to work together, and undermine the facilitator's best efforts to create a comfortable, productive work climate (open, trusting, safe) and to help members progress through their task work (content, agenda, outcomes).

THE NINE TYPES OF GROUP DYNAMICS

1. Stages of Group Development

Groups commonly pass through various stages as their members work together. These stages are generally sequential, with some overlapping. Sometimes groups will "recycle," going back through a previous stage that was left incomplete. The stages relate to both the task maturity of the group as it progresses toward completing its work and the psychosocial maturity of the group as individual or interpersonal needs are resolved.

One popular theory of group development describes these stages in terms of forming, storming, norming, and performing (Tuckman, 1965). Groups begin by members getting to know one another, getting clear about why they are there, getting organized to work, and integrating individuals into the group. Invariably, they face differences and "storm" with one another. These differences might be about "what," "how," "who," or "when" questions. They may be related to issues of power and inclusion, such as who is in charge or who is included, how the group will operate (norms), and how close or personal people will be with one another (Schutz, 1967). Differences also may be related to members' histories with one another or their general attitudes toward group work.

In short, certain assumptions, beliefs, conclusions, and expectations are held by each member about other members, the work itself, and the organization(s) within which they are working. As the issues get resolved and the "storms" subside, groups generally establish agreements on roles, leadership, work methods, timelines, and operating norms, thereby creating their working climate. They are now really ready to perform—to do the work they are chartered to do.

The stages are predictable and inevitable to some extent for every group. They can go quickly or seemingly take forever. The composition, personalities, and maturity of the members play a role, as does the complexity of the task. Each stage has outcomes. If stages are skipped or not completed, the group will likely return to an earlier stage before finishing its work (or may get "stuck" and not be able to finish as a group).

We can also approach group development by breaking it down into five stages:

1. **Polite** (Initial impressions, getting to know one another)
2. **Goal** (Why we're here, what we're going to do)
3. **Power** (Leadership, role, influence)
4. **Work** (Getting the job done)
5. **Esprit** (Rewarding, celebrating, morale)

Productive work requires that the group first deal with the early stages (Polite, Goal, and Power) of group development and not have unresolved issues cluttering the group's task work. Through careful design, you can accelerate the first three stages, enabling the group to address the inherent issues and move through them more quickly.

2. Development of Group Roles

Every group requires two kinds of behavior in order to complete its task and survive as a group. These are referred to as **task and maintenance behaviors** (see Benne and Sheats, 1948). Both are needed and should be appropriately balanced if the group is to realize its potential and successfully complete its work.

Task behaviors help the group define and accomplish its work and reach its desired outcomes. They include:

- Initiating, proposing, or suggesting
- Building on or elaborating
- Coordinating or integrating
- Seeking information or opinions
- Giving information or opinions
- Clarifying

- Questioning
- Disagreeing or challenging
- Testing for understanding
- Orienting the group to its task
- Testing for consensus
- Summarizing
- Recording or capturing content

Members should exhibit and utilize these various behaviors. The facilitator can model the behaviors and support their use by the group.

Maintenance behaviors deal more with keeping the group together, maintaining functional relationships, and strengthening the ability to perform. They include:

- Energizing or motivating
- Gate-keeping or helping people stay included and participating
- Harmonizing
- Agreeing or following another's lead
- Encouraging

- Relieving tensions
- Setting work standards or reminding others of standards
- Compromising
- Observing the process
- Praising others
- Praising the progress of the group

These behaviors must also be present among the members. Their absence leads to breakdowns in group functioning. The facilitator again models, supports, and assists in building these behaviors. It is an important role of the facilitator to deliberately monitor the group for both types of behaviors, identifying imbalances, gaps, and needed changes.

3. Psychosocial Issues

Individuals have a variety of needs and styles as well as interpersonal and social preferences. These "agendas" give rise to a wide variety of issues and related dynamics. These dynamics show up in individuals, between members, among subgroups, or across the whole group.

The most common types of issues affecting individuals and interpersonal relations are:

➤ **Trust** (especially in another's motivation, honesty, safety, and confidentiality or being valued and respected by another)

➤ **Control or power** (the need to have it or the fear of it)

➤ **Inclusion, identity, or status** (the need to be a part of, or to feel recognized or important; the need to know who I am in relation to others)

➤ **Autonomy, dependency, or counterdependency** (freedom from the influence of others, the need for approval of others, or the need to "go against" prevailing thought or authority)

➤ **Tolerance for ambiguity or the need for structure** (uncertainty, evolving answers vs. pinning everything down, the need to structure agendas, processes, etc.)

➤ **Competition** (insecurities, proving worth, being better than another)

➤ **Intimacy** (especially too much or too little; how close and personal is the group compared to "how I want it"?)

The psychosocial arena requires the most experience and skill since there are often deep underlying patterns causing individuals to behave as they do, to have the needs they have, and to deal with others the way they do. As facilitator, your primary interest is in the group's working and progressing. You need to understand these individual and interpersonal issues because they can get in the way of a group's succeeding.

To determine whether any of these issues may be operating in the group, look for repeated signs of the issues by observing people's verbal and nonverbal behavior: what they say and do, and what they do not say and do. For example, a lot of criticism of ideas might suggest competitiveness or control issues; low participation or silence might raise some questions about trust or inclusion; a lot of verbal inputs by a member might suggest some status issues or control needs; and a lot of procedural or methodological discussion might indicate a low tolerance for ambiguity or a need for structure. Also, if issues remain unresolved for individuals, they might begin to display signs of anxiety and defensiveness.

Human behavior is very complex, and a diverse group that includes a variety of personalities will have a complex interpersonal underworld; therefore, it is best to treat what you observe as useful data and not to interpret causality. Treat the possible underlying issues as hunches and keep them to yourself. If the group is unable to address what is going on or the situation gets worse, you may need to talk individually with some members or share some hunches to stimulate group discussion and resolution.

4. Task Progress

As a facilitator, you are always working toward outcomes. The group has a charter, a reason for being, a task to complete, recommendations to make, or ongoing work to perform. The issues on the task side of group life can be just as dysfunctional as issues on the psychosocial side. Essentially, groups need to be clear about, make decisions about, and follow through on four basic issues:

• **What**   *the result will be and the outcomes will look like, what they will do and not do, and what they are accountable for*

- **How** *they will accomplish their outcomes, take the steps they need to take, organize the steps and flow, use specific processes and procedures, and so on*

- **Who** *will do what, will take on what functional roles, will be involved, and so on*

- **When** *they will be done or complete different parts, and when they will meet, report, conduct various steps, and so on*

Groups will often get "stuck" in various task ruts. One purpose of facilitation is to design processes to deal with the various task aspects of the work: data generation, consolidation, and analysis; decision-making approaches; and follow-up techniques. If a group is not making good task progress, it may be due to incomplete stages of development or unresolved psychosocial issues. However, when these issues have been dealt with, the real culprit is probably the process design for the what, how, who, and when. And even when the development of the group is incomplete or psychosocial issues have not been dealt with, the breakdown may still be related to problems in the process design. For example, there might be too many alternatives for members to choose from, endless divergent thinking without converging processes, lack of clarity on the charter, or missing information.

5. Leadership

Group leadership involves more than the simple process of deciding who will be formally leading the session. It is really about who creates and controls the agenda for what the group does and how the work gets done, who gets listened to, and who influences opinions and direction.

Some groups may not have a formally designated leader, in which case leadership will emerge in one or more participants. The key issue is to ensure that group leadership is present, effective, and accepted. Whether emerging, elected, or previously designated, leadership may or may not be effective (e.g., influencing, moving, helping) and may or may not be accepted by the group members. When leadership is not accepted, it is often criticized, challenged, ignored, or countered, and alternative leaders vie for position. When leadership is not effective, these same dynamics can emerge or a leadership vacuum can result.

Groups need leadership. It may come primarily from one person (formally designated or not) or may be shared by more than one person. Without leadership, groups tend to ramble, act in fragmented ways, get stuck in conflict or apathy, and function poorly on their task. Facilitators have to guard against taking over the leadership. The facilitator will need to support or strengthen the effectiveness of formal leaders; support the efforts of effective, informal, emerging leaders when leadership is not in contention; facilitate the resolution of conflicts among members vying for leadership; or help the group identify and establish its leadership. One may help with aspects of leadership, but it is critical for the group to operate with its own leaders and not become dependent on a facilitator who, despite his or her ability to perform all the leadership functions, is not a part of the system and is not accountable for the group's performance or outcomes.

(For some specific pitfalls to avoid and useful tips for helping groups make their decisions about leadership, see Guide I-2: Selecting the Group Leader.)

6. Communication Patterns

Groups develop unique communication patterns. On the verbal side, these patterns include who talks and who talks to whom; the intensity, tone, and inflection of verbal communication; and who talks "after" and to whom. On the nonverbal side, these patterns include who does not talk; expressions of attentiveness, disagreement, boredom, surprise, or agreement; movement (while seated); movement (while not seated); eye contact (when and with whom); and pairings and subgroupings during non-session time (during breaks and before and after formal meeting times).

Paying attention to the communication patterns as they unfold can help you understand underlying dynamics. Communications are often indications of leadership, attempts to dominate, or forms of "counter" behavior. Who talks to whom and who follows whom with some verbal or nonverbal expression often indicate alliances, bonds of influence, or a clear demonstration of differences.

Inflection, tone, or intensity normally provides information on the strength of the opinions, real feelings, and depth of positions. People who do not talk are more difficult to understand because they could be agreeing, they could be disagreeing, they could be uninvolved or disinterested, they could be operating according to a cultural norm, or they could be holding back in response to an intimidating group environment.

Most people are aware that facial expressions such as a smile or a grimace generally reflect what a person is thinking or feeling. In addition, body language—shifting or turning in one's seat, getting up to walk around or leave, leaning forward or back, making eye contact (or having no eye contact)—suggests possible dynamics to be watched or confronted. It is important to remember that whatever you are seeing can have more than one interpretation; a good facilitator needs to consider all of the dynamics and sources of data and not hastily conclude something from observing a few brief behaviors. For instance, a person pacing about the room might be (a) frustrated with what the group is saying, (b) turned on by the conversation and thinking intensely, (c) a little or a lot hyperactive, (d) sleepy and trying to stay awake, or (e) trying to signal that a break is needed.

It is also important to keep in mind that nonverbal behavior can be deceptive. In fact, one meeting expert, Clyde Burleson (1990), asserts that teleconference group members are more capable of "reading" alliances and resistances, and understanding who is satisfied and who is upset, than are group members in face-to-face meetings. Burleson points out that "with no facial expressions or body language to distract, it's much easier to recognize a leader's tone" (p. 178). Whether or not you agree with this expert's assertion, most experienced facilitators will agree that nonverbal behavior is very easy to misread and that interpretations should be carefully constructed.

The facilitator can play an active role in making group members more aware of their communication patterns and focusing attention on productive communication patterns.

7. Participation

Watching participation is similar to watching communication patterns. Ideally, you want people to feel free to fully participate and to participate as much as is needed for the task. Equal participation is generally not natural. However, assuming that the participants are all there because they are valuable resources, it is necessary to facilitate the involvement of everyone and the appropriate level of participation from all participants.

Group process research leaves little question that the highest-performing groups operate with an overall group dynamic that is characterized by equitable participation. Yet groups left to enacting their "natural" patterns will not operate in this state of equity. The absolute necessity of creating and maintaining a healthy and relatively even balance of participation is one of the most compelling reasons for having a group facilitator.

High and low participation are both important to watch for and can have various meanings. High levels of participation can signal enthusiasm and/or discontent. Low levels of participation can indicate apathy, general agreement, or a faulty process design. Uneven participation is more often a problem (e.g., a few members or a subgroup dominating, a few members or a subgroup not participating). The danger in not having appropriate levels of participation is that important information or needed perspectives might be left out, the picture might be incomplete, or biased agendas might go unchecked.

In enabling groups to succeed, facilitators will often have to design or intervene to increase participation, create more even participation, or reduce participation by some while maintaining the involvement of others. (For more specific suggestions for maintaining appropriate participation, see Guide II-2: Encouraging Participation.)

8. Conflict Management

Conflict is inevitable. Heterogeneous groups with a variety of diverse viewpoints, backgrounds, functional interests, and expertise will naturally have differences. How differences are surfaced, discussed, managed, and resolved are critical to the work of the group. It will affect not only the content that gets heard and included but also the ongoing process of the group in terms of creating trust and an open, safe environment.

The expertise and opinions of the participants need to be shared and used. Differences in this process are healthy and useful in pursuing most group tasks, as long as they are managed effectively. Group members generally learn and produce better results by exploring differences and understanding one another's perspectives. Groups are debilitated and unproductive only when conflicts become fights, positions get cemented, adversaries become hostile toward one another, or important points of view get squelched, eliminated, or blocked.

It is the facilitator's job not only to safeguard ideas but also to create a safe atmosphere for the open airing of differing viewpoints. The facilitator is responsible for helping differing parties state their positions, hear one another, engage in balanced, rational dialogue, and involve all group members in resolving issues. Sometimes the conflict needs to be aired and resolved within the group sessions, while at other times, it may be more effective to help the differing parties "off-line" or away from the meeting setting, with appropriate reporting back to the group.

(For procedures, samples, and guides on conflict management, see the subsection "Handling Conflicts and Common Problems With Groups" in Section II.)

9. Decision-Making Processes

A critical part of all group work is decision making. Basically, the members' goal is always to make the best decisions they can with the information they have *(quality)*; to make their decisions as quickly as possible *(speed)*; to make their decisions with a high level of participant agreement *(consensus)*; and to make decisions that get implemented *(commitment)*.

Decisions can be made in many ways. Experts on decision making differ in how they describe different decision methods, yet there is a great deal of underlying similarity. Table 1 shows six common types of decision methods, a description of each method, some of their advantages and disadvantages, and suggestions on when to use them.

There is a great deal of divergence among group process experts as to the number and nature of decision methods. One expert, William Daniels, asserts that there are really only two types of group decision methods: **consultative** and **consensus.** He defines a consensus decision as "any alternative that is determined by **all** members of the group to be superior to the existing status quo," and suggests that the consultative consensus and modified consensus methods described in Table 1 and practiced in many organizations are needlessly confused interpretations of consultative or consensus decisions (personal communication, November 1996). Moreover, he has found no real hard research data to support that these "in-between" decision methods produce results that are superior to individual decisions or that such decisions build stronger support for implementation.

As a facilitator, you can make the determination—on your own or with your group—as to which decision methods will be considered. The facilitator should offer to the group the various means of making decisions and help members clarify which method they will use. This decision-method choice can be made before each decision on the agenda, but it is more appropriately handled as a part of the agenda review at the beginning of each meeting, or—more economical for multi-session groups—during the planning sessions when the charge of the group is clarified. (See Procedure I-2: Developing a Group Charter.)

One way to structure the decision making for a group session is to choose one method as the agreed-upon first choice and one or more methods as "fallbacks." For instance, the primary decision method can be modified consensus; if the group members get

TABLE 1: Decision Methods

METHOD	Advantages	Disadvantages	When to Use
Individual The leader of the group makes the decision.	• Speed • Simplicity • Clarity	• May waste group intelligence • Invites resistance • Lowers motivation for participation • Creates messes	• When one person's content expertise far exceeds that of others • When speed is of paramount concern • When group is conflicted and time is short • When a decision contrary to members' interests must be made
Consultative The leader makes the decision after listening to all group members in a group meeting.	• Allows for input of others without taking undue time • Most cost- and time-effective of all decision methods • Guards against "group-think" • Allows for quick action and high levels of action	• May cause resentment in those whose advice is spurned • Loses quality gain that comes from "give and take" and integration of differing proposals	• When leader is highly expert • When leadership is clear and unquestioned • When leader wants to take advantage of different ideas but does not want to invest the time required to work through to consensus • When leader wants to retain control • When speed is critical
Consultative Consensus The leader consults with other group members, seeking consensus yet still clearly retaining control of the decision.	• Avoids deadlock in decisions • Enables leader to lead, retaining sense of personal control, while still building consensus in group • Group members in some cases may be more likely to support implementation	• Time to attempt consensus • "Murkiness" of mixing two decision methods • Requires considerable skill if not to be perceived as manipulative	• When one person is either highly expert or has a high degree of responsibility for the implementation of the decision • When there is a desire to be collaborative and maintain a participative ethic • When facilitation skills are high in leader or available through neutral facilitator
Modified Consensus The group members each agree upon a decision that all can support or at least "live with."	• Supports a more democratic, participative culture • Forces dealing with all significant conflicting views and opinions in the group • People have belief that it fosters more commitment	• Time-consuming to work through all concerns • Compromises necessary; often does not improve quality • Often tedious to work through the process • No hard data that MC produces more intelligent results	• When group agreement is considered critical • When a participative ethic is highly valued • When all group members are willing to invest the time • On critical decisions that require high levels of agreement • When those who will implement are in the group • When a neutral facilitator is available
Absolute Consensus All group members are in absolute agreement that the decision is superior to what exists in the status quo.	• Produces most intelligent decisions of highest quality • Support for decision is unequivocal	• Groups fail to achieve decision 2 out of 3 times AC is attempted • May take a very long time; often emotionally difficult, stressful	• When the cost of making less than the most intelligent decision is exceptionally high • For strategic, safety, or survival decisions • When the quality of the decision matters more than anything else • When enough time is available
Voting Group members vote on alternative proposals and the alternative receiving the required number of votes (majority, $2/3$, etc.) becomes the group decision.	• Speed—when handled properly • Perceived fairness • Avoids impasses, deadlocks • Anyone can lead • May be only means possible when differences are irreconcilable • Can help build a consensus if used as a process tool	• Creates sides, factions; divides the group • Encourages debate rather than dialogue • Detracts from cohesion of group • Entrenches people rather than expanding group IQ	• When stakes are low; when almost any decision will work • When little discussion or debate is required and any choice will probably work • When consensus cannot be achieved and no leader is available as a fallback decision maker • When you want to "poll" the group about several alternatives and then proceed with alternative selection

stuck there, they can fall back on having the group leader make the decision (consultative); if that decision is intensely opposed by one or more group members, they can fall back on voting on the decision (voting).

Decisions can be made in many ways, and it is important to identify needed decisions and to select appropriate methods. Many groups get into trouble by making decisions too complex, by not making decisions they need to make along the way, or by not being clear on how they will make decisions. For example, members might have different assumptions and expectations about how decisions will be made, only to be surprised, disappointed, or angered when decisions are not made in the way they expected. Also, sometimes too many issues have been loaded into one decision, making it difficult to ever reach consensus.

(For procedures related to decision-making methods, see the subsection "Decision Modes" in Section II.)

REFERENCES

Benne, K. D., & Sheats, P. (1948). The functional roles of group members. *Journal of Social Issues, 4*(2).

Burleson, Clyde. W. (1990). *Effective meetings: The complete guide.* New York: John Wiley & Sons.

Schutz, W. C. (1967). *The FIRO scales: Manual.* Palo Alto, CA: Consulting Psychologists Press.

Tuckman, B. W. (1965). Developmental sequences in small groups, *Psychological Bulletin, 63* (6), 384–399.

PRIMER C

Understanding Process Consultation

PROCESS CONSULTATION, developed by Edgar Schein (1969) and later elaborated on by Brendan Reddy (1994), is an essential arena of knowledge and skill for facilitators. Much of a facilitator's work with a group involves assisting the group in operating effectively and working with processes that are healthy and that enable the group to reach its desired outcomes. Schein (1988) captures that dimension of a facilitator's responsibility in his definition of process consultation as:

> *A set of activities on the part of the consultant that helps the client perceive, understand, and act upon the process events that occur in the client's environment in order to improve the situation as defined by the client.*

Thus process consultation involves intervening in the ongoing flow of work to help a group learn about its processes (and areas associated with its processes) and, on the basis of that learning, taking group action to change the processes in ways necessary for the group's success. Note that:

☞ Process consultation *does not* provide solutions or answers. It leaves the group with the ownership of problems and the responsibility for resolutions. It is distinctly educative in enhancing people's capacity for process management and is therefore nonprescriptive.

For Schein, process consultation can focus on the individual, interpersonal, group, or organizational level.

Reddy (1994) focuses primarily on the small group and defines process consultation as:

> *The reasoned and intentional interventions by the consultant into the ongoing events and dynamics of a group with the purpose of helping that group effectively attain its agreed-upon objectives.*

Thus process consultation revolves around strategic (reasoned and intentional) interventions into the life of the group in order to help it to be more effective. The basic purpose is to help the group understand the processes that are occurring, to assess their effectiveness (against agreed-upon objectives) or dysfunctional consequences, and to engage the group in actively modifying how its members are working on their task and/or interacting with one another.

Processes (as distinguished from content) generally involve **how** individuals, groups, and organizations interact and conduct their work. There are task processes (methods, procedures used to do the work) and interpersonal processes (how people relate to one another). Both kinds of processes are occurring continually in organizational life. Sometimes they help move the group toward the desired outcomes, and sometimes they hinder such movement. Processes that generally require attention are:

- Power distribution
- Commitment
- Communications
- Problem solving and decision making
- Influencing and leading

- Developing norms and culture
- Providing feedback
- Running meetings
- Rewards and consequences
- Evaluation

THE ESSENCE OF PROCESS CONSULTATION

The essence of process consultation is intervening in the group. The facilitator needs to consider several factors in selecting and executing interventions:

- Purpose
- Focus
- Type

- Timing
- Intensity
- Depth

Purpose

Interventions are generally used to contribute to one of the following purposes:

1. **Providing help** to the group members in their thinking and action

2. **Surfacing diagnostic information** that is valid, useful, and leads to insight

3. **Creating ownership and responsibility** on the part of the members for their processes, dynamics, and problem diagnosis/resolution

4. **Developing the group's capability** to surface diagnostic data, to understand and manage its processes and dynamics, and to create functional relationships, norms, and methods of working

All four of the purposes are inherently aimed at producing group learning. The group needs to learn, to mature, and to become more effective over time.

Focus

The focus of an intervention can be an individual, an interpersonal pair or subgroup, or the entire group. The focus will vary based on what you see and what purpose you wish to accomplish. However, it is important to be clear. If you are targeting an individual behavior, do not talk to the whole group. If you are commenting on a group dynamic, do not single out an individual. Facilitator-initiated interventions will usually occur in the group setting, but occasionally you may wish to take individual and interpersonal interventions "off-line," particularly when you believe that working away from the group with the individual(s) involved would be more effective in meeting your intended purpose.

Type

Reddy (1994) and Schein (1988) discuss various types of interventions. The following list of interventions integrates Schein's, Reddy's, and our thinking:

1. **Active listening:** Paying close attention to both what is being said and the processes that are occurring, leading to highlighting, clarification, summarizing, and consensus testing.

2. **Inquiry:** Questions and probes to raise data, focus attention, and/or stimulate diagnostic thinking; surfacing data for the group to look at.

3. **Observation and feedback:** Seeing what is going on with an individual or the group and then (a) describing in behavioral terms what they are doing; (b) reflecting their emotional state; and (c) interpreting the underlying dynamics of what is going on.

4. **Concretization:** Pushing people to be concrete and specific to get beyond generalizations.

5. **Historical reconstruction:** Looking back over events to force a reconstruction and review of what was done and how it was done (emphasizing the process dimensions).

6. **Including process focus:** Building in process analysis periods, feedback sessions, and process discussions.

7. **Cognitive inputs:** Concepts or ideas shared with the group to help members understand something.

8. **Skill building:** Interjecting brief learning activities to enhance the capabilities of the group members in some needed competency (e.g., feedback, problem solving).

9. **Counseling/guidance:** Helping the group or individuals look at themselves and actively engage in solving their own problems.

10. **Designing processes:** Designing and managing activities, methods, or exercises to effectively reach desired outcomes.

11. **Structural alternatives:** Suggesting options for group membership, subgroups, interaction patterns, work allocation, roles and responsibilities, and so forth.

12. **Content suggestions or recommendations:** Providing input or opinions concerning the content the group is working on; recommending what the group should do about some aspect of the group's content.

When designing specific interventions, you can use the following continuum, which reflects the dimensions that characterize different types of interventions:

Non-directive	Directive
Cognitive	Emotional
Reflective (Diagnostic)	Active (Doing)
Exploratory	Confrontative
Participating alongside the group	Participating in the group

For example, **inquiry** is more exploratory, non-directive, reflective, and cognitive and assumes there is group responsibility and that the facilitator is working alongside the group. On the other hand, the **designing processes** intervention is more directive and active. It could be either more exploratory or more confrontative; more cognitive or more emotional. It would probably be in the middle on responsibility and facilitator participation.

Timing

The important timing considerations are to intervene during the following:

— Close to the action of interest when it's fresh and the group can more easily remember and see what is being highlighted.
— When the group can use the information to further its progress.
— When the group is ready, willing, and able to hear and understand; when members are not engaged in something else and are mature enough as a group.

Interventions always need to be aimed at moving the group forward and helping them learn while not distracting the group or taking them off their task inappropriately. Poorly timed interventions may have little effect and can even produce confusion or resistance.

Intensity

According to Reddy (1994), intensity is the facilitator's **intended impact,** the resulting attention or seriousness hoped for from the group. The intensity level (high, medium, low) is controlled by the facilitator through the choice of words, voice tone and inflection, body language (nonverbal positioning, expressions, gestures), and personal emotional delivery. Of course, any intervention might not have the intended effect and can even have an undesirable effect or other unintended consequences (such as rejection or resistance).

Depth

The depth or level of intervention needs to be carefully considered in light of three factors:

➤ What you are trying to accomplish
➤ What the group needs at a given point in time to be able to move forward productively
➤ The group's maturity (level of understanding, skill, learning orientation, ability to hear and assimilate)

A common analogy used to discuss depth and levels is the iceberg, as depicted in Figure 2.

FIGURE 2: "The Iceberg"

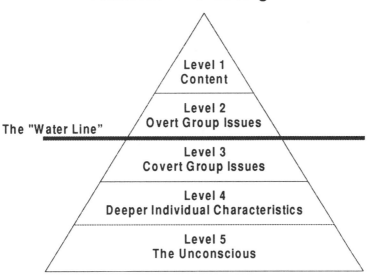

Adapted from Brendan W. Reddy, *Intervention Skills: Process Consultation for Small Groups and Teams.* San Diego, CA: Pfeiffer & Co., 1994.

So that you can better understand the five different levels, let's take a closer look at what they represent:

Level 1: *Content* is focused on the work of the group—its charter, tasks, methods, and outcomes.

Level 2: *Overt Group Issues* comprises the behaviors and interactions you can easily observe, such as conflicts, members being interrupted, lack of participation, communication patterns, and decision processes that members disagree with.

Level 3: *Covert Group Issues* comprises the core issues for a particular group that are not talked about or displayed explicitly. In other words, you can't "see" these. You have to infer them primarily through what you are seeing at Level 2. Typically, these issues relate to inclusion/exclusion, independence/dependence, competence/confidence, control/autonomy, identity/esteem, trust/vulnerability, and intimacy/distance. The group's core issues emerge from the various psychosocial issues of individual members and will therefore vary from group to group.

Level 4: *Deeper Individual Characteristics* includes personality factors rooted in history; deeply held values, beliefs, and assumptions; defense systems; and basic needs and fears. While these issues will, in part, drive what is occurring at Level 2 and Level 3, work at this level is not appropriate in most process consultation situations. Unless you are specifically trained and experienced to work on such deep individual issues, leave this work for those trained to conduct therapy, personal growth groups, T-groups, and the like.

Level 5: *The Unconscious* is not accessible to the individual or the facilitator. These issues and dynamics are deeply hidden and can only be worked with by trained, clinical professionals.

When considering depth, it is important to keep in mind the following:

- The risks of the intervention—being rejected or creating resistance—increase as one moves from Level 1 to Level 5.
- Interventions generally shift from being cognitive to being more emotional as one moves through the levels.
- You should intervene only at the level needed to help the group progress.
- You can intervene effectively only at those levels the group is ready for and is capable of handling.

Process consultation (PC) is a philosophy, a set of skills, and a way of thinking about what is going on and what effectiveness requires. It is useful to the facilitator in the design of sessions and the building of the agenda. However, PC is most valuable in working with groups, particularly in managing data, decision making, and group dynamics.

REFERENCES

Reddy, Brendan W. (1994). *Intervention skills: Process consultation for small groups and teams.* San Diego, CA: Pfeiffer & Co.

Schein, Edgar. (1969). *Process consultation: Its role in organization development.* Reading, MA: Addison-Wesley.

Schein, Edgar. (1988). *Process consultation: Its role in organization development* (2nd ed.). Reading, MA: Addison-Wesley.

SECTION I

PHASE I:
PREPARATION

➡ **Overview**
➡ **Facilitator Resources**

OVERVIEW

Affairs are easier of entrance than of exit, and it is but common prudence to see our way out before we venture in.

—Aesop, 6th century B.C.

You can't hatch chickens from fried eggs.

—Pennsylvania Dutch proverb

The process of successful facilitation starts well before you actually begin facilitating a group. The thinking and action necessary for preparing a group session are just as important as the actual group facilitation. Poor preparation leads to poor meetings. In fact, *most of the problems and difficulties that arise during the group sessions can be traced to some fault in the design or preparation of the session.* Essentially, it is during preparation that contracts, agendas, group processes, and logistics are determined and/or clarified. Weaknesses in any of these elements will eventually lead to problems during the session, when correcting them will be difficult and a hindrance to the group's success.

Good, effective preparation should produce the following outcomes:

1. The group is organized.
2. Membership is determined.
3. Purposes are clear.
4. Roles are clarified.
5. Logistics are planned.
6. The facilitation work contract is clear.
7. Group, work, participants, and context are understood.
8. The agenda is determined and communicated.

THE EIGHT PRIMARY TASKS

In preparing to work with the group, you need to focus on eight primary tasks:

1. Establishing the contract for facilitation
2. Collecting information on context, work, and participants
3. Clarifying the group charter
4. Analyzing stakeholders
5. Selecting group members and the group leader
6. Building agendas for meetings

7. Publishing the agenda and disseminating information
8. Attending to meeting logistics

Task 1: Establishing the Contract for Facilitation

You must begin by establishing a contract with (a) the person or persons in the organization who are responsible for the group you are intending to facilitate, and (b) the person or persons who authorize or approve the group's work.

The general purpose of the contract is to set the facilitation process up for success—to initiate solid planning for the process. More specifically, the purpose of the contract is to ensure the following:

— You understand what your clients expect from a facilitator and what they do not.
— Your clients understand what you expect from them, how you work, and what they can expect from you.

These expectations must be clearly stated, and in most cases, they must be specifically negotiated. Inadequate negotiation of expectations and agreements is a common cause of failure for facilitators. Take the time upfront to reach consensus on expectations, and remember: Adjust the extent of your negotiations according to whom you are dealing with and the situation at hand.

Contract issues to keep foremost in mind include:

- The need to establish such things as timelines and schedules. When will the work be completed? What will be the frequency and sequence of meetings? Decision paths and modes will have to be clarified.

- The nature and membership of the group that you will be facilitating. (Although for complex or extended group work, membership is usually finalized upon completion of a stakeholder analysis.)

- Follow-up work. This should be identified in clear terms.

- How meeting proceedings will be documented; assignment of responsibilities for documenting those proceedings.

- Costs. When applicable, costs must be established. You may need to help your clients identify costs in terms of both personnel time and actual dollars. If you are working as an external consultant/facilitator, you will also need to establish an agreement for the cost of your work. Many internal facilitators also have a cost or fee charge-back system.

- Initial role clarification

  — The meeting leader role should be clarified, and a chair or task group leader should be identified. The meeting leader may, and in most cases should, function mostly as an equal member when conducting task group-style meetings.

— The role of group sponsor should be considered. Often, it is an asset to have a person with management authority sponsor a group and assist in moving group recommendations through the organization's decision-making process. This sponsor is not required to attend meetings, but is enlisted for support before, during, and after the group's work.

Once your planning is completed, you should have a basic contract established with the people whom you will be closely working with. It is good practice whenever possible to put the initial contract in writing. You will need to ensure that all parties are clear on your contract with them and to pursue the authorizations necessary to guarantee that you are able to complete the work.

By establishing some form of a contract, you come to know and understand the nature of the group you are dealing with as well as some of their values, fears, hopes, concerns, and expectations concerning the work ahead and your involvement as a facilitator.

Task 2: Collecting Information on Context, Work, and Participants

You will want to understand the context of the work you are about to do. This means that you must spend time gaining a better understanding of:

- The work of the group
- How the organization in which the work is being performed operates
- The expected outcomes
- How the meetings fit into what the organization is trying to accomplish

You will also want to gain an understanding of the organization's broader history, mission, culture, issues, and crises, as well as the group's history, role, and perceptions.

You may find it useful to interview all or some of the people who will be participating in the meetings. In more complex, longer-term facilitation contracts, you may want to set up some job-shadowing sessions with key people in the business so that you come to understand the business in a more experiential way. It will be helpful to get to know some things about the group members. Have they worked together before? Are they "willing" participants? What kinds of work styles, preferences, and personalities are included?

Task 3: Clarifying the Group Charter

In establishing the foundation for success, your first step is to conduct planning with the people you will be working with to help them clarify their purposes and outcomes for the meetings (or meeting). Two questions are paramount when you are approached for facilitation work:

1. *What is the purpose of the meetings?*

2. *What are the outcomes for the meetings?*

The best way to ensure that you keep on track later on, when facilitating, is to ask these questions upfront and stay focused on them throughout your work.

In formulating the group charter, you will need to consider the basic nature of the group you will be meeting with. There are numerous types of meetings: staff meetings, official board meetings, team meetings (e.g., management team, reengineering team), strategic planning sessions, quality circles, and work group meetings, to name but a few. Each type of meeting has its own set of standard "operating instructions"— procedures that optimize the meeting's effectiveness. The wise facilitator will learn the distinctive features of each kind of meeting and operate in a way consistent with the basic purpose and instructions of a given meeting.

Working with an intact work group that has been regularly meeting for some time would call for a much different type of charter than would either a task force or a new team that has been formed for a specific planning or problem-solving purpose. Daniels (1993) has made a major contribution to our understanding of the distinctions between such groups in his discussion of regular meetings and task group meetings. (If you are not already familiar with these distinctions, you may find it helpful to review Guide I-7: Different Kinds of Meetings: Distinguishing "Task Forces" From "Regular Meetings.") As the contract with your client (Task 1) should reflect the nature of the group, it should also reflect the distinctive features of the type of meeting in which you will be working.

Formulating the group charter is a very critical task. It creates the group's reason for existence and what is expected from its work. In the early stages of forming the group, there is often ambiguity or multiple interpretations about the charter. Early facilitation of charter clarity among the key players will go a long way in helping the group reach its goals.

☞ **For more help, see Facilitator Resources, Section I**

- GUIDE I-1: Chartering the New Team
- SAMPLES I-6 AND 7: Meeting Agendas
- GUIDE I-7: Different Kinds of Meetings: Distinguishing "Task Forces" From "Regular Meetings"

Task 4: Analyzing Stakeholders

Stakeholder analysis is a crucial component of the planning process. If any issue or problem is of such concern to your clients that they are seeking a facilitator to work with their group, then who gets involved is nearly always critical to success. Often, clients tend to narrowly define the membership for a meeting when it would be best to increase participation. When the issues are important, it is best to work with your primary client and a small planning group to perform a stakeholder analysis.

The stakeholder analysis is a way of finding out who has a vested interest in the impending work and the nature and significance of each interest. It is useful not only in determining group membership but also in identifying outside contributors—individuals who, though not group members, have much to offer by way of providing input, assisting data-gathering efforts, approving group issues, and the like.

☞ **For more help, see Facilitator Resources, Section I**

- PROCEDURE I-1: Stakeholder Analysis and Group Member Selection
- SAMPLE I-1: Stakeholder Analysis

Task 5: Selecting Group Members and the Group Leader

The facilitator needs to help the client create the best group composition for the task at hand. In selecting members, it is essential to look for individuals who have the data and expertise to move the group forward and who are critical to follow-up implementation; underemphasis in this area is the most common mistake associated with membership selection. Those whom you choose should be chosen for these five reasons:

1. They are experts or have critical knowledge or data related to accomplishment of the purposes and outcomes of the meeting. They have content knowledge.

2. They know the effects that decisions made by the group may have on key persons or groups needed to implement the decisions. They have data related to the implementation of decisions.

3. They are in roles directly involved in implementation.

4. They have the ability to block decisions made by the group, and their buy-in is needed.

5. They possess personal characteristics or group process skills that will help the group move forward.

All five reasons can be valuable in different situations. It is important not to overemphasize any particular one. Many clients tend to overly stress the fourth reason when selecting members, yet the political selection of members does not necessarily lead to increased buy-in for the decisions of the group. If group members are selected politically, but do not have sufficient expertise, the group may become handicapped by their lack of content knowledge. There is at least some truth to the adage that "every group moves just as fast as its slowest member." The political process of creating buy-in for group decisions can often be better managed through informal communications from meeting leaders and group sponsors to key stakeholders, or through formal review of group recommendations with managers, either individually or at meetings of management groups in the organization.

Task 6: Building the Agenda for the Meeting

Once your contextual understanding of the work is sufficient and the charter and participants are clarified, you are ready to proceed with the planning of your initial meeting with the group. You should build the first meeting agenda by working from the identified purposes and outcomes and crafting a careful, well-planned sequence of activities, including responsibility and time frames for each activity.

You will want to use two types of agendas:

1. A detailed agenda—known as a process facilitation agenda—for your use and that of the meeting leader(s)

2. A simple agenda for the use of the group members

In the process facilitation agenda, critical meeting processes are broken down into steps so that you and the meeting leader(s) clearly understand how the processes work. In the members' agenda, the expected outcomes and the sequence of meeting activities are presented in a clear, brief fashion.

Both types of agendas vary in detail depending on who will be using them. The agendas should be developed with your client(s) or a small planning group who know the participants and organization culture.

> ☞ For more help, see Facilitator Resources, Section I
> - PROCEDURE I-4: Planning Meetings
> - PROCEDURE I-5: Building the Meeting Agenda
> - SAMPLE I-6 and 7: Meeting Agendas

Task 7: Publishing the Agenda and Disseminating Information

Your agenda should be reviewed with, and approved by, your client in enough time so that it can be distributed to meeting participants beforehand, along with any information and materials (e.g., pre-reading, questionnaires, preparation instructions) relevant to the meeting. This will allow participants time to review the materials and to come prepared to the meeting. Pre-publication of the agenda is one of the effectiveness benchmarks of professional facilitation.

Task 8: Attending to Meeting Logistics

The handling of meeting logistics is a core competency for the effective facilitator. Failure to pay attention to logistical detail in the construction of meetings is likely to lead to the meeting's failure to produce the intended results.

The physical arrangements of the meeting room are important considerations. The room should be right for the nature of the meeting, and it should be physically checked out in advance whenever possible. When this is not possible, details regarding the space and furniture arrangement need to be reviewed with the person in the organization who is responsible for making the arrangements. Equipment needs, break times, break set-ups, breakout rooms, temperature, and lighting all should be planned. The wise facilitator will learn to become fastidious about his or her involvement in these logistical issues.

When you are working with other facilitators, you will want to hold a briefing meeting to review the agenda, and to go over each process in sufficient detail, so they are comfortable with handling their facilitation assignments. You should usually count on such a briefing meeting taking about one-half of the total work time planned for the meeting.

Finally, these preparatory planning and contracting steps should not be considered over and done with. The planning and contracting processes are iterative. The wise facilitator will revisit them with clients on a regular basis throughout the process of the facilitation.

A checklist for meeting planning and a guide for room arrangements are included in Section I's "Facilitator Resources." You should review the checklist with your client (or his or her designate) sufficiently in advance so that you are not caught off guard with unexpected complications on the day of the meeting.

> **For more help, see Facilitator Resources, Section I**
>
> - GUIDE I-4: A Checklist for Meeting Planning
> - GUIDE I-5: Meeting Room Designs

Careful, thorough preparation is a key success factor in enabling groups to succeed. The time invested in planning and preparing for the meeting is often the critical determiner of the effectiveness of the meeting.

When your facilitation involves a single event, you will move through the three phases—preparation, working with the group, and follow-up—only once. However, when you are facilitating an ongoing process, you will continually cycle through some tasks in preparation and follow-up each time you work with the group. The tasks may vary from time to time depending on the nature of the next meeting or event.

REFERENCE

Daniels, William R. (1993). *Orchestrating powerful regular meetings.* San Diego, CA: University Associates.

FACILITATOR RESOURCES

Organizing the Group

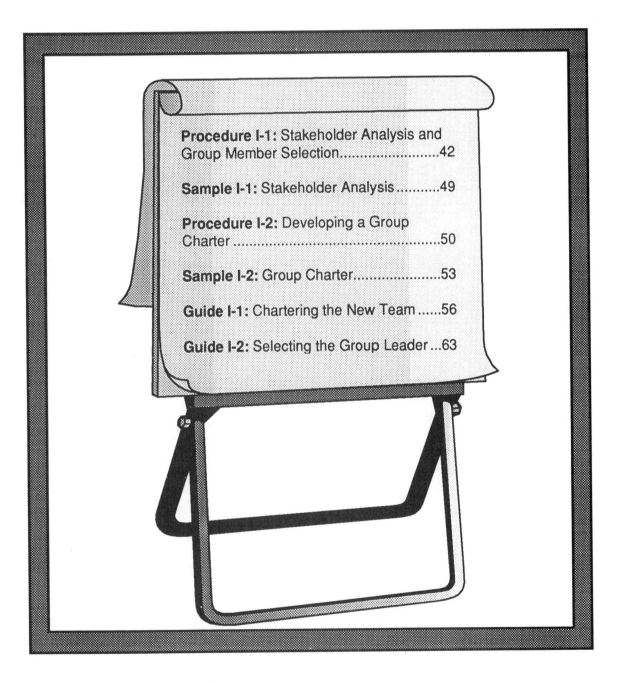

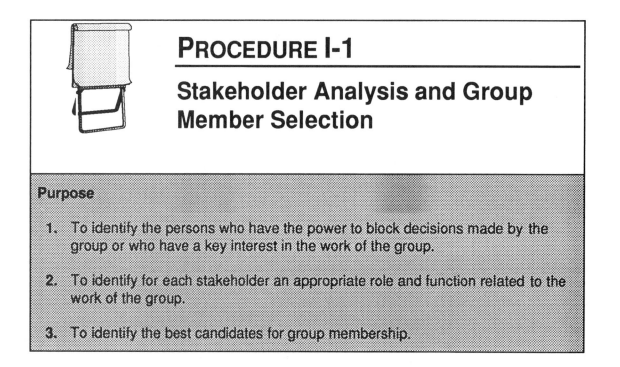

PROCEDURE I-1

Stakeholder Analysis and Group Member Selection

Purpose

1. To identify the persons who have the power to block decisions made by the group or who have a key interest in the work of the group.

2. To identify for each stakeholder an appropriate role and function related to the work of the group.

3. To identify the best candidates for group membership.

Summary Description

A stakeholder is any party who has a substantial interest in your group's work—what you are doing and how you are going to do it. A stakeholder is someone who can block the implementation of recommendations made by the group or who will be significantly affected by the recommendations; stakeholders may be individuals or groups of individuals. It is best to take the time early on to identify these individuals/groups and to decide how your group will relate to each of them.

To conduct a stakeholder analysis, a small planning team meets to identify the stakeholders who care about your group's work and to plan how the group will relate to each one. The most common mistake made by planning teams is to assume that every stakeholder has to be a full-fledged group member. In fact, there are many different options for involving stakeholders, and the purpose of the analysis is to determine the best involvement option for each stakeholder.

When to Use the Procedure

- When your group is being planned
- When your group will be dealing with complex issues that will have an impact on many people
- When the risk of failure is high
- When your group is likely to meet on several occasions or for a significant length of time

Participants

Number: A small planning group of three to five members

Type: The person in charge of the group

The group facilitator, if a facilitator is being used

The organizational sponsor—the person with authority who will help ensure that the group's work is implemented

One or two other persons with knowledge of who might be the stakeholders

Resources *(checkmarks indicate recommended equipment)*

✔ Flip chart and markers

Facilitator(s)

The group facilitator, working with the group leader (or the group leader if a facilitator is not used), leads the planning group through the steps outlined under **Method.**

Time

Approximately 4 to 6 hours as written. Adapt the procedure as needed, basing its time allocation on the group's total meeting time. The following guidelines apply:

Group's Total Meeting Time	Time Allocated for Analysis
1 day	1 hour
20 hours or more	2 hours
40 hours or more	4 to 6 hours

Method

1. The group's purposes and mission or charge statement should be put before the planning group on chart paper.

2. Ask the group: "Given these purposes and this mission, what decisions might come out of our work?"

    Add: "For instance, we might decide to _____. Give me some other examples of decisions that could come out of this group. We might decide to *do what*?"

    Then list all the "We might decide to" choices on the chart paper.

    To guard against these comments prejudicing later group activities, occasionally say, "Or you might decide to [state the opposite or a variation of the suggested decision]."

3. After the group has ventured to offer some decisions, ask: "Now who might have the power to block any of these decisions? Let's list the people and how their official roles or functions relate to our work." Then list all those persons. If members begin naming the whole world, say: "Now let's stop for a reality check. Obviously, lots of people can block a decision. Do we have some past experience or behavior that would indicate that this person could or would really block any decision?"

   Oftentimes members will volunteer group names. For each group mentioned, encourage them to identify the individuals who represent that group in a more or less official way. However, at this point, do not evaluate whether those individuals are stakeholders; allow any responses, suggesting that you will evaluate later.

4. Next ask: "Besides the people we have mentioned, who else really cares about these decisions? Who would be strongly affected by them?" Usually most of the persons who fit this category have already been identified. Again, some planning groups are tempted to list the whole world. Check that all persons listed in this category are stakeholders by asking: "Are you convinced that all these persons have a significant enough interest to be classified as stakeholders? In order to list them, you should have some historical evidence that these people care about the group's purposes in some vital way, or that they might block the decisions or the effective implementation of the decisions."

5. Next ask: "Now do we have any other stakeholders who have demonstrated a positive interest in the group's work?" Or: "Who can or will want to support the group's work?" This might be persons who have volunteered for similar work in the past, persons who are voluntarily pursuing advanced education in the field, or implementers who have already proven to be cooperative and early to adopt innovations related to the group's work. It also might include anyone who strongly holds the same values and philosophy implied by the group's stated purpose(s).

6. To conclude stakeholder nominations, ask: "Do we have available expertise or skills related to our group purposes? Who might have special skills or interests and be willing to commit time to the group effort?"

7. Tell members that what they have done up to this point is identify stakeholders on the basis of four key criteria—the four "I's" of stakeholder involvement:

   ➤ **Influence**   Those with influence to block decisions

   ➤ **Interest**   Those with demonstrated interests in the work of the group

   ➤ **Impacted**   Those who will be affected by decisions

   ➤ **Intelligence**   Those who possess data needed to contribute to an intelligent data base

   Now check to see whether the group feels that all the people on the list are stakeholders. Say something like, "Now, given our criteria, do we agree that each person on our list meets at least one of them?"

A decision matrix can be posted on the flip chart and ratings done on each stakeholder according to the four criteria. Members can "weight" each of the four criteria according to what they think is most important for this group and this task. A sample decision matrix is shown below.

Sample Stakeholder Analysis Chart
Stakeholder Criteria—Score 1–5

Person	Influence	Interest	Impact	Intelligence	Total
James	3	4	5	5	17
Suarez	3	2	1	4	10
Henley	1	2	4	2	9
Jennings	4	2	3	5	14

8. Now you are ready to determine the appropriate type of involvement for each stakeholder you have identified. Below are the possible "involvement options." The planning group will need to select those options they wish to include for the group you will be working with.

    (a) **Regular member of group.** Agrees to attend all meetings of group on a regularly scheduled basis.

    (b) **Member of steering committee or group that will review recommendations.** Meets on a regularly scheduled but less frequent basis to review the recommendations that have been approved by your group.

    (c) **Special liaison to the group.** Agrees to review recommendations of your group at appropriate meeting of his or her constituent group. May also set up special reviews of recommendations from your group at specific checkpoints within his or her group. Does not attend regular meetings of your group, except by special invitation.

    (d) **Standby consultant to the group.** Available to serve on special task forces, but need not attend every session. May attend certain specified meetings to provide information or expertise.

    (e) **Communication liaison.** Receives regular information from your group and provides information to members of his or her constituent group. Responsible for immediate "red flagging" of issues and concerns in own group that relate to your group's work. May be called in to one or more group meetings on a special basis to review alternatives.

    (f) **Ad hoc member of group.** Serves a very specific function on the team (must be clearly specified) and only attends meetings to serve that function (e.g., person from administration in charge of facilities only attends planning sessions related to facilities).

(g) **Group sponsor.** Agrees to advise group on approval of its decisions in the formal hierarchy or his or her system, and coaches group leader on how to ensure that group decisions are approved. Meets on a regularly scheduled basis with group leader. May or may not be a regular member of group (usually is not). Often is group leader's boss.

(h) **Group leader.** Approves all recommendations of group and is responsible for securing approvals of decisions in the formal structure of the organization. Is selected on the basis of having considerable data to contribute to the group and the most time invested in the task, and often because he or she initiated activity related to the task.

(i) **Other roles** as identified by the planning group.

9. Before assigning each of the stakeholders a particular function, review the following criteria for an effective group member. These criteria have been taken from interviews with group leaders and facilitators:

   • Shares the values and philosophies related to the task at hand

   • Is generally respected within the organization

   • Has already demonstrated an interest and "stake" in the issues by taking actions related to the purposes of the group

   • Is willing and able to work and create the time necessary for meeting attendance and take-home assignments

   • Represents a critical stakeholder group

   • Has information and expertise related to the purposes of the group

   • Does not have a "group disability." Willing and able to work in a group. (A significant "group disability" should veto a person as a consistent member of the group, even though he or she might well be involved in one of the other roles listed in Step 8.)

   • Contributes "new blood" to the decision-making process

10. On a flip chart, create a matrix showing roles as listed in Step 8. Assign each stakeholder a particular role and function. Mount the criteria for regular group member selection so planning members can use it for review of each person. (See Sample I-2 matrix; use it as a model for your group memory matrix.)

11. Assign people to other roles you have to fill ([g] through [i] in Step 8).

Notes

1. For the most part, regular group members should already be supportive of the direction you are headed. "Doubting Thomases" should number less than 20%.

2. If your regular group is more than nine, a facilitator is required. If the group is less than nine, a facilitator is helpful unless there is compelling evidence that the leaders can also facilitate.

3. The steering committee is a promising vehicle for managing stakeholder review of recommendations. A steering committee is distinct from a task group and is formed separately. Its members should represent the divergent stakeholder groups. It meets at certain checkpoints to provide the regular group with feedback. Often an existing regular meeting group is the best "steering committee."

    You also can use focus groups for feedback purposes. At critical junctures, your group can take alternative solutions that it has generated to the focus group to receive feedback. Focus groups, unlike steering committees, are most effective when composed homogeneously (e.g., one focus group comprises all the fore-persons in the plant; another comprises engineers; another secretaries; and so forth).

4. When individuals are assigned as liaisons or informants, make sure that a method is clearly specified for how they will review group recommendations. The easiest and probably most effective method for the person in the liaison role is to have a member of your group present recommendations to members of his or her group and register feedback on the spot. A person in the informant role can receive the minutes of each meeting and simply be asked to call whenever there is a concern. The important thing is to be clear **exactly how** persons in every role will interact with your group.

5. Don't be put off by the time required to thoroughly set up a group and use a stakeholder analysis. It will pay off in spades. Think of all the groups and committees that have failed in your experience. These planning steps will enable you to avoid mysterious sabotage of the group's work later. Remember, you have to "go slow" in the beginning to "go fast" in the later stages.

6. Adapt your use of these recommendations to the scale of the system in which you are working. If you are working in a small system with a decidedly clear-cut formal and informal decision method, develop your group in a like manner, ignoring much of this suggested analysis. However, if you are working in a relatively large or complex system or in a system where there have been failures to accomplish similar efforts, you will want to plan with "unnatural" thoroughness, assuming you have the commitment of your group leaders to do so.

7. Aim to select group members who are closest to the issues. Using the tools suggested here, committed groups of intelligent and dedicated individuals, led by someone with "fire inside," will outperform the more traditionally formed groups.

Variation

Here's a variation on stakeholder analysis aimed at group member selection. It is adapted from a matrix suggested by Ken Olsen at the Mid-South Regional Resource Center in Lexington, Kentucky.

Group Membership Decision Analyzer															
Potential Group Members ⬇	Demographics						Content Expertise				Roles/ Personality				
	Minority	Western Region	Central	East	Male	Female	Engineering	Manufacturing	Marketing	Training & Development	Idea People	Implementer	Conciliator	Challenge	Link to

Procedure I-1

SAMPLE I-1

Stakeholder Analysis

Alternative Stakeholder Relationships to Group		
(a) Regular Member (b) Member of Steering and Review Committee	(c) Special Liaison (d) Standby Consultant	(e) Communication Liaison (f) Ad Hoc Member

Stakeholder Representative(s)	Role/Group	A	B	C	D	E	F
Sauter	Finance			X			
Scali	Marketing		X				
Lisagor	Key Supplier				X		
Tezak	Ad Agency Rep		X				
Murray	Marketing	X					
Perry	Manufacturing					X	
Riggs	Printing Contractor					X	
Frankel	Human Resources			X			
Jaffe	VP—Marketing	X		X			
Mazzone	Sales	X				X	
Rogers	Affiliate—Marketing	X					X
Vandersall	Manager—Production			X			
Burns	Manager—Administration	X					
Clark	Manager—Engineering					X	
Greathouse	Marketing	X		X			
Brigham	Harley Account Manager				X		
Jeffrey	Association Director	X					
Thompson	Graphic Designer	X					
Eiber	Manager—Distribution			X			X

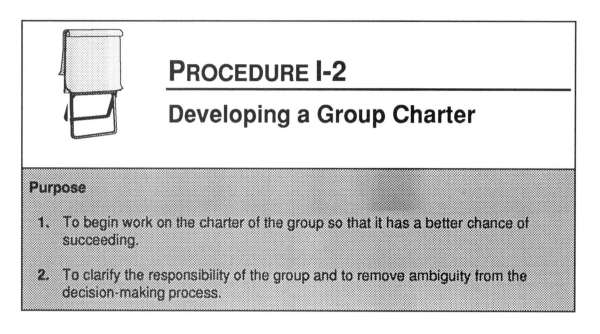

PROCEDURE I-2

Developing a Group Charter

Purpose

1. To begin work on the charter of the group so that it has a better chance of succeeding.

2. To clarify the responsibility of the group and to remove ambiguity from the decision-making process.

Summary Description

Ongoing groups such as self-directed work teams, tasks forces facing complex problems, and special project teams need to take the time necessary to clarify the work of the group if they are to be successful. A group charter statement is an excellent way to clarify the work of the group.

When to Use the Procedure

- When a new task force or team is being planned (approximately six weeks to three months prior to the first meeting)

- When any group is taking on a charge with a considerable degree of complexity that will affect a significant number of players

Participants

Number: A small group of two to five members

Type: The anticipated group leader
The group facilitator
The group sponsor
The manager to whom recommendations will be directed
Others knowledgeable about issues related to task

Resources *(checkmarks indicate recommended equipment)*

    ✔ Flip chart and markers
    ✔ Laptop computer

Time

Approximately 2 to 3 hours. Adapt the allotted time to the significance of the charge of the group.

Method

Every group needs to have a clearly worded statement of its charter and responsibility. You may find the following procedural steps useful for developing such a statement.

1. Brainstorm the purposes of the group. List them on a sheet of chart paper.

2. Prioritize the purposes. Rank them in order of importance according to the priority weighting system you use. Check that the number one purpose can be used as the group's primary purpose, the one purpose that if **not** accomplished ensures the group's failure.

3. As best as you can at this point, indicate the desired future state, or the desired outcomes, that you would like to see result from the group's work. Discuss what you envision as the specific outcomes at this time. Be as specific as you can. Review the outcomes and highlight any that you and members can now agree will surely be needed.

4. Brainstorm the expected barriers to achieving the desired future state or outcomes. Identify problems related to accomplishment of the outcomes, asking something like, "What are the barriers or problems that confront us in accomplishing our outcomes?"

5. Group like problems and condense the statements into a more manageable list.

6. Using the revised list of problems, establish the priorities for each of the problems. Rank them in order of importance.

7. Highlight the top 20% from the total number of problems as the key problems that confront the team. Write these out as "Key Problems."

8. Establish the estimated length of time necessary for the group to accomplish the outcomes.

   Specify one of the following choices:

   (a) The group will disband when it has accomplished its tasks.

   (b) The group will continue in force as a monitoring and problem-solving mechanism after initial tasks are completed.

(c) The decision as to the group's continuance will be reviewed at a subsequent date.

9. Identify the decision maker to whom group recommendations will be submitted and any regular meeting led by that decision maker where recommendations will be reviewed prior to decisions being approved. (Note: This is an important step oftentimes omitted by groups. The failure to precisely identify the decision path for recommended decisions by task groups is a leading cause of the failure of many such groups.)

10. Schedule the first review checkpoint. A review checkpoint is a time when the group's recommendations are reviewed with the person responsible for approving those recommendations. Best practice is for recommendation reviews to take place at a regular meeting over which that person presides.

11. To provide a concluding statement, write a group mission statement of less than 30 words that clearly and succinctly identifies the charge of the group.

12. Review the key data that will be included in the charter statement for the group. Either you or a person assigned from the planning group should record the charter statement on a clean sheet of chart paper. (See Sample I-2: Group Charter.)

13. Schedule a time when, as a group, you will return to the charter statement and make any revisions that seem appropriate. Assign a person responsible for revisiting the charter statement by that date.

Notes

1. It is always something of a dilemma to know how much of the group's work to plan. If you plan too much upfront, before you really get into the work, you often waste a lot of time and effort because you do not have enough data yet about your charter to plan intelligently. If you fail to plan at all and dive into the work, you may be jumping into the jaws of the "group dragon monster," who swallows up well-intentioned teams that have no idea where they are going.

   It is, therefore, a good idea to define the group's work in stages. Do some initial planning, document what you are clear on, and go to work. Then, after you have some experience with the work, return to the planning and work more on the group charter. It is also good to revisit the charter periodically, reviewing and upgrading your approach to the work.

2. One secret to effectively defining the stages of the group's work is to structure and schedule time for this ongoing task. A planning committee can be established for the group and can schedule several planning sessions over the course of time that the group is in force. But be cautious about these planning committees meeting too frequently. They can easily come to be viewed as political structures or alternative subcultures that detract from the group's team character.

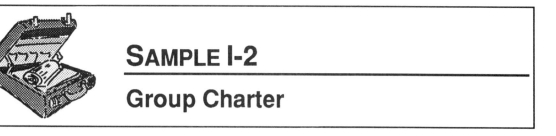

SAMPLE I-2

Group Charter

The mission of the Sagebrush Valley School District Task Force on Violence in the Schools is to identify specific strategies to reduce the incidences of violence in the schools.

Key problems that confront the task force are as follows:

- The lack of paraprofessional staff training to deal with student conflicts in situations where most of the incidents occur. For example, the cafeteria, school buses, student restrooms.

- Insufficient parent/school staff communication on a regular and systematic basis

- A recent rise in the use of alcohol, methamphetamine, and crack cocaine drugs among low-performing students

- Inadequate and insufficiently uniform policies related to discipline in the schools

- The recent advent of gang activities among certain subcultures in the schools

Expected outcomes for the group include:

- A training and development plan for the 19XX to 19XX school year and a subsequent training program for paraprofessional school staff

- Written suspension and expulsion procedures

- Recommended revisions in class scheduling and provisions for staggered release of students

- A cooperative plan jointly developed with the Captain of the Juvenile Division of the Pikeville Police Department

- New policies and procedures on parent/school staff communications approved by the local unit of the California Teachers' Association
- Longer-range recommendations to address root causes of the violence

Term of the Task Force

The task force will disband following presentation of its report on June 15, 199X. The task force will select three members to continue on a District Implementation Team, which will oversee implementation of Board-approved recommendations in the 199X to 199X school year.

Task Force Members

Jane Deville, Director of Pupil Personnel Services, will serve as the group leader. Ben Sanchez, School Psychologist, has agreed to serve as a group facilitator.

Other task force members will be:

— Dr. Jake Rinaldi, Associate Professor of Social Psychology at Pershing State College and the author of a recent report to Congress on school violence
— Suzanne Belcher, teacher and past president of the district teachers' organization
— Captain Sally Montefusco, Officer in Charge of the Juvenile Division of the Pikeville Police Department
— Jan Mendoza, Staff Development Specialist for the state department of education
— Hill Barnard, Assistant Principal, Midview High School
— Laticia Cox, President of the Certified Staff Association
— Jan Fountaine, Principal, Oakview Middle School

Dr. Janet Melville, Assistant Superintendent in charge of Educational Services, will serve as the group sponsor and confer with the group leader. She will only attend meetings of the group when asked to do so for a specific purpose.

The Schedule and Timeline for Completion of Activities

The group will meet weekly for one half-day between 3:00 and 7:00 p.m. for the next three months. One weekend retreat will be held.

Recommendations will be submitted to Dr. Samuel Guerrerro, Superintendent of Schools.

Recommendations will be reviewed at Dr Guerrerro's cabinet meeting. Two such presentations are planned. One presentation will be made when alternative strategies have been formulated, which is expected to happen by mid April 199X. A final presentation of task force recommendations will be made on June 15, 199X.

Final recommendations approved by Dr. Guerrerro will be presented to the School Board at its July 11, 199X meeting.

Costs

The district will provide a catered dinner at each of the task force meetings. The university representative will receive a $750 stipend. Classified employees on the team will receive a $50 stipend per meeting. Estimated costs for two nights' lodging, meals, and conference facilities for the weekend retreat are $2200.

GUIDE I-1

Chartering the New Team

The Purpose of This Guide

This guide's purpose is to provide you with a comprehensive list of questions and issues to consider when chartering a new team. It will also help you think through key issues that will affect the success of the team.

The Importance of the Guide

Chartering a team that is expected to meet a significant performance challenge requires considerations beyond those identified in the procedure for developing a group charter. The upfront time investment in clarifying the team charter should be more substantial. The following checklist poses the key issues for planners of new teams to consider.

How to Use the Guide

Review the list of questions with the potential leader(s) of your group. Check those that you feel should be clarified during the "charter" phase of the group work. You may wish to identify specific dates or times when you want to revisit the list in order to better clarify your charter once you have gotten into the work and have a better handle on it.

It is a good practice to take the list of issues that you have identified to a meeting with the potential group leader(s), any management sponsor for the work of the group, and the person with authority for charging the work of the group. Build the group charter with these people.

QUESTIONS FOR CONSIDERATION

Chartering Issues

1. **Purpose:** What is (are) the purpose(s) of this team? (Use the following only as cues toward developing written purpose statements for the team.)

    ☐ Meet a performance challenge?

    ☐ Define a desired future?

    ☐ Solve a persistent problem?

    ☐ Build a common culture?

    ☐ Foster participation?

(Continued)

Questions for Consideration *(Continued)*

- ☐ Integrate work across functional boundaries?

- ☐ Improve morale?

- ☐ Design or reengineer work systems and/or processes?

- ☐ Design a new product or service?

2. **Present State/Desired Future State**

   - ☐ How would you describe the current or present state that you wish to have an impact on?

   - ☐ Within the present state, are there elements that you want to protect against any changes?

   - ☐ What are some of the elements of a desired future state that you can presently identify?

3. **Performance Challenge:** What are the compelling performance challenges that the team is to address?

   - ☐ Effect on business outcomes or results?

   - ☐ Effect on competitive positioning?

   - ☐ Critical process improvements? (Increases in cycle time, etc.)

4. **Problem Definition:** If known key problems exist, what are the dimensions of these problems?

   - ☐ Where does the problem happen?

   - ☐ When does the problem happen?

   - ☐ What material or equipment is involved?

   - ☐ Who is involved in the problem?

   - ☐ What processes or procedures are involved?

   - ☐ Where and when could this problem be occurring, but it is not?

   - ☐ Is the problem complex?

   - ☐ Does it affect many people in the organization?

   - ☐ Is there a high risk in failing to solve this problem?

   - ☐ Has the problem been persistent?

(Continued)

Questions for Consideration *(Continued)*

5. **Team Mission:** What is the specific mission of the team in 25 to 75 words, including:

    ☐ The basic purpose in a single, simple sentence

    ☐ The ways that the purpose will be accomplished

    ☐ Distinctive features of approaching the tasks of the team

    ☐ The key business outcomes on which the tasks will ultimately have an impact

6. **Natural Deadlines:** Are there natural deadlines establishing time boundaries for the work?

    ☐ How soon must the work be completed or you will be in trouble?

    ☐ How soon is it desirable to complete the work?

    ☐ What is the anticipated date for task completion and final approvals?

7. **Team Membership—Expertise**

    ☐ Who has critical knowledge or data to contribute to the team effort?

    ☐ Who is especially expert in matters related to the purpose and mission of the team?

    ☐ Who from outside the organization is expert in the area and might be consulted with in order to enrich the data base?

    ☐ What are the necessary skills and attributes (both content and process) that will be needed on this team?

    ☐ Could valuable data be gleaned from the following:
    - Visitations?
    - Phone or written surveys?
    - Written requests for information?
    - Reviews of benchmarking standards from other organizations?

8. **Team Membership—Representation**

    ☐ Who is the group representative that will ultimately have to implement any recommendations of the team?

    ☐ Which stakeholders must be represented on the team or failure is likely?

9. **Team Membership—Roles**

    ☐ Are there certain people who should be considered core team members, attending nearly every meeting or function and doing the lion's share of the work?

    (Continued)

Questions for Consideration *(Continued)*

☐ Are there certain people who should be considered staff to the team?

☐ Should certain people be asked to serve as "ad hoc" team members, available to be on call at a specific time?

☐ Will the team have one or more chairpersons? If more than one person is chair, will one be considered lead, or the first point of contact?

☐ Will the team have specific process facilitators? Will they be core team members, facilitating often, or called in when needed?

10. Confidentiality and Communication Issues

☐ What is the agreement related to confidentiality and communication?

1. Complete confidence—Little or no communication occurs until final recommendations are made.

2. Mostly confidential—General communications are made only when data must be provided to ensure task completion.

3. Mostly open—Data is regularly communicated unless doing so would damage someone or lessen the chances of approval.

4. Totally open—All progress and workings of the team are openly published on some type of regular basis and information provided freely and openly upon request.

☐ What reports will be submitted when and to whom?

11. Meetings

☐ Will regular team meetings be held? If so, how often, where, and when?

☐ Who will prepare the agenda for meetings?

☐ Will the agenda be prepublished and materials sent out beforehand to team members?

12. Team Decision Method

☐ What will be the primary mode of making decisions for the team?

1. Absolute consensus
2. Consultative
3. Consultative consensus
4. Modified consensus
5. Voting

☐ What will be the backup method(s) of making decisions if the group fails to come to agreement using the primary decision mode?

☐ Who will make decisions when the group is deadlocked?

(Continued)

Questions for Consideration *(Continued)*

Contracting Issues

13. **Resources**

   ☐ How many person hours in what period of time will be expected for the following people:

   - Core team members?
   - Chairperson(s)?
   - Ad hoc team members?
   - Outside experts or consultants?

   ☐ What training will be provided to the team in order to increase teamwork and process skills?

   ☐ What training will be provided to the group to increase its knowledge of the work associated with its charter?

   ☐ Will travel monies be necessary?

   ☐ Will conference, meeting, or facility costs be involved?

   ☐ Will consultants be retained on a paid basis?

   ☐ Will any materials or supplies be necessary?

   ☐ How will clerical support be provided? Who will do it? How much time will be required?

14. **Management Time Approvals**

   ☐ Should line managers of employees be requested to approve a certain number of person hours for certain team members?

   ☐ Who has the authority to encourage or insist that time be approved from line managers?

15. **Stakeholders**

   ☐ Who could block the work of the team from being implemented?

   ☐ Who could play a major role in supporting the work of the team?

   ☐ Who will have final say over the recommendations of the team?

   ☐ What top authorities could get involved in this work if it was drawn to their attention?

   ☐ Are there certain suppliers who are key stakeholders?

   ☐ Who really cares about the work of the team? Internally? Externally?

   ☐ Who has natural influence related to the work of the team?

(Continued)

Questions for Consideration *(Continued)*

☐ Who really cares about the work of the team but is in probable disagreement about how the team wants to go about doing the work?

16. Sponsors

☐ What persons with political clout want the end result of what the group is working on?

☐ What persons are supportive of the operating principles and distinctive features of how the team wants to do its work?

☐ Who is willing to spend time lobbying for the work of the team to key authorities in the formal organization?

17. Linking to the Formal Organization

☐ To whom will recommendations be presented for approval?

☐ Who must "sign off" on decisions of the team?

☐ If multiple "sign-offs" are required, who has authority over all those who must sign off?

☐ Do your team sponsors have access to that person who has authority over the other persons who must sign off?

☐ How will you make established authorities knowledgeable about the work of the team?

☐ Who will be responsible for cultivating supportive relationships between the team and certain individuals who are central to the approval process?

☐ Will key decision makers approve the charter of the group?

☐ What do you know about the styles of key stakeholders who carry formal decision authority? How might this influence how the team conducts its business?

☐ What regular management team meeting is controlled by the person who has the final approval over the work of the team?

☐ To what regular meetings will the team report to review and seek approval for its work?

18. Implementation

☐ Will this team be responsible for supervising the implementation of team recommendations that are approved?

☐ Who will have the management authority to implement team recommendations?

(Continued)

Questions for Consideration *(Concluded)*

☐ How will implementation authority be "handed off" from team members to implementers?

☐ If the team is not to be responsible for implementation, is there an oversight role it should play during the implementation process? Some other role that ensures the integrity of its original work?

GUIDE I-2

Selecting the Group Leader

Leadership decisions often make the difference between success and failure in a group. The following tips will help you guide the group through key leadership decisions:

❑ Groups will generally move through the stages of group development quicker when the leadership is decided early on. Groups without leaders have a substantially higher failure rate than those that designate a specific leader.

❑ When facilitating a group within a "regular" meeting, such as a weekly staff meeting, it is wise to assume that the person in charge of that meeting is the leader unless he or she specifically designates another leader for the part of the meeting that you are facilitating.

❑ The following are the principal criteria that groups can use to select leaders for specific task groups or task forces. All of the conditions listed below are legitimate reasons for designating a person as a task group leader:

- Expertise: The person has the most expertise in the problem to be solved or the group task.
- Initiation of work: The person is most likely to be called upon to initiate work.
- Workload expectancy: The person will be called upon to do the greatest amount of work.
- Functional responsibility: The person has the most "natural responsibility" for the work in the system.
- Hierarchical status: The person has the highest level of hierarchical status of all group members.

❑ Many groups either fail or "fizzle" if the group leader has a lower hierarchical status than another member of the group. It is safest to appoint as task group leader the member who has the highest hierarchical status in the system in which you are working. If that higher-status person is not made the group leader, the facilitator should assume some responsibility for ensuring that the alternate leadership will not be resisted by the higher-status person before the leadership decision is made.

❑ When the group leader has the highest hierarchical status in the group but clearly does not possess the highest level of expertise in the issue, there is a good rationale for co-leadership of the group.

❑ If co-chairs or leaders of a group are selected, the facilitator should ask that one of the people be designated as the "first point of contact" for the facilitator. This avoids confusion, particularly in the planning of the meetings.

❑ A good practice to adopt early on in the life of a group is to encourage everyone to be a leader, establishing a group culture of shared leadership. This can be done by introducing or reintroducing task maintenance behaviors and asking group members to assert leadership by monitoring the behavior of the group with regard to those behaviors.

A specific practice can be implemented before the meeting when the group goes through the exercise of monitoring task and maintenance behaviors (see Procedure II-2: Monitoring Group Task and Maintenance Behaviors). The group then identifies where it needs to focus attention for this meeting and designates leaders to monitor group performance in these areas.

❑ Some groups prefer to have rotating leaders. Others want to operate leaderless. Caution should be exercised in using a rotating leadership method or establishing a leaderless group dynamic. Groups that successfully use rotating leaders or no leaders usually are working under several of these conditions:

- There is an equality of expertise among group members.

- Group members have equal status within the system.

- If there is a natural or hierarchical leader present, that person has a proven history of successfully yielding authority in group situations.

- There is a simple group process design in place that any member of the group is fully competent to follow. Oftentimes, this process is written and rotating leaders follow the written format.

- The task or performance challenge on which the group is working is relatively uncomplicated and does not involve high numbers of people in the system.

- The culture of the system is highly egalitarian and the egalitarian values are already firmly established in practice. People are "walking the talk."

- The action that results from the group work is usually targeted toward individuals rather than groups or the larger system. That is, each member of the group is free to "take what they like" from the group work and "leave the rest."

- A considerable amount of training has been done within the organization on group leadership and facilitation skills.

FACILITATOR RESOURCES

Setting Group Norms

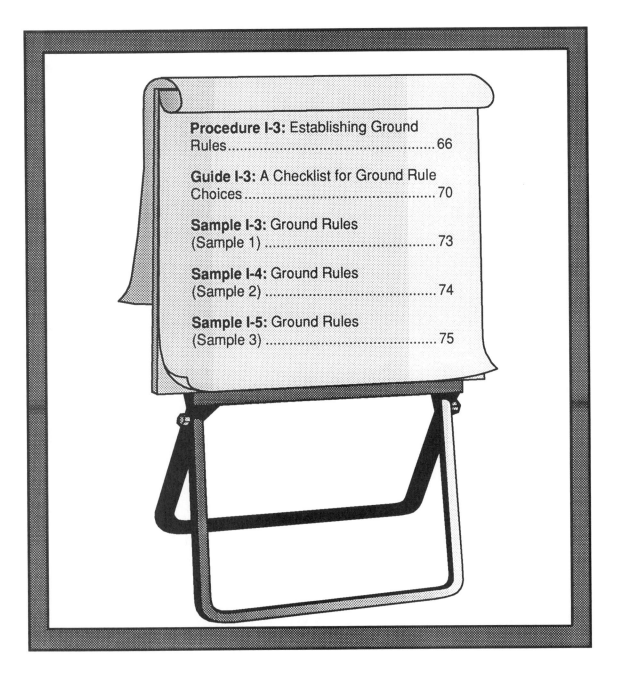

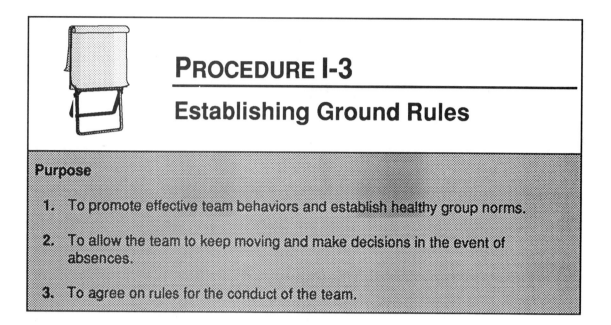

PROCEDURE I-3

Establishing Ground Rules

Purpose

1. To promote effective team behaviors and establish healthy group norms.

2. To allow the team to keep moving and make decisions in the event of absences.

3. To agree on rules for the conduct of the team.

Summary Description

Certain group behaviors will contribute to team productivity. There are also simple rules that make groups (task groups in particular) very effective. These rules are presented to the group, and compliance with the rules is expected.

When to Use the Procedure

At the first meeting of the team or at the initial meetings. Then review the rules for the next one to three meetings and periodically as needed.

Participants

Number: A group of any size

Type: Particularly important with larger groups, ongoing groups, or groups whose members have divergent viewpoints

Resources *(checkmarks indicate recommended equipment)*

✔ Flip chart and markers

☐ Handout—Guide I-3: A Checklist for Ground Rule Choices

Facilitator(s)

One facilitator presents the rules that have been approved by the group leader.

Time

Approximately 3 to 30 minutes at first team meeting; 5 minutes at next one to three meetings; 15 minutes for review after several meetings

Method

Option A

1. The facilitator meets with the team leader or planning group and reviews a list of ground rules to be used.

2. The rules are presented to the group and members are asked if they understand the rules.

3. The facilitator states that these are the rules everyone will be operating with from this point on in the group. He or she checks to make sure everyone is willing to comply with these rules.

Option B

1. The facilitator meets with the team leader and reviews a list of potential ground rules to be presented to the team.

2. The rules are then presented to the team for review. The team then adds any other rules that they feel are needed. From this list, the team selects the rules they wish to operate with. Some teams prefer to get the list down to as few rules as possible. Others tend to adopt nearly all the rules that are presented. A general guideline is to suggest that the ground rules should be eight or less in number.

3. The ground rules may be reviewed at the next couple of meetings, or they may simply be mounted on the wall for the next several meetings. It is not a bad idea to review the rules after several meetings and see if the group has found using the rules valuable and chooses to continue them in force.

Option C

1. The facilitator distributes copies of the handout (Guide I-3) to the group for review and asks members to suggest ground rules that they think would most benefit the group.

2. Group members forward nominations for ground rules that they think would help the group to succeed.

3. The list of nominated rules are prioritized and the group settles on no more than eight rules.

Option D

The same as Option B, but the work is done with a small planning group that is working on formulating the group charter.

Notes

1. How you handle the presentation of ground rules depends on your view of how much the group should be involved in setting the rules.

2. In the purest sense, ground rules are simply rules you play the game by. They are operating instructions for a given activity that enable you to complete the activity without getting hopelessly snagged in argument. Typical ground rules for a pick-up basketball game might be:

   — "Take the ball back behind the line unless the shot misses the rim."

   — "Call your own fouls."

   — "Don't touch the ball after your team has made a basket."

   — "You have to win by 2 points."

   — "Shoot to see who plays when there is an odd number of players."

   Ground rules work best when they are simple and direct, are totally enforceable, and can be imparted to a new "player" in less than 30 seconds. They should also be founded on expert experience from those who already know "the game." This is why it is usually preferable that the rules be presented to the group (and any person who later joins it), rather than be generated by group members who may not have sufficient experience to know what rules are needed.

3. Some facilitators and groups also inject ground rules that are less cut-and-dried, more value-based, and more like basic group principles or desirable norm states for the group. It is up to you as facilitator to determine what types of ground rules will work best for your group and the best way to present the rules to the group.

4. However generated and presented, ground rules do help groups perform better. The following principles are recommended for establishing ground rules:

   1. Keep them clear, simple, and direct.

   2. Make sure they are based on practical, solid experience.

   3. Introduce them quickly and limit discussion.

   4. Enforce them immediately following their introduction.

   If you wish, you can also announce that you will be playing the "referee" role for the group and enforcing the rules. Or you can appoint one or two group members to assume the referee role for the present meeting or for a series of meetings.

5. Sample ground rules are included in this "Resources Section." All these rules have been used in actual meeting situations and have a rationale that supports groups in succeeding.

6. For more information, see Mirja P. Hanson's *Golden Ground Rules* (1996), available from Meeting Needs, 5510 Edgewater Blvd., Minneapolis, MN 55417; (612) 827-3001.

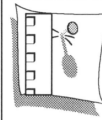

GUIDE I-3

A Checklist for Ground Rule Choices

Directions

The following statements of ground rules have been used in different kinds of meetings. From the list, you may check those rules (no more than eight) that you believe will most contribute to the success of your meeting. Combine and edit rules as appropriate, keeping them clear and direct. The rules can be either:

(a) Chosen by the facilitator before the meeting

(b) Chosen by the group leader or a planning group for the meeting

(c) Selected at the meeting by the group members

❑ No phone calls in or out during scheduled meeting sessions.

❑ Sessions start and end on time.

❑ Commit to being on time for all meetings; if you will be late for a meeting, let the group know in advance.

❑ We stick to the stated times.

❑ Phone messages will be delivered at _____ (lunch, breakpoints, etc.) only.

❑ There will be no group reviews for those not present at any time.

❑ Everyone is encouraged to participate.

❑ All participants are considered equal during these sessions.

❑ One person talks at a time.

❑ Raise your hand to speak in large-group sessions (those with more than nine people).

❑ Every idea and comment is valid.

❑ Before judging the idea, listen to it first as an advocate.

❑ No food or drinks in the meeting area.

❑ Clean up after yourself.

❑ What is said here stays here.

(Continued)

A Checklist for Ground Rule Choices *(Continued)*

☐ Anyone can pass on any activity.

☐ After the meeting, accurately represent the decisions of the group to others.

☐ Every effort will be made to reach consensus.

☐ You are acting as a consultant to the group leader(s), who will make decisions.

☐ Agenda times are flexible. We'll get as far as we get.

☐ All tasks have written outputs recorded in the group memory.

☐ Use the group memory when working in groups.

☐ No lectures.

☐ The meeting facilitator structures time and tasks.

☐ The conference managers (or planning committee) structures time and tasks.

☐ _____ handles the room temperature or other needs of group members.

☐ Some activities are timed. Stop speaking shortly after the timer goes off.

☐ Stay in the room during meeting times.

☐ It's OK to move around when you need to.

☐ It's OK to have fun.

☐ (a) Take your own breaks. There will be no group breaks.

    (b) Breaks will be taken every _____ hour(s) for _____ minutes.

☐ People need not agree.

☐ This is not problem solving, but learning.

☐ All decision are recommendations only, subject to review by _____.

☐ We are here to learn how to think and learn as a collective.

☐ We seek common ground for collective, coordinated action, not agreement.

☐ Personally investigate the assumptions/beliefs underlying your positions.

☐ Suspend predetermined positions to allow the collective intelligence to emerge.

☐ All ideas are held up for consideration, reflection, and inquiry.

☐ There are no taboo topics; nothing is withheld from discussion.

☐ Advocate the best ideas that emerge from the group.

☐ Say what you mean and mean what you say.

☐ Stay conscious.

(Continued)

A Checklist for Ground Rule Choices *(Continued)*

❏ Use "I messages."

❏ Speak first from your own personal experience.

❏ This is a put-down free, safe environment. No sarcasm.

❏ Monitor your participation. (Some need to hold back to allow others to share. Others need to force themselves to share more.)

❏ All ideas are valid.*

❏ Everything goes up on flip charts.*

❏ Observe time frames.*

❏ Seek common ground and action—not problems or conflicts.*

❏ Require mutual respect.**

❏ Realize interdependence.**

❏ Keep an open mind.**

❏ Contribute thoughtful exchange.**

❏ Seek common ground.**

❏ Strive for results.**

❏ Choose effective process.**

❏ Help order chaos.**

❏ Employ human spirit.**

---

 * From: Marvin R. Weisbord and Sandra Janoff, *Future Search: An Action Guide to Finding Common Ground in Organizations and Communities,* San Francisco: Berrett-Koehler Publishers, 1995, p. 49.

** From: Mirja P. Hanson, *Golden Ground Rules,* Minneapolis: Meeting Needs, 1996, p. 4.

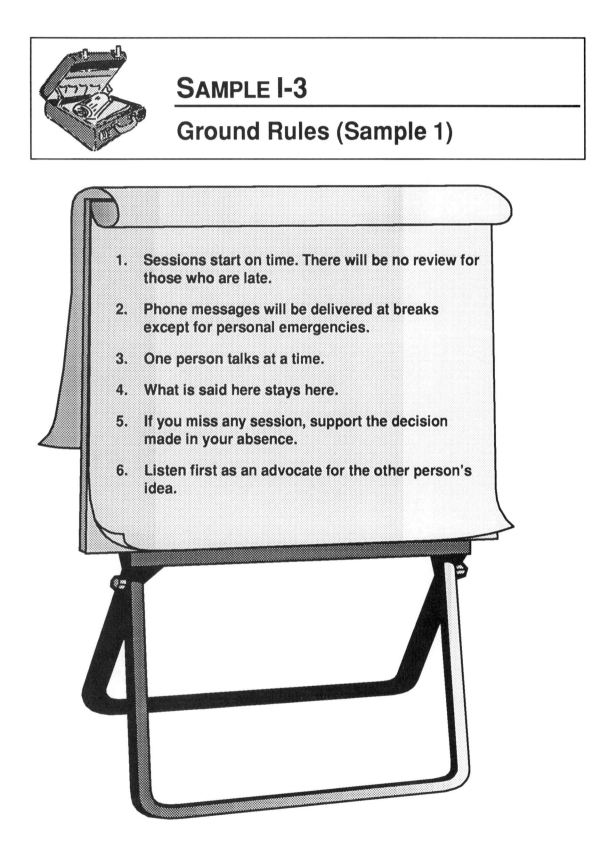

SAMPLE I-3

Ground Rules (Sample 1)

1. Sessions start on time. There will be no review for those who are late.

2. Phone messages will be delivered at breaks except for personal emergencies.

3. One person talks at a time.

4. What is said here stays here.

5. If you miss any session, support the decision made in your absence.

6. Listen first as an advocate for the other person's idea.

SAMPLE I-4

Ground Rules (Sample 2)

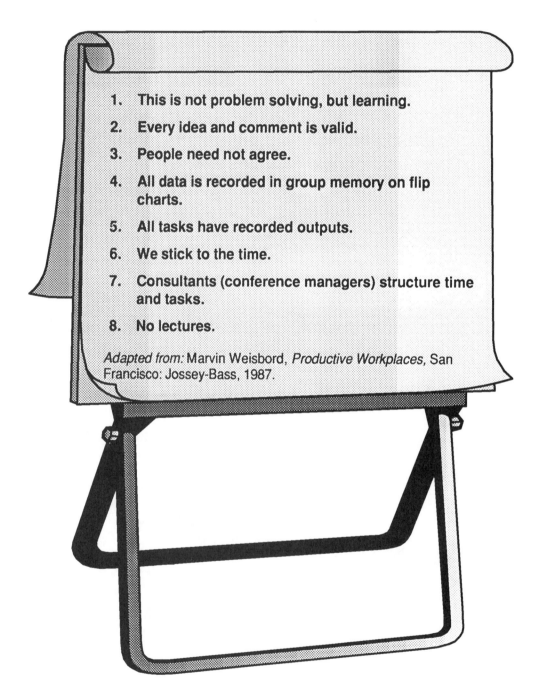

1. This is not problem solving, but learning.

2. Every idea and comment is valid.

3. People need not agree.

4. All data is recorded in group memory on flip charts.

5. All tasks have recorded outputs.

6. We stick to the time.

7. Consultants (conference managers) structure time and tasks.

8. No lectures.

Adapted from: Marvin Weisbord, *Productive Workplaces,* San Francisco: Jossey-Bass, 1987.

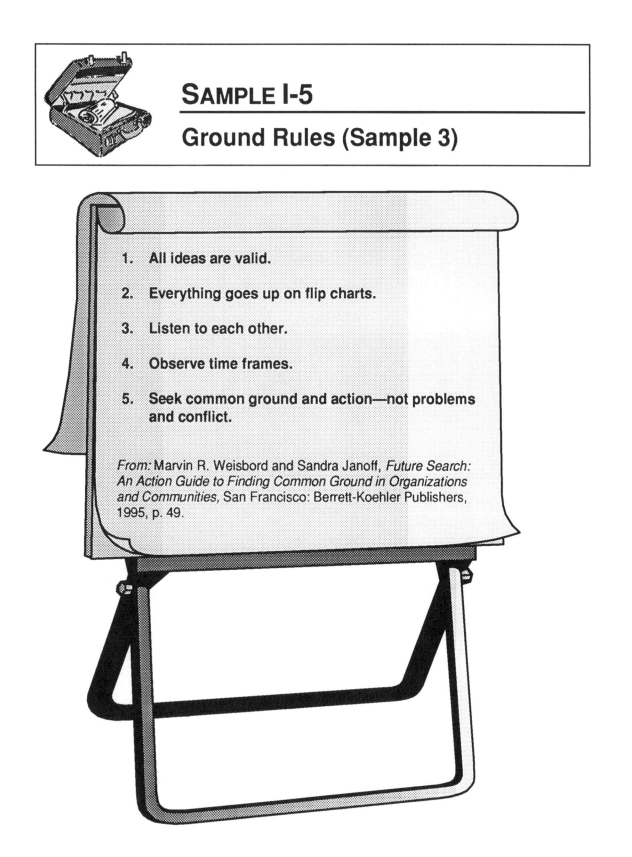

SAMPLE I-5

Ground Rules (Sample 3)

1. All ideas are valid.

2. Everything goes up on flip charts.

3. Listen to each other.

4. Observe time frames.

5. Seek common ground and action—not problems and conflict.

From: Marvin R. Weisbord and Sandra Janoff, *Future Search: An Action Guide to Finding Common Ground in Organizations and Communities,* San Francisco: Berrett-Koehler Publishers, 1995, p. 49.

FACILITATOR RESOURCES

Planning Meetings

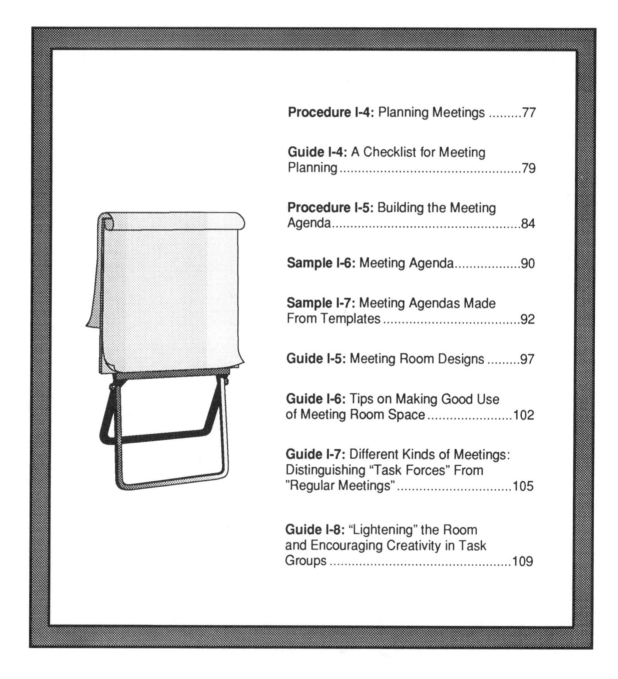

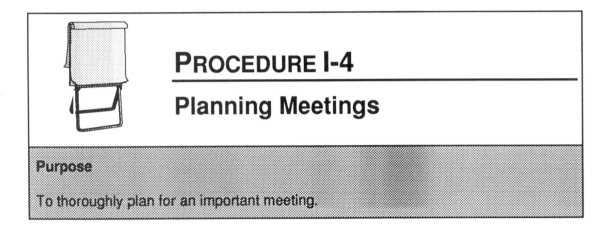

PROCEDURE I-4

Planning Meetings

Purpose

To thoroughly plan for an important meeting.

Summary Description

The 36 questions presented in Guide I-4: Checklist for Meeting Planning relate to the content and logistics planning for the meeting. Many of these questions should be addressed in the course of planning a meeting.

When to Use the Procedure

- Use it after you have committed to help facilitate the meeting. It is best to cover many of these questions by phone or in person as soon as you have agreed to facilitate.

Participants

Number: Usually two: You as the facilitator and the principal person you are working with; others in a meeting planning group may also be involved.

Type: The meeting leader.

Whoever else will be making meeting arrangements.

Resources

☐ Guide I-4: Checklist for Meeting Planning

Facilitator(s)

This procedure assumes that the meeting is complex enough to warrant a group facilitator. Even though the facilitator may not be responsible for many of the meeting planning functions, he or she will be wise to make sure that all the necessary arrangements have been handled.

Time

In actual practice, these planning issues are usually handled over the course of two or three conversations or meetings, the length of which varies according to the length and complexity of the group session(s).

Using Guide I-6 when you plan meetings can reduce the number of times you have to talk about planning issues and reduce overall planning time. It can also help you approach the task more systematically and make costly errors of omission less likely.

Method

1. Convene a small group of people who will be responsible for planning the meeting.

2. Go through the items on the checklist, and respond to the items that you consider relevant to the meeting you are planning.

3. At your first meeting with group members, review the data you have generated, ensuring that all members agree with the decisions that have been made by the planning group.

Notes

1. Before your planning conversations, you may wish to copy Guide I-6 and forward it to the people with whom you will be working.

It may be more appropriate to cover items on the checklist via phone conferences with the people with whom you will be working.

GUIDE I-4

A Checklist for Meeting Planning

Purposes and Outcomes

☐ What is (are) the purpose(s) of the meeting?

☐ What are the intended outcomes of the meeting? At the conclusion of the meeting, what do you expect to leave with?

Meeting Participation

☐ Who has the primary responsibility for ensuring that the outcomes of the meeting are achieved? Who is the meeting leader?

☐ Are there others who must approve the recommendations formulated by the group?

☐ Who has a significant stake in achieving the outcomes of the meeting and/or who might block the implementation of recommendations made by the group?

☐ Who is most knowledgeable or expert within the organization relative to the intended outcomes of the meeting?

☐ Who is knowledgeable within the organization as to how decisions might be received by those critical to successful implementation?

☐ To whom must decisions of the group be communicated, and when must the decisions be communicated?

☐ Is the nature of the meeting's content such that a neutral meeting facilitator is highly desirable or necessary, or should the meeting leader also facilitate the meeting?

☐ Who will decide who should be invited to the meeting?

☐ Who should be invited to the meeting?

☐ Who must review the recommendations of the group for approval? Who should be viewed as the primary person who will review recommendations?

(Continued)

A Checklist for Meeting Planning *(Continued)*

Length and Location

❑ What is the guesstimated number of meeting hours that will be required to achieve the purpose and outcomes for the meeting?

❑ Where should the meeting be held? Is an off-site location desirable in order to control interruptions or establish neutrality?

Meeting Pre-Work

❑ Are there any materials that should be distributed to participants in advance of the meeting? For example:

- Relevant work previously done by others
- Articles or data that will contribute to building an intelligent data base relative to the outcomes
- Instructions for work to be done by participants before the meeting
- Directions to the meeting location; parking instructions
- Assignments to be completed by participants before the meeting

❑ Who will be responsible for preparing the meeting agenda? Approving the agenda?

❑ Who will be responsible for sending out the agenda to meeting participants in advance of the meeting?

❑ Should any people be interviewed or observed before the meeting for the purpose of either (a) building the agenda or (b) helping the meeting leader or facilitator better understand the work?

Facilitation Roles

❑ Which of the following roles will be established for the meeting, and who will play the role?

  ☐ Group facilitator: _____

  ☐ Group newsprint recorder: _____

  ☐ Meeting record-keeper: _____

  ☐ Timekeeper: _____

  ☐ Small-group facilitators:

  _____

  _____

  _____

  _____

  ☐ Equipment operator: _____

(Continued)

A Checklist for Meeting Planning *(Continued)*

Decision Modes

☐ Which of the following decision modes will be our primary way of making decisions in this meeting? (Write #1 in check box.)

   ☐ **Absolute Consensus** (All must agree to support a decision.)

   ☐ **Modified Consensus** (All must be willing to support or "live with" decisions.)

   ☐ **Consultative** (Leader decides following consultation with group.)

   ☐ **Consultative Consensus** (Leader consults with group, seeks consensus, and then makes decision.)

   ☐ **Voting** (By _____ vote; specify majority, two-thirds, etc.)

☐ What will be our "fallback" mode(s) of decision making? (Write #2, #3, etc., in above check boxes.)

Reviews and Approvals

☐ To whom must these recommendations be delivered for review and approval?

☐ By when would we plan that recommendations be submitted for approval?

☐ At what meetings will our recommendations be reviewed, and when would such reviews take place?

	Meeting	*Probable Review Date*
1.		
2.		
3.		

(Continued)

A Checklist for Meeting Planning *(Continued)*

Equipment Required

❑ What equipment is needed for the meeting? (Shade box where equipment is required.)

❑ Flip chart and markers	❑ Chalkboard	❑ Extra pads of newsprint
❑ Overhead projector	❑ Microphone:	❑ Playback
❑ Slide projector	❑ Handheld wireless	❑ Video
❑ Storyboards	❑ Handheld wired	❑ Audio
❑ Wipe-off board	❑ "Lavaliere" microphone	❑ Video camera
❑ Clipboards or laptop writing surface	❑ Laptop computer	❑ Audio recorder
	❑ Computer overhead display device	❑ Other (Specify)

Participant Count/Room Set-Up

❑ How many people are expected to participate?

❑ How should the room be arranged?

❑ Theater style	❑ Rows	❑ Tables and chairs
❑ Classroom style with tables	❑ Circle	❑ Chairs only
	❑ U-shape	❑ Other (Specify)
	❑ Slanted diagonally	

❑ Drawing, diagram, or further instructions attached.

Room and Facility Check-Out Previous to Meeting

❑ Is the wall space adequate for hanging newsprint? Are there any prohibitions against putting masking tape on the walls? Can any paintings or decorations be taken down?

❑ If working off-site, who will be available to handle any problems with the room or supplies (room temperature, equipment, etc.)?

❑ Is there adequate space for separate small-group work areas with flip charts and a large-group meeting area with tables? (This is usually the preferred task group arrangement when sufficient space is available.)

(Continued)

A Checklist for Meeting Planning *(Continued)*

❑ Who receives calls for telephone messages? When do you want messages delivered? At breaks and lunch only? Immediately when received?

❑ Is there a phone in the room? Do you want it operative during the meeting? What calls should be transferred to the room, and who will monitor this?

❑ Where should food and refreshments be set up? If group is "on its own" for lunch or meals, what restaurants are nearby, and where are they located?

❑ If working at hotel location: What is checkout time? Do any special arrangements need to be negotiated to check out later? Are billing arrangements clear?

❑ Is the available equipment exactly what you want, and is it all in working order? Where are the electrical outlets, and will extension cords be needed?

❑ When will the meeting room be set up by hotel staff or others?

❑ What time is the meeting facility available for entry and facilitator set-up? Whom do you see to get in?

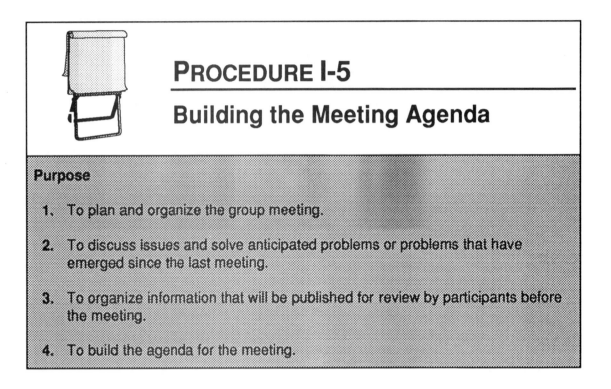

PROCEDURE I-5

Building the Meeting Agenda

Purpose

1. To plan and organize the group meeting.

2. To discuss issues and solve anticipated problems or problems that have emerged since the last meeting.

3. To organize information that will be published for review by participants before the meeting.

4. To build the agenda for the meeting.

Summary Description

A major facilitation role is to support the development of good meeting agendas. You need to ensure that the intentions (purpose and outcomes) for the meeting are made clear and that a carefully thought-out sequence of activities for achieving those intentions is developed. A facilitator process agenda should also be constructed for most task group meetings (see Sample I-6: Meeting Agenda).

When to Use the Procedure

- At least three working days before the meeting

- Best practice: 14 to 21 working days before the meeting

Participants

Number: Usually a small group of two to five members

Type: The group leader

The group facilitator

Others (usually one or two maximum) with skills or knowledge relevant to the meeting that is being planned

Resources *(checkmarks indicate recommended equipment)*

✔ Flip chart and markers

✔ Laptop computer

Facilitator(s)

The facilitator role depends on the experience of the people planning the meeting, the complexity of the tasks to be covered, and the extent to which training is a part of the agenda-building process. The group facilitator most often facilitates the planning session. The meeting leader approves the planning group's recommendation.

Time

At least one-half of the scheduled meeting time. More time is required if problems of substance are to be solved or the issues to be discussed are particularly critical.

Method

1. List on the flip chart the overall purposes of the meeting. Make sure the group takes enough time to be clear on the purposes. Time invested here will save many problems later.

2. List any issues or items that you need to deal with in the meeting to accomplish those purposes. Also, include any news or information items for this meeting.

3. Sort the issues and information items into what you have to deal with in this meeting and what you can deal with another way. The following categories may be helpful:

    ➤ *Now*   Item must be handled this meeting.

    ➤ *Next*   Item can be handled next meeting.

    ➤ *Write*   Assign a person to publish news item.

    ➤ *Delegate*   Assign one or more persons to resolve the issue and bring back resolution to the next meeting.

    ➤ *Task Group*   Assign a leader and members for a task group. Members can be individuals outside regular group.

    Using flip chart paper, write the group's decision next to the outcomes or news items.*

---

* Material in Step 3 adapted from William R. Daniels, *Orchestrating Powerful Regular Meetings,* San Diego, CA: University Associates, 1993.

4. List the anticipated results or outcomes for the meeting—what you want to see come out of the meeting.

   The following words may help focus your outcome statements (remember that outcomes should be listed as objective phrases):

   — Approval of

   — Agreement on

   — Delegation of

   — Recommendations for approval by _____ on _____

   — Definition of the _____ problem or issue

   — Feedback to _____ on _____ operations or performance review

   — Understanding of

   Listing these outcome statement "starters" on chart paper often lends clarity and focus to planning agenda items.

5. Prioritize (rank-order) the outcomes.

6. Where further detail is useful or needed, list the steps you will have to take to achieve each of the outcomes listed. (This is usually desirable for at least the top two priorities.)

7. Transfer all agenda items (outcomes and steps, news items, etc.) to a new sheet of chart paper, listing them by order of priority.

   Hint: News and information items are best left to last on the agenda unless the news or data is critical to the meeting.

   The following list headings may be useful to you:

Item	Person Responsible	Approximate Time

8. For each item, assign a person to be responsible for ensuring that the intended outcome is achieved. Even if the facilitator is leading an activity, one group member should be assigned this role and should monitor the activity.

9. Estimate time allotments.

   Incorporate some slack into the time schedule rather than plan each moment of it. As a rule of thumb, plan no more than 80% of the meeting time.

   Hint: At this point many agenda planners come up against problems with time limitations. A poor (**not** recommended) but frequently used solution is to squeeze the rest of the planning issues into the time remaining. It is better to eliminate some items (save them for another meeting) or to assign issues and problems to individuals or task groups.

10. Check which roles you wish to have in force for this meeting, and be sure those roles are assigned:

   ❑ Leader

   ❑ Facilitator (for entire group)

   ❑ Flip chart recorder (if problem-solving group memory to be used)

   ❑ Minutes-taker/record-keeper

   ❑ Small-group facilitators

   ❑ Timekeeper

   ❑ Process observer (a person assigned to focus on how the group is doing with specific process skills, which will be monitored during the meeting)

11. Check out the leader's preferred way of running the meeting. The following choices may be useful to present:

   (a) **Leader-run: Consultative mode.** Leader runs the meeting, facilitating discussion and making clear decisions before proceeding from item to item. Leader resists involvement in content of decisions; instead, asks questions, seeking consultative data for the decision that he or she will make.

   (b) **Leader-run: Facilitator-assisted.** Facilitator leads group through the items, turning to leader for decisions following consultation with the group. (Note: Using this style, leader is free to contribute to content of discussion, knowing that facilitator will guide discussion and eventually bring discussion back to leader for clear decision.)

   (c) **Leader-run: Periodic facilitator assistance.** Leader operates as in style (a) except for specified items that he or she turns over to facilitator for discussion and problem solving in consensus mode.

   (d) **Facilitator-led: Team-based decisions.** Leader agrees to accept all decisions agreed on by the group. Leader participates fully as an equal group member, with no greater authority than any other member.

   (e) **Leader-run and facilitated.** In this operating mode, the leader functions both as a decision maker and facilitator, choosing when to play which role. Though this is probably the most frequent method of running meetings, it is limited in its effectiveness because the leader usually gets so caught up in the politics and content of decisions that he or she is unable to attend to effective process during the meetings.

   (Note: *Some highly dysfunctional modes of operating are not provided as choices here. One such mode is operating loosely as a "leaderless" group, with no clear guidelines on how the group makes decisions.*)

   Whichever decision mode is used the responsibility for the group remains with the leader. Nothing a facilitator does should confuse this responsibility.

12. Identify the dominant method of making decisions if this has not already been done. These choices are useful:

    (a) **Absolute Consensus:** All must agree to support a decision before a decision is made.

    (b) **Consultative:** Leader makes decision after listening to all advice, points of view, ideas, and recommendations.

    (c) **Consultative Consensus:** Leader makes decision only after listening to views of members and striving for consensus.

    (d) **Modified Consensus:** Group seeks consensus on all items, agreeing to support the decision even though it may not agree with all of the decision. If this definition of consensus cannot be achieved, there is a fallback on the leader for either a decision or a postponement of item.

    (e) **Voting:** Members vote on decisions. Specify whether majority, two-thirds, or other kind of vote determines decision.

Note any agenda items that will be exceptions to the dominant mode for this meeting. For example, your dominant mode is consultative decision making, but the leader feels one item really requires the consensus of the entire group. That item should be marked as an exception. Or suppose your dominant mode is consensus, yet the leader knows that the conflicts are so acute that a clear individual decision followed by an open airing (the consultative mode) is required. That item, too, can be marked as an exception.

13. Identify any materials that will support the meeting, and identify which ones should be sent to meeting participants prior to the meeting.

14. Check to make sure that logistical functions are assigned before the meeting. You may wish to use an action list, with the items printed on the chart paper, or use copies of the Checklist for Meeting Planning (Guide I-4) with items printed for each meeting. A sample action list is shown below with sample items for the first issue.

ACTION LIST		
Item	Person Responsible	By
Have agenda typed and distributed.	Harry	Fri., 6/14
Copy and circulate _____ materials for review.	Seth	Tues., 6/11
Let _____ know to expect assignment on _____.	Bill	Wed., 6/5
Invite _____ to this meeting for presentation on _____.	Ted	Wed., 6/5
Ask _____ to be available for minutes.	Jill	Mon., 6/3
Schedule room.	Jill	Mon., 6/3
Order/bring refreshments.	Nate	Fri., 6/7

15. Establish the time when planning group members will arrive at the meeting, and set up a debriefing time following the meeting.

Variations

1. Facilitators should encourage managers to plan their meetings more carefully and well in advance. One way to do this is to use the "buddy system," whereby an assistant or a group member (selected on a rotating basis) helps the manager with the planning.

   An alternative is to establish a meeting improvement team for a definite length of time, usually three to six months. The meeting improvement team, always led by the person responsible for the meeting being planned, gets together on a regular basis to plan new meetings, debrief the most recent meeting, and ensure that all logistical arrangements are in order for the next meeting. The team also helps ensure that the agendas are published and sent out at least three days before the meeting.

2. Efforts at meeting agenda building are much improved when one group member records the group's flip chart data electronically, using a laptop computer. At the close of the session, a printout is made for everyone, thus making the finalizing of the agenda less cumbersome.

REFERENCES

Daniels, William R. (1987). *Group power II: A manager's guide to conducting regular meetings.* Mill Valley, CA: American Consulting and Training.

SAMPLE I-6

Meeting Agenda

Purposes of the Meeting

- To develop a strategic plan for ongoing and new business
- To improve teamwork among staff
- To reduce anxieties about the uncertain future of the division
- To identify the division's role in new business

Outcomes of the Meeting

- A strategic plan and the action steps for next year
- Concerns aired and addressed
- Team spirit
- Commitment to success for new plans

MEETING AGENDA

DAY ONE

I. Context

- Manager opening: Why we're here.
- Vice President remarks: New business, targets, timelines, bigger picture.
- Manager's perspective: What this means for us.

II. Issues

- Group is asked four questions: "As you listen to this, do you . . .
  — Feel excited about . . .?
  — Feel concerned about . . .?
  — Feel this raises any issues for us? If so, what are they?
  — Have any questions?
- Responses jotted down; group sharing and recording
- Manager and Vice President:
  — Answer any questions they can
  — Comment on concerns; acknowledge issues
- All of the above to be used in their planning

(Continued)

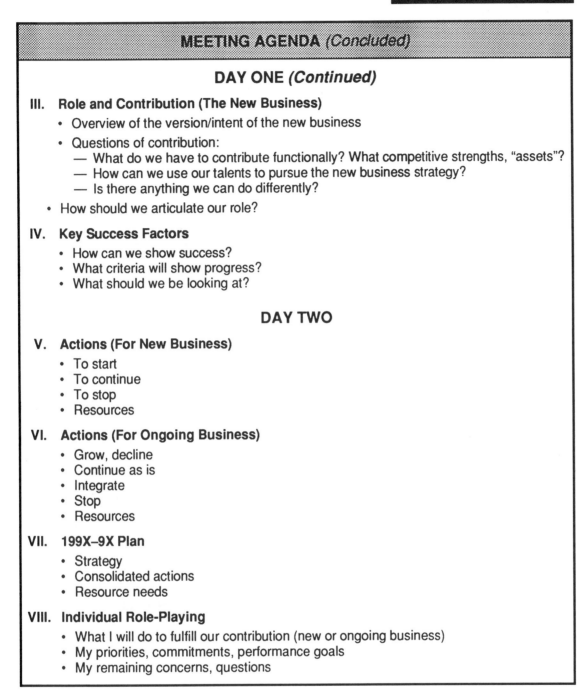

MEETING AGENDA *(Concluded)*

DAY ONE *(Continued)*

III. **Role and Contribution (The New Business)**
- Overview of the version/intent of the new business
- Questions of contribution:
  — What do we have to contribute functionally? What competitive strengths, "assets"?
  — How can we use our talents to pursue the new business strategy?
  — Is there anything we can do differently?
- How should we articulate our role?

IV. **Key Success Factors**
- How can we show success?
- What criteria will show progress?
- What should we be looking at?

DAY TWO

V. **Actions (For New Business)**
- To start
- To continue
- To stop
- Resources

VI. **Actions (For Ongoing Business)**
- Grow, decline
- Continue as is
- Integrate
- Stop
- Resources

VII. **199X–9X Plan**
- Strategy
- Consolidated actions
- Resource needs

VIII. **Individual Role-Playing**
- What I will do to fulfill our contribution (new or ongoing business)
- My priorities, commitments, performance goals
- My remaining concerns, questions

SAMPLE I-7

Meeting Agendas Made From Templates

Creating Meeting Agendas From Templates

We created the following agenda by first using a template from a word processing program and then editing the original version. Most word processing applications have such templates.

This template was made using the table option, but you can also use a column format. If you choose the table option, you will notice that the amount of data on each page tends to vary. This is because the software is designed to keep the material in each table cell together. If you want a more uniform look to your agenda, split the table cells and balance the copy across the pages. Your other option is to create the template using columns instead of a table.

If your word processing software does not offer the template feature, a macro can be created, which becomes your meeting planning template.

If working with templates and macros exceeds your current computer skills, simply create a format on a blank document; then bring up the file each time you want to create an agenda.

Creating a standard template for your meeting agenda preparation is well worth the time invested, particularly if you are frequently called on to create agendas.

WILSON INTERNATIONAL
Human Resources Division Meeting Agenda

MEETING: Team Development Work Session

Overview of Meeting

The workshop offers an initial one-day team development session.

Purpose of the Meeting

1. To resolve conflicts among team members.
2. To develop a more effective team.
3. To improve the group's performance.

Outcomes for the Meeting

We intend this meeting to produce

1. Reduced conflict
2. Effective team functions
3. Improved team performance

Meeting Leader: Alice Sparks **Meeting Facilitator:** Dave Jamieson

Date: March 20, 1996 **Time:** 8:30 a.m. **Location:** Wilson International

Scheduled Time			Actual Time		
Start	Stop	Total Hours	Start	Stop	Total Hours
8:30 a.m.	4:00 p.m.	7 1/2			

#	Activity	Process	Who	Time	Materials
		MEETING PROCESS AGENDA			
1	Introduction	(a) Opening statement by director (b) Opening statement by facilitator (c) Observations and perceptions of the team (d) Feedback on Team Character Inventory (e) Other observations about the team (f) Overview of the plan for the one day (g) Exercise: The things I have done to contribute to the situation The things that might help to change our current situation	Alice, Dave	8:30–8:40	
2	Getting to Know One Another Better	(a) Exercise: Life Line (b) Exercise: Key Achievements (c) Three key achievements, accomplishments, successes in your life that you are particularly proud of	Dave	8:40–9:20	Handouts: – Life Line – 3 Accomplishments

(Continued)

MEETING PROCESS AGENDA (Continued)

#	Activity	Process	Who	Time	Materials
3	Planning for Human Resource Management	(a) Each section head describes the section's key functions and tasks and the problems and challenges it now faces. (b) Each section head describes his or her key goals for the next year. (c) The entire team identifies how various functions, tasks, and goals might have an impact on them and what kinds of support or assistance they could provide to one another. (d) Entire team identifies potential areas/topics for integration of effort. In identifying areas for the team to work on together, they identify topics, issues, or tasks that one individual feel they want or need to work on with some other individual. The second aspect is for anyone in the department to identify topics, issues, or tasks that the entire team should work on together. (e) Director shares philosophy of the department and expectations she has for the role of section heads.	Alice Nate Jill Rocia Janet Sid	9:20–10:20	Worksheet: Section Work Summary
4	Break			10:20–10:30	

(Continued)

Sample I-7

#	Activity	Process	Who	Time	Materials
	MEETING PROCESS AGENDA *(Continued)*				
5	Interpersonal Relations	(a) Each section head completes the following and turns them into the facilitator: As I have interacted with each of the other section heads I would like more of [specify], less of [specify], and I would like them to continue [specify]. (b) Each section head completes the following: I believe the answers to each of the above questions concerning me will be [specify]. (c) Exercise: Learning Styles Inventory.	Dave Nate Jill Rocia Janet Sid	10:30–12:30	Worksheet: Role Negotiation Learning Styles Inventory Survey
6	Lunch		Angie	12:30–2:00	
7	Staff Meetings	(a) When we meet as a staff, the things I like about our meetings are [specify]. (b) The things I do not like about our meetings are [specify]. (c) I think we could improve our meetings if we [specify].	Dave	2:00–3:00	Worksheet: Meetings Analysis
8	Continuation of Interpersonal Relations After Studying the Feedback and Comparing with Their Perceptions of What Others Would Say	(a) Section heads are each given approximately 5 minutes to share their thoughts on what they agree with in the perceptions, what they disagree with, and what they can and will do to build on things people want more of and to eliminate things people want less of.	Dave Nate Jill Rocia Janet Sid	3:00–3:35	

(Continued)

#	Activity	Process	Who	Time	Materials
9	Evaluating the Initial Team Development Session	(a) The key things I learned as a result of this session (b) The things I liked most about this effort (c) The things I liked least about this effort (d) The things we could do to build upon this session (e) I think that as a team we have begun to improve in the following ways	Dave	3:35–4:00	

MEETING PROCESS AGENDA *(Concluded)*

Materials	Person Responsible
Two flip charts, two packs of markers	Alice
Handout: Life Line	Dave
Handout: 3 Accomplishments	Dave
Worksheet: Section Work Summary	Dave
Worksheet: Role Negotiation	Dave
Learning Styles Inventory Survey	Dave
Worksheet: Meetings Analysis	Dave
Bagels, fresh fruit	Angie
Writing tablets	Alice

Sample I-7

GUIDE I-5
Meeting Room Designs

Meeting Room Design	Advantages	Disadavantages
	• Centers attention on the group task. Removes distractions of table items and the barrier represented by a table. • Keeps focus on the group memory (flip chart). • Strongest design for promoting equity among group members. • No one is positioned oppositionally.	• Quite a few people are (at least initially) uncomfortable without a table in front of them. • The table writing surface is unavailable to group members. • It feels awkward until people have tried it a few times.

Chairs in a Semi-Circle—No Table
This is the basic small-group facilitation design deemed by many facilitators as most desirable for small task group work. The flip chart and facilitator are positioned to the side or in front of the group. Clipboards or writing surfaces such as the back of a binder are made available as needed.

When to Use
◆ After the facilitator explains the advantages of the design and asks people to "give it a try"
◆ When you are working with a small task group of six to nine people
◆ At off-sites where the norm is more relaxed and people expect to work differently
◆ Every time you do small-group work, if you can get the norm established

(Continued)

Meeting Room Designs *(Continued)*

Meeting Room Design	Advantages	Disadavantages
The Traditional Meeting Room Best used as the "regular meeting" group design where decisions are reviewed and approved or disapproved. Person seated at the head of the table is the acknowledged authority who is recognized as being in charge of the group. Because these furnishings are found in nearly every office, the design is also frequently used for small task group meetings.	• When the leader is seated at the head of the table, authority and roles are clarified. • Promotes decision making when the leader takes action following the presentation of recommendations. • Is often what is available and requires little set-up. • People are used to the design.	• Is inflexible in terms of breaking group into smaller groups. • Positions people across from one another. Invites cross-talk, opposition. • Directs energy toward head of table rather than dispersing it among members. • Because it is so well known, the design triggers a person's typical meeting behaviors.

When to Use

◆ For most "regular" meetings (e.g., management meetings, staff meetings)

◆ When the meeting time is less than 2 hours

◆ When the meeting is focused on reviewing rigorously developed recommendations and the meeting's purpose is to take action on the recommendations (approving/ disapproving)

◆ When reviewing group standards set as performance targets for individual managers or groups

◆ When quickly dispensing short "news briefs" or "pass-downs" from above

(Continued)

Meeting Room Designs *(Continued)*

Meeting Room Design	Advantages	Disadavantages
Large-Group Task Group Design This design is suitable for many events involving large task groups, such as search conferences or staff planning retreats. Preferably round tables with chairs are positioned in small groups so that work can be done at the tables and easily shared with the larger group. Flip charts are usually positioned at each of the tables as well as at the front of the room.	• Allows both small and large groups to work without changing seats. • Gives everyone a writing surface when needed. • Automatically breaks larger group down into smaller groups. • Can easily work with pairs or trios at the tables.	• Requires a good deal of square footage to set up. • People may have to twist and turn in order to see the front of the room for large-group sessions. • Rooms often do not provide enough space for the design as it is shown here; tables have to be put in the center area, making communication less cohesive.

When to Use
◆ For task-oriented groups of more than 20 but less than 50.
◆ When it is important to have writing surfaces.
◆ For search conferences.
◆ For large planning meetings.
◆ As a standard design for moderately large groups. For groups of over 50 members, it is usually best to do without the tables because they will take up too much space, creating an assembly hall-like atmosphere that can restrict effective communication.

(Continued)

Meeting Room Designs *(Continued)*

Meeting Room Design	Advantages	Disadavantages
Combined Table Set-Up With Chairs for Small-Group Activities This design accommodates both small-group work and large-group discussion. Ideal when training is combined with small-group work or when the table is used as a "decision table" where the group leader "chairs" a decision-making meeting.	• Provides a seating area for large group as well as work spaces for small groups. • Helps the group distinguish between activities appropriate for small task groups (5–9) and larger groups. • Can be used to create separate areas for developing recommendations and reviewing them for official approval by designated leader(s).	• Requires room large enough to accommodate both types of seating areas. • Some people may still not like working in small groups without tables or writing surfaces.

When to Use
◆ For larger groups who will be generating recommendations
◆ When your leader(s) is (are) willing to make immediate decisions in front of the large group, taking advantage of the "decision table" process
◆ When there is a training component combined with small-group recommendations development
◆ Whenever you have a room large enough to accommodate the two different set-ups

(Continued)

Meeting Room Designs *(Continued)*

Meeting Room Design	Advantages	Disadvantages
  The "Herringbone" Facilitation Design This design is good for work with medium-size groups in rooms that are set up with tables that cannot be configured for smaller groups. The slant of the tables is better for task group work than the boxier style where people directly face one another. If you have more people to be seated, you can put additional rows of tables behind the first set of tables in a similar slanted fashion.	• Provides a writing surface during the meeting. • Can still maintain the focus on the group memory. • Small-group work can be conducted around the tables by having people move around on both sides of the table. • Works well when there is a good deal of presentation from the front of the room.	• Takes up a lot of space. Usually difficult to use for groups of more than 14 to 18 without adding a back row. • If you have to set up a back row to accommodate the numbers in the group, several people will be speaking to the backs of the people in the front row(s). • May put undue focus on the facilitator or person in the front of the room.

When to Use
◆ When most of the group members will be spending their time as one group

◆ For groups of 12 to 20 members

◆ When tables cannot be folded up or moved out of the room

◆ For sessions with a shorter duration

GUIDE I-6

Tips on Making Good Use of Meeting Room Space

EFFECTIVELY USING MEETING ROOM SPACE
IDEAS AND TIPS

➡ It is critical for the facilitator to pay attention to the meeting room's physical surroundings. People think and behave better in orderly, arranged environments.

A working standard for professional facilitation is that you arrive at the meeting room **one full hour** before the scheduled start of the meeting. Early arrival will give you a chance to do the following:

- Check on the seating arrangements.
- Switch things around if they do not seem positioned correctly.
- Make sure that you have small tables to put your materials on.
- See that flip charts have enough paper.
- Check markers and make sure they all work.
- Affix masking tape to side of flip charts for ready availability.
- Tape down any loose A-V (audiovisual) cords so no one trips over them.
- Ensure that A-V equipment is in working order.
- Envision each activity you have designed, making sure the space will accommodate it.

You may also wish to put out a welcome sign to greet participants or create some last-minute flip charts for the group.

➡ During the meeting, keep an eye on the physical conditions in the room. Is one group so close to another that their discussions are distracting each other? Are there people who should be invited into the group but who are hanging around the room's perimeters? Are the air circulation and temperature control systems working correctly?

(Continued)

Ideas and Tips *(Continued)*

➡ Although it is important to maintain professional standards regarding the meeting room, do not get too carried away, becoming obsessed with having everything perfect. You want people to feel comfortable in the meeting room, not ill at ease because you are being overly fastidious. One of this book's authors used to get concerned the moment he saw any small detail out of place in a meeting room; that changed, however, when he attended some incredibly effective large-group sessions where people were spread out willy-nilly throughout the meeting room in a seemingly impossible spatial configuration. You need to achieve a balance between paying careful attention to such details and creating a comfortable, relaxed, and safe environment.

Also, in some cases you will have little control over the physical environment. When that happens, remember: It is possible to facilitate extremely effective meetings even in the worst-designed work space.

➡ Don't forget that group memory is critical to task group work. Inexperienced facilitators often fail to go to the trouble (and sometimes moderate expense) of arranging to have enough flip charts for large-group meetings.

Whenever there is a significant amount of small-group work, each group should have a record of its work—its own group memory. Sometimes it is possible to tape flip chart pages to a wall near each group's work space; at other times, it is not possible (because of the spatial arrangement or facility prohibitions). In the latter case, flip charts for the small groups must be secured beforehand.

Also consider, in advance of the meeting, how you will display the charts created by the groups. Find out whether the facility prohibits taping or has certain rules you must follow; then plan accordingly. If you will be conducting the session in a hotel, inquire about the meeting room's wall space. Are there a lot of pictures? Is it OK to take them down? Is it OK to tape things to the walls?

➡ A word on the use of breakout rooms: As a general rule, the best advice is **don't**. Don't use breakout rooms when facilitating large groups unless it is absolutely necessary. Managing people as they are returning from breakout rooms is nearly always problematic. Meeting planners tend to think that using breakout rooms will help small groups concentrate and get their work done better. Perhaps this is true in some cases, but in most cases, the use of such rooms has undesirable results: Small groups misinterpret their original charge, they fail to integrate their ideas, and they feel isolated from the large group rather than a part of it.

Whenever possible, arrange to use a room large enough for the entire group to stay together throughout the session. Noise is not as big a problem as most people think. In fact, the constant "buzz" of small groups at work often creates a kind of group energy and enthusiasm that is lost when people go off to different locations.

(Continued)

Ideas and Tips *(Concluded)*

➡ When facilitating large groups such as search conferences or large planning meetings where several small groups will be working at once, use a microphone if one is available. The amplification of the facilitator's voice brings a clarity and cohesiveness to managing the group. It also saves the facilitator from having to raise his or her voice in order to be heard. Cordless microphones are available now in most meeting locations. It may take some getting use to, but amplifying the facilitator's voice can add value to large-group sessions. It is also a good idea—where the technology is available—to have "traveling" microphones available for small-group leaders to use when they present reports to the larger group.

➡ When ordering room set-ups in hotels or other conference facilities, try to arrange use of the most flexible kind of furniture offered by the facility. Smaller, narrower tables are usually better than the standard (wider, rectangular) tables. Circular tables seem to work well for many types of groups. Whenever feasible, it is a good idea to visit the location and check out the available furnishings as well as the room.

➡ A word for internal facilitators: Getting a "sponsor" who can help make your meeting room space "facilitation-friendly" is often a good idea. If you can align yourself with someone in the organization who has the authority to influence purchasing decisions and the people in charge of meeting room facilities, over time you may be able to significantly improve your organization's meetings by purchasing equipment and arranging space so that the room is conducive to effective group work.

GUIDE I-7

Different Kinds of Meetings: Distinguishing "Task Forces" From "Regular Meetings"

Overview

As a facilitator, you need to be aware of the differences between the types of meetings you will be supporting. The work of William Daniels has greatly expanded our knowledge in this area, focusing on some key distinctions. Daniels raised a serious question in a 1993 work about the efficacy of representationally based planning groups or teams. His research on effective task groups indicates that the most intelligent strategies for change will be designed by those experts who have the essential data to design a new approach or to solve an existing problem.

Daniels has also conducted research on "regular" meetings (staff meetings, management meetings, political council meetings, board meetings) that indicates that these meetings reflect the legitimate power structure of the organization and are the genuine authority base within the organization. He suggests a distinctly separate group of operating principles and procedures for "task group" and "regular" meetings, insisting that they have naturally different purposes, agendas, structures, membership requirements, dynamics, processes, and memory systems. After researching more than 200 "regular meetings," he concluded that six approaches in particular worked well for conducting task forces and regular meetings. The "Distinctions" chart on the next page includes those six approaches along with some differences between task forces and regular meetings.

Daniels (1993) has found that task group work is best conducted **outside** regular meetings and that the effective organization will bring proposals that have been well thought out in task groups to the regular meeting for review and approval, disapproval, tabling, or re-delegation. His research runs counter to the conventional wisdom that task groups should be formed from a broad representational base of stakeholders.

Because many group efforts have been derailed prior to implementation by managers excluded from participation in task groups, Daniels' strategy for integrating task group recommendations into the regular meeting structure for review and decision offers what is, in many cases, a breakthrough strategy for enabling groups to succeed.

Distinctions Between "Task Forces" and "Regular Meetings"

	Task Forces	Regular Meetings
Function	Superior intelligence	Authorization; affirmation of organizational values, structures, roles
Agenda	Problem analysis Decision analysis Planning	Pass-downs (from higher authorities—usually outside the organization) Operations reviews Recommendations reviews News (shortened "bits" of information as opposed to lengthy info shares)
Structure and Membership	Only the necessary experts attend Five to nine members only (or break into groups of five to nine)	All the appropriate members of the designated group All or none at any given level of an organization No numerical limits on attendance
Dynamics	Equity; uninhibited access to every intelligence Uses the "inclusion activity" to establish equity	Role differentiation Status affirmation Uses recognition activities to clarify authorities, roles, etc.
Process	1. Build a common data base. 2. Interpret the data. 3. Resolution.	1. Presentation. 2. Review. 3. Decision. 4. Commissioning (making sure all understand their roles related to the decision).
Memory	Flip charting Publishing	Official records Symbols

Adapted from: William R. Daniels, *Orchestrating Powerful Regular Meetings,* San Diego, CA: University Associates, 1993.

So, you will want to consider the type of meeting in which you will be working. If you are asked to work in one of the more "regular" meetings, such as weekly staff meetings or a regularly scheduled management group that has time limits, it will not be wise to try to tackle complex problem solving. You would be better off encouraging your client to use a task group to perform the problem-solving work, charging the group at the regular meeting, and then bringing its recommendations back to the "regular" group and its leader for official review and approval.

Implications of the Distinctions for Facilitators

These distinctions pose some interesting implications for facilitators. If "regular meetings" are truly distinct from "task forces," as suggested by Daniels, the smart facilitator will integrate the following advice and observations into his or her work:

- As a general operating guideline, strive to separate "task group" problem solving or planning work from the established regular meeting agenda. If task force work (problem solving or planning) is to be conducted in the "regular meeting," create some definite separation for the task force work. (For example, conduct regular business in the first half of the meeting, then break and rearrange the room for the second half of the meeting. Start the second half with an "inclusion activity." Or set special sessions of the regular meeting body that allow for sufficient time to deal thoroughly with the issues at hand.)

- Introduce the distinctions between task forces and regular meetings to members of the regular meeting. Then have them strategize how they can best do the task force work.

- As a general rule, don't try to solve complex problems or do planning within the time boundaries of most regular meetings. Instead, charter a small group of six to nine people at the regular meeting to work as a task group and to bring their recommendations back to the regular meeting for approval by the leader of the regular meeting.

- In most cases, the only type of planning or problem-solving work that can be effectively performed within the time limits of most regular meetings is *initial brainstorming* of either (a) the problem, or (b) potential solutions to the problem. Then a task group can be chartered to take the time necessary to generate more data, analyze the alternatives, and formulate recommendations that are brought back to the regular meeting for review of the group and approval by the leader of the group.

- When chartering specialized task groups, identify which regular meeting group(s) should review the recommendations of the task group and plan for such reviews. To do otherwise often invites problems. Members of regular meeting groups may block implementation if they have not clearly had the opportunity to contribute to the review of proposed solutions.

- Reviewing task group work at regular meetings allows you to more efficiently perform group work. Task groups should be composed *primarily* of those people who have the most data or expertise required to address the charge of the task group. To load a task group with "representatives" of each and every faction affected by a proposed change in the status quo usually reduces the group's creative potential to produce the most intelligent recommendations.

REFERENCES

Daniels, William R., (1986). *Group power: A manager's guide to using meetings.* San Diego, CA: University Associates.

Daniels, William R., (1993). *Orchestrating powerful regular meetings.* San Diego, CA: University Associates. (Formerly published 1987 under title *Group power II: A manager's guide to conducting regular meetings.*)

Daniels, William R., (1995). *Breakthrough performance: Managing for speed and flexibility.* Mill Valley, CA: ACT Publishing.

GUIDE I-8

"Lightening" the Room and Encouraging Creativity in Task Groups

The Purpose of This Guide

Its purpose is to pass along a tip on how you can help put group members at ease, increase their creative thinking, and improve the productivity of the group.

Description

We came up with this tip while working at a major aerospace corporation in Los Angeles. When we went in the room for our meeting, there were toys at all the participant tables. We asked, "What's with all the toys?" The woman in charge of training quickly admonished us with a slight gleam in her eye, explaining that those were never to be referred to as toys but rather as "learning aides." We said, "Well, OK," took a deep breath, and went on with the meeting, hoping we could successfully compete with what looked like perilous distractions for the meeting facilitator.

To our surprise, the learning aides proved not to be distractions at all but seemed to put the group at ease and increase its attention on the tasks at hand. When we got to the small-group work, members seemed freer and more relaxed (and less prone to compete with one another), generating ideas as they juggled Koosh balls, watched colors change in liquid-filled plastic mobiles, and fiddled with Power Ranger-type bendable figures.

We found out that our client organization learned the technique from a training organization in Georgia that specializes in training trainers to train. So we began experimenting with using the learning aides while facilitating other groups. Each time the results were similar. People "mellowed out" and seemed generally more productive.

One director of a consulting organization in Utah, who also serves as a full professor in education at a major university, was quite taken with the effect of this type of learning aide and described the technique as "low cognitive activity while performing higher-order cognitive tasks." This seems to be the real secret. You have to find items that allow people to busy themselves without distracting others. Here are some examples of things that work:

- Koosh balls—balls about the size of a baseball that are soft and fluffy, made from rubber products.

- Liquid-filled plastic containers called snow globes—you turn them over and the "snow" falls.

- "Magic wands" filled with liquid and glittery stars.

- Small wire sculptures that you change into different shapes, available from architectural design supply stores and shops such as Natures Wonder and the Imaginarium.

- Plastic, bendable animal figures, or small statues of cartoon figures.

If you decide to try using such aides in your facilitation activities, keep in mind the following criteria when making purchases:

1. They shouldn't make noise.

2. They shouldn't make you have to think like a puzzle does.

3. They shouldn't be fragile or breakable.

4. They shouldn't roll off the table, wind up, or have movement gimmicks.

Some of the places that carry them are toy stores, novelty shops, art and architectural supply stores, and gift shops.

SECTION II

PHASE II:
WORKING WITH
THE GROUP

➥ Overview
➥ Facilitator Resources

OVERVIEW

*Social Advance depends as much upon the process through which it is
secured as upon the result itself.*

—Jane Addams

To climb steep hills requires a slow pace at first.

—William Shakespeare

*In the hands of vicious men, a mob will do anything.
But under good leaders, it's quite a different story.*

—Euripides, 498 B.C.

This section covers the second phase of facilitation: designing and managing the
actual work with the group. Generally, the facilitator designs the sessions ahead of time
and focuses on managing the process during the session. However, designs often
need to be modified as work is conducted with the group; a process or structure might
need to be eliminated or shortened or an alternative substituted. Section II will help you,
the facilitator, with both the design and management dimensions of the group work.

Good, effective facilitation in this phase should produce the following outcomes:

1. Meeting purposes and outcomes are achieved.
2. Participants worked well together.
3. Participants are satisfied with their progress.
4. Meeting designs are effectively implemented.
5. The facilitation capacity of the group is enhanced.
6. Next steps are clear.
7. Effective group task and maintenance behaviors are observed.

THE SEVEN PRIMARY TASKS

In working with the group, you need to focus on seven primary tasks:

1. Creating a foundation for working together
2. Managing data generation
3. Managing analysis and interpretation of the data
4. Managing decision making
5. Managing group dynamics
6. Evaluating group process and progress
7. Closing group sessions

Task 1: Creating a Foundation for Working Together

It is essential to form a solid foundation for the way that group members work together. To do so, you must ensure that fundamental needs of the members, and the group as a whole, are met. Foremost among those needs for members are the following:

— To feel safe and trust others enough to be open and fully participating.
— To feel there is a meaningful reason for their presence and that they are included.
— To accept the facilitator's role and agree to follow the ground rules for the group's success.
— To take ownership, early on, of the work to be done and establish their commitment to the outcomes and processes.
— To agree on group norms for how they work and interact together.

The start-up processes and structures are critical to meeting such needs and thus to creating a good foundation. For example, openings set the session's tone (light, heavy, firm) and establish who will speak, what they will speak about, and what order they will speak in. Openings can also involve getting acquainted, recognizing each member's importance to the group, and sharing information that encourages trust and equality.

When it is desirable that members operate with equal influence (as in the case of most task groups), you should start the meeting with an inclusion activity. The activity should get everyone participating in a similar way during the first few minutes of the meeting, thereby shaping the norm state of equity.

Group members also need to discuss, clarify, or modify the charter; take ownership of it; and put themselves into the task (e.g., committing their interest, energy, enthusiasm, resources). Reviewing the agenda and design with the group, and obtaining their acceptance, goes a long way toward building trust, ownership, and commitment; it is part of "contracting" with the group.

Another initial activity that helps create a safe environment and encourages inclusion is collaborative work on the group's operating principles. If any critical issues—inclusion, ownership, commitment, safety, and support for purposes, outcomes, and process design—are not dealt with early on, then some members may not participate fully or at all; they may lose interest in the task at hand or may grow tense and anxious.

☞ **For more help, see Facilitator Resources:**
   Section I

   • "Setting Group Norms"

   Section II

   • PROCEDURE II-1: The Agenda Review

Task 2: Managing Data Generation

In all group work, there are data requirements that must be met, such as:

- Obtaining and sharing information
- Generating, organizing, and integrating data
- Consolidating or prioritizing data
- Displaying data

Data management activities may need to be used repeatedly, leading to analysis, conclusions, decisions, or recommendations. Therefore, in facilitation work, it is essential to have a repertoire of methods for generating, displaying, and manipulating data. It is also important to design and facilitate the session in a way that ensures the following:

- Everyone's information gets included.
- Information sharing is complete but not laborious.
- Data generated is meaningful and validated by the group.
- Data is manageable in scope and volume throughout the steps of consolidation, prioritization, and analysis.

Recording and displaying data keep what's important visible to the group and help maintain group focus. Members need an ongoing, clearly visible "group memory" that allows them to concentrate collectively, rather than individually, on the data at hand. Using flip charts or cards (or both) allows easy movement, organization, and regrouping of data. Posting the sheets consecutively on a wall gives the group a broad view of its work process. Both words and graphics can be used to capture information and help members internalize its meaning.

> ☞ **For more help, see Facilitator Resources, Section II**
>
> "Establishing Group Memory Systems" and "Building the Group Data Base"

Task 3: Managing Analysis and Interpretation of the Data

When data has been generated, organized, displayed, and reviewed, the group usually needs to analyze or interpret it for the purpose of drawing conclusions, making decisions, or creating recommendations. In analysis it is often necessary to consolidate, reorganize, or prioritize otherwise voluminous data. The group must understand what's there, make sense of it in terms that are relevant, and prioritize, eliminate, or make other choices so that the data is more manageable and meaningful.

Analysis and interpretation involve dialogue—questioning and clarifying—in order to develop a common understanding (though not necessarily agreement). Interpretation can certainly include more than one perspective, conclusion, or meaning and should bring clarity and understanding to the information before the group proceeds to decision making.

Task 4: Managing Decision Making

At some point in the life of any group, its members will need to make decisions. The facilitator's key to managing their decision making is to be clear about the methods for reaching decisions, as well as about the authority of the group charter.

It is important for you to organize the group's work in such a manner that it progressively and periodically leads to decision points. It is better to pause for several decision points along the way than to wait and expect members to deal with one major decision at the end. Commitment and consensus grow through group decisions. As early on the group makes decisions of a limited scope, members build their ability to arrive at consensus and, later, are better prepared to decide on the broader issues that confront them.

Decisions can be made in a variety of ways, any of which can be useful depending on the situation. The group should be clear on, and comfortable with, their decision-making method. Problems occur most often when there are different expectations or definitions of how decisions will be made or when a group has more or less actual authority than it exercises. The leader can make the decision after group input and analysis, the group can vote on the decision, or the group can use some form of consensus decision making.

> ☞ For more help, see Facilitator Resources, Section II
>
> • "Decision Modes"
>
> **Introduction**
>
> • Primer B: Understanding Group Dynamics and Decision Making

Task 5: Managing Group Dynamics

As group members work together, numerous group dynamics develop and need to be managed. All groups have dynamics related to participation, power, affiliation, status, communication, conflict, decisions, and group roles. Generally speaking, group dynamics are the behaviors and emotions that play out in regard to those dimensions. They can be functional and healthy and help the group to progress with its work; or they can be dysfunctional and unhealthy and hinder the group's progress.

While all group dynamics are a matter of concern for the facilitator, some are particularly important to monitor and manage:

- Participation and equality
- Communication
- Differences and conflicts
- Group roles (task and maintenance)

In managing equality, you should watch for people using status, position, or power to quiet, intimidate, or dominate others. You should also give members equal time and encourage full participation by pulling less active members into the proceedings; this ensures that everyone contributes to the group work and is listened to. The dynamic of equality is most important when planning or solving problems. In these situations role and authority must be clear to all.

Effective communication is related to participation. Who talks, to whom, and how much? What patterns occur? These and other behaviors are important to observe and manage. Communication patterns often reflect the forming of subgroups or cliques or serve to isolate some members. Structuring talk time, sharing the "floor," and moving the focus of communication around the group all help to balance verbal involvement. In addition, nonverbal communication is taking place through facial expressions, body language, and movement. This nonverbal communication often reflects the affective state of participants and sends various other messages of agreement, disagreement, approval, discomfort, and so forth. Lastly, you need to manage listening and understanding. This involves maintaining people's attention, suppressing side talk, checking for clarification and understanding, and recording information accurately.

Differences are inevitable and often healthy for a group. Managing them well as they occur will help you avoid deeper conflicts. Here are some suggestions to keep in mind:

- Acknowledge and clarify differences.

- Give differences equal platforms, thus allowing the group to weigh points of view.

- Give members adequate time to express and hear differing points of view, thus allowing the group to keep differences "on the table" and out in the open.

- When the differences are central to the task of the group, have the group discuss them. When differences are less central to the work, have a private discussion and share the results with the group.

Occasionally, significant differences will surface, usually accompanied by intense emotions. Be prepared for this possibility, and come to the session equipped with a few conflict resolution methods for use either in the group session or outside it.

All groups have task and maintenance needs, and various members need to contribute such roles (Benne & Sheats, 1948). Both types of roles must be balanced to some extent if groups are to make progress on their tasks and to maintain enough cohesion and harmony to stay together. For example, on the task dimension, the group needs members who initiate, clarify, elaborate, instigate, build on others' ideas, set standards, provide information, orient or focus the group, and so on. Regarding maintenance needs, groups benefit from members who support, energize, encourage, harmonize, relieve tension, include others, go along with others, and the like. You should ensure that these roles are present and operating in an appropriate balance.

The better you have designed for and managed key group dynamics, the better the group will function. However, a number of common problems may surface, so be ready to respond. Common situations that need to be handled include:

- A non-participating member
- An overly dominant or controlling member
- Distracting cross-talk
- Expressions of hostility

Tips and methods for intervening in such situations are included in the resources that follow.

> ☞ **For more help, see Facilitator Resources, Section II**
>
> - GUIDE II-2: Encouraging Participation
> - GUIDE II-10: Facilitating Conflict Resolution
> - PROCEDURE II-2: Monitoring Group Task and Maintenance Behaviors
> - GUIDE II-11: Handling Common Problems

Task 6: Evaluating Group Process and Progress

At the end of the group work (i.e., after each session in an ongoing series or at the completion of the group's work), it is important to evaluate aspects of the group's process and progress. These include task progress, charter, purpose and outcomes, processes, and adherence to its operating principles. It is also helpful to evaluate the facilitation effectiveness and the facilitator. Some evaluations might be useful for each session, while others are best made periodically or at the end of the group's work.

Evaluating such dimensions has two main purposes. First, it gives members a sense of their work's completion or progress. Have they fulfilled their charter and accomplished their outcomes, or are they making good progress? Second, it builds in a learning cycle to reinforce what is working well and highlights what needs improvement. Over time, the evaluations help the group become more self-correcting.

Task 7: Closing Group Sessions

Bringing closure to a group's work is important with respect to both task accomplishment and psychological completion. First, the work of the group needs to be reviewed, consolidated, and prepared for the next step. (Next steps will be discussed further in Section III.) The next step might be to do some interim work, to type up the minutes from the meeting, to prepare a report or set of recommendations, or to take some implementation action. Either the work to date or the final work should be understood and agreed on by the group. People also need to be clear about how the group will move to the next step(s) and any roles and accountabilities—either for themselves or for others who will be responsible for implementing subsequent work. Any remaining document preparation, communications, or paper work dissemination should be clarified and responsibilities assigned.

It is also important to design and manage endings. Members of an ongoing group may only need to bring closure to the current meeting and identify the logistics and preliminary agenda for their next session. If the group has reached its final session, then a more explicit ending is necessary. This might include celebrations, appreciations, or various forms of saying good-bye. It could also involve closure with any sponsors or chartering authorities.

For more help, see Evaluation and Group Closure

Whether a group has a single session or multiple, limited, or regular ongoing sessions, the facilitator's work with the group generally involves each of the seven primary tasks discussed above. Parts of the preparation phase are also involved whenever another session is being planned. After any session, it is usually necessary to do some follow-up work, which will be discussed in Section III: Follow-Up.

REFERENCE

Benne, K., & Sheats, P. (1948). The functional roles of group members. *Journal of Social Issues, 4* (2), 42–47.

FACILITATOR RESOURCES

Getting Started Right

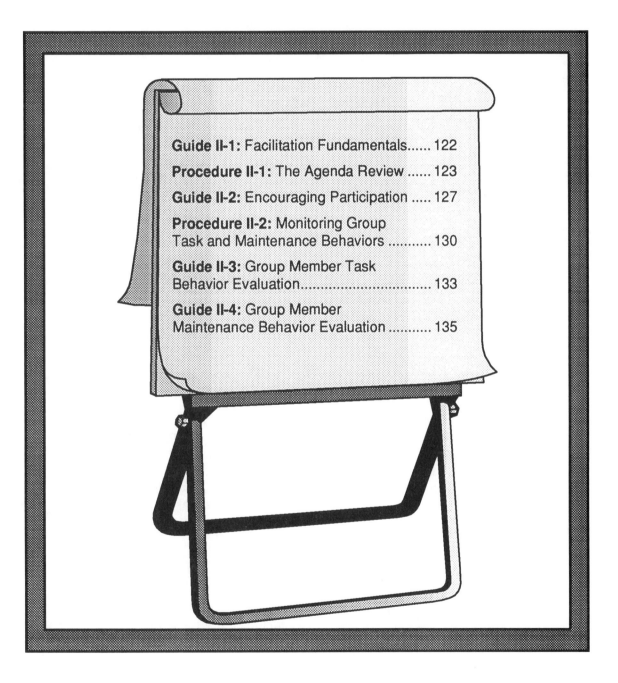

GUIDE II-1

Facilitation Fundamentals

The Importance of Putting Facilitation Fundamentals into Practice

Like most domains, facilitation has a set of fundamental skills that must be faithfully practiced if the facilitator is to enable groups to succeed. Of course, it is possible to lose touch with these skills over time. Therefore, the wise facilitator will regularly review the fundamentals, using this guide, regardless of how long he or she has been facilitating groups.

The Facilitation Fundamentals

There are a number of fundamental skills for facilitating. We reviewed several experts' ideas on the topic and surveyed our own experience to come up with the list below. We have chosen to present the fundamentals as affirmations for the facilitator to review before every session (rather than as diagnostic checkpoints for the facilitator to use after an ineffective session), thus taking a proactive approach.

FACILITATION FUNDAMENTALS: AFFIRMATIONS

☞ **I listen intensely.** I am a model for listening, often paraphrasing and "mirroring" what was said.

☞ **I maintain good eye contact** and stay connected to the group and each of its members.

☞ **I trust in the resources of the group.** I keep **focused on the process** of getting things done; I remain detached from what the group decides to do.

☞ **I always use people's first names.**

☞ **I stay awake, present** at each moment.

☞ **I organize, connect, and summarize data** to achieve closure and a sense of completion.

☞ **I protect each and every idea offered.** I do not allow ideas to be attacked until evaluation time.

☞ **I am a facilitator, not a performer.** My work is being interested, not interesting.

☞ **I encourage everyone** to express themselves, and I validate varying points of view offered. I keep track of who talks and who does not, encouraging balanced participation.

☞ **I am the guide, not the group leader; I support the group leader(s).**

☞ **I am constantly mindful of the outcomes** the group is seeking and **flexible** in my approach to helping achieve those outcomes.

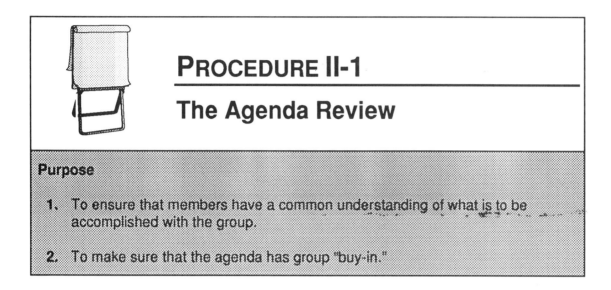

PROCEDURE II-1

The Agenda Review

Purpose

1. To ensure that members have a common understanding of what is to be accomplished with the group.

2. To make sure that the agenda has group "buy-in."

Rationale for the Procedure

One of the most costly errors the facilitator can make is to fail to review the agenda with the group before the work on the agenda is initiated. If you do not review the agenda, you may be confronted by any or all of the following problems:

1. Members do not understand the rationale behind the meeting and have no sense of a cohesive design for getting from one point to another. They become confused and do not think intelligently.

2. Those already inclined not to trust what is going to occur may become more cynical and covertly or overtly sabotage the work of the group.

3. Members may get the sense that someone else is doing the thinking for them and that they just have to follow along; or they may get the sense that nobody's done any thinking and come to expect that the meeting will be pointless, thus contributing toward the possibility that the group will fail.

Some beginning facilitators are reluctant to plan agenda reviews because they have seen groups end up spending all their time arguing over the agenda when it is reviewed. However, if the proper procedure for an agenda review is followed, even substantial changes in agendas can be made with little difficulty and in a minimum amount of time.

Another mistake—one that even seasoned facilitators make—is to become too heavily invested in an agenda. If the facilitator, the meeting leader, and the meeting planners have put much time and effort into the agenda, then one or more of them may grow too deeply attached to the design and (a) avoid the agenda review or (b) become inflexible when group members suggest changes. In either case, group success is compromised. The key is for the facilitator, meeting leader, and others to remain open to amending the design to meet the entire group's needs, regardless of the time and effort invested.

The agenda review is particularly critical to use when facilitating task groups. In many "regular meetings," the agenda is considered the responsibility of the group's natural leader or of an executive committee, and the norm is that the leader controls the agenda. In other regular meetings, a "standing agenda" is used, which serves as a model for conducting the group's work. This is not true of all regular meetings, however, and it is generally still the best practice to review the agenda before a group starts its work.

When to Use the Procedure

- Before any task group starts its work.

- Before the first item of work on the agenda.

- Immediately following the warm-up or inclusion activity. (Some facilitators prefer to review the agenda before the warm-up or inclusion activity. This usually works fine, but conducting an inclusion activity first, before reviewing the agenda, establishes the norm state of equity, which can improve the agenda review by reducing the potential for power struggles.)

Who Presents the Agenda

The leader of the meeting should present the agenda for review. This is far superior to the facilitator conducting the review; it helps minimize problems with the review and ensures that the meeting leader has bought into the agenda. The facilitator can act as a backup support for handling any particular difficulties. Before the meeting, the facilitator can prepare the agenda on flip charts and run through the review process with the leader.

Participants

Number: Any size.

Type: All group members. A group who participated in planning the meeting may play a larger role.

Resources *(checkmarks indicate recommended equipment)*

✔ Flip chart and markers

Time

Approximately 5 to 20 minutes, depending on the level of concern with the agenda

Method

1. When constructing the agenda, always include the item "Agenda Review and Approval." If names are attached to agenda items, put the group leader's name by this item.

2. Post the agenda's major items on a flip chart, even if the group already has a written agenda. Before the meeting starts, list the meeting's purposes and outcomes on the first page of the flip chart; then list the agenda items or activities on the second page.

3. Before moving to the agenda's first activity or item of business, the meeting leader should briefly walk people through the agenda. He or she shares the purposes and outcomes, and then asks: "Does anyone have any questions or concerns about the purposes or outcomes?" Answer the questions and respond to the concerns (see Step 5 below).

4. The meeting leader tears off the first page of the flip chart and posts it in a place visible to all group members. Next, he or she turns to the flip chart's second page and does a quick run-through of the agenda items. The leader then asks: "Do these activities look like they will enable us to achieve the purposes and outcomes?" If concerns emerge, follow Step 5 below.

If there are concerns about the agenda:

5. If the concerns are minor and relatively easy to handle, the leader should immediately suggest the changes, check with the facilitator to see if those are agreeable to him or her, and then check back with the group. If the concerns are more substantial, the facilitator can be "drafted" by the meeting leader to help with the discussion. The facilitator then follows this procedure:

    (a) Draw a line down the middle of a chart page and write "Concerns" at the top of the left column and "Suggestions" at the top of the right column.

    (b) List all the concerns in the left column before asking for any suggestions. Then work through each concern, asking the member who brought it up for a suggestion on how to handle the concern or make a change. If he or she does not have one, ask if others who share the concern can suggest changes. If the suggestions can be implemented and still achieve the purposes and outcomes, suggest that the changes be made and check first with the leader and then with the group for approval. If the suggestions pose more serious conflicts, move to the next step.

    (c) Propose ways of dealing with the concerns or ask members of the planning group to propose a way. Then check back with the group to see if the group is willing to go along with the changes.

    (d) If a resolution on the agenda is not immediately forthcoming, propose either (1) continuing with the rest of the agenda and holding a small-group meeting with the leader and facilitator at the next break to amend the agenda, or (2) taking an immediate break so a small group can "huddle" to propose changes.

    (e) Bring the proposed changes back following the break and check with the group for approval of the changes. Facilitate any final agenda changes.

Notes

1. About nine out of 10 agenda reviews can be handled quickly in the first four steps above, and most discussions that proceed to Step 5 can be resolved fairly quickly. Occasionally, there are some problems that preclude any resolution that will be acceptable to everyone. In these cases, the group leader may need to make a decision and move on.

2. The agenda review process is closely tied to the agenda planning process. If the planning of the agenda has included or has taken into consideration the needs of the various stakeholders and factions in the group, then the agenda review is not likely to be problematic. And if the agenda has been thoughtfully designed, with sufficient (but not excessive) time spent on it, then it is far more likely to be quickly approved.

3. During the agenda review, both the meeting leader and the facilitator need to model an attitude of open-mindedness and flexibility. Don't feel as if the time spent on modifying an agenda is going to keep you from finishing all that you planned. Instead, stay flexible and make the adjustments necessary. Your willingness to change and handle people's concerns will be greatly appreciated by the group and contribute to its eventual success.

4. Though you are a facilitator, reviewing the agenda and making modifications still requires you to act as a participant to protect the integrity of the process. Remember, you have a right and a responsibility not to accept changes in the agenda that you feel will set up both you and the group to fail. Some changes can be genuinely harmful, and you may need to stand your ground against them. The meeting leader must understand your role in this respect, so that any objections you offer will not be interpreted by him or her as a subversion of authority.

5. One way to avoid problems with agenda reviews is to send the agenda out for preliminary review so that group members receive it five to seven working days before the group is to meet. Mark the agenda "Preliminary or Tentative," and ask any member with concerns to forward them to the group leader. Take any such concerns very seriously. If you and the meeting leader do not deal with them to the satisfaction of the person who submitted them, you are likely to be facing a significant force of resistance once the meeting starts.

6. Good agenda reviews require clarity about the group's decision mode and leadership **before you conduct the agenda review.** If the consultative decision-making mode is being used, then the group leader should make any changes in the agenda. If the primary mode involves more consensus decision making, then the group as a whole needs to be in far greater agreement on the agenda.

GUIDE II-2

Encouraging Participation

Groups formed to solve a program or do some sort of planning activity perform far more effectively when they operate in a norm state of equity. A large part of creating and maintaining this necessary dynamic is reliant upon relatively even levels of participation among group members. The following are tactics that the facilitator can use to "level" participation and equalize power, ensuring that the equity and thus the productivity of the group is maintained.

☐ **Divide the group into smaller groups.** Ask the group to break into pairs, triads, or quads instead of keeping them together. Pairs obviously force the most participation.

☐ **Combine small groups in succession until you reach a resolution.** For example, after pairs have met to generate alternatives, have two pairs get together and compare lists, adding other alternatives. Then two groups of four meet together to compare lists, adding alternatives. Or you can use this technique to evaluate a list of alternatives, with the goal being to come up with an agreed-upon number of recommended alternatives.

☐ **Move to round robin participation.** Ask everyone to take a turn offering their thoughts or ideas.

☐ **Call on those who have not been participating.** Look around the room and call on someone, saying: "[Name], I notice that you've been doing a lot more thinking than talking. Do you want to share?"

☐ **Introduce another inclusion activity.** Inclusion activities are typically used at the beginning of a meeting. Their purpose is to establish the norm state of equity. If you feel the required norm state weakening, you can introduce another activity, explaining that you feel the group needs to rebuild the participative atmosphere.

☐ **Acknowledge the participation problem and ask group members to share their feelings.** Say: "I notice that we seem to be having some participation problems here. Can you help us understand what is going on by sharing your thoughts about participating in this group?"

☐ **Ask group members to pause and reflect upon their participation.** Call a time-out for a "participation reflection." Ask everyone to remain silent for a moment and reflect upon their own participation. Have they been freely giving what they have to offer? Have they been talking too much, too little, or about the right amount? What members of the group need to be heard from more? What group task and group maintenance behaviors have they been practicing? What adjustments, if any, do they want to make to maximize the success of the group?

After the moment of silence, you can either discuss people's thoughts, or simply move on. Another option is to use this tactic immediately before the break, having the group pause and then go to break.

❑ **Have group members pair up, interview each other, and report back the view of the other person.** On a flip chart, write a list of questions that represent aspects of the task that members are presently working on. Ask each member to select a partner and interview that person, asking each of the questions. Instruct them to make a note of the answers. Bring the group back together and have each member share his or her partner's perceptions and ideas.

❑ **Review your agenda and change it.** If you get the feeling that the lack of participation may be caused by a flaw in the process, then you need to review the present agenda and see if modifications are in order. This can be done with the whole group, or you can ask the leader and another member or two to join you while others take a break to "huddle" on whether there are needed changes in the agenda or in the processes you are using.

❑ **Call a time-out to strategize.** Just as in an athletic event, you may want to call a time-out to talk with the leader and quickly look at what's not going right, why, and what to do about it.

❑ **Assess and re-assess the equity norm state.**
Draw three concentric circles on a piece of chart paper.

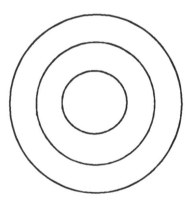

Explain that the three circles represent a "hill of influence" for the group.* People who are participating a lot and perceive themselves as having an impact on the group are closest to the center.

Ask everyone to take a small adhesive note and place it on the flip chart circle to mark where they perceive they have been operating with the group.

Then explain to the group that the research on group process has indicated that the groups that produce the best, most intelligent results are those that operate with a norm state that looks very balanced. (Use x's to represent the people shown in the illustration on the next page.)

* The "hill of influence" concept is taken from William R. Daniels' "Group Power" Training Sessions.

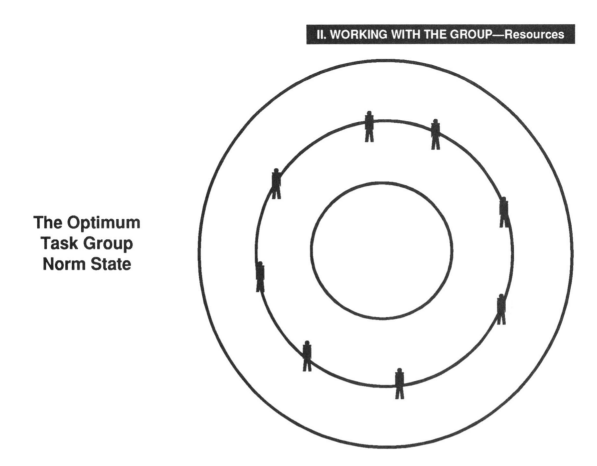

The Optimum Task Group Norm State

Set a timer to go off in 60 to 90 minutes. Tell the members of the group that you will be asking them to place themselves on the chart again.

When the timer goes off, finish whatever activity you have been involved in and have everyone re-position themselves on the "hill of influence." When everyone has finished, discuss what it looks like now and talk about any changes that were made.

PROCEDURE II-2

Monitoring Group Task and Maintenance Behaviors

Purpose

1. To make group participants aware of their response patterns in the group.

2. To encourage participants to adjust their behavior to enhance the effectiveness of the group.

Summary Description

Most people are not at all aware of their style of participating in a group. This procedure is designed to put them in touch with how they are behaving in the group—to see exactly what they are doing, to assess whether it is working or not, and to identify where they need to change to increase the group's productivity. In pairs, group members look at their own and their partner's group behavior by filling out quick evaluations on task and maintenance behaviors. They compare their responses and identify behaviors they need to keep on doing, do more of, or do less of.

When to Use the Procedure

- During the first or second meeting of the group, in order to establish a positive norm state

- When the facilitator notices a dominance of one or two types of responses from team members

- When, as a facilitator, you are charged with helping develop group membership skills in a new team

- Once every five or six meetings for ongoing teams

Resources *(checkmarks indicate recommended equipment)*

✔ Flip chart and markers
✔ Overhead display
❏ Handout—Guide II-3: Group Member Task Behavior Evaluation
❏ Handout—Guide II-4: Group Member Maintenance Behavior Evaluation

Time

30 minutes

Method

1. Distribute the evaluation handouts. Tell participants to take two copies of each evaluation.

2. Give everyone 5 minutes to complete each evaluation of themselves.

3. Ask participants to select a partner for whom they will fill out the evaluations, assessing as best as they can that person's performance.

4. Have the partners meet and compare their self-rankings.

5. Have each pair identify two behaviors that the group needs more of or less of.

6. Ask everyone to work with their partner to identify two behaviors that they, as individuals, need to do more of or less of.

7. In the whole group, identify those behaviors that the group members have been doing well on and need to continue. Write those on a flip chart or transparency.

8. In the whole group, have each member share one behavior that he or she is going to focus on doing more of or less of.

Variations

1. You can copy the evaluations on overhead transparency film and use them as overlays to chart a group's progress. Place each copy over a transparency that shows ratings from an earlier meeting and record the new scores on the top copy with overhead transparency pens.

2. You can have the members fill out their individual forms and identify the behaviors that (a) they need to personally work on doing more of or less of, and (b) the whole group needs to be mindful of increasing or decreasing. Then discuss their responses in the whole group, skipping the paired sharing.

3. Daniels (1990) suggests having the group identify which behaviors are most frequently abused or overused and which behaviors are most empowering for a group. From his experience, he offers three behaviors most overused or abused:

   - Questioning (asking for information and opinions)
   - Giving information or opinions
   - Summarizing (usually group recorder is being too obtrusive and summarizing verbally rather than in writing)

He asserts that these two are most empowering of the group:

- Gate-keeping
- Encouragement

You can structure a "quiz show" type of competition among pairs or small groups. Have them try to identify the three most abused or overused behaviors and the two most empowering behaviors. Then share Daniels' answers with the group.

4. You can share definitions of the behaviors with the group. (Definitions are available from several sources; see Kayser, Daniels, or Bradford in the Reference section.) Have the group build their own specific examples of what the behavior means, trying to identify when each behavior has happened during their session.

REFERENCES

Benne, K., & Sheats, P. (1948). Functional roles of group members. *Journal of Social Issues, 2,* 42–47.

Bradford, Leland P. (1976). *Making meetings work: A guide for leaders and group members.* San Diego, CA: Pfeiffer & Co.

Daniels, William R. (1987). *Group power II: A manager's guide to conducting regular meetings.* Mill Valley, CA: American Consulting and Training.

Kayser, Thomas A. (1994). *Building team power: How to unleash the collaborative genius of work teams.* Burr Ridge, IL: Irwin Publishing.

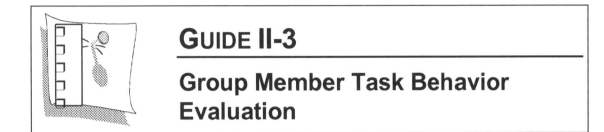

GUIDE II-3

Group Member Task Behavior Evaluation

Instructions: Put an *x* in the box that indicates the degree to which you feel that you have been performing the following group member task behaviors. Samples of comments that typify the task behavior are provided as guides only. Your comments may have been substantially different.

TASK BEHAVIOR	SAMPLE COMMENT	DURING THIS GROUP SESSION, I HAVE PERFORMED THIS BEHAVIOR:			
		Often	Sometimes	Seldom	Not at all
Initiating, proposing, or suggesting	"What if we were to . . ."	Often	Sometimes	Seldom	Not at all
Building on or elaborating	"If I could add to that, I think . . ."	Often	Sometimes	Seldom	Not at all
Coordinating or integrating	"John's idea about . . . would fit well with Ruth's concept of . . ."	Often	Sometimes	Seldom	Not at all
Seeking information or opinions	"Can you tell me more about . . . ?" or "What do the marketing people think about . . . ?"	Often	Sometimes	Seldom	Not at all
Clarifying	"What we meant by that was . . ."	Often	Sometimes	Seldom	Not at all
Questioning	"I wonder what effect this would have on . . ."	Often	Sometimes	Seldom	Not at all
Disagreeing	"I don't see it that way. To me . . ."	Often	Sometimes	Seldom	Not at all

(Continued)

Group Member Task Behavior Evaluation *(Concluded)*

TASK BEHAVIOR	SAMPLE COMMENT	DURING THIS GROUP SESSION, I HAVE PERFORMED THIS BEHAVIOR:			
Testing for understanding	"Let's see. Would implementing this require us to push back our projected implementation date . . . ?"	Often	Sometimes	Seldom	Not at all
Orienting the group to its task	"We've done three items on the agenda. We still have two to go and it's 4 o'clock."	Often	Sometimes	Seldom	Not at all
Testing for consensus	"Does anyone have a problem with . . . ?"	Often	Sometimes	Seldom	Not at all
Summarizing	"We've laid out six key dimensions of the problem and have come up with a few beginning alternatives . . ."	Often	Sometimes	Seldom	Not at all
Recording or capturing content	"Can we make sure that we get Louise's point about cost up on the chart?"	Often	Sometimes	Seldom	Not at all

GUIDE II-4

Group Member Maintenance Behavior Evaluation

Instructions: Put an *x* in the box that indicates the degree to which you feel that you have been performing the following group member maintenance behaviors. Samples of comments that typify the task behavior are provided as guides only. Your comments may have been substantially different.

MAINTENANCE BEHAVIOR	SAMPLE COMMENT	DURING THIS GROUP SESSION, I HAVE PERFORMED THIS BEHAVIOR:			
		Often	Sometimes	Seldom	Not at all
Energizing or motivating	"You know, if we make it through this agenda, we'll have come further than anyone else on this issue."				
Gate-keeping or promoting inclusion	"We're speculating too much about personalities. Let's get back on track." Or, "I'd like to hear from Bill on the customer-recommended upgrades."				
Harmonizing	"I want to look closer at the data and get off the emotional stuff. There's really more that's the same about the two proposals than is different. What's similar is . . . and what's different is . . ."				

(Continued)

Group Member Maintenance Behavior Evaluation *(Continued)*

MAINTENANCE BEHAVIOR	SAMPLE COMMENT	DURING THIS GROUP SESSION, I HAVE PERFORMED THIS BEHAVIOR:			
Agreeing or following another's lead	"I see where Jack's going. If we were to just cut the delivery times, the drivers could make more commission and we might avoid the strike possibility."	Often	Sometimes	Seldom	Not at all
Encouraging	"Aw, c'mon. Let's not quit so easy. Remember where we were last year with the B-17 specs and thought we'd never get them out?"	Often	Sometimes	Seldom	Not at all
Relieving tensions	"You people sure do have a lot of strong beliefs. I believe we ought to take lunch and come back fresh."	Often	Sometimes	Seldom	Not at all
Setting work standards or reminding others of standards	"Before we quit, remember we all agreed we'd hang together with our decisions once we made them. Is there any reason this one is an exception?"	Often	Sometimes	Seldom	Not at all
Compromising	"Well, if we go with a pilot in Mac's department for 3 months instead of the full-blown plan, we can still get the data we need for full implementation in the fiscal year."	Often	Sometimes	Seldom	Not at all

(Continued)

Group Member Maintenance Behavior Evaluation *(Concluded)*

MAINTENANCE BEHAVIOR	SAMPLE COMMENT	DURING THIS GROUP SESSION, I HAVE PERFORMED THIS BEHAVIOR:			
Observing the process	"What I'm noticing is that we're really assessing Jim's proposal before we've thoroughly understood it. Several of my reactions have 'jumped the gun' too— we need all the facts."	Often	Sometimes	Seldom	Not at all
Praising others	"Wow, Beth. I don't see how you got this together for us in just a week. Now we can really move today."	Often	Sometimes	Seldom	Not at all
Praising the progress of the group	"Hey, you know we got through this whole meeting without a single dumb joke or snide comment about Admin. to get us off track."	Often	Sometimes	Seldom	Not at all

FACILITATOR RESOURCES

Establishing Group Memory Systems

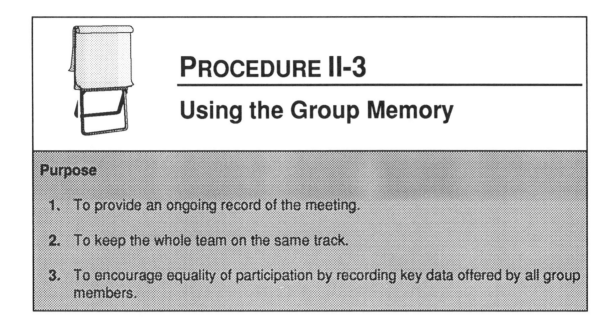

PROCEDURE II-3

Using the Group Memory

Purpose

1. To provide an ongoing record of the meeting.

2. To keep the whole team on the same track.

3. To encourage equality of participation by recording key data offered by all group members.

Summary Description

The group memory is the ongoing record of the task group, logged on flip charts and made clearly visible to all group members. Either the facilitator or a person known as the "recorder" writes the comments and ideas of group members on the flip chart paper.

Recording group members' comments in this way focuses member attention on the group work rather than on individual notes. Data from group members is recorded sequentially on the flip chart pages, which become a temporary record-keeping system for the group. After the meeting, the pages are transcribed and serve as the ongoing meeting record for the group.

In a typical meeting setting, all group members keep their own meeting records, usually in the form of notes. There are two problems with this practice. First, different group members choose to remember different things. The selective memory problem is supported by research, reported by Daniels (1987), that indicates only 30% agreement between any two members of a group who are asked to recall what occurred in a meeting immediately following the meeting. Second, when individuals are focusing on their own notes, they are using an individual, rather than a group, memory system. The group memory encourages collaboration by keeping all members tuned to the same information and data.

The group memory is absolutely essential to complex problem-solving work. If a memory is not used when dealing with complex issues and problems, groups get confused and varying interpretations of what is going on abound. Often, in the absence of a group memory, no resolution occurs or mediocre solutions are begrudgingly agreed upon.

When to Use the Procedure

- Anytime a group is focusing on solving a problem or doing planning that involves complex data

Participants

Number: Task groups between three and 50 members. Larger groups have difficulty seeing flip chart data.

Type: Task group members

Resources *(checkmarks indicate recommended equipment)*

✔ Flip chart and markers

✔ Masking tape

✔ Note cards of varying sizes and colors or colored paper; pushpins; storyboards or bulletin boards (when using storyboard methods)

✔ White boards can be used but are limited as an ongoing memory device for the meeting. Data on white boards can be immediately entered into a laptop computer and printed out as needed. Flip charts are generally considered far more effective as a group memory mechanism.

Facilitator(s)

The facilitator is responsible for overseeing and monitoring the accuracy of the group memory. The facilitator can record group members' comments into the group memory at the same time he or she is facilitating; or a recorder can be used to log the notes (see Procedure II-4: Training the Group Recorder). When a recorder is used, he or she is responsible for accurately representing the comments of group members, without adding any personal interpretation.

Time

The group memory is maintained throughout the meeting.

Time equivalent to about one-half the meeting will be required to transcribe the flip chart notes into a letter-size document.

Method

In order to establish and maintain the group memory, the facilitator should do the following at each meeting of a task group:

1. Identify before the meeting who will be responsible for maintaining the group memory. If subgroups are to be used, think ahead about how the recorder function will be handled in the groups.

If you are working with a recorder who is largely unfamiliar with group recording, review the recorder guidelines (Guide II-5) with the person.

Tip: Keep the group memory in mind when planning task group meetings. Avoid meeting in rooms where you cannot use the wall space to mount flip chart pages. Check with hotels and facility managers to make sure that you will have adequate wall space.

2. Set up the group memory before the meeting.

   Doyle and Straus (1976), who pioneered the widespread use of the group memory technique, recommend that the group memory be placed directly in front of the participants, who are seated in a semi-circle without any tables. An easel can be used or several pages of chart paper can be taped to the wall. The semi-circular seating arrangement is superior for problem-solving task group meetings. It is less appropriate for document or recommendations reviews in a regular meeting setting.

   If subgroups are expected to operate during the meeting, pre-determine where they will be working in the room and station easels with flip chart paper or tape paper to the wall in each subgroup area. It is also a good idea to tear off about 20 to 50 strips of tape and place them on the side of the easel or on walls where the group memory is located. Leave a roll of masking tape at each group memory station.

3. When the meeting starts, explain to the group that the group memory will be used during the meeting to record member responses accurately. It is sometimes a good idea to include a ground rule for how members will use the group memory. For example: "Everything goes up on flip charts."

4. For each agenda item, create a heading at the top of a flip chart page that summarizes the agenda item. Then accurately record the group's data on the appropriate page.

5. Before moving from one agenda item to the next, number each of the flip chart pages. If the data will be used in subsequent parts of the meeting, you can mount the pages on the wall. Some pages may also be mounted to show specific agreements or resolutions the group has made.

   Keep mounted only the data that is necessary for work yet to be completed. From time to time, remove the chart pages that are no longer needed. Leaving too much paper mounted gives a cluttered feeling to the meeting and produces a feeling of information overload.

6. At the end of the meeting, the charts are collected and numbered and a typed record of the charts is made for all group members.

   There are two common ways to store the flip chart pages. One is to fold them. The other is to roll them up and wrap a rubber band, string, or tape around them. Folding is better if you are on the road or need to store them in shelves or a corner of your office. Rolling them up is better if you plan to use them again for display to a group.

Always remember to use a marker to clearly write the contents of the rolled-up or folded papers. Label each set of flip charts clearly on the back of the last page. Then you won't have to fumble around opening up several sets of charts to find the ones you are looking for.

Notes

1. With the recent advent of laptop computers, it is quite feasible to have one member of the group or a support staff person operate a laptop during the meeting and immediately distribute the record following the meeting. The charts' contents should be typed "verbatim," as they appear on the charts. Instruct anyone operating the computer to type in the data as is, making no editing changes. One page per chart should be typed, or a dotted line should be used to indicate where one chart stops and another starts. Diagrams or figures should be drawn by hand after printouts are made.

2. Often, a group member who understands the data is actually a better person to handle the transcribing after the meeting than a support person who is not familiar with the content. A person who was actually at the meeting can also create bridging statements between the flip chart pages or correct minor vagaries or inconsistencies in the charts, although any corrections in the original charts should be approached with extreme caution. If a clerical person is used to transcribe the charts, someone who was actually at the meeting should work closely with him or her to clarify items listed on the charts, to help sequence them, and so forth.

   When giving flip chart pages to a secretary, go over them briefly with him or her and ask for a draft copy to review. Review the draft, noting any corrections or clarifications, and have the secretary enter the changes.

3. Overhead display devices are now available that allow the record to be maintained on the computer and projected, using an overhead projector, onto a wall or screen. This works well for a detailed document review where many minor changes in wording and editing must be made. Yet it is still not superior to the use of flip charts as a group memory, because only one page can be viewed at a time and the pages made by the computer cannot be printed out in large enough type to be visible to the whole group. The use of the technology also may provide a kind of showy audio-visual feeling that is not conducive to a vibrant informal group spirit. At this point, it still seems best in most situations to keep it simple by using flip charts for the group memory.

4. There are machines available that will enlarge letter-size paper to poster size. Also available is a reduction board that allows you to reduce flip chart pages to letter size. These are handy tools for organizations that can afford them but are not essential to the maintenance of a good group memory. (See the "Technological Tools and Applications" section of this book.)

5. A noiseless, simple way of immediately distributing the group memory record is to have one person in the group take legible handwritten notes of all the flip chart pages. These notes can then be distributed to members following the meeting.

6. Commercial boxes are available that allow you to store several rolled-up flip charts vertically. You can also store them in liquor store-type cardboard cartons, wrapping shelf paper around the boxes to make them less of an eyesore in the office.

7. When you are forced to work in a room where you cannot use the wall space, you may have to maintain the group memory on an easel. Here's a tip that allows you to more quickly find parts of the memory that have become "buried" in the chart pad and may be difficult to locate.

    After each agenda item, write the item's name on a large Post-it® note and affix the note to the first page containing data related to that item. After each agenda item, write the item's name on a large Post-it note and "flag" the first chart page containing data for that item. To flag, affix the note to the top right-hand side of the page so that it sticks out from the chart. Affix any subsequent notes in descending order along the edge of the page. Then you can quickly find data from other parts of the meeting.

    You can also use Post-it notes to mark flip chart pages you have pre-made for presentation during the meeting, allowing you to more quickly retrieve them when you need them.

8. Carefully limit any embellishments of the flip chart notes in the transcription process. The group memory is not intended as an official meeting record but should be used as "working notes." Meeting minutes should be unnecessary for task group work. If you have done a good job of recording during the meeting, the group memory should stand alone as a meaningful, ongoing informal record for meeting members. Exercise extreme caution in distributing group memory records to nonmembers. When communicating the work of a task group to a wider audience, a separate document created for wider distribution is usually preferable.

9. Pay careful attention to who is appointed to maintain the group memory. When assigning someone to record at the beginning of a meeting, make sure that the group doesn't "dump" the responsibility on a weaker member, and—in some work cultures—watch out that the group doesn't immediately expect a woman to do the job because of antiquated role-sets about clerical responsibilities.

10. Some facilitators prefer to rotate recorders throughout the meeting to make sure that no one person is saddled with the whole responsibility. This practice helps to maintain the equity role-set for the group. The downside of rotating recorders is that some people don't do it very well or quickly; and additionally, there is an unevenness that interrupts the productive flow of the meeting. Another alternative is to train a few members in proper recording procedures and have them rotate the recording assignment. Yet another alternative is to take the time early on to train all members to properly record the group memory, and then rotate the role.

REFERENCES

Daniels, William R. (1986). *Group power: A manager's guide to using meetings.* San Diego, CA: University Associates.

Daniels, William R. (1987). Personal communication.

Daniels, William R. (1987). *Group power II: A manager's guide to conducting regular meetings.* Mill Valley, CA: American Consulting and Training.

Doyle, Michael, & Straus, David. (1976). *How to make meetings work: The new interaction method.* New York: Jove Books.

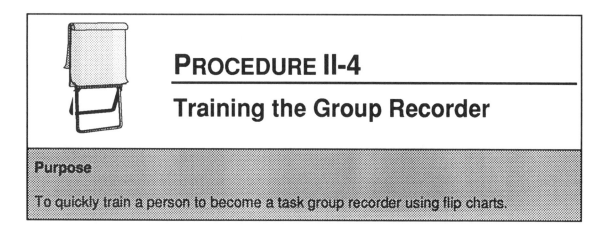

PROCEDURE II-4

Training the Group Recorder

Purpose

To quickly train a person to become a task group recorder using flip charts.

Summary Description

Many task groups choose to use a person other than the facilitator or leader to record information on the group memory. The recorder writes down on the flip chart key comments or statements made by group members. The comments are recorded as close to verbatim as is possible, without any editing or paraphrasing.

The advantage to using a separate recorder is that the facilitator or leader is better able to concentrate on the group. Although professional facilitators can usually perform both the facilitating and recording role (some even prefer to do so), most group facilitators find it is helpful to have a second person recording the data.

When to Use the Procedure

- Prior to the task group session; preferably on a day other than the day of the meeting. At times it may be necessary to train group recorders on the day of the meeting.

Participants

Number: One group recorder for every small group of five to nine people. Recorders may also be used to record large-group discussions.

Type: Group members who volunteer to serve as recorders or separate "neutral" parties not involved in the content of the work of the task group. The person recording should be familiar with the language and nature of the content, but not invested in the outcome of the group work.

Resources *(checkmarks indicate recommended equipment)*

✔ Flip chart and markers

Note: Make sure you have a good set of markers for each of your recorders.

Facilitator(s)

The main facilitator for the meeting should train the recorder(s).

Time

Varies from 15 minutes to an hour for a quick "briefing." A more detailed recorder training session can last from 2 hours to two days.

Method

1. Select recorders prior to the group session. (See notes below for suggestions on selecting recorders.)

2. Go over the guidelines (Guide II-5) with the recorders. Provide them with copies of Guide II-5: Guidelines for the Group Recorder.

3. Immediately following the group session, debrief how it went with the recorders, making sure to offer plenty of compliments on how you observed them following the guidelines for group recorders.

Notes

1. A few myths are associated with the recording role. Here are some dangerous ones:

    a) Anybody can do it.

    b) It's a good job for a clerical or support person.

    c) Many different people can take turns in one meeting.

    d) You don't have to know the business to record accurately.

    Not everyone can be a recorder. It actually requires quite a bit of skill and a reasonable knowledge of the content domain. You have to grasp ideas quickly, listen attentively, be able to quickly discriminate what to record, and then keep listening to what is said as you are writing. In short, it requires a good deal of language ability and verbal skill along with a fairly fast mind that understands the technical language being spoken. Many support staff are unfamiliar with the technical language or do not understand the exact nature of the work, making it difficult for them to handle the recording function. On the other hand, there are support staff members who can perform the role very nicely.

You cannot be a perfectionist and do the job with the speed that is required. People who have to have everything "exactly right" often won't be able to perform as quickly as needed.

Different recorders operate with varying degrees of success and speed, and it can disturb the tempo and sense of continuity of a meeting to have several different people recording. Technically speaking, with the possible exception of very long meetings, it is best to have only one recorder for any work session. As more and more people in your organization master the recording technique, it becomes increasingly workable to have various recorders during one group session. However, many teams, working without a recorder from outside the group, do choose to rotate recorders so that no one person is removed from the content of the discussion too long and the task is democratically shared.

Remember: Groups that develop a competent recording capacity within their organization at least double the speed and output of task groups.

2. The ideal recording solution for an ongoing team working in a task group mode would be to use someone who is not a team member but who knows enough about the task to do a good job of recording. This person might even be from a different department or division and used "on loan" in exchange for the same services from a person in your division. Other methods that have been used include assigning two or three team members to divide up the recording function, assigning a different person for each meeting. It is also an option to have the facilitator handle the recording, provided he or she is comfortable with the dual role.

3. Another tip is to offer several staff persons a brief 2-hour training session on the techniques of recording. The skills required are teachable and can be mastered quickly. A side benefit to organizations that make repeated use of a number of recorders in meetings is that people tend to listen better. If a person spends 10 hours listening to what team members are saying, that person may well surpass the total amount of quality listening time he or she has previously spent in the organization.

GUIDE II-5

Guidelines for the Group Recorder

1. Aim to record exactly what is said without interpreting or editing it. Don't try to "say it better" or add in your meaning.

2. Focus on being invisible. If you are working with another person who is handling the facilitation or leading the meeting, avoid the temptation to help the facilitator facilitate or the leader lead.

3. Ask questions only when you did not hear what was said, or when what was said seems important but was not stated clearly.

4. Write quickly and legibly. Try to make letters 3 to 4 inches tall. Using all caps makes it easier for the group to read the chart. Keep up with the conversation. Don't worry about spelling; take your best guess—don't stop to ask someone how a word is spelled.

5. Keep questions brief and simple. Example: "Would you mind repeating that?"

6. Record key words and phrases exactly as they are said, but don't try to write down everything that is said. Feel free to abbreviate words.

7. Use different-colored markers to make the charts more readable. Record at least every other item in a different color. Experiment with using colors to make the chart more readable.

8. Test all the markers before using them. Discard those that are worn. Use bold-colored markers so your writing is clearly visible to those in the back of the room. Be sure the markers are water-based, so they won't bleed through to the wall.

9. Number the chart pages sequentially. Write the number in the upper right-hand corner of each page. Number the paper before ripping it from the pad.

10. You can draw boxes or circles around key items. Highlight certain words or items with underlining, stars, or asterisks. As you get more used to recording, try using graphics to illustrate points, if you feel comfortable doing so.

(Continued)

Guidelines for the Group Recorder *(Concluded)*

11. Tear off the chart pages slowly, so that they cleanly tear at the perforation all the way across the page.

12. Before the session, tear off 20 to 40 strips of masking tape and affix them to the side of the flip chart. Then, just before tearing off the page, put two pieces of tape on the upper right- and left-hand corners of the paper. Tear off the sheet with the tape on it, and mount the paper on the wall. Keep your own roll of tape handy.

GUIDE II-6

Top 10 Flip Chart Tips and Tricks

Many people feel a bit intimidated when they start to use flip charts, especially if they have bad handwriting or can't draw. No need to worry though. You don't have to have perfect handwriting or be an artist to do a great job of writing on flip charts. You just need to write legibly and accurately keep track of what's been said. Follow the suggestions on the "top 10" list below, and you can look like a flip chart pro on your very first outing.

 Print in large capital letters if you have difficulty with your handwriting. Focus all your attention on listening and writing legibly and accurately.

 Use the "advanced tearing" trick to look like a pro on your first time out. With your left hand, grip the flip chart right above the perforation in the upper right-hand corner of the chart. Press hard with your left thumb to put pressure on the corner. With your right hand, grip the bottom left corner of the page. Tear the page slowly at first, then jerk it quickly. Voilà! A cleanly torn sheet. The mark of a flip chart master! Practice a few times before you start. (Reverse the rights and lefts above if you are left-handed.)

 Never turn your back on a flip chart or walk backwards. Stand facing the flip chart or to the side at all times, except when tearing pages and mounting them. Walking backwards near the chart inevitably leads to tripping over the chart and/or knocking it down—not the sign of the flip chart master.

 Carry white tape with you to cover up any mistakes. One-inch white correction tape is available from your local office supply. Larger rolls are available from architectural supply firms.

 Put two pieces of tape on the page just before you tear it off the flip chart; then you won't have to fumble around with a roll of tape when you get to the wall. When you affix the tape to the wall, "rub it down," using your thumb or a marker cap, so that it adheres well.

(Continued)

Top 10 Flip Chart Tips and Tricks *(Concluded)*

 Hold three different-colored markers in the hand you don't write with, securing them between your fingers. Use bold, darker colors such as black, green, and blue to make the chart more readable. Put the marker back between your fingers instead of laying it down somewhere. Never use more than three colors on one page.

 Stick to basic graphics when you start; for example, use bullets or an arrow for listed items and a border around a page or paragraph that has one "block" of data. You can also use lighter colors like yellow or pink to highlight a key concept or a simple symbol to highlight a word or phase.

Review scores

 Avoid the use of flimsy easels to hold the chart paper. Use sturdy, upright flip charts manufactured for training purposes. Have at least two charts available to maintain the group memory. This allows you to have two people recording data during brainstorming sessions or to separately record sets of data that will be integrated with each other data that will be integrated with each other.

 Have a handy supply of stickers that people can use to indicate choices on brainstormed lists. Different-colored dots and other types of stickers can be purchased at office supply stores. Be creative—use a variety of stickers. For example, give each person four dots and one heart sticker. Assign each dot a point value; reserve the highest value for the heart, which will indicate the "heart of the matter."

 Ask group members to help. They can help hang the charts, set up a new chart pad, title and number the charts, and so forth. This not only promotes participation and enables you to work faster but also gives members the impression that you're a professional with enough self-confidence to ask for help. If you try to do everything, you may find yourself falling behind and missing key data from the group.

GUIDE II-7

On Becoming Marker-Worthy

A marker is not just a marker. The sign of a real facilitator is that he or she takes this small but essential tool seriously. Here are some tips for proving yourself marker-worthy.

▶ Markers are not all equal. The best for use with flip charts are broad-tipped water-based markers. "Vis a Vis" and "Mr. Sketch" are two of the better brand names. Vis a Vis markers last longest, have the best brilliance for broad-tipped markers, and can also be used on overhead transparencies. Avoid the types commonly purchased for children.

▶ Never trust the markers provided by anyone else, particularly hotels or conference centers. Before each use, test all markers to make sure they are still writing clearly, and throw out those that don't. Putting them aside in hopes that they will revive themselves is the mark of a real amateur, with probable tightwad tendencies to boot. If the marker's color starts to fade while you're using it, nonchalantly fling it across the room into the wastebasket, demonstrating that you're a real marker pro.

▶ Buy new markers regularly, especially before any job of a half day or more. Throw out all the light-colored markers, keeping only the bolder, darker colors that are clearly visible from the back of the room. Never write with light yellow, orange, or pink markers.

▶ Include some oversized, super broad-tipped markers in your facilitator kit. They are available in black, red, green, blue, and fluorescent colors. Always buy water-based markers. Permanent markers (both large and small) bleed through the flip chart pages and can stain the wall. Use the giant markers early in the session to boost your credibility. This facilitator tool is sometimes referred to as "the old marker envy technique."

▶ Cap your markers frequently when you are using them. Most markers can be left uncapped about 10 minutes. After that, they will gradually dry up and become useless for the rest of your session. Regularly grabbing a dried-out marker is another sure rookie sign.

▶ The marker-worthy facilitator won't be caught dead with an easel page that ends up in only one color. Use two colors at a minimum, but never more than three. Careful with the cutesy graphics, though. Use drawings appropriately, and don't overdo them.

(Continued)

On Becoming Marker-Worthy *(Concluded)*

➠ Some facilitators hold as many as seven markers between their fingers at one time. We don't advise this. Besides being a real pain for those lacking fine motor skills, it may make you look too much like a process freak whose major talent is juggling different-colored markers. Definitely not someone to be trusted in a strategic planning session.

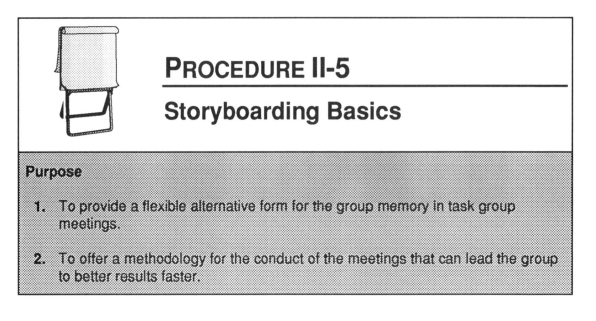

PROCEDURE II-5

Storyboarding Basics

Purpose

1. To provide a flexible alternative form for the group memory in task group meetings.

2. To offer a methodology for the conduct of the meetings that can lead the group to better results faster.

Summary Description

Storyboarding, also known as Displayed Thinking and Discussion Technique (McGartland, 1994), involves organizing complex data by presenting it in a visual, sequential fashion. When used for conducting task group sessions, this technique requires four basic types of tools—a bulletin board, pushpins, index cards, and felt-tipped pens.

The earliest known practitioner of storyboarding is Leonardo da Vinci, who employed it in the form of sketches to conceptualize his paintings. However, the Disney studios are generally credited with attracting widespread attention to the process via its use in animation design, plotting, and sequencing. Later, Disney executives used storyboarding to lay out development and operation plans for theme parks and resorts. The technique has since spread throughout the entertainment industry, and is now regarded by scriptwriters and filmmakers as the standard for creative planning.

Large-scale use of storyboarding in the training/facilitation industry has taken place over the past 20 years. One Pennsylvania consulting company, McNellis, has become the leader in adapting the technique to task group sessions and offers workshops in its sophisticated group process design—dubbed "Compression Planning"—for the use of storyboarding. (For more information, see note on McNellis in the **References** section.)

Here we will cover only the rudiments of the technique, presenting an interpretation of the storyboarding procedure that can be applied to any group session. In this process, note cards and a bulletin board (rather than a flip chart) are used as the group memory device. The session's purpose is identified before the meeting. The group then identifies and orders, in sequence, the tasks that must be completed to achieve that purpose. To build the data base for the session, group members quickly generate data on index cards and pin the cards to the bulletin board. Topic headings are either defined before or after an initial "dump," or output, of data. Basic brainstorming rules apply during the data dump (see Procedure II-8: Basic Brainstorming).

The process described in the **Method** section below assumes the group has a single purpose or topic. The process steps include (1) organizing how the group will accomplish the task, (2) generating data, (3) organizing or sorting the data into classifications, (4) evaluating the alternatives, and (5) planning the implementation of the alternatives.

When to Use the Procedure

- When you want to introduce an alternative method of data generation and analysis to the group

- When you anticipate that a large amount of data will be generated and want to handle the information quickly

- When you have a task group agenda that focuses on planning something

Participants

Number: A small group of six to 12 people is best. (Index cards are difficult to read from a distance.)

Type: Members of a task group.

Resources *(checkmarks indicate recommended equipment)*

✔ Note cards: 5-by-7-inch cards
4-by-6-inch header cards (large index cards)
3-by-5-inch data cards (two to three different colors of each card)
Note: Using different sizes is preferable, but not essential.

✔ Felt-tipped pens—black, red, blue, green for writing data on cards.

✔ 200 pushpins.

✔ Six "Nerf"® balls.

✔ One tape dispenser.

✔ Packages of self-adhesive dots in three colors.

✔ Storyboards or bulletin boards for mounting cards. (Storyboards can be commercially purchased or hand made—see Procedure II-6: Making Your Own Storyboards.)

Facilitator(s)

One person at a time leads the group. Multiple facilitators can take turns as long as they are comfortable with the procedures.

One or two members can be designated as recorders and log on the data cards all the generated ideas; or each person can generate, and record, his or her own ideas using the data cards.

Time

Variable, depending upon the nature of the task. The procedure described below can usually be completed in less than 2 hours.

Method

1. **Set up the storyboard.** Set up the bulletin board or storyboards, making sure they are clearly visible.

2. **Arrange seating.** Arrange chairs in a semi-circle facing the storyboard area. If tables are not to be used, provide a laptop writing surface (notebooks or clipboards).

3. **Identify facilitator(s).** Identify who will facilitate or if facilitators will rotate through the different steps in the procedure.

4. **Identify the group purpose.** Identify the purpose of the session. Print the purpose on a 5-by-7-inch card. Mount that card at the top center of the storyboard, using pushpins.

5. **Explain the purpose and procedure.** Introduce the purpose to the group and briefly share with them how the procedure will work. Pass out the 3-by-5-inch data cards to group members, or assign one or two people to record ideas on the cards. Stress the importance of following the basic brainstorming procedure. Appoint up to six members as brainstorming-rule "monitors," and give them each a Nerf ball. Explain to them that their job is to throw the balls at anyone who breaks one of the basic brainstorming rules during data generation.

6. **Create a header card.** The basic storyboard consists of a purpose card, header cards, and data cards that are subheadings of, or pieces of data relating to, the heading.

Basic Storyboard Layout

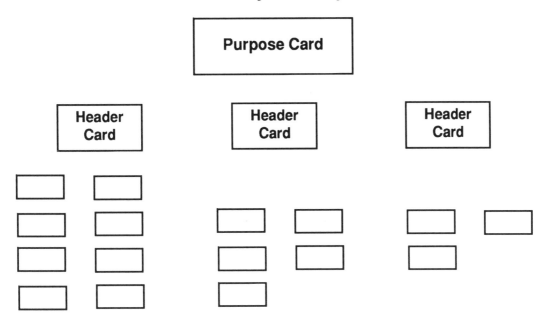

First, make a header card that reads "Steps to accomplishing our purpose," and mount it beneath the purpose card.

7. **Identify the steps necessary to accomplish the task.** Have the group brainstorm the key steps necessary for the group to accomplish its goal. Group members or designated recorders write the steps on the data cards. Record exactly what people suggest. Don't worry about redundancies or sequencing. Pin the cards on the board.

8. **Sequence the steps to accomplish your purpose.** Eliminate redundant steps or combine them on one new card. If several data cards naturally cluster together, create a separate header card and put that cluster under the header card.

9. **Move to your first step.** Move to a different storyboard or a different part of the bulletin board for the next steps. If you don't have enough space, take down the cards you have produced using this method:

   a) Move all cards in a cluster together, re-pinning them to the board so they are vertically aligned, creating rows. The header card should be at the top of the row.

   b) Tape the cards together, running one long strip of tape over an entire row of cards.

   c) Remove the pins from the cards.

d) Tape the rows of cards to a flip chart page if you wish them to remain visible through subsequent steps.

10. **Generate data.** Take each step, one at time, and generate data. Write a 5-by-7-inch card for the step. Mount the card at the top of the board. Then generate alternative data for completing that step. For example, if your purpose is "To design a new process for reporting sales data," your first step might be (written on a 5-by-7-inch card): "To identify what does and doesn't work about our present process." Then you would create two 4-by-6-inch header cards, one for "What's working?" and another for "What's not working?" *Create all topical header cards in question form.*

    Then you would generate data from group members, using 3-by-5-inch data cards for "What's working?" Follow brainstorming rules, not evaluating anyone's notion of what's working. Insert one extra rule. *Generate all data in complete sentences.* This rule forces people to produce whole thoughts that become more understandable in subsequent analysis steps. You can also organize the data as you go, following the procedure described in Step 11 below.

11. **Create headings for data.** As data is generated on data cards, ask, "Is that like anything else, or is it different?" If it's like something else, pin the card beneath the card that has some similarity. After the group has exhausted their ideas, look at the groupings of cards and identify a topical heading for each group. Fill out a 3-by-5-inch topic card that is a different color and put it at the top of those alternatives.

12. **Analyze data.** Move to an analysis phase for the data that has been generated. Members need to agree on what data should remain following the initial brainstorming. You can sort ideas for their level of importance or significance. Data can be merged and reorganized. You can reduce the cards to the "manageable few." You can use the sheets of self-adhesive dots to reduce data or focus on what is most critical.

    Budget time for the analysis phase. At the end of the budgeted time, remove any cards that represent data on which group members were not able to agree in the time available. You can either discard those cards or mount them on a flip chart page labeled "Unresolved Issues." At a subsequent point in your session, you can return to those issues and work on them if any are considered essential to completing your task.

    After the analysis phase is completed, tape the cards together and move them to a flip chart page for subsequent recording onto a computer.

13. **Repeat data generation and analysis for all subsequent steps.** Repeat the data generation and analysis phases for all the key steps you have identified to accomplish your purpose.

14. **Do action planning.** Create a 5-by-7-inch topic card entitled "Action Planning." Create header cards for "Who?," "What?," and "By when?" Fill out data cards for the data under each subheading.

15. **Assign a data recorder.** Assign a person responsible for having the data transferred from the cards to a word processing document. This should be done now or within one to three working days of the time you complete your work session.

Notes

1. The procedure described here allows you to create your agenda for any given purpose "on the spot." When the agenda is planned in this way, you can identify the topic header cards that you will use according to the process steps that you have planned. This saves the group from having to design the process as well as forward and analyze data.

2. Prefabricated storyboards are much better than a single bulletin board. You can work with several boards at once, leaving data on the boards without having to clean one board off and start a new one. You can take them with you to off-site trainings. Specially designed boards also give the process the feel of a professional technique. You can either make the boards yourself (see the next procedure), or order them from a specialty supplier such as McNellis.

3. There is now available on the market a new product that allows you to conduct the storyboarding process using a flip chart and index cards. The product is a repositionable adhesive. This non-toxic adhesive can be sprayed on the flip chart paper; then the note cards can be affixed by just placing them on the paper. The cards can still be moved around once they are affixed. (To find a distributor for the product in your area, call 3M Adhesive Systems Industrial Tape and Specialties Division, St. Paul, MN, at 612-733-1110, Operator 55.)

4. We mean it when we say that this procedure only offers one interpretation of the very basics of storyboarding. The group process applications are far more numerous than we have provided here. If you try out the approach suggested here and feel it has considerable promise, you may want to look into getting more in-depth training in the procedure, available through specialty trainers.

5. You can use the storyboarding procedure for only one phase of your group process work, such as the alternatives generation phase, and then move to another procedure for alternative analysis and selection. The mobility of the cards is a distinct advantage in merging alternatives and arranging them into classifications. Once you have the alternatives neatly classified, you can list them on a flip chart and proceed with subsequent task group processes using the flip charts. Some people prefer to use the technique this way because they feel it avoids the mechanistic feeling that can come about through the extensive use of the basic storyboarding process.

REFERENCES

Higgins, James M. (1994). *101 creative problem solving techniques.* Winter Park, FL: The New Management Publishing Company.

McGartland, Grace. (1994). *Thunderbolt thinking.* Austin, TX: Bernard-Davis.

Nettles, Jack. (February 1989). "Compression Planning" in *US Air* and *Piedmont In Flight* magazines. (Reprint available from the McNellis Company at 1100 Eighth Avenue, New Brighton, PA 15066; 412-847-2120; Fax 412-847-9275.)

PROCEDURE II-6

Making Your Own Storyboards

Purpose

To inexpensively create an alternative form of group memory that can be used to enhance facilitation effectiveness.

Summary Description

Bulletin boards are somewhat limited if you wish to take full advantage of the storyboarding process. They are often permanently affixed to walls or not the right size to use for storyboarding sessions. More important, to use storyboards most effectively, you need to have several boards that can easily be moved about the room, and commercially purchased boards are expensive. So here are some "assembly instructions" for creating your own "homemade" storyboards. In less than 2 hours, you can easily assemble a set of boards that should work well to meet your needs and allow you to practice the technique to the point where you can decide whether or not to invest in more expensive factory-produced boards.

When to Use the Procedure

- After you have tried using the storyboard process and are convinced that you want to use it more frequently in group facilitation sessions

Participants

Number: One to five people.

Type: You can put the boards together yourself, or you can do it as a fun, lighthearted "model-building" project with a group of people who will be facilitating in your organization.

Materials *(checkmarks indicate recommended equipment)*

Available from an art supply store:

✔ Foam boards three-quarters of an inch thick and pre-cut to the size you want to use. Foam board is available in three standard sizes. The 40-by-60-inch size is the most versatile and closest to commercial storyboards. If you plan to travel with the boards on airplanes, you may wish to build some smaller boards that can be checked in more easily on planes.

✔ Putty-like adhesive that can be stuck to the back of the boards.

Available from a fabric store:

✔ Enough cloth to cover the front of the boards and to pull over the back to be attached (e.g., for a 40-by-60-inch board, have a piece of cloth cut about 50 by 70 inches). If you want the fabric to completely cover both the front and back of the board, you will need to buy more fabric. We have always used a black cotton fabric and covered only a portion of the back.

Available from a hardware store:

✔ A staple gun

✔ Staples

Time

You should be able to put the boards together in 1 to 2 hours, once you have gathered all the materials.

Method

1. Visit or call your local art or office supply stores and find out which one has the best selection of foam board.

2. Figure out how many boards you want to make and what size you want them to be.

3. Figure out how much fabric you will need to cover the boards. Fabric is purchased in running yards. Thinking through the math ahead of time will save time when you get to the fabric store.

4. Purchase the materials and get a staple gun and staples.

5. Cut the fabric to the sizes you want for each board.

6. Stretch the fabric out tight around the board; staple it to the back of the board, leaving about 6 inches of space between the staples. This will be easier for two people to do—one holds the fabric tight while the other operates the staple gun.

Affix the putty-like adhesive to the four back corners of the board, so that you can later hang up the board. To mount a board, simply press the corners against the wall. The putty will adhere to most surfaces, although the board may not stay up perfectly. This is one of the limitations of using storyboards: There is no perfect way to keep them up on a wall.

If the facility in which you will be working does not prohibit marking the walls, you can attach a picture wire to the back of the boards and hang them from push pins. However, most facilities will not allow this.

To avoid wall-mounting problems, some facilitators mount the boards on easels or in the flip chart's marker tray.

Note

1. Art supply stores carry zippered vinyl covers that you can use to carry the storyboards. The covers have room for three or four storyboards.

FACILITATOR RESOURCES
Building the Group Data Base

GUIDE II-8

Building the Data Base

Overview

To come up with new solutions and achieve superior results, you must first build a data base that will produce better ideas than those currently driving the status quo.

A part of the group data base will come from the minds of the group members. However, it is often a myth that the ideas that members bring to the meeting from their past experiences will be enough to produce breakthrough solutions for long-standing problems or to generate something new that will make a real difference. An all-too-frequent task group meeting practice is to identify a desired outcome or define a problem, to brainstorm solutions, and then to pick some of the solutions and implement them. This approach will work for some things, particularly if the problem or task is relatively simple and nearly any action will do. But for more sticky, complex situations, you must first bring some fresh data to the table so that you can inject into the collective system the quality input that will yield a previously unimagined result.

Another important reason for building the data base has to do with group dynamics. When you restrict your data base to the ideas that individual members suggest from their own opinions or experience, you concomitantly invite opportunities for personality clashes over dueling opinions. This does not always happen, but it is a danger, particularly when members have some history with one another. When you introduce new or fresh data to the group, you are more likely to be building some common ground for agreement that is not so closely associated with personal opinions or agendas.

The following two checklists offer some strategies for data base construction. You and your group can review the lists and select the ideas that best suit the group's needs. Also provided is a worksheet that can be used to prepare a rough outline of the strategy. A good approach to this activity is (1) to have members work individually on the checklists, selecting the alternatives that they think are valuable to the task at hand, and (2) to ask them to complete a worksheet. Then the group can discuss their ideas, agree on the methods they will use for data base construction, and assign individuals or subgroups to begin collecting the data.

Checklists: Data Base Construction

Data Base Construction Alternatives

- [ ] Surveys
- [ ] Interviews
- [ ] Visitations
- [ ] Readings
- [ ] Personal Histories
- [ ] Journals
- [ ] Workshops
- [ ] Presentations
- [ ] Videos

- [ ] Teleconferences
- [ ] Research Studies
- [ ] Benchmarking Studies
- [ ] Data Base Searches
- [ ] Internet Searches
- [ ] Computer Chat Rooms
- [ ] Brainstorming
- [ ] Idea-Generation Techniques

Resources
(Audiences That Can Be Tapped to Build the Data Base)

- [ ] Experts
- [ ] Implementers
- [ ] Friends and Family
- [ ] First-Line Supervisors
- [ ] Middle Managers
- [ ] Customers
- [ ] Suppliers
- [ ] Colleagues

- [ ] Universities
- [ ] Think Tanks
- [ ] Associations
- [ ] Government Project Teams
- [ ] Group Members
- [ ] Organizational Leaders
- [ ] Competitors
- [ ] Noncompetitive yet similar organizations

WORKSHEET:
Building Our Data Base

STRATEGIES TO CONSIDER

| W H A T | We could [insert construction alternative] . . . |

| W H O M | With, for, by, to [insert audience to be tapped] . . . |

| H O W | Briefly describe how it might work. |

STRATEGIES TO CONSIDER

| W H A T | We could [insert construction alternative] . . . |

| W H O M | With, for, by, to [insert audience to be tapped] . . . |

| H O W | Briefly describe how it might work. |

SAMPLE II-1

Data Base Construction Strategy

Building Our Data Base—A Strategy to Consider

The example provided below is taken from a restructuring group/design team charged with coming up with a way to effectively create cross-functional work teams in the organization.

STRATEGIES TO CONSIDER

WHAT	We could [insert construction alternative]. *We could attend workshops . . .*

WHOM	With, for, by, to [insert audience to be tapped]. *. . . offered by consulting organizations on cross-functional teams.*

HOW	Briefly describe how it might work. *We can break our group into pairs or triads who will attend public workshops offered by consulting organizations and then return to the group to give the design team a 2-hour overview of the workshop highlights.*

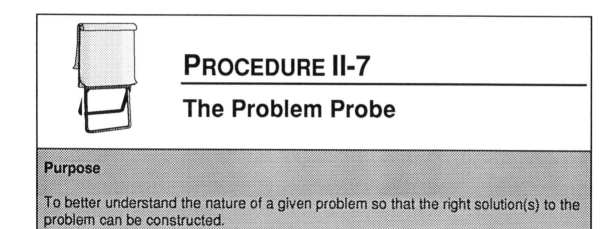

PROCEDURE II-7

The Problem Probe

Purpose

To better understand the nature of a given problem so that the right solution(s) to the problem can be constructed.

Summary Description

Most groups have only a general description of a given problem when they set out to solve it, or group members all have different perceptions. The group adage is "In order to agree upon a solution, you must first agree on the problem." Another rule of thumb used by some group facilitators is "The solution is apparent, once you clearly understand the problem."

Problem-probing techniques allow you to be sure that you have a conceptual handle on the dimensions, boundaries, and nature of the problem. The group is led through a series of cue questions that clarify and define the problem.

When to Use the Procedure

- When a problem is long-standing and there have been several unsuccessful attempts at solving it
- When the problem is complex
- When several different people, functions, departments, systems, or sub-systems are involved

Participants

Number: Five to nine participants

Type: Members of task group charged with solving a given problem

Resources *(checkmarks indicate recommended equipment)*

✔ Flip chart and markers

Facilitator(s)

One person facilitates the group through the cue questions. A separate recorder can be used.

Time

For most problems, 45 to 90 minutes

Method

1. Ask that each group member write down what he or she thinks the problem is. List all the data on a flip chart.

2. Lead the group through a series of probing questions designed to accurately elaborate on the problem. Select a series of no more than eight questions from those that are provided below; check off those questions you want to use in your probe:

   ❏ What happens?

   ❏ Then what happens? (Repeat several times until ultimate consequences are identified.)

   ❏ Where does the problem occur?

   ❏ When does the problem occur?

   ❏ How frequently does it occur?

   ❏ How long has it been going on?

   ❏ What resources are involved in the problem?

   ❏ What systems, processes, or procedures are involved in the problem?

   ❏ Who is most affected by the problem?

   ❏ What other related processes or procedures does the problem have an impact on?

   ❏ When was the problem first identified as being a significant problem?

   ❏ What happened that the problem became so worthy of our attention?

   ❏ Who is the one person or type of person who gets hurt most by the problem?

   ❏ Who has the authority and control to correct the problem?

   ❏ Is this problem much like other problems that have occurred in the past? If yes, does there appear to be a pattern operating here?

   ❏ Where could this problem be occurring but is not? (Inside or outside this particular context, i.e., other departments, other organizations, other countries, other types of situations, other people.)

   ❏ When could this be occurring but is not?

   ❏ Who might have this problem but does not?

   ❏ How did things work before we had this problem occur?

3. Write the selected questions on flip charts, with one question at the top of each chart page.

4. Lead the group through generating data for answering the questions. Record all data without disagreement or comment, and go through all the questions.

5. *(Optional—dependent on time available.)* Go back to each question and ask, "Does anyone have a concern related to any of this data? Do you feel it is inaccurate or unclear?" Either alter those statements so they are acceptable to both the person who had the concern and the person who originally generated the data, or eliminate the statement.

6. Allow some additional discussion related to the problem, noting any relevant comments on the appropriate chart page.

7. Ask the group to write the problem statement so that it fits on one chart page and is expressed in 100 words or less. The statement should conclude with this sentence: "The primary cause(s) of the problem appear(s) to be [fill in cause(s)]."

8. Check to see that the group is satisfied that it has adequately described the problem.

Notes

1. Encourage people to be objective in their identification of the problem—to clearly observe the nature of the problem without becoming emotionally involved in it. You might ask them to imagine themselves hovering on a cloud above where the problem is occurring and describing the problem in clear, objective terms.

2. Insist that people use "I" statements and convey their point of view when describing any problems of an interpersonal nature. They should preface their statements with "It appears to me . . . ," or "The way I feel about that is . . .," or "When *x* occurs, I become *y*," and so forth.

3. One option is to entitle a concluding flip chart page "Desired Future State." Ask group members to describe how they would like conditions to be once the problem is resolved, and ask them if they wish to revise any similar statement they may have generated before undertaking the problem probe.

RESOURCES

Daniels, William R. (1986). *Group power: A manager's guide to using meetings.* San Diego, CA: University Associates.

Kayser, Thomas A. (1994). *Team power: How to unleash the collaborative genius of work teams.* Carlsbad, CA: CRM Films.

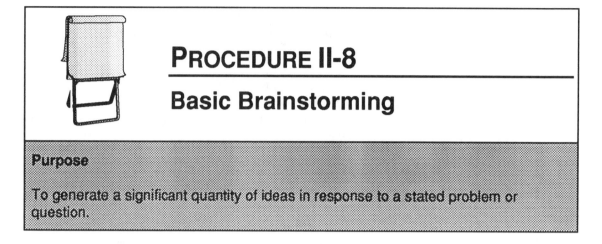

PROCEDURE II-8

Basic Brainstorming

Purpose

To generate a significant quantity of ideas in response to a stated problem or question.

Summary Description

Brainstorming is the most fundamental procedure used to generate data. The group is asked to generate as many responses to a problem or question as they can—usually in a limited time frame. Specific rules are followed in order to prevent group members from inhibiting response because ideas are judged.

When to Use the Procedure

- Anytime that you want to start the "idea flow" in response to a problem or question
- When you want to expand the way that the group views a situation
- When you have a limited amount of time to discuss an issue or problem in a regular meeting and want to avoid unproductive "back-and-forth" discussion that "admires" the problem instead of seeking solutions
- When solutions are unknown or at least "out of immediate reach" of group members
- When several alternatives have been tried (but failed) to solve the problem
- When you want group members to suspend their judgments of one another in order to "get back on track" working as a team

Participants

Number: The advantage of brainstorming is that it can be used with any number of participants.

Type: Group members. As a general rule the facilitator does not generate ideas, but it is possible for the facilitator to generate ideas during brainstorming. However, if facilitator ideas are generated, it is best for the facilitator to abandon any advocacy for the idea in subsequent evaluation activities.

Resources *(checkmarks indicate recommended equipment)*

✔ Flip chart and markers

    and/or

✔ Overhead projector

    and/or

✔ Note cards and storyboards

✔ Laptop computer for recording data (optional)

Facilitator(s)

The facilitator records responses and provides "cues" to stimulate further ideas. A second recorder or a separate recorder (i.e., separate from the facilitator) can be used to speed the flow of data.

The facilitator's skill/experience level is irrelevant to the use of this technique. The most inexperienced facilitators will have success using brainstorming, and the most advanced facilitators will still rely heavily on brainstorming to generate ideas.

Time

Most initial brainstorming exercises take from 10 to 20 minutes. The time can be expanded if the brainstorming is done in stages, following presentation of specific cue questions that are subparts of the problem. After 30 minutes, the process will become tedious unless specific instructions are used to vary the form of the response.

Method

1. Most groups have had some experience with brainstorming. If you don't know the group well, ask how many members have used brainstorming before. It is unlikely that no one will be familiar with this technique, but if so, explain the basic rules for brainstorming, shown in Step 2; otherwise, move directly to Step 2.

2. Ask members to recall the basic rules for brainstorming and ask someone to give you one of the rules. Then have the group generate the rules. Record them on a flip chart. Make sure they identify all the basic rules of brainstorming:

   - Don't evaluate the idea; defer judgment.
   - Quantity is the goal.
   - The wilder, the better.
   - Record each idea verbatim.
   - "Tagging" on or combining ideas as a new idea is OK.

If you prefer, you can present the brainstorming rules on a flip chart or use an overhead with a handout of the rules. (See last page of this procedure for rules printed in a form suitable for use as a handout and overhead.)

Remind the group that there will be plenty of opportunity to evaluate ideas later in a separate activity.

3. Have the group begin brainstorming ideas. Quickly redirect the first members who judge any idea by saying "No judgments," and record the ideas exactly as offered.

Notes

1. Large groups can often be broken down into groups of five to nine people in order to maximize output. Appoint group recorders/facilitators and explain that their job is to record ideas exactly as spoken and to redirect anyone making judgments. When several groups are operating, walk around and monitor the group behaviors, ensuring that ideas are recorded verbatim and that there is no judgmental discussion of ideas.

    The brainstorming exercise is one of the few activities that work well with any size group. You can leave the members in a large group and have people generate ideas. When you do so, it may be a good idea to have two or three recorders working so that the ideas keep flowing without anyone having to pause while they are written out.

2. Cue questions can be prepared ahead of time in order to maximize idea generation. (A general rule is that anyone brainstorming in response to a single question will usually generate between 16 and 22 ideas; this is often not enough data to generate "winning" ideas.) For instance, if the basic question is "How can we improve our handling of incoming phone calls?" you might pose brainstorming questions with five key "cues":

    (a) How the phone is answered
    (b) Technological improvements for handling phone calls
    (c) Setting standards
    (d) Supervision interventions
    (e) Training interventions

    Also, you can have the group first "free-form" responses to the broader question and then look at the responses and categorize them. Next, have them brainstorm more responses to each category or subpart of the larger question.

3. See Procedure II-9: Brainstorming Variations. Many of the methods presented there can be incorporated into the basic brainstorming procedure.

Variations

1. The classic "nine dots" exercise (shown with solution below) can be used to introduce brainstorming. Give group members the instruction to connect the nine dots without picking up their pens or pencils or going over any line twice.

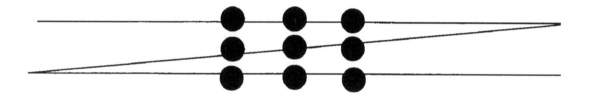

To successfully complete the exercise, you have to go "outside the box" implied by the nine dots. Encourage members to "go outside the box" of their current assumptions and thinking when brainstorming ideas.

Solution:

2. If you want the group to have some fun and know members well enough to be sure they won't abuse one another, purchase enough Nerf balls to give three or four members of each group a ball. Appoint these people as "idea protectors" and have them throw the balls at anyone who offers negative judgments of any idea.

   Pete Zajac, a facilitator with the California Youth Authority, suggests also using the Nerf balls to make sure people are generating one idea at a time and to encourage participation from the entire group. At times, he gives each group one Nerf ball. Then the ball is tossed from one person to another in the group. You only share ideas when you have the ball.

Brainstorming Rules

☞ **Don't evaluate the idea; defer judgment.**

☞ **Quantity is the goal.**

☞ **The wilder, the better.**

☞ **Record each idea verbatim.**

☞ **"Tagging" on or combining ideas into one new idea is OK.**

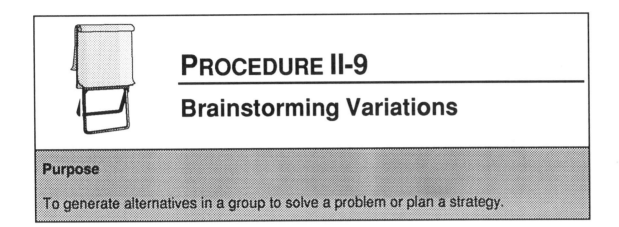

PROCEDURE II-9

Brainstorming Variations

Purpose

To generate alternatives in a group to solve a problem or plan a strategy.

The Importance of Brainstorming Variations

Brainstorming variations are useful because they enable you to vary your methodology so the group does not become bored with basic brainstorming procedures, and because they increase the quantity and quality of ideas that are generated.

We present seven brainstorming variations on the following pages. You can find a multitude of other options in the references noted at the end of this procedure. We suggest that you keep a "stable" of idea-generation variations handy for your work with groups. Each one offers a slightly different spin on brainstorming and adds value to the construction of the group data base. Remember: It is the quality of the group's data base that will determine whether you are able to provide breakthrough results in your work with groups. If you keep working with the same data previously available to the group, then members are likely to get the same results they have been getting from previously unsuccessful efforts to tackle major challenges.

When to Use the Procedure

- When solutions are not obvious, when old strategies have not worked well enough, or when several alternatives will be necessary to solve the problem or meet the group goal

- When you want to break established mindsets

Resources *(checkmarks indicate recommended equipment)*

✔ Flip chart and markers.

      or

✔ Storyboards with index cards, pushpins, tack board.

✔ Index cards and felt-tipped pens are needed for some variations.

Brainstorming Option

Brainstorming Minus Assumptions

Summary Description

This method encourages group members to brainstorm ideas freely, without attachment to the assumptions they have about the issues at hand. The method is used after an initial round of brainstorming. Members are asked to identify their assumptions about the issues and then to hold these assumptions in "suspension" while brainstorming.

Method

1. Explain to the group that it is sometimes useful and "frame breaking" to brainstorm ideas without any attachment to assumptions about the issues.

2. Ask the group to identify their assumptions about the topic and issues for which you are seeking ideas, and record these ideas on a flip chart. (It is usually helpful to prepare a list of sample assumptions related to a separate topic with which the group would be familiar, and to post this list as an illustration.)

3. Point out that the listed assumptions most likely run the whole gamut from "incontrovertible" truths to pure superstition. Explain there is nothing wrong with assumptions—they are not bad things and in fact are useful and often essential to productivity and accomplishment—yet, for maximum group creativity, it is helpful to "suspend" the assumptions for a brief time while seeking new ideas or solutions. Point out the difference between "suspending" assumptions and "letting go" of them. When you suspend assumptions, you don't have to release them from your belief system. It is as if they are hanging above you, suspended in air, but not driving your thoughts and ideas.

4. Break the group into teams of five to nine members and have them brainstorm ideas, now with assumptions suspended, for approximately 15 minutes.

5. Have each group evaluate the brainstormed ideas and identify ideas that they think should be added to the original brainstormed list for further evaluation.

Variations

1. To dramatize the idea of suspending the assumptions, you can hang the lists from the ceiling by attaching long pieces of masking tape to the flip chart pages.

2. For a more interesting variation (provided you have an open-minded group), ask members to identify the assumptions they were operating with during the initial brainstorming, and write these on the left side of a flip chart page. Draw a line down the middle of the chart page, and then ask them to identify the opposite assumption. Tear the chart page off. Fold it over so only the opposite assumptions are visible, and ask the group to brainstorm new ideas using these assumptions.

Brainstorming Option

Segmented Brainstorming

Summary Description

Each person is given a specific assignment to brainstorm alternatives to a part of (or one dimension of) the problem, strategy, or task. Each dimension of the problem is written on a stiff card. Their responses are written on index cards. The cluster of these cards is mounted under the "header" card. The group then goes through each "part" and adds additional alternatives.

Method

1. Post the problem, strategy, or task at the front of the room.

2. If you have not broken down the problem into parts, do so. Strategies and tasks can be divided into subparts.

3. Assign each member a part (or dimension) of the problem or a subpart of a strategy or task, and give each one about 10 index cards and a colored felt-tipped pen. Ask members to generate as many alternatives as they can for their assigned part.

4. Give everyone time to generate their lists.

5. Mount all the cards at the front of the room.

6. Taking each part in turn, ask group members to generate additional alternatives for consideration. Write these ideas on cards and post them.

Brainstorming Option

Round Robin Brainstorming

Summary Description

The facilitator asks each person in turn to generate ideas.

Method

1. Post the problem, strategy, or task.

2. Post any further elaborations such as dimensions of the problem or subparts of the task you are trying to achieve.

3. Ask each person to generate a list of ideas.

4. Pick a method for taking turns and have everyone take a turn until all the ideas are posted.

Brainstorming Option

Anonymous Alternatives Generation

Summary Description

This technique allows group members to share alternatives anonymously, thus eliminating associations of a personality with an idea. It requires two recorders to write down all the ideas and a person (usually the facilitator) to pick up note cards from the participants. Individuals generate ideas anonymously, writing them on note cards. The cards are collected and recorded in random order on flip charts.

Method

1. Post the problem, task, question, or desired outcome on a flip chart.

2. Pass out index cards to group members and ask that they record their ideas on the cards. The only requirement is that the idea be written legibly and in a complete sentence. Instruct members to put each card facedown in front of them after they have recorded a response. Allow 20 to 30 minutes for individuals to generate responses.

3. The facilitator goes around the room, picks up the cards as they are completed, and delivers them to the two recorders, who then rewrite the ideas on flip charts or post them. The recorders should be situated in the back of the room, with the flip charts turned around so that no one can see the ideas as they are being recorded.

4. After all the cards are recorded, the flip charts are moved to the front of the room. The facilitator walks the group through each idea and makes sure that members understand it. The person who generated the idea has the option of explaining the idea or remaining anonymous.

Variation

You can insist that no one reveal authorship of any idea, thus ensuring an anonymous discussion and subsequent analysis of each idea.

Brainstorming Option

"Be Somebody Else"

Summary Description

Group members role-play while they are generating ideas. Several options are available for "being somebody else" during idea generation.

Method

1. Post the data for the problem, issue, or strategy at the front of the room.

2. Have members divide into pairs and discuss the issues and how they would approach dealing with the problem or doing the work.

3. During idea generation, partners reverse roles and generate alternatives that they believe would meet the approval of the other member of the pair.

4. After the list of alternatives is generated, check with members and see how closely their partners came to "reading them right."

Variations

1. Have the group list people whom they have known and admired—ones who are familiar to everyone in the group. Each member then picks someone from the list to role-play during idea generation.

2. Make a list of famous people who are admired by members of the group. Have everyone pick one person to role-play during idea generation.

Brainstorming Option

Idea Derby

Summary Description

Small teams of pairs, triads, or quads form to generate as many ideas or solutions as they can. The goal is purely volume. Teams have a set time to generate as many ideas as they can. The team with the most ideas wins.

Method

1. Post the problem or challenge on the flip chart.

2. Divide the group into teams. Make teams of two, three, or four members.

3. Review the rules of brainstorming (see Procedure II-8: Basic Brainstorming). Explain that all ideas are valid, but that one team can call a foul against another if they think the team "cheated" in some way. The facilitator should act as referee. If you want, you can devise a prize or reward for the winning team.

Brainstorming Option

Guided Imagery

Summary Description

Group members are led through a relaxation exercise and guided imagery by the facilitator after they have identified the "end point" of the activity or problem-solving process. Alternatives resulting from the guided imagery experience are generated.

Method

1. Post the problem, task, or strategy at the front of the room.

2. Have the group precisely identify the final step or end point of solving the problem or completing the task. For example, suppose your problem is developing a winning proposal. You might identify the end point as the telephone call through which you learn that you got the proposal.

3. The facilitator leads the group through a guided imagery exercise using the script provided next (in Guide II-9) or an alternative script. The end point the group has identified is used to fill in the blank space on the script.

4. Immediately after finishing the exercise, members silently write out all the ideas that occurred to them during the experience, as well as other ideas that spin off from the experience.

5. In "round robin" style, have each person share his or her ideas. Record all ideas on flip charts.

REFERENCES

Higgins, James H. (1994). *101 creative problem solving techniques: The handbook of new ideas for business.* Winter Park, FL: The New Management Publishing Company.

Van Gundy, Arthur B. (1992). *Idea power: Techniques and resources to unleash the creativity in your organization.* New York: AMACOM.

Von Oech, Roger. (1992). *The creative whack pack.* Stamford, CT: U.S. Game Systems.

Weiss, Donald H. (1988). *Creative problem solving.* New York: AMACOM.

GUIDE II-9

Guided Imagery Script

The Purpose of This Guide

When used properly, guided imagery is an effective tool for generating ideas. The facilitator encourages people to relax and then gives them verbal prompts that elicit ideas relevant to the group task. There are many variations on how to do guided imagery. The script below, provided for the facilitator's use, is simple and has proven to be effective in many different settings. You may want to adapt it to include other techniques with which you are familiar.

THE SCRIPT—

You, the facilitator, say the following:

We are going to do an exercise that will help us imagine creative solutions to our task at hand. Most of you have probably done some sort of guided imagery before. Some people like it; others don't. Regardless of your past experience, be open to the chance that this might help us see some new possibilities.

I want to offer a kind of ground rule here. You don't have to do any part of the process that you are uncomfortable with. For instance, I will be suggesting that you close your eyes. If you're not comfortable with that, you can keep your eyes open.

I will be putting you through a few simple exercises to help you relax. Then you will be invited to go to a peaceful, restful spot and imagine the desired state that we are looking for. It will take only a few minutes. Then, in the group, we will discuss what you saw and log any ideas that might contribute to our work.

Now, I'd like to ask you to sit up straight in your chair, with both feet on the floor. Put down anything that you are holding. If you are wearing glasses, take them off. Rest your hands comfortably on your legs. Close your eyes and be still for a moment.

[Pause for about 30 seconds and allow people to be still; then continue.]

Now pay attention to your breathing. Slow your breathing a bit and exhale slightly longer than you inhale.

[Pause for about 30 seconds as people slow their breathing; then continue.]

(Continued)

THE SCRIPT *(Continued)*

[During the next part of the exercise, pause for about 10 seconds between your tension-and-release instructions.]

Now, we will move through your body, relaxing different muscles. First, your toes. Tense your toes now. **[Pause.]** *Now release the tension. Notice the difference.*

Tense your calves and lower leg muscles. **[Pause.]** *Now release the tension. Notice the difference.*

Tense your thighs and upper leg muscles. **[Pause.]** *Now release the tension. Notice the difference.*

Tense your buttocks muscles. **[Pause.]** *Release the tension. Notice the difference.*

The lower part of your body is now relaxed.

Tense your abdominal muscles. **[Pause.]** *Now release the tension. Notice the difference.*

Tense your chest muscles. **[Pause.]** *Now release the tension. Notice the difference.*

Tense your upper back muscles. **[Pause.]** *Release the tension. Notice the difference.*

Tense your shoulder blades. **[Pause.]** *Now release the tension. Notice the difference.*

Now your neck muscles. Tense the neck muscles. **[Pause.]** *Now release the tension.*

Now the muscles in your face. Tense your facial muscles. **[Pause.]** *Let go of the tension. Notice the difference.*

Now your head. Notice where any tension in your head is located. Pinpoint the location. Feel the tension. **[Pause.]** *Now let go of the tension there.*

Now your entire body is more relaxed. Notice any remaining tensions and let them go.

Now imagine that there is an elevator here in the room. You are waiting for the elevator. It arrives here and you get into the elevator. You are going to go down several floors, and when you get out of the elevator, you will walk into a peaceful, restful place that you enjoy.

The elevator is going down . . . 10 . . . 9 . . . 8 . . . 7 . . . 6 . . . 5 . . . 4 . . . 3 . . . 2 . . . 1. The elevator stops. The doors open and you walk out into one of your favorite outdoor locations.

Look around and notice what the environment is like. Sit or lie down and relax.

(Continued)

THE SCRIPT *(Concluded)*

Now imagine that

_____

_____

_____

_____

_____

[Write the outcome you are seeking in the space above. Examples: "Imagine that our team is functioning at full productivity. We are producing astonishing results, working together better than we ever have before." "Imagine that we now have a product design process that is quicker than ever before, that people feel fully empowered, and that there is acceptance and buy-in throughout the company for the new design." "Imagine that we are all at a special luncheon where we are being presented with the Baldrige award for organizational excellence."]

[Continue script.]

- *What does it look like?*
- *Who is there? Who is involved?*
- *What happened?*
- *Notice what it took to produce the results.*
- *What were the key elements involved in making the breakthroughs?*

[Allow people about 2 or 3 minutes of silence to imagine the scenario.]

Now it is time to leave this setting and return to the room. Allow your mind to return to the pleasant surroundings. Relax for a moment before leaving.

[Allow about 20 seconds of silence.]

Now, when you get up, you will notice the elevator. Walk over to the elevator and press the button to return. The elevator comes. The door opens and you get in. You are now going back up in the elevator. First floor . . . second floor . . . third floor . . . fourth floor . . . fifth floor . . . sixth floor . . . seventh floor . . . eighth floor . . . ninth floor . . . and you arrive at the tenth floor.

The door opens and you step out of the elevator. You are now back in the room. You can open your eyes and return to the room.

[Wait a moment for everyone to adjust to their return to the room.]

PROCEDURE II-10

Introducing Groups to Dialogue

Purpose

To introduce a group to the concepts involved in dialoguing and to prepare them for an initial activity in dialogue conversations.

Summary Description

This procedure involves using several different tools to illustrate the concepts and the principles of dialogue. It prepares the group for and incorporates Procedure II-11: Reflective Listening.

David Bohm is known as one of the premiere thinkers on the concept of dialogue. In his small book *On Dialogue* (1990), he writes:

> I give a meaning to the word "dialogue" that is somewhat different from what is commonly used. The derivations of words often help to suggest a deeper meaning. "Dialogue" comes from the Greek word *dialogos.* *Logos* means "the word," or in our case we would think of the "meaning of the word." And *dia* means "through"—it doesn't mean two. A dialogue can be among any number of people, not just two. Even one person can have a sense of dialogue within himself, if the spirit of the dialogue is present. The picture or image that this derivation suggests is of a stream of meaning flowing among and through us and between us. This will make possible a flow of meaning in the whole group, out of which will emerge some new understanding. It's something new, which may not have been in the starting point at all. It's something creative. And this shared meaning is the "glue" or "cement" that holds people and societies together.

> In a dialogue, however, nobody is trying to win. Everybody wins if anybody wins. There is a different sort of spirit to it. In a dialogue, there is no attempt to gain points, or to make your particular view prevail. Rather, whenever any mistake is discovered on the part of anybody, everybody gains. It's a situation called win-win, whereas the other game is win-lose —if I win, you lose. But a dialogue is something more of a common

participation, in which we are not playing a game against each other but with each other. In a dialogue, everybody wins.

Bohm suggests that the purpose of dialogue is "to communicate coherently the truth." William Isaacs (1993) suggests that in order to effectively engage in real dialogue, there must be a safe "container" created for the conversation that allows everyone to share their opinions and surface the assumptions underlying their opinions without hostility.

Dialogue conversations are undertaken in a quest for meaning without regard to a particular outcome. In fact, it is important that the conversations be taken on with no intent other than to gain meaning and understanding relative to the issues at hand. The objective, if there is one, is to take in all the opinions and expose them to view without subjecting them to the filters of judgment. The conversation requires a willingness of those participating to open their minds to all possible views, holding their judgments in abeyance. Only when all the opinions and assumptions have surfaced is there an opportunity for some kind of real and meaningful change.

Meaningful dialogue conversations require that each member look at the things that he or she has assumed to be true, that is, personal assumptions about the issues at hand. And after understanding those assumptions, every member attempts to suspend those assumptions while taking part in a process of inquiry and reflection.

The procedure described below is intended to **introduce** the group to the dialogue process. It should give group members a sense that their conversations can exist on an entirely different level—one that, in yielding a deeper sense of meaning, can lead to a richer and ultimately more useful collective intelligence and thus the possibility of breakthrough strategies and win-win solutions.

When to Use the Procedure

- When you are working with a group that is divided on some key "hot button" issues
- When you want to deepen the level of conversation
- When you want to openly confront conflict in a group in search of a common ground for action
- When you want to break people's conversational habits and patterns related to a particular topic or issue

Participants

Number: About 12 is best for dialogue groups, but the technique can be used with any size group.

Type: Members of any type of group.

Resources *(checkmarks indicate recommended equipment)*

✔ Flip chart and markers
✔ Playback unit
✔ Overhead projector
✔ Video that illustrates the principles of dialogue
✔ Other: See **Resources** for Procedure II-11: Reflective Listening
❑ Handout: At least one paper on dialoguing technique. The Isaacs paper (see **References**) is highly recommended.
❑ Transparencies of the four job aids included with this procedure

Facilitator(s)

The facilitator introduces the concepts of dialoguing, using the job aids that accompany this procedure and following the instructions under **Method** below. Procedure II-11: Reflective Listening is then explained to the group. The facilitator answers any questions about the Reflective Listening activity and then leaves the group alone to complete the activity. The facilitator can join the group, or can circulate among members if there is more than one group.

Time

Ninety minutes for both Procedure II-10 and Procedure II-11.

Method

1. Read some background material on dialogue. This is a weighty yet exciting concept, and it is important to develop a personal enthusiasm for the possibilities of dialogue technique. See **References**. Especially recommended are the Isaacs and Schein articles and the Senge and colleagues book.

2. Using the job aids included with this procedure, introduce the meaning of dialogue and the purposes of dialogue to the group.

3. Show a videotape that illustrates many of the principles of dialogue. Before starting the video, explain to the group that you now want them to see an example of dialogue and to think about the principles illustrated by it. (See **Notes** section for a suggested video.)

4. Title a flip chart page "Principles of Dialogue," and invite the group to identify some of the principles that they observed in the video. Record the principles on the chart.

5. Show "12 Principles of Effective Dialogue" on the overhead, and review the principles with the group. Note where similarities occur between the group's list and the transparency.

6. Explain that the group will now do a kind of "warm-up" exercise for dialoguing. Then follow the instructions for Procedure II-11: Reflective Listening. Keep the group size under 12 for the exercise (groups of 10 to 12 work best). Before members begin the exercise, show the "Suggestions for Dialogue" job aid.

7. Bring everyone back into the large group following the Reflective Listening exercise. Ask members what they noticed about the process and the experience.

8. Conclude by heading a flip chart page "Possible Applications" and asking the group when and where they think using dialogue might enhance their work with other groups.

Note

1. The film *Dances With Wolves,* readily available on videotape, contains an excellent scene illustrating many of the principles of dialogue. In this scene, a Sioux tribe meets and discusses what to do when the white man comes. (The dialogue is spoken in the Sioux language and translated into English subtitles.)

   If you decide to use this videotape, preview it first. Before playing the tape, set your VCR's digital counter at zero. When you find the scene, note the counter number so that you can easily locate the scene again when presenting it to the group. The scene is less than 3 minutes long. We were introduced to the tape by colleagues Alysia Vanitzian and David Hetrick after they had seen it used in a workshop conducted by The Dialogue Group (see **References**).

REFERENCES

Bohm, David. (1990). *On dialogue.* Ojai, CA: David Bohm Seminars.

Isaacs, William N. (1993, autumn). Taking flight: Dialogue, collective thinking, and organizational learning. *Organizational Dynamics, 22*(2).

Schein, Edgar. (1993, autumn). On dialogue, culture, and organizational learning. *Organizational Dynamics, 22*(2).

Senge, Peter M.; Kleiner, Art; Roberts, Charlotte; Ross, Richard B.; and Smith, Bryan J. (1994). *The fifth discipline fieldbook: Strategies and tools for building a learning organization.* New York: Doubleday.

Teurfs, Linda, & Gerard, Glenna. (1993). *Reflections on building blocks and guidelines for dialogue.* Laguna Hills, CA: The Dialogue Group. (To order this material from the publisher, write 23010 Lake Forest Drive #342, Laguna Hills, CA 92653; or call 714-497-9757.)

The Meaning of Dialogue

What Does Dialogue Mean?

A commonly held interpretation of dialogue is:

"A mechanistic and unproductive debate between people seeking to defend their own views against one another."

(William Isaacs)

The actual derivation of the word is:

GR: *Dia* + *logos* = **"meaning flowing through"**

Dictionary definitions useful when facilitating groups are:

"A frank exchange of ideas or views on a specific issue in an effort to attain mutual understanding."

(Webster's)

or

"A free interchange of different points of view."

(Funk & Wagnalls)

The Purposes of Dialogue

- To establish a field of genuine meeting and inquiry (which can be called a "container").

- To create a setting in which people can allow a free flow of meaning and vigorous exploration of the collective background of their thought, their personal predispositions, the nature of their shared attention, and the rigid features of their individual and collective assumptions.

- To explore the experience of meaning embodied in a group of people.

From: William N. Isaacs, "Taking Flight: Dialogue, Collective Thinking, and Organizational Learning," *Organizational Dynamics, 22*(2), 1993.

12 Principles of Effective Dialogue

1. You become conscious of your assumptions.

2. People reward each other for searching for the meaning behind ideas.

3. People work to discern the pattern of the collective experience, learning how to think together.

4. Differences are welcomed and sought out for explanation.

5. A metaphorical container is constructed big enough to hold diverse allegiances, experiences, and opinions.

6. Previously taboo subjects can be raised in a safe and meaningful inquiry.

7. There is no agenda. Agreement unfolds as it does.

8. Different reasons support the direction that emerges.

9. Fragmentary thinking becomes organized into a whole.

10. We view a complex problem with "new eyes."

11. Cross-talk is discouraged.

12. The process has a beginning, but no end. Change happens when it does. There is no "hurrying the harvest."

Suggestions for Dialogue

☞ **Suspend assumptions**

☞ **Observe/listen to one another**

☞ **Listen to your inner voice**

☞ **Slow the discussion and search for the underlying meaning**

—Contributed by David Hetrick, Los Angeles

PROCEDURE II-11

Reflective Listening

Purpose

To introduce group members to dialoguing technique and to encourage deeper conversations prior to problem solving or group discussion.

Summary Description

Group members individually take turns reflecting upon a question posed by another group member, sharing their thoughts, and then posing a question to the next person.

When to Use the Procedure

- Prior to generating ideas or building the group data base in problem-solving groups

- When there are significant differences among group members; before group members have had a chance to become positional and "entrenched" in their ideas

Participants

Number: Less than 12 is best, but the technique can be used with any size group if time permits.

Type: Suitable for any group that will be continuing to work together or that is charged with solving a problem of any complexity.

Resources

An object that can be passed from person to person. The object should be made of natural materials and encourage reflection. "Rainsticks" purchased in specialty stores can be used, as can a "talking stick" made with a small tree branch and feathers.

Facilitator(s)

One facilitator introduces and explains the technique.

Time

It usually takes an average of 2 to 3 minutes per person.

Method

1. Introduce the method. Explain that it is used before discussion or problem solving to encourage reflective conversations that stimulate group members to listen carefully to one another's point of view and experience base.

2. Ground rules are stated:

   - Only one person speaks at a time.
   - No interrupting, correcting, or helping.
   - Suspend judgment, especially of yourself.

3. Summarize the process: One group member is given the talking stick (or rainstick) and asked to generate, after a moment's reflection, a broad question related to a topical area. The member pauses (if using a rainstick, the pause can be the length of time it takes for the beads inside the stick to fall when the stick is turned), responds to the question, poses another question to the person sitting next to him or her, and passes the talking stick to that person. The second person reflects on the question, taking as long as needed to answer the question, and responds; then he or she pauses, thinks of a question for the next person, and poses it. The process continues until everyone has had a turn.

4. Ask the group to discuss what the experience was like for them and what they noticed about the activity.

Notes

1. The facilitator follows the same ground rules as participants. Don't try to help anyone respond. Occasionally during the exercise, a person will totally go off the topic or not "get" the question. Just allow the exercise to proceed without giving any corrective feedback.

2. You might want to ask someone who has demonstrated that they are knowledgeable about the topic to reflect on and pose the first question of the process.

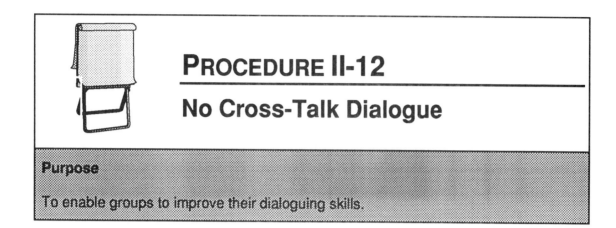

PROCEDURE II-12

No Cross-Talk Dialogue

Purpose

To enable groups to improve their dialoguing skills.

Summary Description

The "No Cross-Talk" rule is drawn from the conversational practices traditionally used in 12-step meetings such as those of Alcoholics Anonymous and Narcotics Anonymous. It is a powerful group norm that enables members to share their ideas and feelings without fear of being attacked or judged. The facilitator introduces the "No Cross-Talk" rule to members and then allows members to discuss a particular topic using the newly established conversational norm.

When to Use the Procedure

- When you are helping groups practice dialoguing
- Before engaging in a nominal group process in order to enable everyone to clarify their present feelings and positions related to an issue or topic
- When there is no necessity for group agreement or an action, but members are looking for guidance or ideas for their own use related to a topic or issue

Participants

Number: Between seven and 30 persons may participate in a discussion.

Type: All members of a group.

Resources *(checkmarks indicate recommended equipment)*

✔ Overhead projector or flip chart
✔ An electronic timer with a soft reminder tone

Facilitator(s)

The facilitator introduces the procedure, explains the timekeeping rules, and then turns the floor over to the participants. During the activity, the facilitator is responsible for enforcing the "No Cross-Talk" rule and, if necessary, reminding members of the rule. When the time for the activity is up, the facilitator leads the group in a short debriefing.

Note: No group recording of any kind should be done during this procedure.

Time

Sixty to 90 minutes

Method

1. Define the "No Cross-Talk" rule:

   "'No cross-talk' means sharing your experiences, concerns, feelings, opinions, and hopes related to a particular issue or topic without referring to, or reacting to, any other group member's sharing and without evaluating what has previously been said."

   Ask if everyone understands the rule and if there are any questions.

2. Explain that there is no need for the group to come to any agreement. Members should feel free to share their observations, opinions, and experiences without regard to what others might think or feel. Everyone is free to make use of other members' experiences, and is encouraged to "take what you want and leave the rest."

3. Ask a group member to serve as the timekeeper. These are the basic timekeeping rules: (a) The timer should be set for either 2, 3, or 4 minutes per person (the setting should be the same for everyone), and (b) after the timer goes off, the timekeeper resets it for 1 more minute. Decide on the first time setting and explain the rules:

   "Everyone will have [2, 3, or 4] minutes to share. The timer will go off after that, reminding you that you should wrap up your sharing. The timer will go off again in 1 minute, at which time you stop sharing and give the next person a turn."

4. Present the following options for how to rotate the sharing, and ask the group which option they would prefer:

   (a) When a person is done sharing, he or she calls on someone else who wants to share.

   (b) When a person is done sharing, he or she picks someone else to share.

   (c) The group member who starts the sharing calls on people.

   (d) The group member who starts the sharing calls for a show of hands from those wanting to go next and then selects someone.

5. Other rules for the sharing:

   • Do not ask questions.

- Do not share a second time until everyone who wants to share has had a chance.

- Own your own messages by using "I" messages. Avoid telling others what to do.

- Feel free to pass if you do not wish to share. There is no need to give any reason for passing.

- We stop after _____ minutes.

6. Have the group select a topic or issue members wish to discuss.

7. Check for any questions, clarify the topic or issue to be discussed, and ask, "Who would like to start?" If no one volunteers, pick someone who you think will be a good model and ask that person to start.

8. As the activity proceeds, monitor the group to ensure that everyone is observing the "No Cross-Talk" rule. If anyone breaks the rule, remind him or her of the rule.

9. When time for the activity is up, tell members to stop; then hold a short debriefing session during which members share their observations of the activity.

Notes

1. Before conducting this procedure, you may want to observe the "No Cross-Talk" norm in action by attending an "open" 12-step meeting (open meetings can be attended by anyone). Check with directory assistance for the phone number of a group that holds such meetings; then call to find out when and where open meetings are held. Make sure you specify that you are interested in discussion group meetings (as opposed to "speaker" meetings). Attending a meeting may give you insights into how you can hold group discussions that require minimal facilitation.

2. Twelve-step meetings work best when the topic is related to one of the program's simple, guiding principles, such as "gratitude" or "working with others." In an organizational setting, you might select company values or key operating principles for topics.

Variations

1. For a variation, ask one person to speak for 10 minutes on a broad topic (you decide the topic). The speaker should conclude by narrowing down the topic to something more specific or by asking a question about a part of the topic that interests him or her. For instance, let's say the broad topic is "our work overload problem." After 10 minutes, the speaker might say, "I'd like to hear about how people handle responding to a work request when they are already overloaded." Topics of this kind will produce rather practical discussions. You can also use the variation for "hot button" issues such as "the new organizational structure" or "the upcoming labor-management negotiations."

"No Cross-Talk" Definition

" 'No cross-talk' means sharing your experience, concerns, feelings, opinions, and hopes related to a particular issue or topic without referring to, or reacting to, any other group member's sharing and without evaluating what has previously been said."

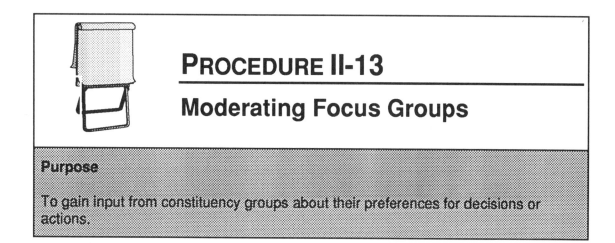

PROCEDURE II-13

Moderating Focus Groups

Purpose

To gain input from constituency groups about their preferences for decisions or actions.

Summary Description

Stewart and Shamdasani (1990) provide us with a brief history of focus groups. Developed shortly after World War II, and originally called "group depth interviews" or "focused interviews," focus groups were used by the entertainment industry to gauge audience responses to radio programs. Groups were asked to listen to a program and to press a red button when they had a negative reaction to something they heard and a green button when they had a positive reaction; then, after the program, group members were asked to discuss why they liked certain aspects of the program and disliked others.

The group process technique came into widespread use in the world of consumer market research. Currently, it is employed in almost bonanza-like proportions throughout the world, although it is frequently misused or not used as originally intended. Today, there is a tendency to call many groups "focus groups" when in fact they are not true focus groups. Real focus groups are actually underutilized by most organizational developers and group process specialists. This is unfortunate, for if understood and used properly, focus groups can be an indispensable tool for enabling groups to succeed.

The best way to understand focus groups is to look at several characteristics that distinguish the group from other group process tools. These distinguishing characteristics are as follows:

- *Agreement is not necessary or even desired in the focus group.* You are only trying to accurately record the opinions of members so that their thoughts and feelings can be analyzed for some future decision or action. The purpose of the process is research toward quality decisions, not decision making.

- *Homogeneity, not heterogeneity, is most often sought.* Groups are usually conducted with one particular type of person, not a variety of representatives or "stakeholders." This homogeneity helps group members feel comfortable in airing their true feelings.

- *Focus groups are used as a research/evaluation tool.* Usually groups are given specific options for evaluation rather than asked to generate ideas or options. There are times, though, when focus groups are used for idea generation.

- *Issues discussed are limited.* An in-depth knowledge about a limited number of issues is sought.

- *Groups are small.* They are usually between six and 12 members.

- *Homogeneous, multiple groups are conducted.* Whenever possible, multiple groups are used to avoid the research error that can occur from certain people dominating the group or the group's not being truly reflective of the constituency.

- *A neutral facilitator moderates the discussion.* A neutral facilitator, not connected to any formal decision-making authority, acts as a moderator and interviewer.

- *Their duration is usually 1½ to 2 hours.* Meeting time is limited, yet long enough to deal with a few issues in depth.

- *Responses are recorded in detail.* A detailed recording is made of the full range of positions and opinions, and then analyzed later in order to provide an in-depth qualitative research basis for subsequent decisions.

- *Questions are pre-formulated to create the agenda.* A series of mostly open-ended questions is generated. The questions usually move from general to specific considerations.

When to Use the Procedure

- When you want to test several alternative courses of action with a given group that will be critical to the success of implementation

- When you are using "consultative" decision making (See Procedure II-15: Consultative Decision Making)

- As an alternative discussion technique for a group during the decision analysis phase of task group work

- In order to determine the best questions for a written survey

- With systems change design teams, when they are gathering data toward the change or are in the alternative evaluation phase of their work

- Anytime that you want to be sure that a given group has been "heard" and their positions and opinions taken seriously

- When little data is available regarding the positions and interests of a given group, or when the data that is available is questionable

Participants

Number: Six to 12 participants

Type: Members of a given constituency group

Resources *(checkmarks indicate recommended equipment)*

✔ Flip charts and markers.

✔ Video camera and/or audiotape recorder. (Test the microphone to make sure that it will pick up and clearly record the conversations throughout the room.)

✔ Laptop computer and operator.

Facilitator(s)

One person acts as the moderator/interviewer. If you will be using flip charts to record data, have two recorders. A stenographer can substitute for the group recorders. One person should be included as an assistant to attend to the video/audiotape recording.

Time

Each group is given 1½ to 2 hours for the activity.

Method

The method described below is an adaptation of the model for designing and using focus groups proposed by Stewart and Shamdasani (1990). The model has eight basic steps:

1. **Problem Definition—Formulation of the Research Question**

2. **Identification of the Sampling Frame**

3. **Identification of Moderator**

4. **Generation and Pre-testing of Interview Guide**

5. **Recruiting the Sample Group**

6. **Conducting the Group**

7. **Analysis and Interpretation of the Data**

8. **Writing the Report**

The steps are used as a framework for the following procedure, which is provided as a guide to the conduct of focus groups:

1. **Problem Definition—Formulation of the Research Question**

   First, clarify the purpose of the focus group. It is called a focus group because it is to be focused. What do you want to focus on? What is the research question you want to answer, the problem you want to clarify, or the types of alternatives you want evaluated? What information is sought, and why do you want it? Write a clear statement of the group's purpose.

2. **Identification of the Sampling Frame**

   A sampling frame is a list of people whom you deem representative of the group that you are seeking data from. Identify the numbers in that population and how you will reach them. Determine what percentage of those people you want to include in your group(s). Determine how many groups you will conduct, and try to interview multiple groups whenever feasible. At this point, also identify the data sources or data bases from which you can get the names, addresses, and phone numbers of participants. It is also wise to identify a targeted date "range" when you will conduct the interviews. The date(s) you select should allow enough time to do a good job of recruiting the participants (Step 5).

3. **Identification of Moderator**

   Identify a moderator for the group whom members will perceive as neutral and not attached to any position related to the questions that are asked. Avoid using as moderators people with higher organizational ranks than those being interviewed or people who work with participants on a day-to-day basis. It is important that the moderator be familiar with and able to speak "the language" of the participants. If need be, you can have two moderators co-facilitate: one who is a neutral facilitator, unfamiliar with the technical nature of the information you seek, and another who is less skilled as a process facilitator but knows the nature of the data to be discussed.

4. **Generation and Pre-testing of the Interview Guide**

   Next, brainstorm a list of questions that you want the group to answer. If specific product designs or attributes, alternative strategies, or some form of optional choices are to be presented to the group, identify ways that the options will be clearly introduced and explained. If you are trying to capture people's experiences in coping with a specific problem, break your questions down into parts that help cue the total experience. For example, if the problem is the "too long product development cycles," break it down into components such as design, development, and testing. How have you reduced cycle time in the design phase? In the development phase? In the testing phase?

   Then select your preferred questions to use. Ask those questions of a general and less structured nature before you ask more definite specific questions. For instance, "How have you felt to date about your product development cycle?" Then later: "Please give us your position on the effectiveness of test markets we currently use." Estimate the time it will take to use each, and schedule these questions on the agenda. Leave enough unspecified time so that you can explore interesting responses as they occur. Interviewing is an art form as well as a science, and you want to be able to use the intuition and instincts of the moderator to cue the highest quality of data.

If you can, try out the agenda with a sample group or a mock group and revise your questions and schedule on the basis of the tryout.

Finally, write up your interview guide for use during the group.

5. Recruiting the Sample Group

Make a list of potential group members. Candidates can be selected either (a) randomly, (b) according to a specific list of criteria, or (c) by some combination of (a) and (b). The questions in the interview guide represent one form of criteria for recruitment. You want people who will be able to provide data in response to the questions.

The way that you recruit your sample group depends on how necessary it is for the sample to be randomized. When randomization is less necessary, you can use "ready-made" groups, available through regular meetings conducted in organizations, support group meetings open to the public, church group meetings, and the like. You may be able to "tag" on to the existing agenda of these gatherings, saving considerable recruitment time—provided that linking to such meetings does not skew your sample in some way that will negatively affect the integrity of the data you collect.

After you have selected the date and location of your meeting, a letter of invitation should be prepared. The letter should include the purpose of the meeting, the location of the meeting, starting and ending times, and any incentives that are provided for participation. Incentives may be small participation stipends, travel allowances, child care, meals, snacks, and so forth. Even small incentives may have a significant positive effect on attendance.

The letters should then be sent. Confirmations of attendance can be handled by enclosing a response form or telephoning people shortly after they receive their letter to see if they will be able to attend. The latter method is preferred as long as resources are available to make the calls.

It is wise to "book" more people than you need. You should "overbook" anywhere from 10% to 100% of your targeted population, depending on the expected difficulty in getting people to follow through and attend.

The day before the meeting, calls should be made reminding people of the meeting and reconfirming attendance.

6. Conducting the Group

The following is a basic outline for the conduct of the group:

(a) Welcome the group.

(b) Have people introduce themselves and tell a little bit about themselves and their personal experience as it relates to the issues under discussion.

(c) Review the purpose of the group, the type of questions that will be asked, and what will be done with the data.

(d) Establish a "norm state" or environment where people feel comfortable and safe expressing themselves.

(e) Explain the recording methods. Usually, written releases for audio or video recording are not necessary; but if you deem them necessary, obtain them.

(f) Following the interview guide, present questions to group members, one by one.

(g) Following each question presented, probe for more information as appropriate.

(h) Stop 5 minutes before the end of the scheduled time (regardless of whether all questions have been covered), summarize, and thank people for their participation.

Step c is critical to the focus group's success. People need to be assured that the environment is safe and that they are free to express themselves. Stress that there is no need for agreement in the group. You want to know each individual's thoughts, feelings, and positions on the questions presented. Be specific about the confidentiality issues involved, letting people know who will see the data, whether names will be attached to the data or not, and if names are attached to all or some of the data, who will have access to this information.

Make sure that you explain each person's role (e.g., participants, observers, assistants, recorders).

Make the ground rules for the discussion clear by stating them explicitly. They can be either written on a flip chart and reviewed, or just reviewed verbally. You might consider these suggested ground rules (also see Guide I-3: A Checklist for Ground Rule Choices):

1. Share your thoughts, feelings, and positions, regardless of whether they agree with those of other group members.

2. Focus on your own feelings, thoughts, and positions. Avoid referring to the comments of others.

3. Share freely and openly, and remain conscious of allowing others plenty of "air time."

4. Stick within the time frames for responses if time frames are specified.

A good technique suggested by Stewart and Shamdasani (1990) is to start the discussion by having each member relate some personal anecdote connected to the issues under discussion. This sharing will serve to increase rapport in the group and break down inhibitions.

Another useful starting technique is to pose a fairly general question (one to which everyone can respond) and then to ask each person to briefly share his or her ideas about that question. This "breaks the ice" for those who are more inhibited and might wait until much later in the meeting to share their thoughts.

Each moderator will handle the interviewing in a personally unique style. The critical facilitation skills involved are (1) actively listening to the responses, thus validating each response provided, and (2) probing for more information via effective questioning, as appropriate. For the most part, moderators should restrict themselves to making responses in these two areas; they also should be vigilant about keeping their own "air time" to a minimum. Techniques for soliciting information from the group may be varied. Here are some useful choices:

1. Go around the room, asking each person in turn to respond.

2. Ask everyone to respond, allowing people to answer in whatever order they prefer. Check to see that everyone has responded.

3. Ask for a specific number of people to respond. "I'd like to hear from about three of you on this."

4. Following one person's response, ask, "Is there anyone with a significantly different view?"

5. Following one response, ask for an indication from the group as to how many people feel the same way or have the same position.

6. Use some technique for calling on people in a random fashion. For example, use a pack of index cards with people's names on them and pull a name (or two or three) and ask that person to respond.

7. Just ask for responses, and allow everyone who has something to say to respond.

8. Before starting, specify the amount of time for a response. "I'd like to hear from each of you for no more than a minute on _____."

9. Ask people to respond to written survey question(s) before responding verbally. Then ask them to share why they responded the way that they did.

The moderator needs to keep an eye on the time and periodically check to see how he or she is doing on time, adjusting the interview guide questions as necessary.

It is important to end the focus group on time. This demonstrates to group members that you will keep your agreements and encourages trust in the process and in the moderator. End with a summary of the process and acknowledge group members for their participation and for the quality of the data that they offered.

7. **Analysis and Interpretation of the Data**

You should start your analysis by going back to the original intent of the study. What was your purpose? What were the questions for which you were seeking data? Your analysis, in simple terms, provides whatever answers you found to those questions. The process of analysis can be explained by Robert Yin's statement of what data analysis is: "Data analysis consists of examining, categorizing, tabulating, or otherwise re-combining the evidence, to address the initial propositions of a study" (1984, p. 99).

After focus group interviews, you generally end up with a considerable amount of mostly anecdotal data that forms the basis for "qualitative research." It is easy to get stuck forever on trying to process all the data. So, practically speaking, it is important to look first at your original purposes and questions. Then look over the data that you have. Think about how much time you have for data analysis and select ways of analyzing the data that fit your practical time constraints and most directly contribute to answering your original research question. If you just dive into processing the data, you may find yourself hopelessly trapped in a seemingly never-ending task. Think about what will be the most useful and least time-consuming analysis of the data.

Krueger (1994) offers four ways to analyze the data and suggests selecting one before you conduct the group. The four ways are as follows:

1. *Transcript-based analysis.* The entire meeting is transcribed and the transcription is analyzed.

2. *Tape-based analysis.* The audio or video recording is listened to carefully and the highlights of the data are transcribed, creating an abridged transcript for analysis.

3. *Note-based analysis.* Notes taken at the meeting (either on flip charts or by a transcriber) are analyzed, using the audio or video recording, to double-check accuracy.

4. *Memory-based analysis.* The interviewer/moderator verbally presents the results to the group or individual client(s) almost immediately after the meeting, using notes taken as aids, but mostly relying on personal recall of the meeting.

One method of processing the data is to take a transcription of the data and begin "cutting and pasting" responses in the transcript, placing the response under one of the research questions originally posed.

A similar quick analysis can be performed by coding each of the responses according to which research question is addressed by the response. Then the questions are listed with the responses following.

Once the initial tabulating/processing of the data is complete, some analysis of the data's meaning needs to be done. This content analysis becomes the second step in formulating a report. The methods of analyzing responses for meaning in qualitative research are numerous and beyond the scope of a guide such as this. Suffice it to say that some work needs to be done in response to the "What's it all mean?" type of question. Krueger (1994) suggests seven general guidelines for analyzing the content:

1. *Consider the words.* (Look at the actual words used and the meaning of the words.)

2. *Consider the context.* (What was the stimulus that triggered certain types of responses?)

3. *Consider the internal consistency.* (Look for how consistent the responses remained throughout the interview. Was there a shift in opinion at some point?)

4. *Consider the frequency or extensiveness of comments.*

5. *Consider the intensity of the comments.*

6. *Consider the specificity of responses.* (Specific, experience-based comments receive more weight than vague opinions.)

7. *Find the big ideas.*

The next step is to complete the analysis of themes, trends, and patterns that appear to have occurred throughout the conduct of the group(s). Finally, the implications of the data for future decisions and actions should be identified. Suggestions for further study or recommendations on the subsequent steps of reaching a decision may be specified. These interpretations of data should be succinctly noted for inclusion in the focus group report, the final step in the process.

8. Writing the Report

The first step in writing the report should be to think about whom the report is to be prepared for and the appropriate response for that group. Report formats and length should vary according to the targeted readers. The following represents a suggested outline of components that should be included in the report:

I. **The introduction.** Includes a description of the primary purpose of the focus groups, the composition of the groups, the period over which the groups were conducted, the moderators and other key personnel involved with collecting the data, and the locations of the groups.

II. **The statement of the problem and the key questions that were asked of group members.**

III. **The results or findings.** The results or findings should be organized into categories. One way to report the findings is to repeat each key question, followed by a summary of the data associated with the findings. Or the data can be presented according to the "big ideas" or major findings that were found after the data analysis was conducted. Sample verbatim quotes that are representative of each of the findings are often included to explicate the findings.

IV. **Major themes.** The themes of the findings should be identified. These are the major "threads" that tie together the individual findings that are reported.

V. **Limitations.** This section should be a forthright noting of all the limiting factors that should be considered when looking at the data reported. If there are certain holes in the data, these should be pointed out. If intact groups were used to collect the data, the limitations inherent in this approach should be pointed out. If only one group was used or the sample was small and possibly unrepresentative, these factors should be pointed out.

VI. **Implications of the data; recommendations.** The implications of the data for future actions or decisions should be noted. Recommendations for further study, research, or analysis should be made. Specific recommendations toward a given decision may or may not be included in the report, depending on whether such recommending was a part of the group's original charge.

An appendix that provides the original data or the data analysis can be attached to the report.

Finally, an executive summary should be written to preface the report.

Notes

1. Focus group techniques have not historically been addressed in books about group facilitation skills. We, the authors, feel that the proper use and understanding of focus groups can significantly add an important dimension to group work and to the repertoire of tools available to the group facilitator. Focus group techniques have typically been "hidden" from organizational development trainees because of the methodology's place in advertising and market research.

2. Focus groups, though time-consuming when rigorously implemented, represent an alternative way to gather data toward quality decisions. The collection of data via focus groups represents an excellent way to encourage participation in the organization without requiring the group to come to any form of consensus. On the other hand, the focus group techniques can be used to gather data for building consensual decisions.

REFERENCES

Krueger, Richard A. (1994). *Focus groups: A practical guide for applied research* (2nd ed.). Thousand Oaks, CA: Sage Publications.

Stewart, David W., & Shamdasani, Prem N. (1990). *Focus groups: Theory and practice* (Applied Social Research Methods Series, Vol. 2). Thousand Oaks, CA: Sage Publications.

Yin, Robert K. (1984). *Case study research.* Thousand Oaks, CA: Sage Publications.

FACILITATOR RESOURCES

Decision Modes

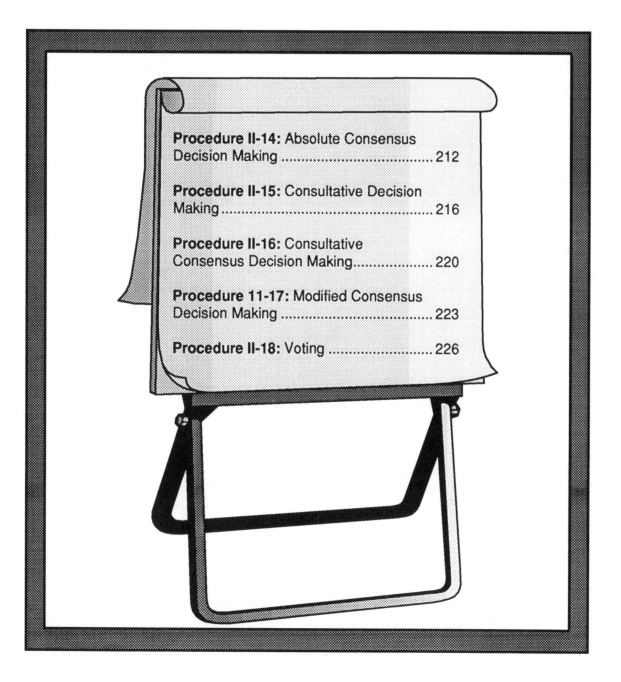

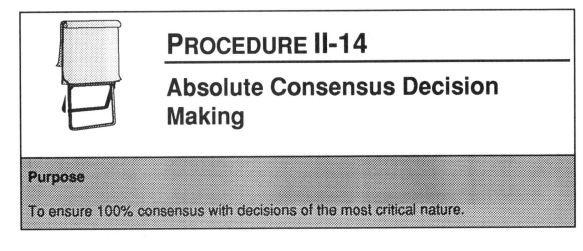

PROCEDURE II-14

Absolute Consensus Decision Making

Purpose

To ensure 100% consensus with decisions of the most critical nature.

Summary Description

Absolute consensus requires that all group members not only can live with a decision, but that they actively support the decision and are convinced that the decision is superior to the existing status quo. Absolute consensus is thus synonymous with unanimous agreement.

Absolute consensus decisions are usually time-consuming and require intense discussion and analysis. These 100% consensus decisions are best reserved for especially critical agreements, such as agreement on the organization's mission statement, the company's values, or the decision to enter a new line of business.

There are two basic criteria for employing absolute consensus:

1. The risk of making the wrong decision is exceptionally high.

2. It is essential that there be no pocket of resistance from any group member who fails to support the decision.

The group first agrees upon the necessity of making an absolute consensus decision and commits to the time needed to make the decision; then the group moves through a process, either structured or unstructured, to arrive at a decision that all members agree is the best decision possible.

When to Use the Procedure

-   When the risk of failure or of making the wrong decision is extremely high

-   When active support for the decision is required of all group members who will have a part in implementation of the decision

Participants

Number: Absolute consensus is usually successful only with small task groups of five to nine members. Larger groups risk weaker consensus, with some members agreeing to compromise decisions.

Type: Those persons who have a key stake in the decision and/or will hold significant responsibility for implementing the decision.

Resources *(checkmarks indicate recommended equipment)*

✔ Flip chart and markers

Facilitator(s)

The facilitator clarifies the outcomes that the group must achieve, assures commitment to the process, presents process options for arriving at the decision, and, if the group requests assistance in facilitating a process, leads the group through the process steps.

Time

There are two options for handling the time requirement. One is that the group agrees to meet for whatever time it takes to reach a decision. The other option is to specify a time limit for building absolute consensus. If everyone doesn't agree at the end of that time, the group either (a) abandons the challenge, (b) suggests an alternative person or group to make the decision, or (c) moves to a backup method for making the decision, such as voting, consultative decision making, or consultative consensus.

Method

1.   Check with the group to make sure that all members feel the need to make the decision by absolute consensus. Then share the definition of consensus:

   "Consensus means that all members of the group agree that the alternatives proposed are superior to the existing status quo. If any member of the group believes that the existing status quo is better than the proposed alternative(s), the status quo will be the group's decision."

2.   A time agreement is established. Either a specific time for making the decision is set or the group agrees to take whatever time is needed to make the decision. For example: "We'll meet every morning from 7:00 to 9:00 until we reach a decision." Or, "We'll meet today and, if necessary, next Thursday for the whole day, and see if we've made the decision." Whichever option is chosen now, the group should keep the alternative in mind until the decision is actually made.

3.   The group decides on any backup decision methods, should it fail to arrive at an absolute consensus.

4. The group charge is clearly specified by developing outcome statements for the charge.

5. The group decides at this point if it wishes to proceed in a facilitated manner or to operate as a self-directed group. If members prefer facilitation, you should offer process options, review them with the group, and get approval on the process from every member, thus illustrating the absolute consensus agreement.

    If the group prefers to operate unfacilitated, you can still help the group identify some process options before "turning them loose."

Subsequent steps assume that the group has asked to be facilitated.

6. Once the process agreement is made, the facilitator lists the process steps on a flip chart and labels the list "Consensus Agreement #1." All subsequent agreements are numbered in order so that the group can sense success as they are building consensus.

    Every member signs the agreement. The facilitator prepares a chart indicating what the signatures mean. The agreement definition should read something like this:

    > "I am in agreement with this decision. I agree that the alternatives are superior to the existing status quo, and I support the decision."

7. The facilitator moves the group through the process steps, using the tools in this guide to help members arrive at agreement. As agreements are achieved, they are numbered and mounted on flip chart paper on the wall.

8. When the group has completed all the process steps, the facilitator checks with members to make sure that everyone agrees that the outcomes have been achieved and their charge has been completed.

Notes

1. Absolute decision making is difficult for groups and for the facilitator; therefore, it is important that the group makes it clear that it wants the help of a facilitator. If the group doesn't actively ask for help, members are likely to direct frustrations at the facilitator rather than concentrate on the task at hand.

2. One option is to have the group dedicate a given amount of time to coming to the decisions itself and then request facilitation assistance if necessary.

3. The facilitator should take plenty of time to design the processes that will be used for the meeting. A rule of thumb for all meetings is that process-planning time be at least equal to the time allotted for the meeting. When facilitating absolute consensus sessions, it is wise to increase planning time significantly.

4. Longer-than-normal breaks are often useful in absolute consensus sessions to give people time to detach from personality and emotional issues and refocus on the best decision. Specific conflict resolution procedures can be found in Section II's Facilitator Resources, "Handling Conflicts and Common Problems With Groups."

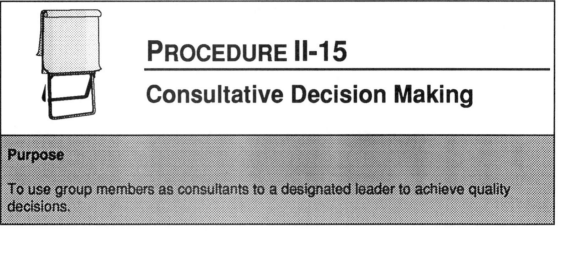

PROCEDURE II-15

Consultative Decision Making

Purpose

To use group members as consultants to a designated leader to achieve quality decisions.

Summary Description

There is an old-time management adage that says, "Usually the only difference between a slow decision and a fast decision is the amount of time it takes." There is another adage, sometimes heard about working groups, that illustrates a limitation of group decision making: "Any group will only move as fast as its slowest member." Both adages hold at least some truth. Yet, just because several people are involved, you do not necessarily have to move slower, particularly if you take advantage of the consultative decision method.

Consultative decisions mean that the group is providing consultation and advice to one group member, the person who has the responsibility for choosing the ultimate course of action. The "long and short" of the decision method is that a problem, question, or issue is raised; the group leader asks the group to help clarify the issue, draws suggestions and advice for correction or solution, and selects which of these ideas will be implemented.

When to Use the Procedure

- When there is at least one person with a clear command of the content under discussion, or when one person's expertise is clearly superior to that of other group members.

- When you want to utilize the expertise of a group of individuals but must do so quickly.

- When there is no compelling need to take the time required by absolute or modified consensus.

- When the group leader has a clear responsibility for action in the matter and prefers to retain personal control of any decision reached with the aid of a group.

- Most of the time, if you want to make decisions with a maximum of economy and effectiveness. This is the best "price value" method for making decisions in a group. However, if your group or organization has placed a high value on building consensual decisions, the technique will need to be used more sparingly.

- When you want to avoid "group-think," which results in a diminished quality solution because of ineffective group process.

Participants

Number: No size restrictions. The method is more flexible than consensus methods and can be used with any size group.

Type: All members of the group, with one clearly identified group leader. It is clear from the start that decisions will be made by only one group member.

Resources *(checkmarks indicate recommended equipment)*

✔ Flip chart and markers

Facilitator(s)

Facilitation is a choice. Although consultative decisions are often unfacilitated, it is usually desirable to use a facilitator to introduce the technique to a new group. The use of a facilitator also guards against the unintended but natural tendency of group members to perceive the method as arbitrary or autocratic.

Time

Usually less than 2 hours for any given issue

Method

Consultative decisions are often just as effective as modified consensus decisions and, in many cases, even more effective because you get a decision that accesses the collective intelligence of the group without having to take the time to negotiate consensus. The consultative decision method relies on the leader to make key decisions after consultative input has been received from the "experts" in the group.

There are several reasons why this method is effective. First, the leader of the group usually feels at ease, knowing that he or she remains clearly in control and will be able to accept or reject any suggestions. Second, there is little or no need to go through decision-process negotiations, which may end up diluting the "punch" of the original notion and take quite a bit of time. Third, the decision method encourages the use of clear individual accountability systems in the organization while allowing for participation. In a way, this is clearly the most time- and cost-effective version of "participative management" that can be employed by an organization.

Here are the steps to making a consultative decision:

1. The leader shares the written charge of the group, recording it on the flip chart.

2. The leader shares his or her initial tendencies or biases toward action/resolution with the group. These become boundaries for the recommendations that the group should produce. The leader may also wish to indicate how shaky those boundaries or initial "tendings" are. For example: "You could probably convince me to go with totally different alternatives here. I'm not sure I'm on the right path at all." Or, "I have given this part of the solution a good deal of thought, and I doubt that you'll be able to sway me much on this."

3. The leader takes the group through the standard steps for nominal group process if a problem is to be solved, or some other planning procedure if an advance plan is to be formulated. Alternatives are then generated by the group.

4. The leader selects alternatives for further review. When the alternative generation phase is completed, the leader eliminates unacceptable alternatives or selects favored alternatives for further consideration. The leader may or may not state why these decisions are being made. At times, it is best not to rationalize why alternatives are eliminated or selections are made.

5. The group is led through some type of decision analysis procedure with the alternatives that are acceptable for consideration by the leader.

6. The leader asks the group to address any remaining concerns. After carefully listening and weighing the results of the analysis phase, the leader lets the group know where he or she stands on the results or how close an acceptable decision is, stating any remaining concerns with favored alternatives. For example: "I really like the results of your analysis here. I think I'm leaning heavily toward alternative number 5, your most preferred option. Yet, I am still concerned that _____. Who's got an idea on how to get around that?"

7. Following this discussion of concerns, the leader offers a decision for review by the group. Once all such concerns are resolved to the leader's satisfaction, the chosen alternatives are listed as decisions and actions that will in fact be implemented. The leader checks for support for the decision(s). At this point, some leaders still prefer to check with their consulting "experts" to ensure that the solution meets each person's minimum standards for acceptance. For example: "OK, that's how I see it. I think this will work really nicely. But I would like to know if you all feel you could support this resolution. Is there anybody who can't support it?" If there is someone who can't support the decision and the leader feels it's critical for that person to provide support, the procedure can be shifted to a modified consensus approach to deal with that person's particular concern.

Notes

1. This method is underutilized by most groups. Many people fear that the method undermines group participation principles. This does not have to be the case. However, if the method is not carefully handled, it can be viewed as arbitrary or autocratic, particularly in cultures with high expectations for consensual decisions. The following tips will guard against the method being interpreted negatively by the group:

   ➧ Make sure that there is an explicit agreement with the group to use the method for a given meeting or decision.

   ➧ Use the method with a variety of group leaders, not just the person with the highest hierarchical status in the group. When doing so, make sure that the person with the highest status explicitly and genuinely agrees with someone else acting as the group leader and having authority to make the decision.

   ➧ Use a facilitator to introduce the method, explaining the rationale for its use and walking the group through its first few steps.

   ➧ Do a group process review at the close of the decision process. Ask members, "How did the consultative method work for everyone?" Listen to any concerns and adjust accordingly.

2. This method can be used as a backup when the group appears to be struggling with reaching a more consensual decision **and** it is not absolutely necessary that there be consensus for a given decision. In many cases, what is needed is action and a decision, not consensus. This may be the case if the issue is not particularly complex or it does not affect a great number of people.

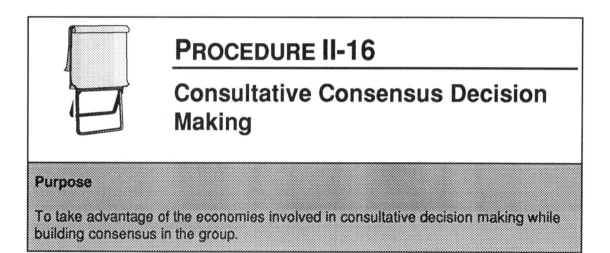

PROCEDURE II-16

Consultative Consensus Decision Making

Purpose

To take advantage of the economies involved in consultative decision making while building consensus in the group.

Summary Description

Consultative consensus decisions, just as the name implies, represent decisions that combine consultative and consensus decision techniques. It is clear from the start who will make the decisions, yet the group leader or facilitator makes a special effort to have the decisions represent a growing consensus that emerges from the collective intelligence of the group.

The acknowledged decision maker or decision makers are generally those who either have higher hierarchical status than other group members, have superior experience or expertise, or simply have a clear primary responsibility to execute the task at hand.

When to Use the Procedure

- When one person or a few group members have greater stake in, or superior expertise in, the issue under consideration or the task at hand

- When one person has been designated as having primary responsibility for a project or task and it is necessary to move quickly toward completion

- When the group values both clear-cut authority for decisions and high levels of participation

Participants

Number: The procedure can be used with small task groups or larger groups. About 25 people is usually the manageable limit.

Type: Participants may be either members of a task group or members of a regular group (e.g., management group, staff group).

Resources *(checkmarks indicate recommended equipment)*

> ✔ Flip chart and markers

Facilitator(s)

The group leader usually facilitates *and* leads consultative consensus decision making. A group facilitator can be used to introduce the technique to a group or to support the group leader by facilitating the session so that he or she can concentrate on the decision-related content.

Time

Consultative consensus decisions usually run anywhere from 30 to 90 minutes, but there is no real time restriction.

Method

1. Before the group meets, the decision to use the consultative consensus method needs to be clearly understood by group members. The best way to do this is to publish and distribute the agenda with the purpose and outcomes of the session, stating clearly that decisions will be made by consultative consensus.

2. The group leader posts the charge of the group, clearly identifying the outcomes expected for the group session.

3. The leader states any initial position or tendencies toward a decision that he or she presently holds, letting the group know if he or she holds any strong biases or predispositions toward action.

4. The leader helps the group move through a process designed to arrive at the necessary decisions. Nominal group process is often used, but the meeting can also proceed less formally. Two essentials have to occur. First, the group needs to build a data base that captures, and integrates, the intelligence of individual members. Second, the group must generate alternatives and discuss the pros and cons of the alternatives.

   What distinguishes consultative consensus decisions is that the group leader puts forth extraordinary effort to listen and clearly understand the data generated by the group. The leader focuses on building group consensus from the advice and consultation of group members.

5. As group members build the data base for the decision, the data is recorded on flip charts by the leader, the facilitator, or another member.

6. When the group leader feels that sufficient data has been gathered, he or she indicates so to the group and asks members if they feel comfortable moving on to alternative generation. The group then moves into the alternative generation

phase. The leader should be careful not to judge or edit the responses of group members offering alternatives.

The leader should wait to add any personal alternatives until members have generated their alternatives. Delaying any personal input allows the leader to focus on listening and hear the other members' advice.

7. Following a discussion of the alternatives on the use of decision analysis procedures, the leader either asks members if they sense that group consensus is emerging or offers a personal analysis of the consensus that does appear to be emerging.

8. If the emerging consensus of the group conflicts with the previously held notions of the leader, it is often wisest to postpone a decision until the leader has had the necessary time to reflect upon the options presented by the group. A postponement may also be in order if the group offers discordant or confusing opinions.

If, however, the leader does not sense such a conflict, he or she selects, and states, what seems to be the most personally comfortable decision that also represents the emerging consensus of the group. The leader states his or her reasons for the proposed decision and then checks with members to see if each is able to support the decision.

Notes

1. Consultative consensus works best when there are no intense time pressures to make a decision. The leader needs to feel free to take the time necessary to become personally comfortable with the decision and to make sure the group is comfortable with the decision.

2. Consultative consensus decision making may well stretch out over several meetings with the leader meeting with members individually or with two or three others between group meetings to develop his or her decision.

3. The real difference between consultative decisions and consultative consensus decisions lies in the intent of the group leader to forge a consensus among group members. In consultative decisions, the group understands (or should understand) that the leader may make a decision contrary to the ideas of the group. When operating in the consultative consensus mode, both the group and the leader are committed to using the group's collective intelligence to "grow" a decision that will be superior to any individual decision the leader might make.

4. Consultative consensus decision making relies on the group leader's listening skills. Group members must feel that the leader is truly hearing the advice that they are offering and is genuinely open to influence. Group members must accept the prerogative of the leader to make the decision and realize that though consensus is sought, the leader will retain the final say and make the decision.

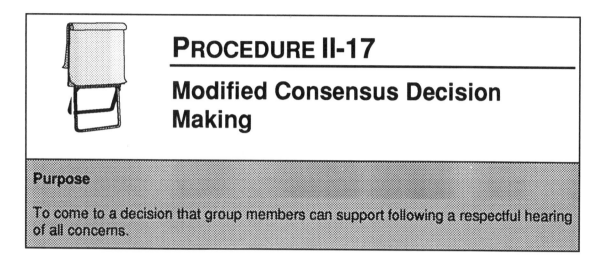

PROCEDURE II-17

Modified Consensus Decision Making

Purpose

To come to a decision that group members can support following a respectful hearing of all concerns.

Summary Description

The most stringent definition of consensus decisions insists that all members of the group agree with the decision before any approval is made by the team or task force. These types of consensus decisions are time-consuming and often unreachable. To reach absolute consensus when it involves complex data will usually require anywhere from 2 hours to several days. Most groups do not have this kind of time. And in at least half of the cases where unanimous consensus decisions are attempted, the group will end up in a hopeless deadlock with at least one member not being able to agree. Though this most stringent form of consensus decision making will still produce the best group decisions, it is not realistic for a group to come to unanimous consensus on each decision it must make.

Modified group consensus is a decision procedure that enables a group to achieve a type of consensus that ensures that each member of the group is willing to support the decision.

When to Use the Procedure

- When it is important that all team members support the decision

- When the decision represents some key or pivotal component of the task group's work

Participants

Number: This procedure works best with a small task group of five to nine people. It becomes tedious with larger numbers.

Type: Members of the task group.

Resources *(checkmarks indicate recommended equipment)*

✔ Flip chart and markers

Facilitator(s)

The facilitator leads the group through the steps. The chairperson or team leader is responsible for the approval of the eventual decision. The method usually becomes too cumbersome for the group leader who is operating without a facilitator, though some team leaders choose to master the method and use it for key decisions.

Time

Between 15 minutes and 2 hours, depending on the complexity of the decision, the divergence of views, and the group dynamics.

Method

1. Begin with a list of alternative ideas that have been developed. Ask for a group member to "nominate" one idea that the group can seriously consider adopting.

2. Appoint the originator of the idea as the leader for the further development of the idea.

3. Ask group members to brainstorm added data that would strengthen this idea. Record on the flip chart.

4. Check with the idea's originator to see that the integrity of the idea is still maintained if the suggestions made by group members are added to the original idea. Scratch out any suggestions that the idea's originator feels detract from the original conception.

5. When the alternative is classified on the flip chart, ask, "Given this alternative as presented, is there anyone who would have a serious concern about supporting it?"

6. If no concerns are expressed, say, "As there are no concerns expressed, I assume we have an alternative that everyone can support. Could each of you please come up and sign the chart, indicating your willingness to support the alternative?" Then each individual goes to the chart and writes his or her initials on the chart page.

    If concerns are expressed by any individual, deal with the concerns one person at a time, saying, "Please tell us your exact concern." The concern is recorded exactly as expressed by the group member. Next, you should say, "Who has an adaptation or amendment to this alternative that would address this concern?" List any suggestions. Then say to the person with the concern, "Do any of these adaptions address your concern so that you could now support the alternative?" If an adaptation is acceptable to the objectioner, ask the group, "Could everyone now accept the alternative as adapted?" Keep testing alternative adaptations in this manner until one is found acceptable by the whole group. Deal with any concerns held by other members in the same way until all concerns have been resolved satisfactorily and each member can "sign" the agreement noted on the flip chart, indicating the willingness to support the alternative.

This process may look like it would take forever, but in actual practice, most concerns can be resolved within a matter of minutes. For some more difficult agreements, the facilitator may need to vary the acceptance query to the group a bit and say, "We're having a little trouble with this one, and we still need a decision so we can keep moving. Is this an alternative that everyone can live with for now?" Then the facilitator asks if the group needs to schedule a review of the decision at a later date, while accepting the alternative as a recommendation at the present time. If a review is seen as necessary, the facilitator writes on the flip chart "To be reviewed [date]"; then the group members sign.

Notes

1. Group consensus can often be achieved without the use of this specific process. The process is an excellent tool to have available when group consensus does not emerge naturally. It is often useful for new groups that have not totally jelled and need to have demonstrated to them that they will be able to successfully work through differences to achieve a consensus decision.

2. The facilitator needs to exercise a good deal of judgment when working groups through this process. On some key decisions, it may be important to take more time and look for alternative ideas that are superior to the original idea about which concerns have been raised. At other times, it is necessary to work out a compromise among conflicting alternatives. Compromise solutions usually come quicker than seeking alternatives that truly integrate conflicting ideas, creating a superior alternative. Yet, there are instances when the additional time is well spent, and times when it isn't. These judgments become easier as the facilitator gains experience.

3. When the facilitator senses that the group is "stuck" and not really coming up with adequate alternatives to resolve conflicts, several choices are available. One is to take a short break and ask everyone to come back fresh in a few minutes. Another is to break the group into pairs or triads and have them informally discuss how to create acceptable and superior alternatives to the suggestions under question. Yet another alternative is to move on to another agenda item and later return to the issue on which the group is divided. And finally, the facilitator can suggest a backup method such as the group leader or another member making a decision that can be viewed as "temporary" until the group is able to review it at a later point in time. For more deadlock-breaking strategies, see Section II's Facilitator Resources, "Handling Conflict and Common Problems With Groups."

4. This procedure begins to pale in its effectiveness if it is overused, for it can make the group sessions seem too mechanical.

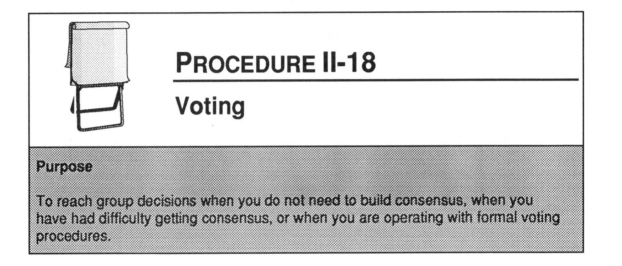

PROCEDURE II-18

Voting

Purpose

To reach group decisions when you do not need to build consensus, when you have had difficulty getting consensus, or when you are operating with formal voting procedures.

Summary Description

Voting is not the preferred alternative for most group decisions because it interferes with the development of a participative culture, is not supportive of team building, and tends to entrench people in their positions rather than unleash the group's collective intelligence. However, there are times when voting can be helpful to groups. Simple, nonbinding "straw voting" can be a useful way to eliminate least-preferred alternatives, and actually helps to build consensual decisions. This procedure will focus on handling voting decisions so that the minimum amount of damage is done to the group spirit when the decision method is employed.

Voting procedures vary widely, but the following principles are suggested for use when voting decisions are made:

- ➥ Have the group decide when voting should be used as a technique.

- ➥ Determine the definition of a majority (e.g., two-thirds) before the vote.

- ➥ Handle voting with as much speed as possible, and limit discussion and debate.

- ➥ Make the decision options clear and state them in writing.

- ➥ Before voting, check with all group members to ensure that they will comply with the voting decision whether they like it or not. You can also ask group members to agree to refrain from privately objecting to the decision outside the group.

- ➥ Consider voting confidentially to prevent divisiveness.

When to Use the Procedure

- When participating in regular meetings where *Robert's Rules of Order* (see *Note* 3) are standard operating procedure

- When you want to arrive at decisions quickly and other more time-consuming methods of decision making are unnecessary

- When the group has difficulty reaching consensus and voting is used as a backup method (e.g., when consensus-building techniques seem too arduous or not worth the effort, given the importance of the decision)

- When you need to narrow down the field of alternatives for consideration

Participants

Number: No numerical limits.

Type: The whole group or certain members of the group (e.g., those with the most expertise on the issue or those who feel most strongly) may be selected to vote.

Resources *(checkmarks indicate recommended equipment)*

- ✔ Flip chart and markers
- ✔ Paper ballots if voting is done confidentially
- ✔ Red, yellow, and green index cards—one of each for each participant

Facilitator(s)

The facilitator's role is to make sure that the group agrees to use voting as a method and then to handle the brief discussion of alternatives and the voting.

Time

From 5 minutes to an hour

Method

1. Check with the group to make sure there is agreement to use voting as a procedure. Also make sure everyone agrees to comply with the vote and to refrain from subsequent private objection.

2. Determine who will vote. In most cases it will be the whole group, but at times the group may agree that certain members possess more issue-related data and should be the ones to vote. You can also ask, "Who feels qualified to vote on this issue, has a strong opinion, or wants to vote?"

3. Determine the definition of the winning vote (e.g., majority, two-thirds).

4. Clarify the decision alternatives by posting them on the flip chart.

5. Conduct a time-limited discussion of the issues. Begin by asking, "Who would like to advocate for one of the alternatives?"

6. Check with the group to see if members feel it would be best for them to vote confidentially or visibly.

7. Set the time limit with the group, using a timer. Stop the discussion when the timer goes off.

8. Take the vote and announce the decision.

Notes

1. A "straw vote" can also be used, meaning that members vote to assist the group in making a consensual choice. Members can be given x number of votes to place beside alternatives presented on a flip chart. The top 20% of the vote-getting options can then be discussed further to see if a consensus decision can be achieved. This is an excellent consensus-building technique, but remember that it may eliminate a creative possibility or a "piece" of the solution that only one or two individuals understand.

2. One alternative technique that works well is to give each member three index cards. One is green for "yes," one is red for "no," and one is yellow for "We need to talk more." Members simply hold up one of the cards to indicate their voting choice. We heard of this technique from Walt Ross, co-founder of the Legacy Alliance Consulting Group.

3. *Robert's Rules of Order* (1876), though perceived by some as old-fashioned, contains an exquisite voting procedure used by many organizations. Many floundering groups unable to reach decisions have become resuscitated following introduction of *Robert's Rules* for meetings. *Robert's Rules* also enables a larger group to proceed through a series of structured steps toward action. The problem is that the procedure tends to create factions and eliminate many creative alternatives, which become victims of rule by majority.

    The perceived neutrality of the person conducting a *Robert's Rules* meeting is critical to the success of the procedure. Therefore, it may be wise to consider using a neutral facilitator to handle meetings conducted in this fashion. However, the main advantage of the technique is that it gives the natural leader of the group a clearly scripted procedure to follow for making decisions, thereby eliminating the need for facilitation.

REFERENCE

Robert, General Henry M. (1985). *Robert's rules of order.* 1876. Reprint, New York: Jove Books.

FACILITATOR RESOURCES

Handling Conflicts and Common Problems With Groups

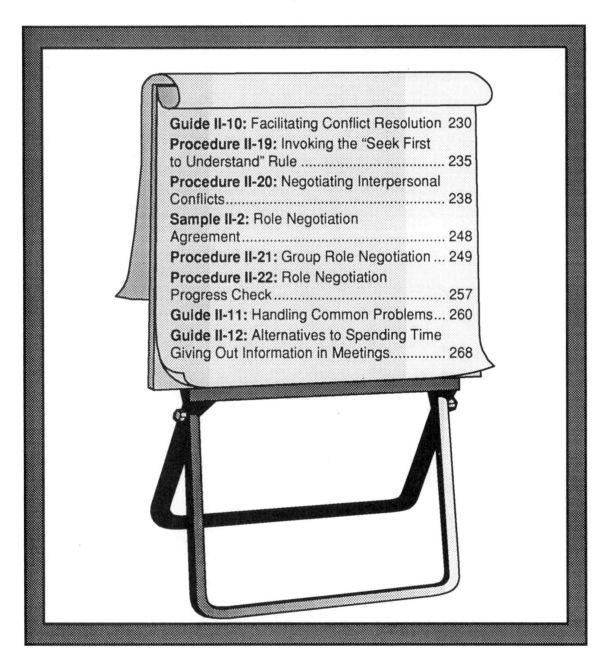

GUIDE II-10

Facilitating Conflict Resolution

STRATEGY 1—*Pinpoint conflicts.*

Identify the specific points of conflict. One way to do this is to first identify what is similar about the views and then what is different. List the similarities and the differences on a flip chart. Showing people that they do not see everything differently helps them approach the conflict more analytically and less negatively.

STRATEGY 2—*Identify options for handling conflicts.*

Differentiate conflicts that must be resolved from those that are less critical. Keep in mind that there are several ways to handle conflict, as illustrated below.

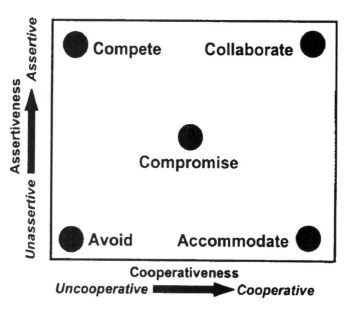

It is sometimes helpful to remind the group of the alternative ways to handle conflict and then to ask the conflicting parties or individuals involved in a conflict which method seems the most appropriate in their particular case.

STRATEGY 3—*Point out the positive aspects of conflict.*

Help the conflicting parties feel it is safe to have different views. The facilitator needs to have a neutral (even positive) view toward handling conflicts. Remind members that the group is working as an open marketplace of ideas, with room for all points of view, and that all views need to be fully understood. You may mention that conflict can afford us the opportunity to refine our views and even our lives. As Thomas F. Crumb, in *The Magic of Conflict* (Simon & Schuster, 1987), simply and succinctly explains:

> *"Conflict is the sandpaper that allows us to smooth the rough edges of our life."*

If you wish, share with the group some of the benefits of conflict:

- Understanding and Respect
- Real Dialogue and Sharing
- Feelings Aired Out
- Increased Energy and Motivation
- Increased Self-Awareness

- Creativity
- New Ways of Doing Things
- Appreciation for Differences and Diversity
- Opportunity to Change Bothersome Things

STRATEGY 4—*Differentiate positions from interests.*

Encourage members to focus on their interests rather than on their positions. A *position* is a specific solution, strategy, or alternative—a way of doing something. Positions are specific solutions that a person advances to meet a need or an interest; they answer the question "What do I want?" An *interest* is a need or desire that a person wants satisfied. Interests answer the question "Why do I want that?"

To get members focused on interests, conduct the following quick exercise:

1. Ask the two conflicting parties to stand. One of them states his or her position. The other then asks "Why does that matter to you?" three times. The facilitator records the answers on a flip chart. The roles are reversed and the process is repeated.

2. The two parties (perhaps with the entire group) review the answers to see what can be done that will be congruent with the **interests** of each party.

Here is an example of the question-and-answer process:

Jan: My position is that we should bring in a new rep who focuses only on high-tech businesses.

Jack: *Why does that matter to you?*

Jan: Because 30% of our potential customer base is in high tech and we don't have anyone who really speaks their language. Only 8% of our customers come from high-tech businesses.

Jack: *Why does that matter to you?*

Jan: Because we have to expand our volume if we're to meet our targets.

Jack: *Why does that matter to you?*

Jan: We've never had any targets this ambitious. If we don't do some things radically different, we'll never achieve our new expectations.

For a variation on this method, ask the parties to:

1. State their positions and interests, as shown above.

2. Identify the "major theme" of each other's position and interests.

3. See if there are alternative ways that both parties' interests can be met.

If you wish, the entire group can participate in *(2)* and *(3)*.

STRATEGY 5—*Use the "and" test to see if the two views are totally incompatible.*

Have members determine if the conflict is irreconcilable. Take the two positions that seem in conflict and link them into a compound sentence using the conjunctive *and.* For example: "We should hire a rep who focuses on high-tech business **and** we have to cut our department budget by 25% to conform to the President's edict." The group then brainstorms alternatives to decide if the two views are indeed incompatible.

STRATEGY 6—*Point out the negative consequences of failing to deal with significant conflicts.*

Make sure members understand how important conflict resolution is. Conflicts, when not dealt with, can lead to major problems.

Conflicts that are not dealt with in the group usually do not just lie there, unresolved. The conflict is likely to escalate. An Australian group specializing in conflict resolution suggests that most conflicts progressively escalate through five steps from 1) beginning **DISCOMFORTS,** to 2) **INCIDENTS,** to 3) **MISUNDERSTANDINGS.** These misunderstandings create an atmosphere of 4) **TENSION** that finally results in a full-blown 5) **CRISIS.*** The later that you intervene to resolve the significant conflict, the more difficult resolution becomes.

STRATEGY 7—*Surfacing value differences.*

Help members understand the importance of surfacing value differences. Some conflicts originate from serious differences in the parties' values. If these differences are not surfaced and understood, severe interpersonal antagonisms could develop and hurt the group's chances of succeeding. Shown below is a good example of serious value conflicts, offered by Jan Abbott and Warren Rose, two labor-management consultants. It illustrates the problems faced by many organizations when they try to bring labor and management people together.

Cultural Attributes	
UNION COUNTRY	**MANAGEMENT COUNTRY**
• Egalitarian	• Hierarchical
• Democratic decision making	• Factual decision making
• Brotherhood	• Individualism, competition
• Mutual protection	• Performance
• Seniority	• Control
• Challenge pay and benefits	• Profit
• QWL	• Productivity
• Past and precedent rules	• Now, what works
	• Flexibility

From: Jan Abbott and Warren Rose, "Changing the Adversarial Assumption: New Approaches to Labor-Management Relations," *Vision/Action: The Journal of the Bay Area OD Network,* September 1991.

The facilitator needs to keep an ear tuned to conflicts as they emerge and to assess whether the conflicts are largely rooted in value differences. The process of surfacing value conflicts is inevitably uncomfortable and will be resisted by any group member who leans too heavily toward the "We're one big, happy family" mindset. Yet, if value differences do not surface, members may misinterpret one another's views, with the conflict-escalation cycle moving into full force, hampering the group's chances to succeed.

---

*From: The Conflict Resolution Network—Chatsworth N.5 W. 2057, Australia.

When differences are perceived within a context of respect and appreciation for diversity, members can better understand one another's actions and blindly heated discussion can be transformed into real dialogue. To facilitate such dialogue, encourage members to stop attacking one another's values and to shift to understanding the value culture of others. It is only with this mutual understanding of value differences that the path can be cleared to find some common ground for action.

PROCEDURE II-19

Invoking the "Seek First to Understand" Rule

Purpose (A Conflict Resolution Method)

To reduce conflict between two members who are "stuck" in their positions and not listening to each other.

Summary Description

Stephen Covey (1989, 1994), though known more as a personal development writer and trainer than a group process expert, has offered a simple tool for resolving conflicts that can be of enormous benefit to the group facilitator. Covey asserts that nearly every two-person conflict can be resolved by one simple procedure: invoking a communication rule that says, "You cannot make your point until you restate the point of the other person to his or her satisfaction."

When you see two members becoming entrenched in their conflicting positions, you stop the discussion, point to the necessity of members listening to one another in order for groups to succeed, and ask the conflicting parties to do an exercise that requires them to hone their listening skills. When the two members agree to participate, you put the "Seek First to Understand" rule on a flip chart and ask them to proceed with the discussion. You then monitor the discussion, making sure that no one proceeds to make a point until the other person is satisfied that he or she has been "heard." The discussion proceeds in this way until both parties feel they have fully expressed their standpoint and have been heard.

When to Use the Procedure

- When group members are becoming entrenched in their conflicting positions
- When two people in the group are obviously becoming frustrated with each other
- When you want to shift the group "norm state" toward genuine listening and respect for one another's ideas

Participants

Number: Two participants

Type: Members of a task group or team

Resources

✔ Flip chart and markers

Time

Between 10 and 20 minutes

Method

1. When you notice from the tenor of the group's conversation that a logjam is starting to appear, stop the group and point to the need to listen to one another in order for the group to succeed. It is sometimes useful to drive home the point with a quote. Here are a few you might choose from to help make the point:

   Three-fourths of the miseries and misunderstandings in the world will disappear if we step into the shoes of our adversaries and understand their standpoint. — Mahatma Gandhi

   Conversation in the United States is a competitive exercise in which the first person to draw a breath is declared the listener. —Nathan Miller

   Everybody wants to talk, few want to think, and nobody wants to listen. —No attribution

   One of the best ways to persuade others is with your ears—by listening to them. —Dean Rusk, Former U.S. Secretary of State

   It is the province of knowledge to speak, and it is the privilege of wisdom to listen. —Oliver Wendell Holmes, American writer and physician

   Let every man be quick to hear, slow to talk. —New Testament, James 1:19

   The road to the heart is through the ear. —Voltaire

   Know how to listen, and you will profit even from those who talk badly. —Plutarch

   A good listener is not only popular everywhere, but after a while he knows something. —Wilson Mizner

   No one ever listened himself out of a job. —Calvin Coolidge

2. Ask two conflicting members if they would be willing to complete an exercise that would help the group move toward a resolution of the issues. Emphasize that the two volunteers will be working to improve the performance of the entire group.

3. Write on a flip chart the "Seek First to Understand" rule: "You cannot make your point until you restate the point of the other person to his or her satisfaction." Ask both members if they understand the rule. (For our purposes here, we will refer to these members as Member A and Member B.)

4. Ask Member A to start making his or her point. If Member B interrupts, remind him or her of the rule and have Member A finish.

5. Have Member B state Member A's point.

6. Ask Member A if he or she is satisfied that Member B got the point—not only what was said, but the essence of the point (which includes feelings associated with the point). If Member A is not satisfied, ask Member B to try again. If he or she needs to hear more, have Member A make the point again.

7. Once Member A feels he or she has been heard, Member B makes a point and the process is repeated.

8. After both members have fully established their standpoints, ask them if they are feeling any differently than when they began and if they can share the difference in their feelings.

9. Proceed with your agenda, using whatever processes were planned to bring the group to agreement.

Variations

1. The "Seek First to Understand" rule can be invoked for the entire group. In this case, no one proceeds to make a point until he or she can restate the previous speaker's point to the speaker's satisfaction. When using the rule with the whole group, proceed until everyone has had a chance to express his or her personal view.

2. You may wish to first model the procedure with two members of the group, putting them in front of the other group members. Then the rule can be invoked with the rest of the group until all points of view have been heard.

3. Following the first pair, demonstrate "seeking first to understand." Other group members can pair off and try the exercise.

REFERENCES

Covey, Stephen R. (1989). *The seven habits of effective people.* New York: Simon & Schuster.

Covey, Stephen R.; Merrill, A. Roger; and Merril, Rebecca R. (1994). *First things first.* New York: Simon & Schuster.

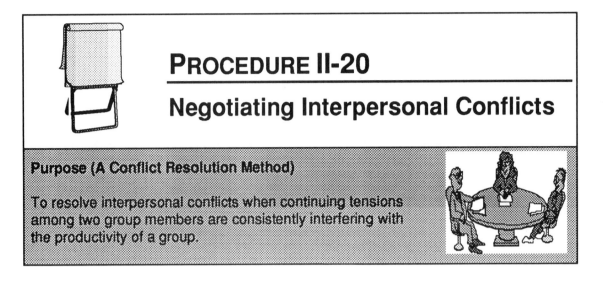

PROCEDURE II-20

Negotiating Interpersonal Conflicts

Purpose (A Conflict Resolution Method)

To resolve interpersonal conflicts when continuing tensions among two group members are consistently interfering with the productivity of a group.

Summary Description

Some groups become significantly "stuck" on interpersonal conflicts. These conflicts may be rooted in situations that preceded the group effort (i.e., they may have a history), or they may be newly developed, occurring among members who are working together for the first time. In either case, many of these conflicts are best handled away from regular group meetings. The facilitator's role expands to include those of mediator and negotiator so that the parties involved can directly confront the problems at hand.

One of the most useful interventions in these situations is role negotiation, a technique developed by Roger Harrison (1972a, 1972b). Role negotiation is based on two key assumptions:

1. That most people prefer a fair, negotiated settlement over a state of unresolved conflict

2. That the conflicts stand the best chance of successful resolution if the facilitator focuses on negotiating common-sensical "behavior" agreements rather than probes for the complex interpersonal psychological dynamics underlying the conflicts

Harrison emphasizes that his technique makes one basic assumption: Most people prefer a fair negotiated settlement to a state of unsuccessful conflict (1983, pp. 158–164). The people involved in the conflict must be willing to invest some time and make some concessions in order to achieve a solution. It may also be necessary for the conflicting parties to be directed or encouraged to participate in the intervention by their superiors.

The model that is described under **Method** below is an adaptation of the Harrison Role Negotiation intervention, which we have used successfully on several occasions. It essentially calls for (a) separately interviewing each group member involved in the conflict, (b) having each member fill out a negotiation worksheet, (c) meeting with a facilitator to negotiate a written behavioral agreement, and (d) following up with the members for two weeks to six months to see how the agreement is working out and renegotiating, as necessary.

When to Use the Procedure

- When tensions between individual members are impeding the progress of the entire group

- When personality conflicts are getting in the way of group productivity

- When long-standing interpersonal conflicts emerge as a major cause of problems (following interviews or surveys conducted with group members)

Participants

Number: The procedure is typically conducted with two people and a facilitator, but can be adapted for groups (see **Variations**).

Type: Members of a team who are having trouble working together and who must continue to work together.

Resources

❑ Role Negotiation Worksheet
❑ Role Negotiation Agreement form
❑ Role Negotiation Agreement Progress Check form (from Procedure II-22: Role Negotiation Progress Check)
❑ A private conferencing space

Time

Between 45 minutes and 2 hours for each interview with the facilitator and person involved; one hour for the facilitated negotiation; 20 minutes for group members to fill out their worksheets. Extend the time if the negotiations take place over more than one session (see **Variations**).

Method

1. The intervention is offered as a possible conflict resolution model. Each party involved must agree to participate. Approach each one individually, briefly explain the nature of the intervention, and let them assess whether they think it would be useful.

2. If both parties are willing to participate, schedule a 2-hour time period. To avoid undue anxiety, schedule it as soon as possible. Often the best time is immediately following their agreement to participate, if both parties are available. Arrange to

have a private, neutral space for the session(s). Do not meet in either party's office.

3. Ask each party to fill out the Role Negotiation Worksheet as completely as possible. It is best if the worksheets are filled out in separate rooms.

4. Visit briefly with each person. Check their worksheets to be sure responses are in specific terms. People often have trouble with one or more of the behavioral categories. Coach them as necessary, helping them clarify their specific requests. You may need to ask them to give specific examples of the behaviors/actions they prefer less of. Have them add those examples under the change request they have already noted.

   Also, make sure each person has rank-ordered the importance of the change requests by filling in the "Priority" columns of the worksheet.

5. Ask both parties to come into the room you have designated as the meeting room. (Make sure that you have arranged to have privacy and that there will be no interruptions or intrusions.)

   Explain that this is an interpersonal negotiation session and you will be acting as a facilitator. It is not "therapy," and you are not a qualified therapist, and the outcome of the session is for both of them to agree to some new conditions for working together. (If you *are* a qualified therapist, see Note 1.)

   Share the ground rules for the role negotiation session. Tell them: "Here are some recommended guidelines to follow for this session":

   ◆ **Use "I" statements** whenever possible. Describe the effects that the other person's behavior has on you. Say "When you _____, I _____." (Facilitator can give example.)

   ◆ **Be specific** in your description of what the person does or doesn't do. Make direct requests of the other person to be some specific way or to do some specific thing. **Be willing to give in order to get.**

   ◆ **Be willing to answer "yes" or "no"** to the other person's change request. Don't justify your actions, defend yourself, or point out the other person's part in the problem when a request is made of you.

   ◆ **Exchange requests and promises one at a time.** You must get something "quid pro quo" from the other person after you have agreed to give something. There must be an equal number of agreements for each person.

   ◆ **No characterizations or name-calling.**

   ◆ **Don't raise your voice.**

   ◆ **Listen without interpreting what others say.** Don't search for underlying meaning or motivations behind the other person's behavior. Don't speculate on his or her motives.

♦ **It's all right to be emotional. It's not all right to stay stuck in the emotions.**

♦ **No physical contact,** either positive or negative.

♦ **Understand first, before responding.** You must demonstrate that you have heard what the other person says to the satisfaction of that person before you disagree with anything.

Ask if they have any questions about the rules. Check that each person is willing to comply with the ground rules for the session.

6. Have the parties read their worksheets to each other. One person reads his or her entire sheet; the other person listens without questions. Then the roles are reversed.

7. Give each person a chance to ask for clarification of any of the items. Monitor the questions carefully to make sure they are only questions that help one person understand what the other means.

8. Explain that you will now begin the process of negotiating specific agreements between the two parties (for our purposes here, Member A and Member B). Use this process:

   • Ask Member A to identify his or her highest-priority change request; ask the other member to listen carefully. Next, ask Member A to expand on the request by citing specific examples of the behavior.

   • Ask Member B to demonstrate his or her understanding of the change request by feeding back the request in a way that demonstrates the understanding. See if Member A is satisfied that Member B understands; if not, have Member B try again.

   Repeat the process, this time having Member B share his or her highest-priority request.

9. Once they understand each other's request, ask both parties if they would be willing to make an agreement based on the two requests. Explain the format of the agreement: "[Member A] will do *x* and [Member B] will do *y*." If both agree, write down the agreement legibly, using the given format.

   If one party agrees to the number one request of the other, but the other is not willing to return such agreement, then move on to the second-priority change request of the party whose first request was turned down.

   If neither party agrees, then move on to both parties' second-priority change request and repeat the process explained in Step 8.

10. Move through the parties' priorities, in order of ranking, using the same process to negotiate agreements. Log the agreements, as they are made, on the Role Negotiation Agreement form (or on a sheet of paper if you prefer). Don't get hung

up on trying to negotiate an agreement that they are reluctant to engage in. Just keep moving through the items, negotiating as many as you can.

Keep in mind that you do not necessarily have to get the parties to "swap" same-priority requests. Follow the guideline that each party should receive the same number of "promises" (i.e., agreements) by the end of the session.

You may not have to go through all the requests. You likely will reach a point when (a) time is running out, or (b) it is obvious that the parties have achieved a much healthier working agreement. At that point, read the agreements back to them and see if they are willing to commit to keeping the agreements. Ask them if they are satisfied that the agreements are enough to substantially change the way they have been working together. See if there is anything missing from the agreements that will significantly hinder the chances of them working without the "cloud" that presently hangs over the relationship. Negotiate further if changes are needed.

11. You now should have a handwritten list of their agreements. There should be exactly the same number of "promises" made by each person. Take the list and immediately make three copies, one for each party and one for you.

12. (Take this step if time permits and the following seems to be a good idea.) Ask the parties to go back to their individual rooms and to review the agreement carefully, making sure that it works for them and that no additions or deletions are needed. These few moments of solitary reflection allow each person to think about the agreement without feeling rushed or pressured.

13. The parties review the promises they are willing to make to each other. If something is still missing for either of them, additional requests can be made. Write the changes on all copies of the agreement, or re-copy the agreement to reflect any changes. Ask each party to sign all three final agreements.

14. (Optional.) Ask the parties if either of them would like to make any specific apologies. (This can work out very positively if both parties equally admit their wrongs; however, it can become a problem if one person believes he or she was more forthcoming and yielding than the other. The healing character of plain old apologies should not be underestimated, though, and it can substantially increase the effectiveness of the intervention.)

15. Set dates for follow-up facilitated discussions about how the agreement is going. The first date is usually between two and four weeks after the initial agreement and the second date about four to six weeks after the first follow-up. However, in some cases, you may want to follow up much more quickly. Have all parties write the appointments in their calendars. Clarify who will initiate the contact and arrange for the room or teleconference.

16. Explain that both parties will be held accountable for adhering to the agreements. Give them each a copy of the Role Negotiation Agreement Progress Check (for this form, see Procedure II-22: Role Negotiation Progress Check). Ask them to file

the Progress Check form with the agreement so they can fill it out before the first review session.

17. "Validate" each party for his or her courage and determination in confronting difficult issues. Give each person the opportunity to "validate" the other for participating and to say what he or she appreciated about the other's behavior during the session.

18. Conclude by warning them that implementing and living the new promises may feel somewhat awkward and contrived. They may feel resentful about living up to some of the expectations. Emphasize that the success of the intervention lies in their ability to act in line with the agreements on the paper, no matter what they think or how it feels. The craziness will continue to the extent that they violate the agreements. If they act in line with the agreements, over time they will think and feel better about each other. This is a case where you have to "act yourself into the right thinking," not vice versa.

Notes

1. The guideline for these sessions is: "You don't go where you're not qualified to go." This means that you stick to your role as mediator and not try to be a psychologist if you aren't licensed to do so. Keep the sessions focused on behavioral exchanges of expectations. Some facilitators are licensed mental health professionals and may feel comfortable dealing a little more with feeling states and such during the sessions. If you're qualified, this can enhance the sessions, so long as you don't move too far afield from negotiating very specific down-to-earth "action agreements" that will give the parties behaviorally specific guidelines for future interactions.

2. Don't expect these sessions to feel good. Nor should they result in verbal abuse or the infliction of injurious pain to either party. They are mediation sessions designed to clear the air and create a new relationship based on keeping your word about specific requests and promises. They should feel like difficult and courageous communications that produce a feeling of possibility. The goal isn't warm fuzzies and hugs. Both parties are trying to achieve a reasonably productive working relationship minus the pervasive tensions that interfere with work getting done.

3. The facilitator can help mediate the exchange of requests and promises. You may suggest a modification of the request that stands a better chance of being accepted. For example, "Bill, instead of asking Megan not to disagree with you in front of others, why don't you narrow your request a bit and ask her not to disagree with you immediately after you have said something in the staff meeting. Would that be acceptable to both of you?" Or you may see a natural "exchange" of promises that is a logical trade to propose.

4. If one party balks at a request, you can ask the person what concern is keeping him or her from complying with the request. For example:

Facilitator: Megan, what is your concern about complying with Bill's request for you not to disagree with him in front of others?

Megan: Well, I can't guarantee that I won't disagree all the time. I would feel totally shut down and manipulated. It doesn't seem fair.

Facilitator: Bill, do you understand that concern?

Bill: Yes, it sounds like it's too all-encompassing for her. I think that's her concern.

Facilitator: Megan, does that cover your concern?

Megan: Yes, that's about it.

[Then ask the original requestor to generate an alternative request.]

Bill: OK, how about if you just don't immediately disagree with something I suggest in the staff meeting?

Megan: OK, I can do that. I can wait to say my piece as long as I can react honestly with my point of view before any action or decisions are made.

Bill: Yes, that can be a part of it, too.

Facilitator: OK, it looks like we have a deal here. Megan won't immediately disagree with something Bill says in the staff meeting, but she is free to share her view on the issue before any action or decision is made. Is that OK with you both?

Bill: Yes.

Megan: Yes.

Facilitator: OK, I'll write that one down.

5. There are some cases where more than one group member will have difficulty with the same individual. It is usually best to conduct separate, one-on-one negotiations in these cases so that the playing field is level for each negotiation. Another alternative is to conduct a group role negotiation. (See Procedure II-21: Group Role Negotiation.)

Variations

1. One variation is to ask each party to fill out a second worksheet, in addition to the Role Negotiation Worksheet, on which they record what they think the other party will say about them with respect to the three Role Negotiation questions. You have them share both worksheets during the negotiation process.

2. This intervention can also be conducted with a whole team. See this section for a description of a variation of the intervention with the whole team.

3. More than one session can be conducted. Sometimes, there is an advantage to approaching the negotiations more deliberately. Here is an alternative approach:

    (a) Interview the parties individually to review process and gain agreement to participate.

    (b) Conduct the first session, negotiating one request only. Ask one person to make a request and to explain the request in some detail; have the other person listen, asking clarifying questions only. Check that the person making the request feels that he or she has been heard. Then do the same with the other person's request.

    (c) Negotiate agreements related to the single issue only. Schedule a second meeting.

    (d) Begin the second meeting by having the parties comment on what they have appreciated about the other person's efforts to keep their agreement. Then repeat the process in (a) and (b) above. Either continue with the process, working on two other requests, or schedule yet another session to continue the work.

    (e) Conclude the sessions when both parties feel they have negotiated agreements sufficiently to rebuild a productive working relationship. Schedule a follow-up session as suggested in the **Method** section.

REFERENCES

Harrison, Roger. (1972a). Role negotiation: A tough-minded approach to team development. In W. Warner Burke & Harvey A. Horstein (Eds.), *The social technology of organization development* (pp. 84–96). San Diego, CA: University Associates.

Harrison, Roger. (1972b, spring). When power conflicts trigger team spirit. *European Business,* 57–65. [Or see Harrison, 1983.]

Harrison, Roger. (1983). When power conflicts trigger team spirit. In Wendell L. French, Cecil H. Bell, Jr., & Robert A. Zawacki (Eds.), *Organization development: Theory, practice, research.* Plano, TX: Business Publications Inc. [Or see Harrison, 1972b.]

Walton, Richard E. (1968). Interpersonal confrontation and basic third-party functions: A case study. *The Journal of Applied Behavioral Science, 4*(3), 327–343.

Role Negotiation Worksheet

Directions: First, fill in the behavior-actions in the three areas below. Then rank-order your responses in both the second and third sections, prioritizing them on a scale where 1 is the most important to you, 2 is the next important, and so on.

Things about _____ that I appreciate—that support me in doing my job. Things that this person should *keep on* doing.

Behavior, Action

Things I wish this person would do *less of*—things that make it more difficult for me to do my job.

Priority	Behavior, Action

Things I wish this person would do *more of*—things that would help me to do my job more effectively.

Priority	Behavior, Action

Role Negotiation Agreement

_____ agrees to:
Name of Party

1.

2.

3.

4.

5.

_____ agrees to:
Name of Party

1.

2.

3.

4.

5.

To be reviewed on _____/_____/_____   @ Time_____A.M./P.M.
                 Day Month Year

I agree to adhere to this agreement to the best of my ability:

_____ and _____
          Signature   Signature

Date signed: _____/_____/_____   Witness: _____
             Day Month Year

SAMPLE II-2

Role Negotiation Agreement

Ricky agrees to:

1) Thoroughly listen to Jan's suggestions in staff meetings before reacting.
2) Ask Charice (Jan's secretary) to help out with clerical work overload, when she can.
3) Not "badmouth" corporate office in regional sales meetings she conducts.
4) Be in the office two whole days a week.
5) Complain to Jan directly and not go around her.

Jan agrees to:

1) Let go more and delegate more assignments to Ricky that will be carried out by regional sales staff.
2) Include Ricky on the front end in plans that will affect regional sales people.
3) Come to most of the informal social events that occur at corporate.
4) Return Ricky's voice and E-mail messages promptly.
5) Support Ricky's efforts to develop team spirit amongst corporate clerical staff.

To be reviewed on *12/10/98* @ Time *2:00* P.M.

I agree to adhere to this agreement to the best of my ability:

Ricky Venudo and *Jan Pitts-Dreyer*
Signature   Signature

Date signed: *11/20/98*   Witness: *Sherry Feliciado*

PROCEDURE II-21

Group Role Negotiation

Purpose (A Conflict Resolution Method)

To resolve conflicts among group members while they remain in the group rather than conducting one-on-one "off-site" negotiations.

Summary Description

This procedure borrows from the Harrison technique for role negotiation described in Procedure II-20: Negotiating Interpersonal Conflicts. Each group member fills out a Role Negotiation Worksheet for every other member in the group; then the completed worksheets are exchanged. Each person records his or her data on a flip chart.

When to Use the Procedure

- When there are multiple conflicts among group members (i.e., the conflicts cannot be traced to a few members but are widespread throughout the team).

- When the relationships within the group are so strained that members are willing to confront the difficulties.

- This procedure is also helpful for the "healthy" group that is committed to learning more about how personal behavior affects others so that all can work together with maximum effectiveness.

Participants

Number: The number is best kept to between eight and 12 participants.

Type: Members of a group that will be continuing to work together for some time in the future.

Resources *(checkmarks indicate recommended equipment)*

✔ Flip chart and markers

□ Handout: Role Negotiation Worksheet, found in Procedure II-20.

□ Enough wall space that each member can post his or her flip chart page.

□ Flip chart pages on which are recorded the ground rules for interpersonal negotiation and the steps of the negotiation process (see **Method** section, Step 12)

✔ A small portable copying machine, or carbon paper if a machine is unavailable

Time

A minimum of 4 hours. Extend the time if more than two or three personal negotiations are planned.

Method

1. Write the purposes of the activity on a flip chart:

   1. To negotiate work agreements that will help each person work more productively in the group

   2. To better understand how others see us and to bring our own "picture" of ourselves into closer alignment with the "picture" that others have of us

   Briefly comment on the purposes, if you wish. The Johari Window model of the communication process can be useful here. Each of us interacts with other group members in a communications climate that is comprised of four "windows":

2 Known to Self Unknown to Others	1 Known to Self and Others
4 Unknown to Self or Others	3 Unknown to Self Known to Others

- **Cell 1** represents those aspects of ourselves that are perceived by both ourselves and others.

- **Cell 2** represents aspects of ourselves or feelings toward others in the work group that we know about but keep hidden from others.

- **Cell 3** represents aspects of ourselves of which we are unaware but that are communicated clearly to others.

- **Cell 4** represents those aspects unknown to either ourselves or others.

Through this exercise, group members learn more about Cell 3 and, where appropriate, how to reduce the size of Cell 2 (Huse, 1975).

Our capacity to be an effective team player is, in large part, determined by our ability to align our self-image with the image that others have of us, and thus to close the "perception gap" in relationships. This procedure helps us develop such ability.

2. Review the steps in the process carefully with the participants. On a flip chart, write the bold-faced descriptions of the following steps:

   (a) *Fill out worksheets.* Fill out one Role Negotiation Worksheet for each person in the group. Sign your name on each worksheet you complete. (Pass out worksheets here.)

   (b) *Deliver the worksheets* to other members of the group.

   (c) *Read your data and post it.* Record the data you receive from other group members on a flip chart page. Post your flip chart page where it will be visible.

   (d) *Code the data: ✔ = negotiable, ? = ?, x = no.* Check any item you are presently willing to work on. Put a question mark beside any item you do not fully understand. Put an x beside any item you are definitely not willing to do.

   (e) *Share the data.* Each member shares his or her chart and the data. At this point members can ask clarifying questions about any question-marked items.

   (f) *Schedule individual negotiations.* Each member selects up to three other members with whom he or she wants to negotiate requests and promises. They fill out an "appointment card" for the conferences they need to have.

   (g) *Conduct individual negotiations.* Group members individually negotiate their exchange of requests and promises, following directions that will be provided before the individual sessions.

   (h) *Share the agreements.* Each group member shares the negotiated agreements made with the rest of the group.

3. Explain to the group that they will have a chance to see the process demonstrated before they start it with their first partner.

4. Tell everyone that they will have _____ minutes to complete one worksheet for each individual in the group. (Allow about 4 minutes per person in the group.) Ask them to complete the worksheets.

5. When time is up, ask members to make sure they have signed their name to each form and to deliver the worksheets to each individual.

6. Have everyone take a few moments to read the data.

7. Ask members to write the data on a flip chart page. Explain that they can put an asterisk beside any data that is repeated nearly verbatim.

8. Next, ask members to code the data using the symbols that are shown on the group flip chart.

9. Have members, one by one, share their data and how they coded it. Give everyone a chance to ask *clarification* questions. They can ask what someone meant by the data, but they are not to agree or disagree with it.

10. Ask for two volunteers from the group who actually want to "kick off" their negotiation with support.

    If no one volunteers, ask for one volunteer who is willing to demonstrate the process with you, "role-playing" issues related to someone external to the group. Ask the volunteer to think of somebody who is not in the group and to write down three things that he or she wants that person to do more of or less of.

    Then walk through the process with the volunteer(s), negotiating agreements as you go, while other group members observe. (For a guide, see Procedure II-20: Negotiating Interpersonal Conflicts.)

11. Explain there will be three rounds of individual negotiations. Individual members should schedule their rounds according to whom they feel they most need to deal with. Have them mill about and fill out their "dance cards" (appointed negotiation times) for rounds 1, 2, and 3. Some people may not feel they need three rounds. Others may feel they need more. Ask them to go along with the process for now and to schedule three interactions. If, after the process is completed, they still feel they need to talk to others, arrangements can be made to do so.

12. Set out enough Role Negotiation Worksheets for each of the negotiations (e.g., if there are 10 people, you will need at least 100 worksheets). Using the flip chart page you prepared beforehand, share **the interpersonal ground rules for the negotiation process.** Tell members: "There are several rules that are recommended for this process. They are designed to make the process both safe and effective. Here are the rules:

    ◆ **Use "I" statements** whenever possible. Describe the effects that the other person's behavior has on you. Say "When you _____, I _____." (Facilitator can give example.)

◆ **Be specific** in your description of what the **person** does or doesn't do. Make direct requests of the other person to be some specific way or to do some specific thing. **Be willing to give in order to get.**

◆ **Be willing to answer "yes" or "no"** to the other person's change request. Don't justify your actions, defend yourself, or point out the other person's part in the problem when a request is made of you.

◆ **Exchange requests and promises one at a time.** You must get something "quid pro quo" from the other person after you have agreed to give something. There must be an equal number of agreements for each person.

◆ **No characterizations or name-calling.**

◆ **Don't raise your voice.**

◆ **Listen without interpreting what others say.** Don't search for underlying meaning or motivations behind the other person's behavior. Don't speculate on his or her motives.

◆ **It's all right to be emotional. It's not all right to stay stuck in the emotions.**

◆ **No physical contact,** either positive or negative.

◆ **Understand first, before responding.** You must demonstrate that you have heard what the other person says to the satisfaction of that person before you disagree with anything.

Suggest a simple **negotiation process.** Mount the flip chart page you prepared beforehand, making sure it is visible to all members.

◆ One person makes a request (ideally, the most important request first).

◆ The second person says "yes" or "no" to the request.

◆ Repeat the process if necessary, until you have your first "yes." Write down the request as your first agreement.

◆ Then the second person makes a request.

◆ The first person says "yes" or "no."

◆ Repeat the process if necessary, until you receive your second "yes."

◆ Continue until you feel you have sufficient agreements or until time is called.

◆ Set a follow-up time and date to review the process. You can request a third group member to facilitate the follow-up. Record the time and date on the Role Negotiation Agreement and write it down in your personal calendars.

Run through the process steps one more time. Create an example, using the names of two members, to illustrate how the process might work. For instance, "Let's say that Jack and Caroline were negotiating. Jack will make the first request, probably the one most important to him. Then Caroline will . . ." and so forth.

Emphasize the "quid pro quo" nature of the process. Each person should get something for giving something, and the exchange should be even.

13. After answering any questions about how the process works, start your first 30-minute session. After 20 minutes, remind people they have 10 minutes left to complete their agreements, sign them, copy them, and schedule a follow-up session. Let people know you are available for individual coaching if they request it. Also let them know you will be moving around the room and may be listening in on parts of their conversations.

14. Conduct the remaining two 30-minute sessions in the same manner.

15. Bring together the whole group. Have members take turns sharing the agreements they personally have committed to.

16. Pass out the Role Negotiation Agreement Progress Check form. Explain that they can use the worksheet if they feel it will be helpful. Allow everyone a few moments to schedule follow-up progress checks that they feel would help them follow through on their agreements.

17. Conclude with this exercise (see Hart, 1989). Tell members: "Look around the room at the faces of your fellow group members. Think about each person and what you appreciate in him or her." Then select a member and ask the others to offer positive feedback to that member. Work through the entire group in this manner. Be sure to allow enough time so that everyone, including you and any other facilitator, receives at least three positive comments.

Notes

1. This process is designed to be led by a well-experienced facilitator who has conducted other conflict resolution work with groups. If you don't feel ready to handle the process on your own, team up with someone in order to acquire the requisite experience.

2. Even if you have significant experience handling groups in conflict situations, you will probably want to read some of Roger Harrison's works (see **References**) to feel fully comfortable implementing this process.

3. The process is not as scary as it may appear upon reading it. Although neither fun nor comfortable, it is manageable if implemented carefully according to the above procedure. In fact, you will probably be surprised at the lack of difficulties you encounter.

4. Move around the room during the individual negotiations and eavesdrop on the conversations. Sense the feeling states of the individuals. Provide support where it may be needed.

5. At some point in the procedure, mention that we are primarily dealing with the negative side of each person's ledger of attributes and weaknesses. Tell

members: "You may be shedding some light on the 'dark' side of who you are so that you can grow positively. It is important to keep in mind that there is another whole side to who you really are." Making this point serves as a good introduction to the final activity in the procedure.

Variations

1. Instead of scheduling all the individual negotiations at once, you can have members pair up at the beginning of each 30-minute round.

2. Here is an optional activity that you may include just before you move on to Step 17. It is based on the folk adage that every failing we can see in others is a failing that we possess ourselves. This is quite a valuable bit of wisdom, and a stunning personal realization to come to.

   To start the activity, ask members to reflect a moment on the changes they asked others to make. Was there a pattern to their requests? Did they ask similar things of different people?

   Suggest that they may find it valuable to "try on" the idea that the failings we can see in others are the failings that we have ourselves. Invite members to see if the idea "fits" for them. If it does, apply the idea to their present situation, suggesting that the weaknesses they have perceived in others may be the very weaknesses they themselves need to work on—that the real gift of the day may be the sight of their own flaws in the "mirror" of others. **Underscore the value of the experience**, explaining that once we see such flaws, we can adjust and correct them. Emphasize that we have real control and power over our behavior (which we do not have over others' behaviors) and can *choose* to change.

3. Have members each fill out two Role Negotiation Worksheets: one that lists what they appreciate and want from the other person, and one (sometimes called an "empathy" list) that states what they think the other person will appreciate and want from them. If you use this option, pass out twice as many copies of the Role Negotiation Worksheet.

4. Another optional activity is to ask everyone to list the origins of people's troubling behaviors. How do we come to pick up these less-than-desirable aspects of our behavior and personality? Forming such a list should enable members to see that most of these origins have little to do with making personal choices. Behaviors in us that others see as troubling are often "survival" behaviors that we have acquired in response to something that happened to us over which we had little control.

   This activity will help those who tend to be ashamed of any imperfection to better accept the data they may be receiving.

   A final point to make is that although we are not always responsible for what happened, we do need to be responsible for cleaning up these left-over behaviors if we are to continue learning and growing.

REFERENCES

Harrison, Roger. (1972a). Role negotiation: A tough-minded approach to team development. In W. Warner Burke & Harvey A. Horstein (Eds.), *The social technology of organization development* (pp. 84–96). San Diego, CA: University Associates.

Harrison, Roger. (1972b, spring). When power conflicts trigger team spirit. *European Business,* 57–65. [Or see Harrison, 1983.]

Harrison, Roger. (1983). When power conflicts trigger team spirit. In Wendell L. French, Cecil H. Bell, Jr., & Robert A. Zawacki (Eds.), *Organization development: Theory, practice, research.* Plano, TX: Business Publications Inc. [Or see Harrison, 1972b.]

Hart, Lois. (1989). *Saying good-bye: Ending a group experience* (2nd ed.). King of Prussia, PA: Organization Design and Development Inc.

Huse, Edgar. (1975). *Organization development and change.* St. Paul: MN: West Publishing Co. (See Chapter 8.)

Luft, J. (1961). The Johari window. *Human Relations Training News, 5*(1), 6–7.

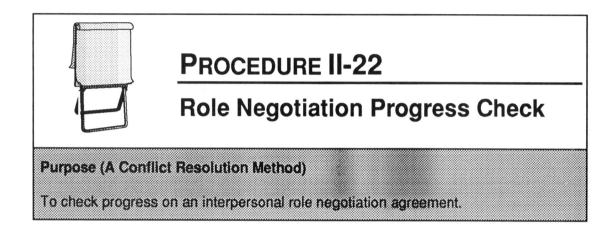

PROCEDURE II-22

Role Negotiation Progress Check

Purpose (A Conflict Resolution Method)

To check progress on an interpersonal role negotiation agreement.

Summary Description

Two group members who have negotiated an interpersonal work agreement meet to discuss progress on the agreement, to revise the agreement as needed, and to schedule further progress checks as needed.

When to Use the Procedure

- About two to six weeks after the establishment of a role negotiation agreement
- After the initial progress check, as needed, until both parties feel they have done what they can using the role negotiation strategy

Resources *(checkmarks indicate recommended equipment)*

✔ A nearby copy machine or carbon paper
☐ The completed and signed Role Negotiation Agreement worksheets
☐ The Role Negotiation Agreement Progress Check

Facilitator(s)

A third-party facilitator can mediate the meeting. This can be either a group member acceptable to both parties or the facilitator who assisted with the original agreement.

Time

Thirty to 60 minutes

Method

1. Each party fills out the Progress Check before the start of the scheduled meeting.

2. The agreement items are reviewed one by one, alternating between parties. Each person's number one agreement is reviewed; then the number two item, and so on. See how congruent members' progress ratings are, but don't try to reach consensus on what the ratings should be. Just review them and have each person explain why those particular ratings were chosen. Both parties are responsible for listening to each other's reasons for the ratings and understanding those reasons.

3. Each party shares the "What I most need to work on" portion of the Progress Check.

4. Each party adds data to the "What I most need to work on" portion, depending on what he or she heard from the other party.

5. Make any revisions that might upgrade the agreements. Change the originals as needed and have each party initialize any changes. Make photocopies of the agreements if changes are made.

6. Determine whether or not a subsequent progress check is needed. Schedule the next progress check and write it in the calendar. (Most successful negotiations require at least two follow-up progress checks.)

Role Negotiation Agreement Progress Check

Directions: Write an abbreviated description of the agreements that you and your work partner established in your initial role negotiation session. Then estimate the progress that you think you have made and you think that your partner has made. Use these guidelines to rate the progress.

5 — **Outstanding.** Done everything necessary to make the change. The problem no longer exists.

4 — **Commendable.** Have really worked on this one. There is almost no difficulty remaining.

3 — **Considerable Progress.** Considerable effort has been made. Still occasionally problematic.

2 — **Little Progress.** Some limited effort has been made. The problem still exists, for the most part.

1 — **No Progress.** No effort has been made and no progress has been observed.

_____ agrees to:
Name of Party

Score	Statement
1.	
2.	
3.	
4.	
5.	

_____ agrees to:
Name of Party

Score	Statement
1.	
2.	
3.	
4.	
5.	

What I most need to work on now is:

GUIDE II-11

Handling Common Problems

About This Guide

Because so many different types of people interact in **groups**, problems are inevitable. These difficulties prompt virtually every author who writes about facilitation to include a section on dealing with problem people or situations. The overabundance of such writing gave us pause for thought when it came to covering the topic in our book. We also considered that, based on our experience, 98% of all the problems anticipated by beginning facilitators simply don't happen if the group sessions have been carefully designed and planned. In fact, one of the most important messages we can convey about such problems is this:

> **You handle the vast majority of potential group problems through careful design and planning, before the group ever convenes—not during the session by using an arsenal of tricks.**

Having delivered that message, we must also acknowledge that even the most skilled facilitator will face some problems with certain group members or with unpredictably difficult situations. This guide identifies 16 of the most common problems that must be dealt with. Some are difficult situations involving the group, while others involve inappropriate or unhelpful individual behaviors. We have described each common problem by highlighting how it manifests itself in group situations; then we offer some facilitator actions for dealing with the challenge. Primers B and C on Group Dynamics and Process Consultation are also helpful in handling group problems. (See Introduction.)

Difficult Group Situations

1. **Waning Group Energy, Interest, or Attention.** There are many reasons why a group might start to lose energy, including fatigue, the time of day, environmental conditions (heating, background noise), the content becoming less interesting or relevant for the whole group, individual members going off on a tangent, or unsurfaced differences that distract participants from the present conversation. The key manifestations of this situation are:

   • Low participation

- Slow participation and pace; sluggishness

- Less feeling, passion, or energy in conversation; flat

- Nonverbal cues, including physical withdrawal, lying back in seat, turning away, staring off, or focusing outside the group

When you are confronted with this type of situation, **try one or more of these options:**

(a) Ask the group what is going on.

(b) Provide descriptive feedback on what you see; **ask why.**

(c) Increase your own energy, animation, pace; alter voice tone/inflection.

(d) Take a short break.

(e) Ask the group if this (what is being discussed at the time) is working, helpful, and on track.

(f) Ask the group what it would like to do.

(g) Have the group do something physical (walk, stretch, etc.).

2. **Unresponsive Group.** Sometimes, a particular activity or task seems to fall flat; members respond with only silence, a few superficial statements, or some form of questioning or whining about having to do the activity. There could be many reasons for such a situation, ranging from poor placement of the activity in the agenda sequence or a design that seems inappropriate, confusing, or too complicated to resistance related to where the task is leading (e.g., sensitivity of a subject, political vulnerability, fear of retribution).

In these situations, it is often helpful to try one or more of the following:

(a) Ask the group what is going on.

(b) Provide descriptive feedback on what you see; ask why.

(c) Try a different way to start the activity or discussion.

(d) Take a short break; ask a few individuals why they are silent or do not seem to want to do the activity.

(e) Ask the group if what has been proposed is needed, or helpful, or not possible right now.

(f) Ask members if they have any suggestions as to how to do it differently.

(g) Ask the group what it would like to do.

(h) Ask individuals to respond.

3. **The Group Keeps Going Off the Agenda.** Some groups seem to have trouble staying on the subject or following the agenda. They may just lack discipline, or they may be thinking of other agendas (personal) or disagree with the agenda, or for some reason want to avoid the task.

When this group behavior occurs, try one or more of these options:

(a) Refer people back to, and re-orient them to, the agenda.

(b) Ask members if they feel the current discussion is helpful or necessary.

(c) Point out the behavior and ask why the group is going off the agenda.

(d) Offer to change or re-order the agenda.

(e) Ask if the current conversation is important to everyone or if it can be postponed until after the meeting and then handled by a few members of the group.

(f) Ask the group what is going on.

(g) Take a break. Start back on the agenda after the break.

4. **Only Part of the Group Participates.** Many factors can contribute to this problem, such as:

- The topic of discussion may be relevant only to some members.

- The group composition may be wrong.

- The participants may be intimidating others.

- Political barriers may be keeping some members from expressing themselves (e.g., hierarchy, unpopular differences).

- The quiet ones are "checked out."

- The quiet ones are attentive and processing what they are hearing.

In these kinds of situations, it can be useful for the facilitator to do the following:

(a) Ask if others have information or opinions to share.

(b) Structure the discussion so that everyone gets to talk.

(c) Ask if the quiet ones feel connected to the discussion.

(d) Point out that only some people are contributing, and ask why.

(e) During a break, ask quiet members why they are not participating.

(f) Ask if the current conversation is important to everyone or if it can be postponed until after the meeting and then handled by a few members of the group.

5. **The Group Is Getting Highly Emotional.** Sometimes group discussions get heated or highly sensitive. Emotions such as anger, hurt, or fear are openly expressed. Voices get louder. Tension and nervousness increase. Even tears appear. When a group gets emotional, it's not necessarily a bad thing. It can just be part of someone's passion, ownership, or commitment to specific ideas or views. It could also be part of healthy debate that is highly relevant to the task. On the other hand, it can become destructive when the emotional expression is

personally hurtful, personality-based, or exceeds the bounds of the group and its work.

When a highly emotional state emerges, it is often helpful to try these options:

(a) Let it go. Watch how the group handles it. Determine if it is task-related and relevant to the group's progress.

(b) Take a break. Ask everyone to relax and come back with some input.

(c) If you see people acting uncomfortable, ask why.

(d) If just a few are emotional, see if the discussion can be held privately or whether or not it's really important for all to hear.

(e) If the conflict is escalating and not moving toward a natural resolution, intervene with a conflict resolution technique.

Difficult Individual Behaviors

Invariably, there will be people in the group who cause problems through inappropriate or unhelpful behaviors. While each situation is unique, there are some general guidelines to follow when dealing with such individuals in the group setting:

1. When possible, talk to them privately to point out the problem and coach them toward more desirable behaviors. Approach as a friend and ally, not as an authority figure.

2. Focus on a specific desired behavior.

3. Don't judge a person's behavior as right or wrong.

4. Try to maintain the balance between protecting the group from the distracting behavior and protecting the individual from undue attack.

5. Accept what they're doing. Describe it. Ask about it.

6. Legitimize their feelings, perceptions, or rights.

7. Work with their issues when it will be productive for the group, or defer the issues to a time when the group is likely to perform well, despite the distraction.

8. Be sure to have ground rules and norms for participation, so that the group can self-monitor. Refer to the group for enforcement when someone is out of line.

In addition to the general guidelines, there are other specific actions you can take when a problem behavior pops up. Some of the more common behaviors and possible responses are listed below:

1. *Dominating the Discussion.* A person talks too often, too long, or too loud, making it difficult for others to participate.

➤ Stop the person, thank him or her, and say you'd like to hear from someone else.

➤ Call attention to the agenda and time frames.

➤ Break eye contact. Move away from the person. Stop giving him or her focused attention.

➤ Move closer and closer to the person, maintaining eye contact. Get in front of him or her. The problematic behavior will start to stand out (even to the person).

➤ Summarize what the person has said and move to someone else.

➤ Give the person a time limit.

➤ Before the discussion starts, pose a standard for the length of comments. For example: "Let's hear from a few people for no more than 2 minutes each."

➤ When you know in advance that an individual or individuals tend to dominate a group, propose a ground rule at the beginning of the session that everyone "monitor the air time." Explain that for some, this means talking less; for others, it means talking more.

➤ Introduce an inclusion activity to get everyone participating.

2. ***Inserting Personal Agendas.*** A person continually inserts a concern, a disagreement, or an alternative or additional agenda item. This is often annoying if it's repetitive and distracts from the group task.

➤ Ask the person how what he or she is saying relates to the current agenda item.

➤ Record the point, thank the person, and move on.

➤ Ask the person what he or she wants the group to do with the input.

➤ Give the person a time limit.

3. ***Repeating the Same Point Over and Over.*** Sometimes people get so caught up in something they care about that they can't let go of it and begin to sound like a "broken record." This is often a variation of number 2 above.

➤ Acknowledge the importance of the point and the person's passion, advocacy, or determination.

➤ Demonstrate that he or she has been heard and the point recorded.

➤ Explain how and when the point will be dealt with.

➤ Ask directly if the person can "let go of it for now."

➤ Give the person a final time-limited opportunity to make the point.

4. *Talking off the Subject.* Sometimes people are out of synch with the agenda and regularly talk about things that are irrelevant to the group's task or are out of sequence with the agenda.

   ➤ Ask them to relate what they are saying to the *current* agenda.

   ➤ Ask if the group can come back to their point and record it on a "parking lot" sheet.

   ➤ Ask others if they have anything to add to what the person said.

   ➤ Stop them. Tell them it's not appropriate now. Bring it up later under a different part of the agenda.

5. *Having Side Conversations.* There are always people who have to make private comments to one another or carry on another meeting with their neighbor.

   ➤ Invite them to share what is being said.

   ➤ Stop the conversation, be quiet, and look at the people talking.

   ➤ Ask them to stop.

   ➤ Ask if they would please join the group.

   ➤ Move closer to the people having the side conversation.

   ➤ Repeat the topic under discussion and ask if everyone can focus on having just one conversation at a time. Say, "Let's have one conversation," or "Let's all focus on the same thing."

   ➤ Point out that the whispering or talking is distracting.

6. *Being Constantly Negative or Antagonistic, or Presenting a Hostile Demeanor.* Some people are nay-sayers, doubters, and cynics. Nothing is okay and nothing will work. They always seem skeptical. Their negative expressions may be either verbal or nonverbal.

   ➤ Acknowledge their points of view.

   ➤ Make a special point of thoroughly paraphrasing their view the first couple of times they speak. Stick very close to their exact wording.

   ➤ Point out the negative pattern.

   ➤ Ask if there is any part of the work that they feel good about.

   ➤ Ask for their opinions about what is needed. Record the opinions. Ask the group to respond.

7. *Interrupting Others.* When people cut off others who are speaking or jump into a conversation too soon, they disrupt the flow of information and show disrespect for the other person. These interruptions can be verbal or highly distracting nonverbal expressions. Even when there is a ground rule against this, it still seems to happen.

   ➤ Enforce the related ground rule.

➤ Stop the interrupter and ask him or her to wait while the group allows the speaker to complete his or her thought or point.

➤ Ask people who feel impatient to write down their thoughts rather than blurt them out.

➤ This happens most frequently in larger groups, which tend to give members the feeling that they may not get a chance to speak. When your group has nine or more members, establish a hand-raising rule. As people raise their hands, say, "OK, we'll hear first from [member's name], then [member's name], then [member's name]," and so on. Make sure you follow through in calling on people in sequence.

➤ Be neutral and consistent. Don't let some interrupt but not others.

8. *Non-Participation.* Some people remain silent in group meetings. They seem unable or unwilling to speak up. They may be timid, fearful of something, or unsure of themselves and what they have to offer. Sometimes they drop out, withdraw, or work on something else.

➤ Talk to them privately at another time. Find out their problem.

➤ Call on them by name. For example, "John, we haven't heard from you on this. Could you share your thoughts with us?"

➤ Thank them when they do contribute.

➤ Turn to them when the agenda moves to an area that you know they can address with confidence, conviction, or expertise.

➤ Early in key conversations, have everyone respond briefly in turn to a specific cue question intended to stimulate discussion.

9. *Attacking, Criticizing, or Picking an Argument.* Some people go after other members or the facilitator to argue or personally attack. Sometimes this is just counterdependence, aimed at discrediting or trying to change what the group is doing.

➤ Describe, nonjudgmentally, what the person is doing.

➤ Ask if the criticism or judgment (attack) is based on something that has occurred in the meeting.

➤ Stop any argument. Ask for and record a statement of each position. Engage other group members in discussing their positions.

➤ Ask the person what the group could do to respond to his or her concern.

10. *Clowning.* Sometimes a person may overuse humor, act silly, or joke about everything. These are usually attention-getting behaviors if they are regular and patterned. Once in a while these behaviors can, of course, be helpful in infusing the group with energy.

➤ Ignore the behavior and the person.

➤ Ask the person to stop it.

➤ Describe what is going on and point out its distracting quality.

➤ Talk to the person privately, after the meeting or during a break.

➤ If the person has really disrupted the meeting, take a break. Talk to him or her. Come back with a structure and focus on the agenda.

11. **Attendance Problems.** Some people repeatedly arrive late or leave early, miss meetings, or make a habit of ducking in and out. These actions disrupt the group, delaying or halting its progress.

➤ Take the time to get an attendance commitment from the group. Enforce it.

➤ Speak to the person outside of the meeting.

➤ Don't review anything or stop the meeting for such people.

➤ Suggest either or both of these ground rules: "Members agree to support any decision made in their absence," and/or "There will be no reviews for people absent at any time."

➤ Ask members to announce if, when, and why they have to leave, come late, or miss a meeting.

➤ At the beginning of the meeting, review the scheduled times and ask if there is anyone who will not be able to be there for any part of the meeting.

➤ Ask one of the group members to update someone on a break.

➤ Have the group leader ask these members to come to meetings regularly. If they can't do that, replace them. Ask those who can't regularly participate to suggest replacements in the group. Avoid allowing "temporary" replacements to fill in for another member.

GUIDE II-12

Alternatives to Spending Time Giving Out Information in Meetings

Top 10 Reasons Not to Spend Time Giving Out Information in Meetings

10. It's boring.
9. It may seem egocentric and damage leadership credibility.
8. Most people won't remember the information.
7. You promote misinterpretation; if people do recall information, their memories are partly—and sometimes totally—inaccurate.
6. People usually don't listen.
5. People resent it.
4. There are more effective ways of giving data in less time.
3. Usually there's nothing new.
2. Only a few people need to know it—not everybody.
1. It seldom results in constructive action.

WHERE LESS IS MORE
TIPS ON HOW TO GIVE OUT LESS UNNECESSARY INFORMATION

First we need to make clear that what we are referring to as undesirable is the use of meetings to disseminate information. We are not talking about building a data base for task group work, which is indispensable to making those groups effective. We are suggesting that facilitators discourage the information dissemination so common in regular staff meetings. Research shows that the average accurate retention rate of such information is about 20%. To make better use of meeting time, consider using these strategies:

➡ Time-limit information dissemination and stick to the limits.

➡ Place any information items close to the end of the agenda.

➡ Screen information items that go on meeting agendas by asking the questions that follow:

(Continued)

Tips on How To Give Out Less Unnecessary Information *(Continued)*

1. Is there any significant action to be taken now, in this meeting, as a result of the information?

2. Does this information imply that some sort of action should be taken by a majority of the participants in the near future?

3. Is this the only way that participants can get this information in a timely manner?

4. Do more than two-thirds of the people in the meeting need to know this?

5. Will a significant number of the participants be in some kind of trouble if they don't get this information here, right now, in this meeting?

➡ If you can't answer yes to at least two of the questions, then don't use the meeting time to disseminate the information. Find another way.

➡ When you have detailed information that group members will find valuable for the meeting, send it out in advance of the meeting, and ask everyone to read it before the meeting.

➡ Ask group members to put their information items in "headline" form, capturing the essence of the information in 13 words or less. There are several ways to handle the headlines. Here are a few:

- Go around the room and ask members to share any information headlines that they feel other members would be interested in.

- Do the above, but right before a break. You may want to extend the break time so that members who are interested in the information can find out more about it and informally network with one another. The same strategy can be applied at the end of the meeting. For example, 30 minutes before scheduled closure, have members share the headlines; then those who have questions or seem particularly interested in the information can mingle after the meeting.

- Here is a method developed from Daniels' (1990) "For Your Information" technique. Ask everyone to record their headlines on a sheet of flip chart paper and to identify their respective contribution by signing their name to it. (If chart paper is not available, use regular paper and have members put the sheet on a table.) Then use break time or a prescribed amount of "networking" time to follow up on questions or pursue interest in the information.

(Continued)

Tips on How To Give Out Less Unnecessary Information *(Continued)*

- Have everyone put their headlines on a flip chart **before** the break. Tell members to initialize any item they want to hear more about during the meeting. If more than half the group initialize an item, give the person who wrote the headline a set number of minutes after the break to speak briefly and answer questions about the item.

➡ You can suggest that the meeting leader(s) impose a standard that no more than 5% of the meeting time be devoted to information dissemination unless there is some compelling reason to do so.

➡ There are, of course, notable exceptions to the guidelines proposed here. However, when these exceptions occur, there is usually a rationale for having a separate session that focuses on handling the information well. Examples might be the announcement of key restructuring efforts or the rolling out of significant organizational change. The presidential press conference format is a fairly effective format for handling this type of information dissemination.

➡ If circumstances are compelling enough that you must devote a significant amount of time to disseminating information, then make sure that members accurately understand the information and process it correctly. To push the usual 20% accurate-retention rate higher, it will be necessary (a) to have members actively respond to the information in a way that will help them process the information, or (b) check in some way (either formally or informally) to make sure they have understood the information.

➡ Daniels (1990) suggests several good techniques for compressing information dissemination and making it more productive (as noted earlier, his "For Your Information" technique is the source of the headlining-idea method). Here are thumbnail sketches of three of his other techniques (for more detail, see Daniels, 1990, pp. 65–72):

- *Start, Stop, Alert* asks everyone to quickly share in headline form (a) what's starting (what's new), (b) what's stopping (what's at an end), and (c) what to be on the alert for (what's on the horizon—good or bad).

- *Highlights/Lowlights* asks everyone in the group to share at least one highlight (significant good news, accomplishments worth notice) and at least one lowlight (significant bad news, problems or failures worth notice or as a learning opportunity). The leader discourages anyone from passing.

- *For the Good of the Order* asks everyone to take a turn sharing "significant good news or accomplishments on behalf of the organization worth noticing." These might be personal accomplishments or the accomplishments of others. Again, the leader discourages passing.

(Continued)

Tips on How To Give Out Less Unnecessary Information *(Concluded)*

Here are a few other ideas for compressed information sharing that follow procedures similar to those described in the three Daniels' examples:

- *Working and not*—What's working and what's not

- *Breakdowns*—What's not working for me and what kind of help I think I need

- *My goals*—The three most important things I have to accomplish this week

- *CSFs (Critical Success Factors)*—My critical success factors for the week: what I most need to be or have in order to accomplish my goals this week

- *Give and take*—How I've been of service and who's been of service to me

- *Accomplishments and Targets*—Where I started with [target], where I am today, and where I still have to go; or where we started with [target], where we are today, and where we still have to go

REFERENCES

Daniels, William R. (1987). *Group power II: A manager's guide to conducting regular meetings.* Mill Valley, CA: American Consulting and Training.

FACILITATOR RESOURCES

Evaluation and Group Closure

PROCEDURE II-23

The Task Group Process Review

Purpose

To check the progress of a group and consciously plan process improvements on a continuous basis.

Summary Description

Most successful groups periodically review their work and evaluate its effectiveness. This procedure provides a checklist of items for reviewing the effectiveness of any given group. Group members are asked to respond "yes" or "no" to each of the items. Next, they share their "no" responses with one another, first limiting discussion to understanding why an item was marked "no." The group then prioritizes items most in need of corrective action and plans specific actions for correction. Group members conclude by validating themselves for the things they have been doing right.

When to Use the Procedure

- Whenever it seems necessary. A rule of thumb is to stop and do a group process review after every 20 hours that a group has been meeting.

Participants

Number: No numerical limits

Type: Any group that will be continuing to work together for a significant period of time

Resources *(checkmarks indicate recommended equipment)*

✔ Flip chart and markers
✔ Copies of the Task Group Process Review List (see Guide II-13)

Facilitator(s)

One person acts as group facilitator, leading the discussion and recording the data. There is not usually a need for a separate recorder.

Time

Between 1 and 3 hours, depending on the problems identified

Method

1. Have group members write out their answers to the questions on the Task Group Process Review List and mark the appropriate response. Go through each item on the list. Ask if any member marked the item "no."

2. Record that item on the flip chart for discussion. Go through all the items without discussion, noting those items for which any "no" responses were recorded.

3. For items marked "no," listen to each individual rationale for a "no" response. Again, go through the complete list of questions before discussing solutions or actions.

4. Ask group members to identify which items they believe are most in need of discussion and action planning for correction. Discuss potential solutions and actions. Record the actions on an action list, noting the specific action, who will do it, and when it will be done.

5. Ask if there are other issues that the group should consider and plan corrective action for.

6. Conclude the discussion by noting what the group has been doing right. Record these strengths on the flip chart. Ask members to identify the positive things that they believe have most contributed to their success. Remind everyone that it is important to focus on continuing to do those things that have contributed most to the group's success.

Notes

1. You may wish to add or delete questions for the purposes of your group. Two or three group members might review the questions suggested, adding others they feel are important and deleting those that they feel are less important for consideration. You could create a few simple categories for discussion, such as "Meeting Preparation," "Facilitation Effectiveness," "Group Member Process Skills," and "Political Considerations," and review those categories. Another alternative is to create a simple positives-and-negatives list. You can list group positives (+'s) and group negatives (–'s), or group "strengths" and "concerns."

2. This analysis can be conducted by a subgroup and the recommendations for corrective action presented to the whole group for approval and action.

3. Another alternative discussion format is to simply ask the question, "How are we doing working as a team?" Then ask each member to respond to the question, and note the highlights of members' responses on the group memory. Move into discussion and action planning after everyone has had their say.

4. If the group has established group operating principles, these can be reviewed. Each member marks each of the principles "yes" or "no," and the above process steps are followed.

5. It is best to do this activity after a group has gone through the "norming and storming" group phases and has become productive to some degree. This usually takes between three and five meetings.

6. Some groups may prefer to acknowledge the things they have been doing right or those items receiving positive responses before moving on to the corrective action.

GUIDE II-13

Task Group Process Review List

Answer *yes* or *no* to the following items:	YES	NO
1. Group members are working together well.	☐	☐
2. Enough tasks are getting produced to meet our timelines in the charge for the group.	☐	☐
3. The group dynamic norm of equality is well in force. (No big shots.)	☐	☐
4. We have the right people to get the data we need.	☐	☐
5. The agendas are getting out far enough ahead of time. Group members come prepared to the meetings.	☐	☐
6. We are effectively using time between meetings to have individuals or small teams produce products that give the group a sense of progress.	☐	☐
7. The manager to whom this group will provide recommendations is well informed and pleased with the progress of the group.	☐	☐
8. The group feels comfortable with the balance between content and process during the meetings.	☐	☐
9. Who makes decisions in the group is clear, and there is little ambiguity about authority.	☐	☐
10. The group is not being held up by obvious personality conflicts between two or more members.	☐	☐
11. There is little or no "eggshell-walking" during the meetings.	☐	☐
12. Team ground rules are in effect and consistently adhered to.	☐	☐
13. All team members show up on time and stay until the end of the meeting.	☐	☐
14. Action lists are followed up on from meeting to meeting.	☐	☐
15. The physical meeting arrangements are as good as we need them to be to maximize group productivity.	☐	☐
16. Group memory notes are recorded and sent out within three working days following the meeting.	☐	☐
17. Meetings start and end on time unless the group requests that they go longer.	☐	☐

(Continued)

Task Group Process Review List *(Concluded)*

Answer *yes* or *no* to the following items:	YES	NO
18. Written products coming from the group are clear and understandable (for draft) yet rich in content.	☐	☐
19. Group members agree that the work being produced is superior in quality to what any individual could produce.	☐	☐
20. A good variety of processes are being used. The same process isn't being overdone so that the group becomes bored with routine.	☐	☐
21. Flexibility is exercised in who attends meetings, depending upon what type of expertise is needed.	☐	☐
22. Political considerations are not interfering with the development of the best possible product.	☐	☐

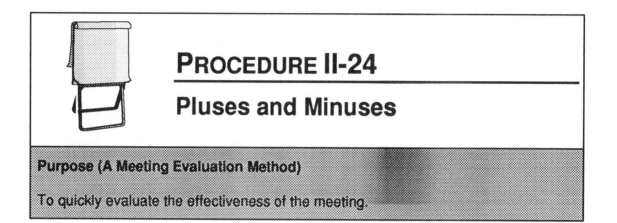

PROCEDURE II-24

Pluses and Minuses

Purpose (A Meeting Evaluation Method)

To quickly evaluate the effectiveness of the meeting.

Summary Description

One of the quickest methods for evaluating meetings is also one of the most effective. About 5 minutes before the close of the meeting, the group lists the pluses and minuses of the meeting on a flip chart.

When to Use the Procedure

- Immediately before adjourning a group session

Participants

Number: For task groups between two and 25 members

Type: All group members

Resources *(checkmarks indicate recommended equipment)*

✔ Flip chart and markers

Time

Approximately 5 minutes

Method

1. Draw a line down the center of a flip chart page. At the top of one column, write "+'s." At the top of the other column, write "–'s."

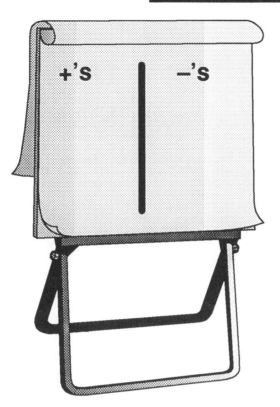

2. Ask the group, "What were the pluses and minuses of our session today?"

3. Record each suggestion verbatim, just as it is offered by a group member.

4. Adjourn the meeting.

Note

1. You can avoid the negative connotations of "minuses" by using the heading "Improvements" or "Let's remember next time . . ." It may be particularly important to amend the heading, and your language in general, if the group (or the facilitator) has had some rough moments during the meeting. Using this alternative language ensures that you do not reinforce a pattern of complaining or give too much negative criticism.

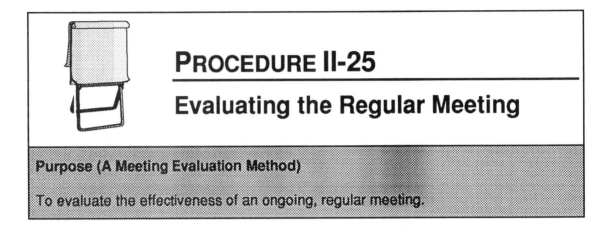

PROCEDURE II-25

Evaluating the Regular Meeting

Purpose (A Meeting Evaluation Method)

To evaluate the effectiveness of an ongoing, regular meeting.

Summary Description

Ongoing, regular meetings (such as staff and management group meetings) can benefit from a slightly different approach to evaluation. According to Daniels (1990), these meetings, if conducted effectively, have functions, membership structures, agendas, processes, and memory systems that are distinct from task group or problem-solving meetings. The overall purposes of these meetings should be to maintain and strengthen the existing culture, values, standards, and roles of the organization while producing clear-cut decisions and authorized actions.

Creative solutions to problems and carefully thought-out plans should be developed for the most part outside of these regular meetings in small "think tanks" or task groups composed of those persons most familiar with the issues and those who have the best specialized expertise. These solutions should then be brought to the regular meeting for review and approval.

Because research suggests that meetings are not a cost-effective way to present information, the effective regular meeting will also limit information sharing to "news briefs" and quick announcements of forthcoming events; thus, in the usually scant meeting time available, the group can focus on approval of the carefully thought-out recommendations and the review of operational standards that must be maintained and strengthened if the organization is to succeed in its mission.

The 25 evaluation questions in the accompanying handout are designed for periodic use by the regular meeting group to monitor and assess the group's effectiveness.

When to Use the Procedure

- When a group is working to teach itself the distinctions between effective regular meetings and task group meetings

- For the first six times that a regular meeting group is being coached to learn the "Group Power" method of operating

- Monthly or quarterly for any intact work group

Participants

Number: Varies according to the size of the meeting

Type: Members of a regular meeting group such as a management or staff team

Resources *(checkmarks indicate recommended equipment)*

✔ Flip chart and markers
✔ Overhead projector
❑ Handout: Regular Meeting Evaluation Guide

Facilitator(s)

The meeting leader (or person in charge of the group) hands out the evaluation or asks another team member to do so. If you are using a consultant to coach the group on the Group Power methodology, the consultant may handle the evaluation process.

Time

Five minutes at the end of the meeting; 10 minutes at the start of the next meeting

Method

1. At the close of the meeting, hand out an evaluation form to each member of the group.

2. Ask members to look over the form and see if they have any questions. Answer any questions.

3. Ask everyone to fill out the form before leaving the meeting.

4. Have the data compiled before the next meeting of the group.

5. Present the composite data on an overhead transparency at the beginning of the next meeting. Ask everyone to scan the data for a moment or two.

6. Have group members suggest things that the group should "keep on doing," "do more of," or "do less of" in this meeting. Post suggestions on a flip chart page.

Notes

1. The evaluation is set up to yield a potential score of 100. If you wish, you can post the composite score received by the group and chart the subsequent group scores as an indication of progress in the conduct of effective regular meetings.

2. This evaluation is most useful for intact regular groups such as staff or management teams. There are other groups, such as cross-functional project teams, that are part regular group and part task group. The evaluation may be less appropriate for these "hybrid" types of groups.

REFERENCES

Daniels, William R. (1987). *Group power II: A manager's guide to conducting regular meetings.* Mill Valley, CA: American Consulting & Training.

Regular Meeting Evaluation Guide

Directions: Rate each item as best as you can. If it has not occurred, give it a 1 rating.

REGULAR MEETING QUALITY INDICATOR	RATING			
Before the Meeting	*Yes*			*No*
1. The agenda was planned ahead.	4	3	2	1
2. The agenda was distributed prior to the meeting.	4	3	2	1
3. All members were present.	4	3	2	1
4. Formats for operations reviews and recommendations reviews were prepared before the meeting.	4	3	2	1
5. Information relative to the agenda was distributed before meeting.	4	3	2	1
6. The room was set up properly.	4	3	2	1
During the Meeting	*Yes*			*No*
7. Decisions passed down from other authorities were checked for understanding and compliance.	4	3	2	1
8. News items and announcements were presented quickly in abbreviated format.	4	3	2	1
9. Problem-solving discussions were limited to brainstorming, delegated to be handled outside the meeting, or sufficient time was allocated for thorough analysis.	4	3	2	1
10. Recommendations were reviewed fairly and with appropriate scrutiny.	4	3	2	1
11. Clear decisions resulted from recommendations reviews.	4	3	2	1
12. Specific standards were used to review operations.	4	3	2	1
13. Recommendations and/or operations reviews were reviewed objectively without feelings of personal attack or acrimony.	4	3	2	1
14. Operations critical to the success of the group's work were reviewed.	4	3	2	1
15. The person responsible for making decisions was clearly specified.	4	3	2	1
16. Group members intelligently reviewed recommendations and operations outside their primary responsibilities.	4	3	2	1
17. There were no interruptions or intrusions. No calls were taken during the meeting.	4	3	2	1
18. There was no side-talk or distracting commentary.	4	3	2	1
19. Decisions and actions were logged in writing.	4	3	2	1
20. Action lists from previous meetings were reviewed for completion.	4	3	2	1
21. The agenda was completed or it was consciously revised well before the end of the meeting.	4	3	2	1
22. The meeting started and ended on time.	4	3	2	1
23. All permanent members arrived on time and stayed from the start to the end of the meeting.	4	3	2	1
After the Meeting (Rate your last meeting for these items)	*Yes*			*No*
24. A record of the meeting was promptly distributed.	4	3	2	1
25. The meeting effectiveness was evaluated prior to the close of the meeting.	4	3	2	1
Meeting Effectiveness Rating = Total Score	**Total Score**			

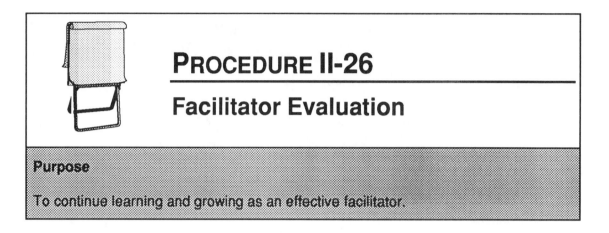

PROCEDURE II-26

Facilitator Evaluation

Purpose

To continue learning and growing as an effective facilitator.

Summary Description

The facilitator needs feedback, just as the group members do. During this procedure, the facilitator asks all members of the group to fill out a copy of the Facilitator Evaluation and briefly discuss the results with the facilitator.

When to Use the Procedure

- With ongoing groups; approximately once every three months
- Whenever you feel that the feedback would be useful

Resources *(checkmarks indicate recommended equipment)*

- ✔ Flip chart and markers
- ☐ Handout: Facilitator Evaluation form

Facilitator(s)

You can handle the facilitation yourself, or you can ask someone from the group to facilitate the session so that you can focus on interacting with group members.

Time

Approximately 20 to 25 minutes

Method

1. Explain that is helpful for your own professional development to have group members evaluate your work. Also explain that it can enhance the effectiveness of their work if you know how you can best support them.

2. Pass out copies of the Facilitator Evaluation form and ask everyone to complete them. Allow about 6 to 8 minutes for them to complete the form.

3. While members are working on the form, label four flip chart pages with the four questions at the end of the Facilitator Evaluation.

4. When everyone has finished, ask members to share their responses to the four questions. As members share this data, record it on the flip chart pages and ask probing questions. Explain that you want to understand exactly what the responses mean. Don't be either defensive or apologetic. Just focus on getting the data.

5. Conclude by thanking the group for providing you with the opportunity to learn and grow. You may want to suggest some ways that group members can support you in being the most effective facilitator you can be. For example: "Ralph, would you be willing to help me out on remembering to do group evaluations by pointing to your watch when there are 30 minutes left in the session? Could you do that for our next two sessions?"

6. Ask everyone to hand in the forms.

Variations

1. You can just have the group respond to the four questions without filling out the form.

2. After members have filled out the form, tell them what your personal standard is for facilitator ratings. Ask them to specify, for any substandard rating, what it would take for them to be able to rate you at the standard or higher in a subsequent evaluation.

3. You have the choice of having members sign the forms or not.

4. After members have filled out the form, pass out 4-by-6-inch note cards. Ask them to write on one side of the card the one or two most helpful things that you have been doing. Ask them to write on the other side the one or two most helpful things that you could do more of or do less of. Have members turn in only the cards when they are finished.

5. You can leave the room and have people work as a group, coming up with ratings on the items that they all pretty much agree with as well as answers for the four questions that follow the items. Then, after a specified amount of time, return to the group and review the feedback with the group.

Facilitator Evaluation

Part 1. Directions: Rate each item according to your experience with the Group Facilitator.

FACILITATOR EFFECTIVENESS STANDARD	RATING Yes				No
1. Presents directions clearly.	5	4	3	2	1
2. Balances participation by bringing others out.	5	4	3	2	1
3. Remains neutral on issues under discussion.	5	4	3	2	1
4. Listens intently.	5	4	3	2	1
5. Enforces ground rules fairly as needed.	5	4	3	2	1
6. Reviews agendas for sessions before the session begins.	5	4	3	2	1
7. Uses a variety of interesting, useful processes that keep people engaged.	5	4	3	2	1
8. Remains flexible while staying within designed structures and processes.	5	4	3	2	1
9. Promotes sufficient interaction between members of the group.	5	4	3	2	1
10. Maintains group memory in an orderly fashion.	5	4	3	2	1
11. Records data from group members accurately.	5	4	3	2	1
12. Gives all suggested ideas equal consideration and attention.	5	4	3	2	1
13. Is respectful and considerate of group members.	5	4	3	2	1
14. Keeps us on task without being overly directive.	5	4	3	2	1
15. Reasonably adheres to established time limits.	5	4	3	2	1
16. Helps us to confront our differences and come to resolution.	5	4	3	2	1
17. Brings closure to one item before moving to the next. Makes sure actions and decisions are clearly specified.	5	4	3	2	1
18. Has supported me in being an effective team player.	5	4	3	2	1
19. Evaluates the effectiveness of each group session before the end of the session.	5	4	3	2	1
20. Supports us in following through on commitments to action.	5	4	3	2	1
Meeting Effectiveness Rating = Total Score	Total Score _____				

(Continued)

Facilitator Evaluation *(Concluded)*

Part 2. Directions: Please respond to the following statements.

The things the facilitator does that most help us as a group:

The things the facilitator does that have most helped me to be an effective group member:

Things the facilitator could do more of or less of that would support our group's effectiveness:

Things the facilitator could do more of or less of that would support me in being an effective group member and team player:

GUIDE II-14

Handling Closings With the Group

Overview

Every group session should have an appropriate closing. The nature of the closing will vary considerably according to the situation. Handling closings effectively is a sign of facilitation mastery. The most frequent mistake that is made by both novice and seasoned facilitators is to concentrate so intensely on the task at hand that there is only a rushed 3 or 4 minutes at the end of the session to do a hurried evaluation of the session or to set the next meeting date. Failing to properly close often leaves the group feeling incomplete and can inadvertently create a frenzied type of norm state that does not serve the group.

Carefully planned closings should be built into the agenda, and the facilitator will be wise to exercise the discipline to modify or shorten the agenda rather than to neglect closing activities. Every effective group session needs a good beginning, productive work accomplished toward the agenda, and a proper closing. It is important to stay in touch session by session with the type of closings that are needed and to plan your meetings without shortchanging the endings. Several types of closings and some tips for handling closings effectively are provided here.

TYPES OF CLOSINGS

Closing activities fall into one or another of the following categories:

1. *Evaluations.* The group evaluates its work and the adequacy of the agenda and suggests process corrections for the following session (see the meeting evaluation methods in this section). From time to time, group members evaluate their own effectiveness in contributing to the group (see Procedure II-2: Monitoring Group Task and Maintenance Behaviors; Procedure II-23: The Task Group Process Review; and Procedure II-25: Evaluating the Regular Meeting).

2. *Clarifying Action Assignments and Responsibilities.* The action plans that the group has made are clearly specified with clear accountabilities for completion. Individuals may want to make contracts with themselves or other group members to complete action assignments or to perform some kind of learning assignment.

3. *Summarizing the Work of the Group and Looking Ahead to Next Steps.* A brief summary of the work should be made by the facilitator or a group member, and the group should agree on the logical "next steps."

4. ***Sharing Positive Feedback and Giving Acknowledgments.*** Nearly every session should have as a part of its closing some form of positive, encouraging feedback to the group. The form of the feedback might vary, but the feedback itself remains an important motivational element in enabling groups to succeed. During some sessions, it may be appropriate to give out awards, certificates, or prizes for participation.

5. ***Saying Good-Bye.*** Saying good-bye can be done in a variety of ways for groups that are disbanding or not coming back together for a considerable period of time. There may also be times when expressions of sorrow or remorse become important ceremonies in the act of saying good-bye to someone or something.

6. ***Staying in Touch and Monitoring Work Progress.*** Group members may find it necessary to stay in touch with one another in order to coordinate actions that have been planned. Or group members may wish to use one another as support for accomplishing tasks that they have been assigned. A phone/address list may be valuable to distribute to members; they may need to coordinate calendars for phone conference dates or subgroup meetings.

7. ***Looking Ahead.*** Outcomes or agenda items for the next session may need to be identified. Rotating assignments may need to be made (e.g., who's facilitating, recording, hosting). Upcoming milestones or goals may need to be announced. Group members may need to be reminded of an important event or a particular type of "work season" that is coming up that may have an impact on the work.

8. ***Stakeholder Communications.*** People who have a stake in the work of the group may need to be informed about what has occurred during the group session. The timing and method of communication may need to be clarified, as well as information about who will be communicating what to whom.

9. ***Staying in Touch with Key Values and Principles.*** You may wish to invoke one of the group's (or organization's) guiding principles as a reminder before members "go forth" to do their work. Though not appropriate in the secular organization, some adaptation of the closing prayer or a type of "principles benediction" can help people keep in touch with their guiding principles and values.

TIPS ON CLOSINGS

➡ Resolve to handle endings properly, and plan an appropriate time for closing activities. Stay alert to the time when you are nearing the end of meetings and modify the agenda, if necessary, to allow time for proper closings. Emphasize to the group the importance of ending meetings properly. Ask group members to make a similar resolution in the form of an agreement that allows for proper closure. For instance, "We agree to stop every meeting _____ minutes before the scheduled ending time to allow for a cohesive completion of the meeting."

➡ Establish ending rituals that are repeated at each meeting, such as reviewing the action list. Vary other types of closing activities from meeting to meeting. Keep a resource guide of good closing activities on hand so that you can quickly come up with a variety of ending activities.

➡ Have different group members handle different parts of the closings for you. One person can summarize the meeting. Another can lead a quick plus-and-minus evaluation. Another can suggest a validation activity. This is particularly important when you are committed to maintaining an egalitarian group norm for the group.

➡ If you are working in a group with its supervisor present, ask that person regularly (or occasionally) to validate the group and group members for their effort and accomplishment. Before the meetings, coach the leader on the importance of his or her role as "cheerleader" and group motivator.

➡ Remember closings particularly when the group has been experiencing difficulty or the session has had its share of rough moments. In these cases, it can be debilitating to the group to end the meeting on a sour note. It may not be appropriate in such cases to try and cheer anyone up. The closing in such a meeting might include a frank discussion of each person's regrets about the meeting and hopes for future meetings. Repeating some of the ritual closings during such times says to the group, "We may have had a rough time, but we're still together as a group." Failing to do so may lead people to question the efficacy of the group itself.

➡ Look at group closings as a critical period for building a positive, supportive spirit in the group. Emphasize the validations and encouragements far more than the judgments and evaluations, and make sure that you take time now and then to recognize that empowering and encouraging the group are priorities.

➡ Use the list "Types of Closings" as a regular resource when planning group sessions and meetings. Scan the list when you are planning the agenda and include those types of closings that seem most appropriate to your agenda and to the current status of the group.

SECTION III

PHASE III:
FOLLOW-UP

➡ **Overview**
➡ **Facilitator Resources**

OVERVIEW

Life always gets harder toward the summit—
the cold increases, responsibility increases.

—F. Nietzsche, *The Antichrist,* 1888

When you get right down to the root of the meaning of the word "succeed,"
you find it simply means to follow through.

—F. W. Nichols

The reward of a thing well done is to have done it.

—Ralph Waldo Emerson

After the group session, the facilitator has a number of follow-up tasks to complete. The nature of this follow-up work will vary depending on the type of work the group was doing and whether the session was a one-time event or part of an ongoing series of meetings. Also, the facilitator's role in the follow-up will depend on the contract and the client's role and resources.

Good, effective follow-up work should produce the following outcomes:

1. The meeting record is produced and distributed; group outputs are completed.
2. The results of the group's work are communicated to members, sponsors, and stakeholders.
3. Approvals of results are obtained and announced.
4. Next steps are carried out.
5. The need for further group work is determined.

THE FIVE PRIMARY TASKS

In following up work with the group, you need to focus on five primary tasks:

1. Preparing the meeting record and outputs
2. Communicating with and informing others
3. Obtaining approvals of the group's work
4. Monitoring interim and implementation work
5. Identifying the need for additional group work

To better understand what follow-up work involves, let's take a closer look at each of these five tasks.

Task 1: Preparing the Meeting Record and Outputs

During group work, data is generated, gathered, and consolidated. Alternative actions and other information logged on the group memory are essential for group follow-up and important to anyone who must report on, or create minutes from, the meeting; therefore, it is highly useful to have the group memory copied. Also, new or ongoing responsibilities are usually identified during the group work, and their implementation and follow-through will be more likely if a group contract is drawn up (establishing who will be doing what next and by when), recorded, and distributed to members.

Outputs play an important role in the following:

— Keeping a common picture in front of the group members
— Preventing misinterpretations
— Reinforcing commitment
— Documenting accountability
— Providing a vehicle for informing or including others not involved in the group sessions

As facilitator, you may have either a small role or a large one in preparing these outputs, depending on the client's resources and your contract.

Task 2: Communicating With and Informing Others

Often a group's work will have an impact on others, will benefit from the involvement of others, or will require others to do something. Making contact and managing the communication with others need to be planned. Who will talk with whom? When? Who should receive copies of your output documents? Who requires face-to-face conversations? Should a special session be used for informing others? These and other considerations need to be examined and orchestrated. Timing could be important, as well as what is shared and by whom. At this point, the group is generally engaged in an "influence process," so how that process is designed can make a big difference.

Task 3: Obtaining Approvals of the Group's Work

In most cases, the group's work will be subject to explicit approval by some outside individuals or groups. Other individuals or groups may need to review the work and be in basic agreement with it. When groups are not the "senior team" or they cut across the organization, there will usually be a need to bring their results to the organizational hierarchy and obtain approvals. These approvals may involve a whole stage of work, a final product, specific recommendations, or requests for funding.

It is incumbent on the group to prepare and educate those whose approval is needed. Ongoing communication with all stakeholders, starting before sessions actually begin, can be an important factor in winning approval.

The more explicit and public the approvals, the better. Recommendations from groups should be scrutinized according to their importance and priority for the organization. The recommendations review process is often one of the least developed group processes in the organization. When done well, this process can lead to improvements in the group's work, unquestioned approvals, and therefore more focused implementation. If the process is skirted, serious problems may arise when it is time to implement a group's recommendations. To encourage the development of recommendation reviews, we have designed a thorough procedure for conducting a recommendation review, which is included in Section III's "Facilitator Resources."

☞ **For more help, see Facilitator Resources, Section III**

• PROCEDURE III-1: Reviewing Recommendations

Task 4: Monitoring Interim and Implementation Work

The work of monitoring primarily involves having three things:

• A communications system through which you can find out what work has been done and what happened as a result

• A way to capture new ideas

• Decision checkpoints, and persons accountable, to ascertain whether modifications, corrections, or new strategies are needed

You, as facilitator, may handle the monitoring work, or it may be undertaken by someone from the client's staff. In either case, the work must be done.

In monitoring, you want to be timely in discovering any problems and be agile in responding. You also want to know reactions of others, whether your plans are falling into place, or if a new perspective or changed conditions warrant adaptation in the what or how of the work you're trying to accomplish.

If the group that does the original work is not the same group that implements the recommendations and decisions, then some formal link between groups should be established for the implementation stage so that the original group can stay in touch with the work as recommendations and decisions are carried out. This link might be a structural variation or an additional system or process. For example, some original group members might form an oversight evaluation team whose charge is (1) to look at the effectiveness of implementation, and (2) to provide feedback to managers in charge of the implementation. Or original group members can be assigned as consultants to teams that are implementing recommendations.

In addition, some methods should be plugged into the implementation phase so that the integrity and zeal of the original work will remain in force as implementation proceeds. If these allowances are not made, the original group may feel its work has been implemented in a watered-down or careless way and thus become cynical about group work—a mindset that will hinder the organization's movement toward using groups effectively.

Task 5: Identifying the Need for Additional Group Work

Finally, the group identifies additional needs for group work. These needs may result from any of the following:

- The group has been unable to successfully address some part of the work. Members are not completely satisfied that they have addressed some issue or aspect of the work.

- The group has uncovered problems that need to be solved that are related to, but are not included in, its charge.

- New information surfaces that needs to be integrated into the group's work.

- The group has been working against a deadline and ran out of time to do a part of the work.

- Group members were significantly deadlocked on some issues, and the resolution of these issues needs to be addressed elsewhere.

- Group members have identified some opportunities that would add significant value to their work, but they have not had the time and/or lack the necessary expertise to follow through on the opportunities.

The group may wish to recommend how the continued group work should be addressed: who should be involved, what the charge of that group should be, and an estimated length of time that it would take to do the additional work. In some cases, the group members may recommend that they themselves be charged to pursue some of the needed additional work. These work needs should be presented, along with the original recommendations, when the group presents its final recommendations review.

FACILITATOR RESOURCES

Meeting Records

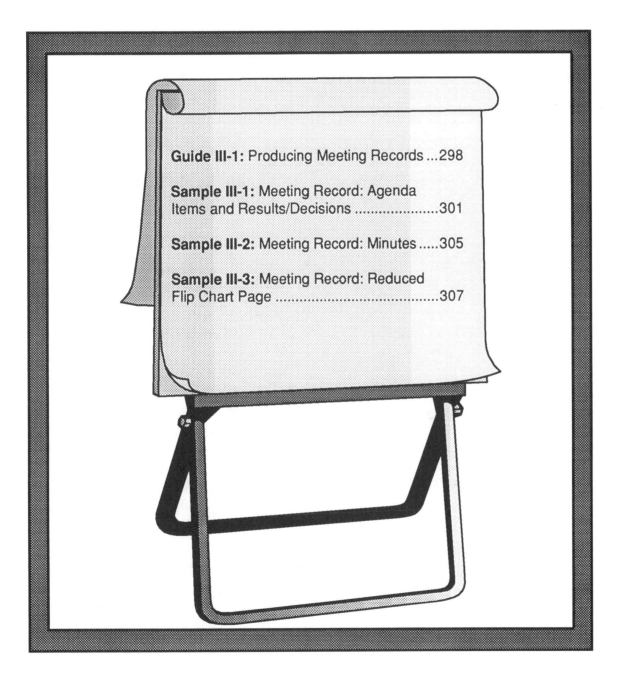

GUIDE III-1

Producing Meeting Records

About Meeting Records

Whereas the task group records its work in the form of the group memory, the regular meeting group records its outputs in a meeting record, or "minutes." Copies of the meeting record are then distributed to group members.

There is one critical function of the meeting minutes: to clearly convey what decisions were made and what subsequent action will be taken. Long-winded, near-verbatim recordings of minutes are seldom necessary and are indeed a waste of time for most meetings. A good record of a regular meeting is generally confined to one page; it is an action record, not a diary.

Before the start of the meeting, the meeting's leader should assign a person to record the minutes. The person chosen should be one in whom the leader has confidence that the decisions and actions taken in the meeting will be accurately represented.

Each regular meeting should have a form for the recording of the minutes. If the meetings take place regularly inside an organization, the form should follow an organization-approved format.

Meeting-Minutes Format Choices

One simple format is to record the agenda item and the decisions made, along with an action list of subsequent tasks and assignments related to the items under discussion at the meeting. This format is shown on the following page.

Other types of data that can be incorporated into meeting minutes include:

- Members present; members absent; others attending
- The leader of the meeting
- The time, place, and length of the meeting
- The next meeting date
- Summaries of discussions

Meeting-Minutes Format: The Simple Version

[Name of Meeting]	Date:	
Agenda Item:	Decision(s):	
1	1	
2	2	
3	3	
4	4	
Subsequent Actions	**Person(s) Responsible**	**Date Due**
1		
2		
3		
4		
5		
6		

TAKING REGULAR MEETING-MINUTES
IDEAS AND TIPS

➡ The task of taking the minutes (i.e., the role of minutes-taker) should be assigned before the start of the meeting.

➡ If the outcome of an agenda item seems unclear, or if it might be subject to multiple interpretations, the minutes-taker should ask the leader to clarify the decision.

➡ A good practice in the regular meeting is to review the decisions and subsequent actions before the group adjourns. One way to do this is to have the minutes-taker review his or her notes, summarizing the recorded information for the group and the leader. This method gives the leader and the group the opportunity to hear what is being put into the record of the meeting and immediately correct any misunderstandings.

➤ If discussions of issues are included in your minutes, keep them in summary form and related to the major points of the discussion. Avoid interpreting or describing the nature of the process of the discussion (e.g., "After a lengthy discussion . . .").

➤ Describe decisions accurately. Don't refer to decisions as "the group decided" if it is really the meeting leader who made the decision.

➤ For most regular meetings conducted today, there is no need to delay the distribution of minutes. Minutes can be taken on a laptop computer, summarized at the end of the meeting, and printed immediately so that members can take copies with them when they go. An alternative to using a laptop is to simply write the decisions and actions on a meeting-minutes form and then photocopy the minutes at the close of the meeting.

➤ If the meeting is particularly crucial and it is anticipated that the information will go out to a wider audience, it might be wise to delay the distribution of minutes until the leader has had a chance to carefully review the minutes and check the language used to describe the decisions.

➤ Rotating the taking of minutes may not be such a good practice, even though some meeting experts suggest doing so. It is absolutely essential that meeting minutes accurately reflect the decisions made in the meeting and do so in a style and manner that the leader of the regular meeting prefers. Minutes-taking is usually done best by people who are in close "sync" with the leader, have good language skills, and are trusted by the group to accurately record the data and conclusions of the meeting.

➤ A flip chart can be used to display the key decisions and actions in the regular meeting. The chart can be reviewed immediately prior to the end of the meeting to check its accuracy and make any final modifications.

➤ There are meeting leaders who keep minutes-taking especially simple by keeping their own handwritten notes and distributing copies of the notes at the end of the meeting. This strategy isn't for every meeting or every leader, but it does work well in some cases.

➤ Tape recorders should be avoided in all but the most official of regular meetings, such as official public reviews or hearings.

SAMPLE III-1

Meeting Record: Agenda Items and Results/Decisions

MEETING RECORD

Divisional Reorganization Steering Group

February 27, 1997

Purpose of the Meeting: To prepare for the March 17 meeting of the Reorganization Task Force

Outcomes for the Meeting: We intended to leave this meeting with:

- Instructions to the vision-writing team for final revisions in the Division Vision Statement

- Approved-of changes to be put in revised mission statement for the LACOE Division

- The names of the work groups that will be formed, a broad charge for each work group, and leaders or a process for selecting leaders for each group

Meeting Leader:

Meeting Facilitator(s):

Members Attending:

NAME	TITLE

Others Attending:

Members Not Attending:

Primary Decision Method: Consultative to leader

Date: Thurs., February 27th   **Time:** 10:00 a.m. to 4:00 p.m.   **Location:** County Office 110A

Scheduled Time			Actual Time		
Start	Stop	Total Hours	Start	Stop	Total Hours
10:00 a.m.	4:00 p.m.	6 hrs.	10:15 a.m	4:15 p.m.	5.5 hrs.

Meeting Agenda		
#	**Agenda Item, Intended Outcomes**	**Results, Decisions**
1.	Announcements • Any news updates regarding change, instructions, data for the vision review • Attendance: who's here when • Ground rules	One person absent. Ground rule is "Support any decision made in your absence."
2.	Agenda review and review of previous meeting of task force • Approved agenda	Agenda approved. Last meeting reviewed.
3.	Review drafts of the vision statement, respond to any questions regarding the vision document • Understanding of the items included in drafts of the vision document	Group members each read draft materials; question period continued until everyone understood the data.
4.	Steering group recommendations review of vision statements • Preferred choices for one-liner statement • Strengths and weaknesses of vision draft • Instructions for further revision • Tim's approval of changes	One-liner vision statement selected: "Expect the best." Noted strengths and weaknesses of vision draft. *Strengths:* ◆ Guiding principles ◆ Value statements ◆ Good content

(Continued)

Meeting Agenda *(Continued)*

#	Agenda Item, Intended Outcomes	Results, Decisions
4.	Steering group recommendations review of vision statements *(Continued)*	*Suggestions:* ☞ Connect it better. ☞ Include short two-page vision in guiding principles. ☞ Fewer values. ☞ Be less wordy, more succinct. ☞ Clarify audience. ☞ Eliminate repetition. ☞ Organize it. ☞ Have it read as "one voice." ☞ Don't hurry to get it pretty. ☞ Text should speak to "Expect the best."
5.	Mission statement revision • List of suggested changes that are agreed to by the steering group • Charge to complete mission statement revision and scheduled time to do the work: Date by which draft to be submitted to Tim for review • Who will review mission statement and vision previous to 3/17	Mission statement revised as follows: "We provide instructional programs, consultation, and professional development to school districts, their students with special needs, and families in Los Angeles County."
6.	**LUNCH**	
7.	Calendar of meetings for the remainder of the school year: Task Force Steering Group 1st Meeting of Team Leaders • Dates for task force and steering group meetings for remainder of year • Suggested steps for work improvement teams • Things to include in agenda for team leaders • Due date for first set of change recommendations	Not completed.

(Continued)

Meeting Agenda (Concluded)

#	Agenda Item, Intended Outcomes	Results, Decisions
8.	Presentation of data from various groups forwarding change data; keep on, more of, less of: LACOE Administrators Staff Development Group Task Force • Themes of the data identified to date • Additions to data from review of district directors' data	Themes of the data were presented, then categorized into clusters which would make for a work improvement team. Group members then used a decision matrix to arrive at the numerical values appearing beside each item in the attached "Work Improvement Teams" document.
9.	Identification of potential work groups, evaluation of alternatives, selection of alternatives • Number of work groups to start with • Criteria for selection of work groups • Names of the work groups and a broad charge for each • A leader for each group or a process for selecting the leader • Membership and member selection process • Schedule for development of recommendations • Support to group leaders	The work groups were prioritized using the decision matrix method. Criteria used to select the groups and weights provided for each group were: • Speed (can finish by 6/30/97)—weight $2x$ • "Big Pow" significant impact—weight $2x$ • Within control of special ed division—weight $3x$ Names, leaders, member selection process, schedule not completed.
10.	Next steps and action list review • Clear on steps to complete vision, mission, work group formation, and agenda for 3/17 meeting of task force	1. "Tweak last statements"—Gloria, by 3/4. 2. "Mail vision, values, gp's to six people (Gigi, Joan, Jenine, Angie, Dana, Walt)"—Vicki, by 3/5. 3. Develop review form—Tom, by 3/4.

SAMPLE III-2

Meeting Record: Minutes

ORGANIZATIONAL CULTURE DESIGN TEAM MINUTES
October 27, 1997

MEMBERS PRESENT

Ron	Rod	Sam
Mo	Denise	Paul
Kari	Scott	Doug
Joe	Al	Woody
Jessica	Arlene	Dave Jamieson

MEMBERS ABSENT

John
Jack
Dave
Mike
Bob
Gil

VALUE STATEMENT

Captain Bruce Kidder discussed how he presented the Value Statement to West Side Station. Six commanders were chosen to make presentations to the General Staff Meeting on October 4 at GHRC North, Executive Conference Room.

Interpretation of the value statement policy varies in different stations/divisions, based upon the commander's presentation and enforcement. It is their obligation to support, get on board, reemphasize, and internalize. Focus on specific "happenings" to talk about/command, place no blame, use the approach of here's how we can progress, and believe it.

FUTURE MEANS

A. Push drive for commanders to encourage subsequent steps, ideas, recognitions, and commendations:

  • Generate ideas—what can we do/others do; how to implement.

  • Find a way to encourage commanders' operationalizing!

B. How to get things happening—what role do we play?

  • Office of the Sheriff—Executive Staff emulate role for others in their everyday performance.

  • Command staff, captains, lieutenants, and sergeants—immediate supervisors will have influence on troops.

  • Deputies perceive "succeed vs. survive."

  • Incorporate values in E.R.'s; identify people who are living specific values; use reward approach, i.e., Station/Commander's Award.

  • Board of Deputy Chiefs' meetings—emphasis, don't overdo—needs balance. Enforce, enforce—"You need to practice it yourself." Open, honest communication/risk. Need a buy-in by all Deputy Chiefs—needs to be discussed at a Board of DC's meeting.

TASK GROUPS

The four task groups need to be updated. Report on group meetings and task plans by next meeting on November 13, 1997.

UNIT REPRESENTATIVES

Design Team members/unit representatives were reassigned (see attached list). Members are to contact station/division unit representatives and commanders to confirm appropriate personnel.

NEXT DESIGN TEAM MEETING

  • Meet with the Board of Deputy Chiefs/Design Team meeting November 13, 1997, 9:00 a.m. to 4:00 p.m., Main Conference Room East.

  • Focus on issues we all agree on and have the power to work on (identify issues).

  • Discuss the commanders' communication/visibility.

Prepared by Arlene S.

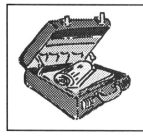

SAMPLE III-3

Meeting Record: Reduced Flip Chart Page

PILOTS

1) GROUP = CROSS FUNCTIONAL, CONTINUITY CONSISTENT IN PROCESS,

2) PURPOSE - QUALITY CHECK ON CONTENT NOT PROCESS NOT A DECISION CHECK OR DESIGN REVIEW

3) TIME - AFTER EXEC OVERVIEW BEFORE

4) CHARACTERISTICS -
   - EXPERIENTIAL
   - METHOD ENUMERATED IN CONTRACT
   - DEFINED → BOILER PLATE

5) ACCURACY -
   - "I AM SATISFIED"
   - 98%

6) LEADERS' GUIDES - WHO DOES IT?
   - EXPENSE/TIME IN CONTRACT
   GUIDLINES FOR FORMAT

FACILITATOR RESOURCES

Reviewing Recommendations

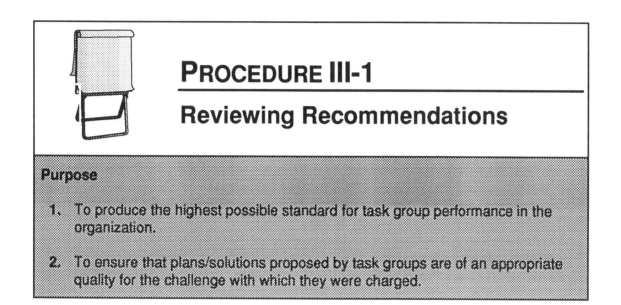

PROCEDURE III-1

Reviewing Recommendations

Purpose

1. To produce the highest possible standard for task group performance in the organization.

2. To ensure that plans/solutions proposed by task groups are of an appropriate quality for the challenge with which they were charged.

Summary Description: The Need for This Procedure

Most organizations do a lousy job reviewing recommendations from task groups or, for that matter, even reviewing the work of individuals. In many cases, management reviews of task group work decimate the work, leaving members with the feeling that *anything* they do will be reduced to virtually nothing. And oftentimes, management-directed "peer reviews" don't really produce a more desirable outcome. Again, members are left with a feeling of futility—that whatever they do will get shot down.

When the authorized decision makers in an organization do a poor job handling the recommendations of task groups, they inadvertently discredit the specific task group. Even more costly is the effect that such mishandling has on the total organization. People begin to question the value of working in groups, and groups are set up to fail before they have their first meeting, because no one believes that the group can really make a difference.

A much-needed role for the task group facilitator is to be the "protector" of the ideas that are generated by the task group. To successfully play this role, the group facilitator must take these steps:

    a) Set up a rational, fair, and thoughtful review of the recommendations of the task group when the group is initially charged.

    b) Prepare the reviewers of the recommendations to play a productive role in the recommendations review process.

c) Clarify the decision path that will be followed with respect to acting upon and authorizing the work of the group.

d) Help the task group set up their presentation of recommendations, and have them actually rehearse the presentation.

To perform these functions, the professional group facilitator will first clarify the decision path to be followed with key decision makers **before** the group even begins meeting (see Procedure I-2: Developing a Group Charter). Decisions should be made with the task group leader and an organizational sponsor of the work as to how recommendations will be reviewed, when, and by whom.

If the organization is truly serious about using groups successfully, it will recognize the need to handle official decisions well and be willing to commit to a training design for managers and management groups on the effective review of decisions. The **Method** section offers a rough outline for such a training design.

The most effective and the healthiest way to review recommendations is to do so at the regular management and decision-making meetings. Guide III-2, which follows this procedure, focuses on preparing for and delivering presentations of recommendations reviews at regular meetings.

When to Use the Procedure

- Initially, during the charge phase of the task group

- For groups charged with a complex task: at specific stages of their work, before moving from one stage to another

- When the task group has completed its work and is ready to seek official approval of the recommendations

Participants

Number: Varies according to the activity

Type: —Members of regular management review groups

—Sometimes, larger groups, such as entire staffs

—Special interest groups such as union boards

—The members of the task group themselves

—The task group sponsor and the task group leader

Resources *(checkmarks indicate recommended equipment)*

✔ Flip chart and markers

Facilitator(s)

The facilitator plays multiple roles. He or she arranges for meetings of the task group leader and organizational sponsor, coaches the task group on preparing the presentation, and, during a training phase, facilitates recommendations reviews at regular management meetings, coaching the meeting leader ahead of time on how to handle the recommendations review.

Time

About 1 hour before the group begins meeting with the organizational sponsor, the task group leader, and a key person who will authorize decisions

Approximately 1 hour for a task group recommendation at a regular meeting

Method

The following steps describe a method for facilitating the establishment of a quality review process for task group recommendations in any given organization (the method assumes that a thorough review process for such recommendations has not yet been established):

1. Identify the person who has the ultimate authority to approve or disapprove recommendations from the task group.

2. Meet individually with that person and schedule a date for the recommendations review at the appropriate meeting of his or her managers. The management "sponsor" for the work of the task group should also attend this "pre-meeting" with the decision maker.

3. Go over the review process with the decision maker (see Step 7 below) and gain his or her approval for the process. Make any suggested modifications in the process and agree on an approximate amount of time that the review will take.

4. Provide the decision maker with a list of recommendations review questions and request that he or she distribute them to the regular meeting members at the meeting before the recommendations review. Offer to attend the meeting in order to explain the process and the questions.

   Ask the decision maker if any members of the regular meeting should be individually briefed prior to the recommendations review.

5. Schedule and conduct individual briefings with anyone whom the decision maker or members of the task group feel should be briefed.

6. Meet with the task group to prepare for the recommendations review. The group leader takes the group through the following steps:

(a) Review the recommendations of the group. Share any feedback obtained from individual briefings and consider whether or not to make modifications in the recommendations. Agree upon the recommendations that will be presented.

(b) Review the list of questions for recommendations reviews, and organize the presentation.

(c) Determine how you will present the data (e.g., on flip charts, overheads, charts).

(d) Assign roles for the presentation and any assignments necessary to prepare for the presentation.

7. Attend the decision maker's scheduled regular meeting and make the presentation. The following are recommended steps for conducting the review at the meeting. The leader of the regular meeting (i.e., the authorized decision maker) should be responsible for following the process, not the facilitator, sponsor, or task group leader.

To begin, the task group leader and/or team members should do the following:

(a) Present the process that the group used to arrive at its recommendations.

(b) Answer any questions about the process.

(c) Present the recommendations of the task group.

(d) Answer any questions about the actual recommendations.

Then the process is completed in this way:

(e) The regular meeting leader asks meeting members to offer their evaluative comments on the recommendations presented.

(f) Following the evaluation discussion, the meeting leader authorizes action on approved recommendations, rejects any that were disapproved, and delegates any further work.

GUIDE III-2

Preparing and Presenting Recommendations

The Purpose of This Guide

This guide's purposes are to support the group in preparing the delivery of their recommendations to a body of reviewers, and to provide the reviewers with cues for thoroughly reviewing the recommendations.

Why This Guide Is Important

Most organizations do not do a very good job of thoroughly and fairly reviewing recommendations developed by a group that has been charged with a task. Thus, shallow solutions or "group-think" may become a dangerous operating norm. If people are to come to respect the work of groups, the quality of the work that occurs in the group must be held to a high standard. The guidelines suggested here offer one way to bring the expected quality of group work to a higher standard.

How to Use the Guide

Have the guide questions available to the task group when it is preparing its report or recommendations so that members can respond proactively to as many points as possible. The questions should also be made available to the group that will be reviewing the task group recommendations so that they can use the questions as guides for formulating their own questions of the presenting group or individual.

PREPARING AND DELIVERING
A RECOMMENDATIONS REVIEW
QUESTIONS FOR CONSIDERATION*

A. Relationship to the Original Charge

A1   What was the original charge of the group? Was it clear?

A2   If there were departures from the original charge, how did those occur and were they authorized adequately?

---

*Recommendations review questions suggested by William Daniels were used as source material for this list. See William R. Daniels, *Group Power II: A Manager's Guide to Conducting Regular Meetings,* pp. 63–64, Mill Valley, CA, 1987: Amercian Consulting and Training.

A3   Did the group remain within the boundaries of the original charge?

A4   Did the group appropriately look at the systems, processes, and procedures related to its work that are necessary for successful completion of the charge?

B. The Sufficiency of the Data Base Used to Construct Recommendations

B1   Were the best available experts used, given the complexity of the task?

B2   Were outside experts consulted? If not, would such consultation have been feasible and appropriate?

B3   Were available internal experts who were not members of the team consulted?

B4   Was sufficient "implementer" expertise present within the group? That is, were there people in the group who had sufficient knowledge of how the recommendations would be received when "the rubber hits the road"? Were people involved who are closest to the work?

B5   Was there sufficient group time, and were there enough resources devoted to establishing the data base prior to the generation of alternatives?

B6   Were appropriate and available alternative data bases searched for information? (For example: associations, professional literature, competitors, benchmarking studies, best practices reports, past work of analogous individuals, groups within the organization)

B7   Was the level of effort devoted to constructing the data base appropriate to the complexity of the task with which the group was charged?

B8   Did the group gather and confront any unpleasant data related to the task, including information suggesting its own participation in the problems?

B9   What methods were used to prevent the group from becoming too insular in its thinking?

C. The Adequacy of the Process Used to Generate Alternatives and Make Decisions

C1   Was the time devoted to generating the recommendations sufficient in relationship to the complexity of the task?

C2   Was the desired outcome(s) or future state clearly identified?

C3   Was a specific process designed and used to arrive at the recommendations?

C4   What methods were used to ensure that alternatives were creative and fresh?

C5   What decision mode was primarily used—absolute consensus, modified consensus, consultative consensus, consultative, or voting? What is the level of group consensus with respect to the recommendations presented?

C6   Were key problems adequately defined and confronted?

C7   Were specific criteria generated upon which to consider alternatives generated? Were the criteria weighted or prioritized?

C8   Was a variety of methods used to generate the alternatives? (For example, group brainstorming, research between meetings, interviews with outside experts)

C9   Did the group have adequate support and facilitation in working through conflicts?

C10 Do some of the recommended alternatives represent common ground or integrated solutions that resulted from doing the work necessary to resolve conflicts?

C11 To what extent did group members feel they were participating as equals?

C12 Were stakeholders thoroughly identified? To what degree were they kept informed of the work of the group? What was the rationale for informing or not informing stakeholders?

D. Consideration of Issues Related to Implementation

D1   Were past experiences related to the task considered?

D2   Was the current culture within which the alternatives would be implemented considered? Are the recommendations consistent with the present values base, or is some departure from the values base indicated? Current policy? History? Tradition?

D3   Were the effects upon the key stakeholders related to the task considered?

D4   Were preferred alternatives tested for probable consequences upon implementation? What are the probable roadblocks to implementation? Are recommendations presented for dealing with those roadblocks?

D5   What changes will be required in present structures, systems, processes, or procedures in order to implement the recommendations? Are these changes feasible and does the implementation timeline allow for making the changes?

D6   Is a specific schedule for implementation presented, and if so, does it reflect the considerations above?

D7   Were interviewing or focus group techniques used to test preferred alternatives?

D8   Are the resources necessary to implement the recommendations clear? Are the resources available?

D9   Are all recommendations within the control of the authority of the person reviewing the recommendations? Will other approvals be necessary prior to implementation?

D10 Is it clear who will be responsible for implementing the recommendations? Are recommendations included on who should be accountable for implementation? Have these people been consulted regarding their views on the adequacy of the alternatives?

D11 Is there a need for an implementation group to be charged with implementing the recommendations?

D12 How will the handoff or transition from the task group to the implementer(s) be handled?

D13 What aspects of the work of the group still need to be addressed? Who should be charged with completing this work by when?

D14 Were both the benefits and drawbacks of the proposed solutions presented?

D15 Are the action steps required to implement the solutions clearly spelled out with specific schedules for implementation?

GUIDE III-3

Communicating With Others

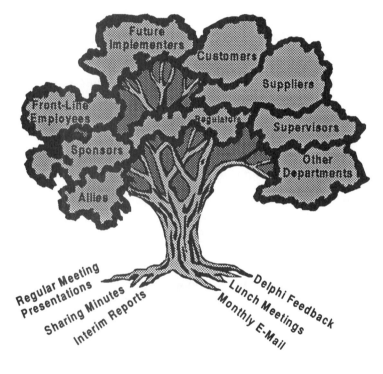

About This Guide

Many groups never see their ideas and recommendations carried through to implementation because they run up against the proverbial "not invented here" brick wall.

Disturbing as it is to the keen rational mind, many people are not as interested in seeing the best ideas implemented as they are in feeling as if they were a part of the process of arriving at the conclusions that are being advanced.

Another way of looking at it is that many people just don't *understand* why the alternatives being proposed really are thoughtful and intelligent, because they have not witnessed the development of those alternatives and have not observed the processes that were used to arrive at certain conclusions.

| Data Collection | Stakeholder Review | Data Analysis | Stakeholder Review | Alternatives Generation | Stakeholder Review | Alternatives Selection | Stakeholder Review |

Quality communication needs to take place with stakeholders during the process of working with the group **and** in the "follow-up" phase when certain recommendations are approved and ready to be implemented. The nature of the communications may vary considerably according to which phase of work the group is in. Before the group has completed its charge and is working to either collect data, generate alternatives, or analyze and select alternatives, stakeholder communications should be as active as possible. Meetings can be held with stakeholder groups, and they can actually contribute data to the process. Or stakeholder groups can review the group at the completion of each phase of the work. A time period for stakeholder communication can be set aside following each specific phase.

The review process need not always be so systematic or calculated. Yet some amount of planning should be done during both Phase I: Preparation and Phase II: Working With the Group to allow for effective communications with stakeholders. A number of key planning questions need to be asked:

- With whom do we need to communicate?
- Who will be responsible for communicating with that individual or group?
- When should the communication take place? How often? What intervals?
- How will the communication take place? What will be the nature of the communication?

The methods of communication can be quite varied. Here are some different ways that groups can communicate with various constituencies or stakeholders:

1. Groups can contribute data or brainstorm ideas to be further considered by the stakeholder group.

2. Reports can be written and then sent out to others. Follow-up meetings can be held to answer questions and receive feedback.

3. Group members can make presentations at regular meetings of certain stakeholder groups.

4. Informal lunch discussions can be scheduled with key stakeholders at occasional, planned intervals.

5. Written feedback processes can be used; that is, a report or document can be sent out for review requesting written feedback. All the feedback can then be documented and sent out again for further response (e.g., prioritization).

6. There can be planned one-on-one meetings at critical points. Each member of the team is assigned certain individuals with whom the member will meet regularly to communicate the work of the group.

7. E-mail messages or faxes can be sent on a regular basis.

8. Interim reports can be constructed specifically for distribution to others.

9. Meeting minutes can be posted on bulletin boards or at key locations (e.g., above the drinking fountain).

10. Carefully planned large-group meetings can be held to announce the results of the work that is to be implemented.

When the group has agreed on the solutions it is recommending for implementation, it needs to plan for the implementation—or at least recommend how the recommendations will be implemented. An important part of this planning is to devise communications strategies through which the work of the group will be adopted or put into action. The nature and detail of the communications strategies will vary depending upon the complexity of the group charge. One example might be the following implementation "communication plan" recommended by a group that met to design a new purchasing work process.

New Purchasing Work Process Communication Plan

(a) Memo generated from president and director of purchasing announcing meeting of all department heads to review the new purchasing work process.

(b) Corporate services director and Purchasing Work Process Review Team leader present the new process and schedule for implementation to all purchasing agents at a special meeting.

(c) Corporate services director, Purchasing Work Process Review Team leader, two purchasing agents, and two department heads make a panel presentation on the new Purchasing Work Process at the June managers' meeting.

(d) Survey feedback form assessing the effectiveness of the new process distributed to all purchasing agents and department heads in September.

(e) Revisions in process communicated at October managers' meeting.

FACILITATOR RESOURCES

Implementation Planning

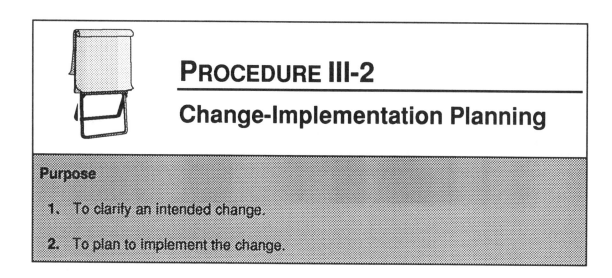

PROCEDURE III-2

Change-Implementation Planning

Purpose

1. To clarify an intended change.

2. To plan to implement the change.

Summary Description

This procedure assumes that a group has been working for some time on certain identified changes. The process enables project or team leaders and management decision makers to clarify exactly what still needs to change, how the changes will be implemented, who will be responsible for each change, and what resources are necessary to fully implement the intended changes.

When to Use the Procedure

- Following a period of concentrated activity during which needed changes have been identified. This initial activity is often carried out by design teams or specialized work groups.

- When organizational decision makers are immediately available to make decisions.

Participants

Number: Five to nine participants

Type: Decision makers who control resources; team or project staff who have been working on designing needed changes

Resources *(checkmarks indicate recommended equipment)*

- ✔ Flip chart and markers
- ✔ Storyboards
- ✔ Note cards, pushpins, and other storyboard tools, if storyboards are used

Facilitator(s)

One person acts as a process facilitator for the activity. This can be a professional facilitator or a group member who is skilled enough to focus on process rather than the content of the decisions.

Time

The agenda below can be accomplished in 4 to 6 hours.

Method

1. Inclusion activity options:

   (a) Have the group create a "Proud of" list and a "Sorry About" list. First, list the major accomplishments of the work of the team or the project and prioritize them. Then do the same for regrets.

   (b) The same as above, but use the list headings "Accomplishments" and "Remaining Concerns."

   (c) Make a timeline of the course of the project and major events, milestones, and notable occurrences. Place large note cards on the floor, marking the time in weeks, months, and/or years. Have participants fill out smaller note cards for events, milestones, occurrences. Then post the cards, using pushpins or tape. Flip chart pages and Post-it notes can also be used.

2. List the changes that need more work to be fully implemented. For example: "To track the progress of graduates and feed outcome data back to practicing educators and vocational rehabilitation personnel." Or: "To outsource our present sales function."

   Note: No more than seven such changes should be tackled in one implementation-planning session.

3. Clarify the current state and the preferred future state for each identified change. An example follows:

Establish Graduate Tracking System

Present State	Future State
Little or no graduate outcome data available to practicing school-age personnel.	Annual data report published in July tracking progress of minimum 20% of graduates out of school 3 to 5 years.
No mechanism for practicing personnel to adjust planned programs on basis of graduate outcome data.	Special education directors (60%), local area vocational administrators, and training personnel in both agencies receive in-service "train the trainers" on options for feeding back data to local implementers.
No clear assignment of personnel responsible for tracking graduate outcome data.	Outcomes-tracking team of one educator and one vocational rehabilitation specialist allocated .20 FTE each to oversee data collection process in each educational regional planning area. Thirty data collection technicians hired statewide to work with local teams. One full-time person oversees entire program statewide.

4. Clarify the strategies that will be necessary to achieve the preferred future state, and assign those who will be responsible for implementation of both the overall change and each key strategy. The first assignment should be for the persons with overall responsibility for the change. In the subsequent discussions, other group members act as consultants to the person(s) with overall responsibility for the change. Only key "springboard, first-start" strategies need be planned for implementation at this time.

Change and Strategies	Person(s) Responsible (First is lead)
Establish Graduate Tracking System	Jan V., Ted R.
Looking closely at Connecticut and Oregon systems, produce report and recommendations.	Bill T.
Establish .50 FTE state-level position and secure 3-year funding for position.	Jan V., Ted R.
Develop 5-year proposal for 80 to 20 split funding project, leveraging available vocational rehabilitation funds.	Jan V., Ted R., Bill T.

5. Establish the processes and mechanisms by which the change will be managed. For example:

A transition-implementation team will be formed to meet for 2 hours each month for six months and quarterly for one year thereafter to oversee this change and others we have agreed to. Members of the team will include the DVR Director,

Assistant Director, Special Education Director, SEA person in charge of transition, and the person hired to oversee implementation of the tracking system.

or

A monthly teleconference will be held to oversee implementation. [Players same as above.] Three face-to-face meetings will be held at six-month intervals.

or

The implementation of the strategies will be managed within the monthly management meeting at DVR. The DVR Director, Special Education Director, and Transition Specialist will meet at least bi-monthly prior to reviews of the project at the monthly DVR management meeting.

and

Three times a year, strategy progress updates will be published in the statewide SEA newsletter that goes out to all school districts. Similar updates will be published at least three times in the Director's monthly letter that goes to local DVR administrators.

6. Clarify who will be responsible for seeing that each implementation process is carried out.

7. Identify the resources that will be needed to execute the change and who will be responsible for providing them. Resources should be specified in time and/or money. A sample is shown below.

Resource Support	Time and/or Money	Person(s) Responsible (First is lead)
Best Practice report from three states	20 days	Bill T.
Statewide coordination position .5 FTE	$24,000 $6,000	Jan V., Ted R.
Produce 80 to 20 cost share plan	10 days	Sandy P., Jill R.
Computer programming subcontract	Design—5 days $15,000	Bill T., Ted R.

8. Using a "What, When, Who" action list format, list any next steps for moving toward implementation and who will be responsible for each step.

Notes

1. You can use either flip charts or storyboards to facilitate the meeting. If you opt for storyboards, use one board to clarify the present state and the desired future state. Use another board to complete the remainder of the planning; make "header cards" for "Strategies, Processes, and Mechanisms," "Resource Support," and "Person(s) Responsible."

2. If the planning of specific responsibilities is especially critical, you can use Procedure III-3: Responsibility Charting to plan specific strategies, activities, and persons responsible. The responsibility-charting procedure, though tedious, produces a more thorough list of the specific responsibilities of the various players.

3. Change-implementation meetings absolutely require the presence of persons who have control of the resources necessary to implement the change. Do not attempt to plan the specific implementation of the change strategy without these people present.

4. Often this type of meeting implies a transition or "handoff" of responsibility from a design group or project team to established management. It may be useful to plan an activity that dramatizes this handoff. A transition "ceremony" helps the original group let go of past attachments and makes clear the new management responsibilities for the change.

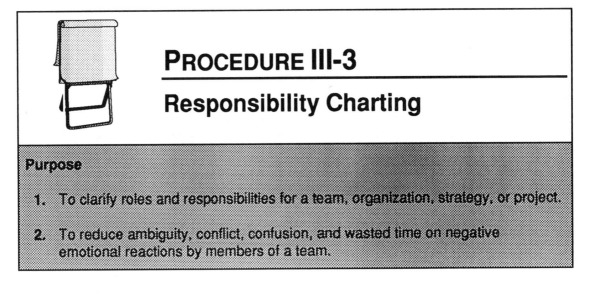

PROCEDURE III-3

Responsibility Charting

Purpose

1. To clarify roles and responsibilities for a team, organization, strategy, or project.

2. To reduce ambiguity, conflict, confusion, and wasted time on negative emotional reactions by members of a team.

Summary Description

Responsibility charting clarifies who is responsible for what on any given task, activity, decision, or behavior. More importantly, the distinctive type of responsibility is clearly specified. A list of tasks, activities, decisions, or behaviors is made on the vertical axis of a matrix. Then the responsibility classifications are listed across the horizontal axis of the matrix. Team members proceed through each of the tasks, determining who should have which type of responsibility and filling in the cells of the matrix (Melcher, 1967; Beckhard and Harris, 1987).

Responsibility charting is one of the most flexible tools available to the consultant, facilitator, or team leader. It can be used in innumerable ways, such as:

- To organize a new team to get a job done, specifying who is needed to do what.

- To estimate who and how many staff are needed to perform a given task.

- To chart decisions. Levels of decision-making authority can be clarified using the chart.

- To prioritize functions in an organization, as shown under **Method** below.

- To unravel power and authority issues when two or more team members are engaged in power struggles. A facilitator usually helps members open communication lines, express what has been unsaid, and identify what has been impeding their past efforts.

- To contribute toward a quality management plan or plan of operation in detailed proposals or requests for funding.

When to Use the Procedure

- When a new team is forming

- When a group is having difficulties with role ambiguities or conflicts in a given situation

- When a project or strategy is being planned

- Immediately prior to or following an organizational restructuring

- As part of the process when a new job is designed or job descriptions are reviewed

- A few weeks following major activity on any task that involves change

Participants

Number: No more than nine people at any one time

Type:
— Persons who will have responsibilities to carry out relative to a change, task, strategy, project, or job

— A leader who will be responsible for approving decisions of the group

— All group members or a selected task group of members, who then present their recommendations to the entire group

— (Optional.) A stenographer to capture details that are too time-consuming for you to record on charts as you go along

Resources *(checkmarks indicate recommended equipment)*

✔ Flip chart and markers

Facilitator(s)

This is a procedure that requires facilitation from a neutral party who is removed from the responsibilities that are being charted. The team leader is responsible for the product. The facilitator should be responsible for teaching the team the process.

Time

Responsibility charting is best done in 2-hour segments, using as many segments as needed to clarify the task.

Method

1. The facilitator introduces the responsibility classifiers to the group. The leader of the group or the facilitator can specify beforehand which classifiers should be used; or team members themselves can select which classifiers to use.

Responsibility-Charting Classifiers

Classifier	Description	When to Use
OR: Overall Responsibility	Overall responsibility indicates that a person needs to maintain an overall responsibility, even if he or she did not initiate the task and does not spend the most time on the task. There must be a good reason why authority on the task needs to stay with this person.	On extremely high-visibility or dangerous tasks. When a person's job would be in jeopardy if a mistake were made here. CAUTION: Use sparingly, only when necessary. ORs can lead to accountability confusion.
PR: Primary Responsibility	Primary responsibility indicates that a person is in charge of a specific task, activity, decision, or action. This person has the main responsibility for the successful completion of the task. Usually he or she either (a) clearly knows the most about the activity, (b) has initiated the activity, or (c) spends the most time on the activity.	Always use this classification for each and every item on the chart.
MA: Must Approve	A "must-approve" function means that this person must grant approval before any significant action is taken or a decision is made regarding this task or activity. An approval function means that consensus is required between this person and the person with the OR and PR before any action is given the time necessary for consensus.	When two key people involved have had a history of power struggles related to the activity. When the task is critical and consensus is essential for success or error is highly dangerous. CAUTION: Use discretion. Many approval functions can be an indication that there are low levels of trust in a group.

(Continued)

Responsibility-Charting Classifiers *(Concluded)*

Classifier	Description	When to Use
SR: Specific Responsibility	This means that someone has a responsibility for a specific "piece" or part of the task. This part is critical to the successful execution of the task or will require a significant amount of time and will not be done by the person with primary responsibility. The nature of the specific responsibility should be clearly identified in notes that accompany the chart.	When there are key functions that need to be performed by someone other than the person with primary responsibility. When you want to divide a task into parts and have different people responsible for different subtasks.
MC: Must Consult	A must-consult function means that this person must be consulted on any significant action that is taken or decision that is made. This person does not have to agree with the action that is finally taken but has to provide input toward the decision. It is up to the PR-holder to consult with this person and to initiate contact.	When someone has expertise or data that is critical to quality execution of the task. When someone is working on a task that is interdependent with this one. When someone has a strong desire to be involved.
MI: Must Inform	This means that a person must be informed immediately following the completion of any significant task. The classification is reserved for particularly critical information functions. It should not be used for all information or to the point where the designation becomes so undiscriminating as to be useless.	When not being informed might cause severe embarrassment to the person or cause problems for the activity related to the person. When someone requests to be informed because he or she specifically wants to have the information out of some key interest or necessity. Do not include people here who need to be informed just for the sake of keeping them up to date.

These are the responsibility classifications that we have found most useful in our work with groups. Here are some others that can also be used:

- **Operating Responsibility**—Used synonymously with Primary Responsibility above

- **General Responsibility**—Used synonymously with Overall Responsibility above.

- **May be consulted**—Implies that consultation is not mandatory. Is at discretion of person with PR.

- **Must be notified**—Synonymous with "Must Inform"

Here is one example of a responsibility chart with one cell completed.

Outsource the Sales Function						
Responsibility	Jack	Nan	Sergio	Bill	Ted	Beth
Identify available contractors	MC	SR	PR		MI	MA

The alternate format is shown below.

Outsource the Sales Function						
Responsibility	Overall Respons.	Primary Respons.	Specific Respons.	Must Consult	Must Inform	Must Approve
Identify available contractors		Sergio	Nan	Jack	Ted	Beth

2. List all the items to be charted. These may be goals, objectives, critical success factors, tasks, decisions, actions, broad functions, or even departments or organizational units. This step can be done either with individual interviews prior to a meeting or with the entire group involved in a team setting.

   (Optional.) Following the above, you can insert an analysis step during which the data is studied and problem/discussion areas are identified for discussion.

3. Have members practice with a few simple functions in the organization that are clearly understood. Or practice with a fictional example of some particular task that is separate from the work at hand (e.g., planning a party).

4. Ask members to identify their present responsibilities with regard to a given item, and/or what level of responsibility they think they should have.

5. Select a group to take a first stab at coming up with an agreed-upon set of responsibility definitions. The group should be composed of fewer than nine members. It can include selected individuals who are most familiar with the data to be charted and/or who have the analytic/managerial skills to best manipulate the data, or it can comprise all members of a given group or work team. You can use the activity as a team-building intervention if all team members are involved. For each item, the "PR" is handled first. If the person with the PR is in the group, then he or she can become the leader in determining what the remaining responsibility classifications will be. The group proceeds through each item, charting each type of responsibility.

6. After the charting is completed, conduct an action-planning session during which members list all the new tasks that need to be done to implement the new agreed-upon plan. Specific actions, persons responsible, and due dates should be charted.

Notes

1. Again, the tool is remarkably flexible. It can be used very quickly "on the spot" to establish clear responsibility for some task, action, or decision, or it can be used as an elaborate and comprehensive organizational intervention.

2. When introducing the process, explain to the group that at times it may be tedious and laborious and at other times, tensions may rise because the group will discuss issues of power and responsibility that have been delayed too long. Suggest that although this is not the most "uplifting" process tool, you believe they will agree that the time and emotional energy will pay off in much more defined, less ambiguous activities that are far more likely to succeed.

3. Making up flip chart pages during this procedure can be cumbersome, so prepare several pages ahead of time. This is one procedure that works well using a laptop computer and an overhead display device. The form can be created in table form as a template to be used during the session, with the data immediately entered in the cells. This cuts down considerably the clerical time required to transpose data from flip charts for distribution to the group. If you try this procedure, use a recorder who is familiar with both the responsibility-charting procedure itself and the flip charts and/or computer software used. The negotiations involved in the process require the facilitator to concentrate on the group dynamics, and having to deal with equipment can get in the way of the interactions.

4. Some software applications will let you organize table or spreadsheet data according to name or responsibility classifier. If you use such software, you can make printouts for particular classifications of responsibility or of each individual's responsibilities (Turner, 1996).

REFERENCES

Beckhard, Richard, & Harris, Ruben. (1987). *Organizational transitions: Managing complex change* (2nd ed.; pp. 104–108). Reading, MA: Addison-Wesley.

Melcher, Robert D. (1967, May/June). Role and relationships: Clarifying the manager's job. *Personnel Magazine,* 33–41.

Turner, Jean G. (1996, April). Tips—Keeping a database with tables. *WordPerfect for Windows,* 67–68.

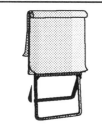

PROCEDURE III-4

Scheduling Meetings With Groups

Purpose

To schedule group meetings in an efficient and painless way.

Summary Description

During meetings, groups tend to waste a lot of time scheduling the next meeting. Several different dates and times are proposed, but one or two members can't make it, and the search goes on, often frustrating everyone. This simple technique solves the problem.

The facilitator prepares a calendar of the possible dates on a flip chart. Members are asked to mark on the chart the times they definitely cannot attend. A date and time is then selected from the times when everyone is available or the fewest members are not available.

When to Use the Procedure

- When the group members are likely to have several conflicting engagements

Resources *(checkmarks indicate recommended equipment)*

✔ Flip chart and markers

Method

1. Write the potential meeting dates on a flip chart page, dividing each date in half for "A.M." or "P.M." For example, if you are planning over a three-week span, you would use a chart similar to the one shown on the next page.

2. Pass out markers and ask members to come up to the flip chart and put their initials on any A.M. or P.M. when they have appointments that **cannot** be rescheduled.

3. Members look at the chart and select the date and time that is best for the meeting. Neatness of the drawing on the flip chart obviously matters little here. The important thing is to quickly get the choices up on the chart with enough room for everyone to initial when they cannot be present.
See the example on the next page.

Potential Meeting Dates

11/6	11/7	11/8	11/9	11/10
A.M.	A.M. Sarah	A.M. Javier	A.M.	A.M.
P.M. Betty Sarah	P.M. Ben	P.M. Jack	P.M. Ben	P.M. Betty
11/13	**11/14**	**11/15**	**11/16**	**11/17**
A.M.	A.M. Jack Ben	A.M. Sarah Ben	A.M. Ben	A.M.
P.M.	P.M. Javier	P.M. Sarah	P.M. Javier Betty	P.M.
11/20	**11/21**	**11/22**	**Holiday**	**Holiday**
A.M.	A.M. Sarah Jack	A.M. Jack	A.M. X	A.M. X
P.M. Betty	P.M.	P.M. Ben Javier	P.M. X	P.M. X

SECTION IV

SPECIAL MEETINGS

➡ Overview

➡ Facilitator Resources

OVERVIEW

In addition to the facilitation tasks, outcomes, and resources that are needed in working with any group on any task (see Sections I to III), there are specific procedures and tools for facilitating a variety of "special meetings." These are meetings that, although common in *type,* are special in *purpose.*

We have presented in Section IV a number of facilitation resources for special meetings, placing them in a category called Planning Meetings and Tools.

Here is a brief forecast of what you will find.

Planning Meetings and Tools

It is becoming commonplace to do more planning for meetings and to involve more people in that planning; thus, facilitators are regularly called upon to design and facilitate various types of meeting plans. The Facilitator Resources in this section include general procedures that can be easily modified to fit your special purpose, including procedures for the following:

— Developing mission statements
— Creating values and vision statements
— Conducting strategic planning
— Analyzing critical success factors
— Using Gantt charts for planning

FACILITATOR RESOURCES

Planning Meeting and Tools

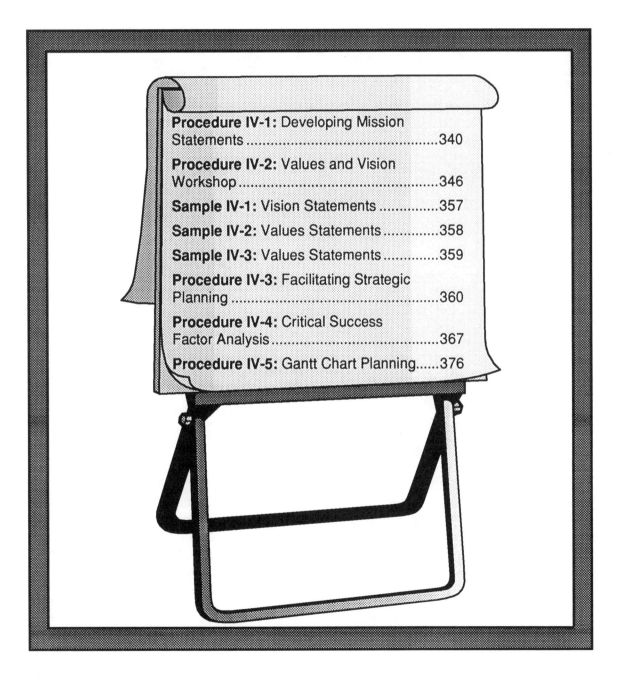

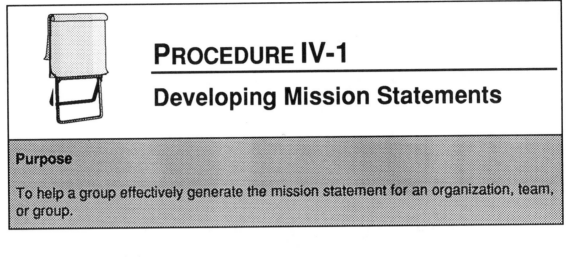

PROCEDURE IV-1

Developing Mission Statements

Purpose

To help a group effectively generate the mission statement for an organization, team, or group.

Summary Description

A mission statement is a concise statement that establishes the direction for, and the boundaries of, the work of a group. It tells what the group does and why the group has been formed.

Small task groups usually generate mission statements. A group's first step is to identify the following:

- The business that it is engaged in
- The customers or clientele that are served
- The group's primary purpose
- The key outcomes that will determine success
- The services that are provided
- The distinguishing characteristics of the services
- (Optional.) The way outcomes or impacts are measured

The group identifies alternative statements for each of these areas. Members then discuss the alternatives and come to consensus on the conceptual content for the mission. A great deal of data is generated and subsequently condensed into a concise mission statement. In some cases, quality standards for mission statements are presented and other mission statements are critiqued. Draft versions of the statement are prepared and reviewed. The statement is finally approved by absolute consensus of all members.

When to Use the Procedure

- During organizational strategic-planning sessions

- When generating the charge of a group or task force

- When you want to clarify the work of a cross-functional team

Participants

Number: Five to nine group members

Type: Organizational mission statements are usually generated by the top management group of the organization. Team (or group) mission statements can be generated and reviewed by the whole team or can be generated by a subgroup and then reviewed by the entire team.

Resources *(checkmarks indicate recommended equipment)*

✔ Flip chart and markers

Facilitator(s)

One facilitator works with the group. The facilitator should be familiar with the work yet still be able to maintain strict neutrality on the content of the mission statement. Separate recorders can also be used.

Time

Approximately 2 to 6 hours

Method

1. Provide the group with an overview of the process and the steps that will be used. Ask the group to identify the reasons why formulating a mission statement is worth the time that is being allocated to its development. Check to see that everyone understands and supports the process.

2. Identify the overarching purpose of the work. Head a flip chart page "We exist to . . ." Have the group generate alternatives and come to agreement on one overarching purpose statement for its work.

3. Identify what business or businesses the group is in (i.e., what characterizes the work of the group). Write "We are in the _____ business" on the flip chart. Agree on one or more answers. If you have more than one, rank them by priority.

4. Identify the services the group performs or products it produces and for whom. Create two columns on the flip chart page:

Services or Products   *For (customer or client)*

Have the group generate alternatives and agree upon the "core services or products" and key customers or clients.

5. Identify the distinguishing characteristics of the services or products. Write "What distinguishes our services or products?" on the flip chart. Generate the data and reach agreement on the "distinguishing characteristics."

6. Identify the critical outcomes that the group will use to measure the success or failure of its mission. Write "We gauge our success by the extent to which. . ." on the flip chart. Generate data and agree upon the critical outcomes.

7. (Optional.) Identify how the group will measure the critical outcomes. Write on the flip chart "We measure our success in achieving critical outcomes by. . . ." Generate data and agree upon measurement mechanisms.

8. (Optional.) Review quality standards for mission statements. Ask the group to generate what it feels are quality standards for mission statements. Check these standards to see if they include some of the following typical standards for mission statements:

   — Values-based
   — Jargon-free
   — Ennobling and spirited
   — Create a demanding performance challenge
   — Clear and direct
   — Distinguish you from others
   — Measurable

Then have the group evaluate a few mission statements using the criteria it has generated. You can provide members with examples from your own files or use the following:

From the IRS: *"The mission of the Internal Revenue Service is to collect the proper amount of tax revenue at the least cost; serve the public by continually improving the quality of our products and services; and perform in a manner warranting the highest degree of public integrity, efficiency and fairness."*

From a major health care system: *"[This HMO] will ensure highly satisfied members by offering easily accessible, quality healthcare services that are sensitive to our members' needs."*

From a soft-drink manufacturer: *"To bring refreshment to a thirsty world and to create shareholder value for all our associates."*

From a health-food chain: *"We are committed to offering the highest-quality natural foods, related products, service, and information which optimize and enrich the health and well being of the individual as well as the planet."*

From the pharmacy of a healthcare provider: *"Our mission is to contribute to the health and satisfaction of members by providing appropriate medications, information, and professional services."*

From the U.S. Department of Education: *"To ensure equal access to education and to promote educational excellence throughout the nation."*

From a state education division: *"The purpose of the Division of Student/Family services is to ensure that all [state] students achieve a high level of learning through the provision of a coordinated array of flexible services to students and families."*

From a county educational agency: *"We are a leading regional educational agency providing leadership, programs, and services to prepare an educated citizenry for the 21st century."*

9. Next, offer these options for generating mission statements:

    (a) Work individually to generate statements.

    (b) Work in two-person teams to generate statements.

    (c) Delegate the generation of statements to a group member or writing team of two or three members.

    If *(a)* or *(b)* is selected: Allocate 20 minutes for individuals or teams to come up with draft statements. Then have two individuals or teams meet and come to agreement on one statement. Repeat the process until you end up with only two statements. Post both statements on flip chart paper; then have the group compose one statement from the two statements.

    If *(c)* is selected: Decide on a meeting date for when the statements will be reviewed.

    Be sure to agree on the desired length or word count for the final mission statement. Also, some members may prefer to work from a format. If so, provide them with the Mission Statement Format Worksheet at the end of this procedure. Although this format is not really suitable for generating a statement of 15 words or less, it does allow most groups to consider the critical questions of the mission in one statement.

10. If some additional wordsmithing is needed, assign someone to make changes without altering any conceptual agreement. Agree on a time to review the mission and come to absolute agreement on the statement.

11. Meet to have each member of the group agree on the wording of the statement. Have each member sign the statement, indicating his or her agreement.

Notes

1. This process is designed for groups that can gain value from carefully examining their mission. It may be too lengthy for some groups and need substantial adjustment. Tailor the length and nature of the process to the needs of your individual client.

2. Explain that even extremely short missions require careful thought and analysis. The process is designed to ensure that there are no ambiguities that will detract from the clarity of the final statement.

3. If your group has had a good deal of experience constructing mission statements, caution members against assuming that they do not need to clarify the data in each of the categories before constructing a statement.

4. Though mission statements are often generated in a single top-level management session, there is a definite trend toward involving more stakeholders, over a longer period of time, in the development of mission statements. Some organizations take the initial statement to focus groups at all levels of the organization. Others review the statement in all management meetings. Others go even further, developing the statement from ideas "grown" from the bottom up. Still others develop the organizational mission and department missions simultaneously. It is not uncommon for the development of a mission statement to take several months to complete rather than several hours.

Mission Statement Format Worksheet

We exist to *(primary purpose and the business we are in)*:

_____

_____

_____

_____

for *(primary clients or customers listed in order of significance)*:

_____

_____

_____

_____

in order to *(core services)*:

_____

_____

_____

_____

believing that *(critical values)*:

_____

_____

_____

_____

so that *(key outcomes that determine success)*:

_____

_____

_____

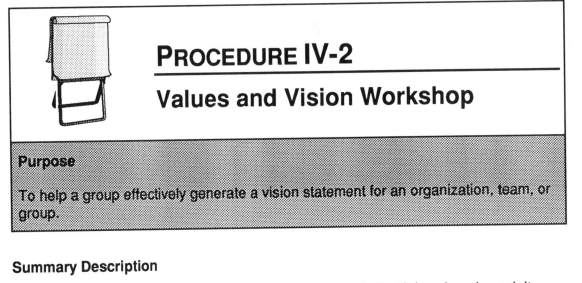

PROCEDURE IV-2

Values and Vision Workshop

Purpose

To help a group effectively generate a vision statement for an organization, team, or group.

Summary Description

The most distinguishing feature of the vision statement is that it is values-based. It shows group members what conditions are like when they are working their mission and living within their work-related values. The vision integrates the group's core values into the work statement and clearly presents to the rest of the world who the group is and what it is all about.

The vision statement is distinct from the mission statement in several ways:

- The mission statement tells group members precisely what the group's intended work is; the vision statement provides the group with a clear, inspiring word picture of what the work looks like when performed in its desired state.

- The mission statement tells the group exactly who its customer is; the vision statement tells the group what the customer looks like when the ideal relationship with the customer is realized.

- The mission statement clarifies the exact nature of the services or products to be provided; the vision statement indicates what it looks like when those services or products are being delivered or produced in the way that group members believe they should be.

- Mission statement writing is mostly a science or a craft; vision statement generation is much more of an art.

Vision statements take many forms. Some are little more than a phrase—"A Coca-Cola within arm's reach of everyone in the world," or "Service with respect" (from a local police department). Some comprise two or three sentences, and still others are anywhere from a page to a dozen pages in length. Kotter (1996) suggests that the critical success factor for the good vision statement is that it can be communicated in 5 minutes or less.

There are many ways to produce a vision statement. Here we are going to present a model that we believe is uniquely practical, given most organizations' capacity and available time for group work. It is a one-and-a-half-day workshop with five parts:

1. The Mission Review (Day 1)

2. Core Values Identification (Day 1)

3. Present State Analysis (Day 1)

4. Vision Data Generation (Day 1)

5. The Vision Review (Day 2, in a follow-up session)

This model assumes that the organization has a mission statement that is no more than three years old. If this is not the case, mission statement work (see Procedure IV-1) should be completed before the workshop.

When to Use the Procedure

• Immediately before a major strategic-planning effort

• Following the generation of a new or revised mission statement

• During the early stages of a planned organizational change effort

Participants

Number: From 12 to 25 group members (numbers can be larger, but time should be extended slightly to allow for management of the larger group)

Planning team of three to five

Type: Top managers, other managers, and a few front-line people

Resources *(checkmarks indicate recommended equipment)*

✔ Flip chart and markers
✔ Overhead projector
✔ 3M spray adhesive
✔ (Optional.) Butcher paper
✔ Standard-size paper in three different colors
✔ Black marking pens
✔ Laptop computer

Facilitator(s)

One facilitator has primary responsibility. With groups larger than 25, two facilitators should be used. The primary facilitator should be familiar with the work yet able to maintain strict neutrality on the content of the vision statement. The primary facilitator can also serve as a coordinator for others who share in the planning and facilitation of the vision workshop. The facilitator can be either internal or external. An internal facilitator can be used as long as he or she is not directly attached to the unit that is developing the vision statement.

Time

One full day and a half day

Where

Conduct the workshop off-site. It is extremely important to distance the groups from normal work pressures, phones, and intrusions.

Method

1. *Six weeks before the workshop:* Determine who will be invited to the vision workshop, set a date, and arrange for an off-site location. Find an off-site meeting room with sufficient wall space to carry out the activities described in Steps 6 and 7.

2. *Five weeks before the workshop:* Draft a letter of invitation to the workshop and send it to those invited.

3. *Two to four weeks before the workshop:* Convene a small planning team of three to five people to plan the workshop. Meet for a half-day planning session.

4. Send out a copy of this procedure to members of the planning team and ask them to review the procedure before they come to the meeting. You can also send out other materials on building vision statements (see **References**).

5. At the half-day planning meeting:

   ❑ Review this procedure and any other materials.

   ❑ Determine if the present mission for the organization or unit is adequate or if it needs to be reviewed or modified at the vision workshop.

   ❑ Make any design modifications necessary to meet your particular needs.

   ❑ Consider whether to make the following decisions or to present choices to the larger group and have them make the decisions:

      • The nature of the final statement(s) that will be turned out. Determine the length, whether there will be just one statement or alternate forms, and so on.

      • Who will do the work, between the Day 1 and Day 2, on editing and readying final drafts to present to the group for approval. Also, who will do any mission statement redrafting for presentation to the group on Day 2.

- Identify several "core work processes" that are critical to the performance of the group work. These processes will be introduced in the values-building session.

- Identify the subcategory areas or "elements" of the vision for which data will be generated. Then identify which of those areas will be targeted for the formation of work improvement or process improvement teams.

- Determine the record-keeping method(s) that you will use and whether or not you will attempt "on-the-spot" word processing of data generated. Identify equipment needs and assign a person responsible for procuring and getting them to the meeting site.

- Determine whether you want to use flip charts, storyboards, or a combination of both.

❏ Establish any ground rules that you want to have for the workshop (see Guide I-3: A Checklist for Ground Rule Choices and Samples I-3 to I-5: Ground Rules).

❏ Identify persons responsible for facilitating each of the activities in the workshop sessions.

❏ Assign a person responsible for writing up a process agenda for the workshop (see Sample I-6: Meeting Agenda).

❏ Review logistics and preparations for the meeting (see Guide I-4: Checklist for Meeting Planning), and assign persons responsible for various workshop preparations.

❏ Have the group nominate two to four people to be a writing group that is charged with taking the data from the flip charts and creating draft values and vision statements. The criteria for soliciting these people is important. Each person in the writing group must:

- Be trusted by the group to accurately represent the thinking of the entire group

- Be a good writer—at least one person should be an excellent writer

- Be able to write with feeling and passion

- Know the work well

❏ Have the group plan a "celebratory" event to conclude Day 2 of the workshop. Assign one person responsible for coordinating the celebration.

6. Day 1 of the Vision Workshop

7:30 A.M. *Room Preparation and Set-Up*

Arrive and set up the room. Arrange two work areas: one area for small-group work with spaces for groups of six to eight participants and one large-group space. Station a flip chart and markers at each small-group space. Station two flip charts at the front of the room. Cover each of three walls with sheets of flip chart paper (or a long sheet of butcher paper) sprayed with 3M adhesive; this setup will be needed for the Present State Analysis exercise of the workshop.

8:30 A.M. *Introductions, Agenda Review, and Ground Rules*

Have the group leader welcome everyone and share why the work that is about to be done is important. Introduce the planning group and have one of its members go over the agenda for the day. Answer any questions on how the processes will work. Check with the group on acceptance of the agenda. Share the ground rules established by the planning group. Introduce any people who are new to the group.

9:00 A.M. *Mission Review*

Review the organization's mission statement or your revision of the statement. Have members break into small groups. Ask them to look at the mission closely and to note on a flip chart their answers to these two questions:

1. What does this statement say or imply about the following?

    — *What business we are in*
    — *Who our customer is*
    — *What services or products we offer*
    — *Key distinctions about how we go about doing our work*

2. What's missing from the statement or not in touch with where we are now?

Note: An option is to analyze the mission statement before the workshop, provide the workshop group with answers to the first question, and simply have the group respond to the second question.

9:20 A.M. *Large-Group Mission Review*

Bring everyone to the large-group area and post the groups' notes regarding the mission statement. Briefly share the data from the charts; then announce who will be looking at the mission to do revisions in the interim between this first session and the final session.

9:35 A.M. *Core Values Identification*

Introduce the values-building session. Speak briefly about the importance of defining the key values by which the group (organization, unit, team) operates; then take the following steps:

1. Explain that members will re-form their small groups to brainstorm values with respect to:

    *   Values related to the core processes of our work. (Share the core processes identified by the planning group and invite the group to add any others they believe are critical.)

    *   Values related to our customers and users.

    *   Values related to the services and/or products we provide or produce.

- Values regarding our employees.

- Values regarding management, the role of managers, and how we get things done.

- Values related to critical organizational goals or priorities.

Provide the following cue phrases to start each values statement:

—We believe   —We care about
—We believe in   —We value

2. Have each small group reduce the data generated in all the values areas to no more than five key values. (Provide the groups with suggestions on processes to reduce the goals.)

10:00 A.M. *Core Values Identification (continued)*

3. In the large-group setting, have one spokesperson for each group review their five values with the rest of the group. Check for understanding of the values only at this point. Record the values on a flip chart at the front of the room.

4. Have the group combine any values that appear to overlap.

5. Use a straw-voting procedure whereby each member shares his or her choices for the top five value statements. Two of these five votes will be what the member considers to matter the most in the performance of the work, the "heart of the matter."

10:45 A.M. **BREAK**

11:00 A.M. *Core Values Identification (concluded)*

6. Over the break, tally the votes and rearrange the value statements in the order of the votes they received. Take the top seven values and check for agreement on those values. See if you can make any changes to the statements, such as inserting portions of other statements (keep simple; revised statements should not be cumbersome). Check for agreement. Point out that a narrative will be written on the values and that nearly all the data can be included within descriptions of the key values. Suggest that two or three members work on drafting the values statements as well as a short paragraph saying what each value means for review at the subsequent session.

11:30 A.M. *Present State Analysis* (Organizational Audit)

Before starting the analysis, make sure setup directions have been followed (see *Room Preparation and Set-Up*).

1. Introduce the exercise by explaining to the group: "We will be analyzing our present state. We will use a simple form of analysis, identifying (a) what we as [an organization, a division, or a unit] do well and should remember to **keep on doing,** (b) what we need to do **more of,** and (c)

what we need to do **less of**." Write these three categories on the posted chart paper (or butcher paper), one category per wall.

2. Distribute the three sets of different-colored paper; each member should receive 10 sheets of each color (30 sheets in all). Explain that one color is for the things "we need to *keep on doing,*" another for what "we need to do *more of,*" and another for what "we need to do *less of.*"

   To give members a point of reference, put these headings on a chart page:

   - The core values we have identified

   - The core processes of our work

   - Our services or products (list services or products)

   - Our operations (how we go about doing business)

   - The resources and support we receive in performing our work

   - Our relationships with customers, constituencies, and stakeholders

   - Our people who do the work (employees, human resources)

   - How we are organized to perform the work

   Ask everyone to generate up to 10 items for each of the three categories (keep on doing, do more of, and do less of). Explain that they should print the items in large bold letters, one item per sheet of paper. (Have members use black marking pens so their writing will be clearly visible.) Ask them to mount the items on the walls, according to category, when they are finished.

12:15 P.M. LUNCH

(Optional.) If the timing goes as planned, it is possible to have three pairs of planning group members cluster the items in like categories over the lunch break.

1:15 P.M. *Present State Analysis (concluded)*

3. (Time limit: 15 minutes.) Have group members walk around the room and view all the comments. Suggest to them that they look for common themes in the data.

4. (Time limit: 20 minutes.) Reassemble the group and list some of the common "themes" of the data on a flip chart.

5. Consultant shares the themes of the data collected to date, asking the group for sample quotes to illustrate each theme. The theme and the sample quotes should be written on flip charts.

<u>2:15 P.M.</u> *Vision Data Generation*

1. Before the session, the planning team should create "elements" of the vision. One element might focus on performance evaluation, another on customer relationships, and so forth. Assign two members of the planning team to be particularly vigilant regarding the data recorded in the present state analysis. During the break, have these two people move about the room, checking to see if there are other vision-element areas that should be added on the basis of the data that has been generated. Then create a separate group memory area for each vision element. If you don't have enough flip charts for all the elements, create group memories by affixing several sheets of chart paper to a wall. Rearrange chairs so that there is an equivalent number in each vision-element area.

2. Write this instruction on a flip chart or an overhead projector:

   "When we are performing our mission with excellence in this area, operating within the core values we have identified, we are . . ."

   Then have the whole group brainstorm a few sample responses in one of the small-group areas so that everyone becomes familiar with the process.

3. Explain to the group that most members will have the opportunity to complete two rounds of data generation, working in a different area for each round. They can pick which two areas they want to generate data for, but the seating in each area will be limited to the number of chairs stationed there so that every area receives some attention. Explain that one or two people from the first-round group will stay in the group to serve as "ambassadors" for the data generated during the first round. The "ambassadors" explain the data generated in the first round to the new group in the second round.

   Review the instructions for each round: Members first should brainstorm any and all responses; then, after the brainstorming has "dried up," they should see which items are agreed upon through consensus.

4. Make sure that everyone understands the instructions; then have members move to the areas and generate first-round data.

5. Conduct the second round, modifying the data generated in the first round.

6. Have members return to their original groups and review the data for agreement. One member of the planning group will act as a facilitator for the discussion. The groups have 20 minutes to modify items and/or check for consensus.

7. Present each group's data for review by the large group. Don't allow members to change any data at this point, as there won't be time. The sharing has to be quick and crisp—no more than 5 minutes per vision element.

8. Share a few sample "one-line" vision statements (see Sample IV-1: Vision Statements). Ask members to generate one-line statements (on cards in the large group).

9. Share any statements generated in the large group and have people record the data. If time is available, do one round of straw voting on the one-liners.

<u>4:45 P.M.</u> *Closure*

1. Present a brief preview of Day 2, the follow-up meeting.

2. If you have not already done so, present the planning group's recommendations as to who will prepare the values and vision statements for review on Day 2. Obtain the group's approval of the "writing group." Have the writing group meet after the workshop and set dates for its writing session.

3. **Interim Work**

   The "writing group" recommended by the planning team and approved by the entire group should meet soon after Day 1. The soonest would be that same night of Day 1, preparing for Day 2 of the workshop on the next day. The longest interim period between Day 1 and Day 2 of the workshop should be about three weeks. The longer the interim between Day 1 and Day 2, the greater the risk of losing momentum.

   The writing team should have a transcription of all the data generated at the Day 1 meeting. From this data, members should agree on what should be written by whom. Then they should take some time to do individual drafts. The individual drafts should be reviewed by the whole group for conceptual agreement **and** agreement that each writer accurately represented the thinking of the larger group. These agreements should be made by the group and the drafts should be turned over to one person for re-writing to present to the entire group.

   The length, content, and form of what is written will vary from group to group, but the following four elements are typical of what many successful groups have produced:

   1. *No more than seven key values statements.* These should be complete sentences describing the value clearly. Then the sentences can be reduced to single words, if that type of brevity is valued.

   2. *At least one paragraph for each value that elaborates on what the value means.* The meaning and implications of the value should be made clear through a short description of what this value means to the group in its work. As a group, the writers can brainstorm and include several bullets under each value. Then one person writes the paragraph.

   3. *A one-sentence vision statement.* This is a single sentence that captures the meaning of the entire Day 1. If the writing group is not definite on a single choice, it may be wisest to present about three choices for review by the whole group.

4. *A short narrative vision document.* Single sentence vision statements can be too limiting. A brief narrative that captures the essence of the themes from the Day 1 vision work adds enormous value. This statement should be uplifting and ennobling. The length is less important than the result that people are moved when it is read. After they read the statement, they should be able to say, "That's a place where I want my son or daughter (loved one) to work."

7. **Day 2 of the Vision Workshop**

   The Values and Vision Review

   1. Post the values and vision work done by the writing group. Print the work on flip charts or blow up the typed copy and make posters, if you have enlargement equipment to make posters.

   2. Ask someone to read the copy in front of the entire group.

   3. Do an initial gauge of the group's support for the statements. If support for the statements "as is" is exceptionally strong, you can shorten and perhaps even eliminate Step 4 below. Adjust the nature of the review that you do according to the level of support shown for the values and vision statements.

   4. Depending on the size of the group, have the whole group or small groups review the work in two stages. First, it should look to see if the statements are clear. Anything not clear should be posted on a flip chart. Second, it should look at the content of the statements. Are they:

      • An accurate representation of the work of the group?

      • Sufficiently compelling?

      • About right in form, style, and length?

      • Something each member is personally proud of?

      Any concerns related to any of the statements should be noted, along with any suggestions for change or amendment.

   5. Review the needed clarifications, concerns, and suggested changes. Seek consensus in the group for any changes. Avoid doing any wordsmithing with the large group. Instead, note the nature of the concern and a general way that it can be handled. Leave re-writing to individuals.

   6. If the changes are simple enough to be done quickly over a break, take a break and have one or two writers make the changes. If the changes are more substantial, note the concern and the general strategy for dealing with it on a Post-it and affix the Post-it to the flip chart or poster.

   7. In the large group, ask everyone to re-review the statement as it now exists. Negotiate quickly any remaining concerns. Ask every member to come up to the front of the room and sign their names on the charts, indicating their support for the statement, with any changes noted on the Post-its.

8. Determine when the group would recommend that the statements be reviewed for possible revision. Write on the charts (To be reviewed _____ [date]).

9. If the authorities who must officially review the statement are present in the room, ask them if they prefer to (a) adopt the statement immediately or (b) submit it for any other key review. If such reviews are needed, try to schedule the dates of the reviews and determine which members of the group should present the recommended statements for review.

10. Conduct the celebratory closing activity planned by the original planning group.

REFERENCES

Kotter, John. (1996). *Leading change.* Cambridge, MA: The Harvard Business School Press.

Nanus, Burt. (1992). *Visionary leadership.* San Francisco: Jossey-Bass.

Nanus, Burt. (1995a). *The vision retreat: A facilitator's guide.* San Francisco: Jossey-Bass.

Nanus, Burt. (1995b). *The vision retreat: A participant's workbook.* San Francisco: Jossey-Bass.

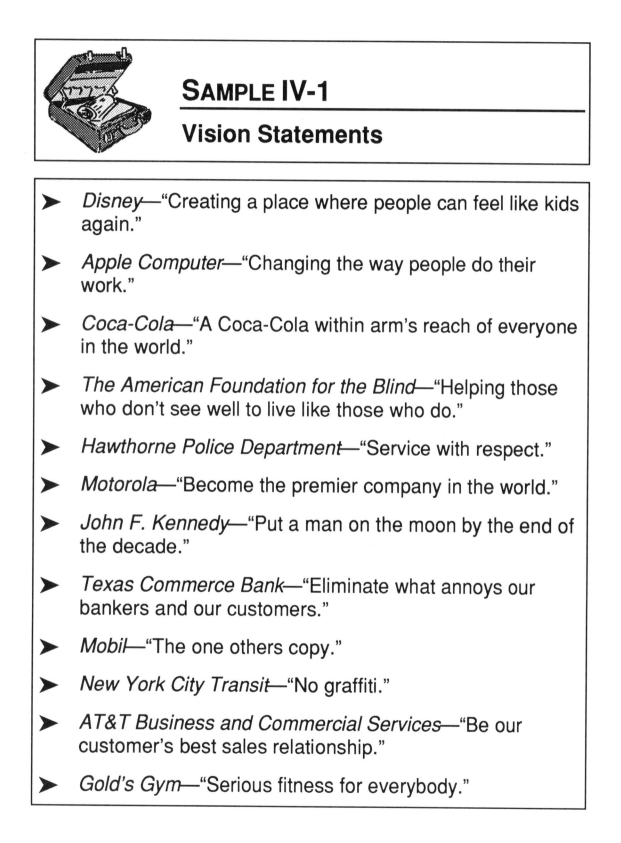

SAMPLE IV-1

Vision Statements

➤ *Disney*—"Creating a place where people can feel like kids again."

➤ *Apple Computer*—"Changing the way people do their work."

➤ *Coca-Cola*—"A Coca-Cola within arm's reach of everyone in the world."

➤ *The American Foundation for the Blind*—"Helping those who don't see well to live like those who do."

➤ *Hawthorne Police Department*—"Service with respect."

➤ *Motorola*—"Become the premier company in the world."

➤ *John F. Kennedy*—"Put a man on the moon by the end of the decade."

➤ *Texas Commerce Bank*—"Eliminate what annoys our bankers and our customers."

➤ *Mobil*—"The one others copy."

➤ *New York City Transit*—"No graffiti."

➤ *AT&T Business and Commercial Services*—"Be our customer's best sales relationship."

➤ *Gold's Gym*—"Serious fitness for everybody."

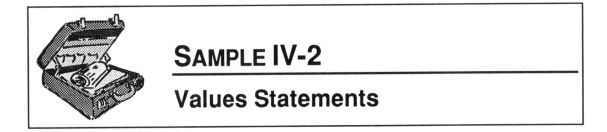

SAMPLE IV-2

Values Statements

From a law enforcement agency:

1. We believe in strong, effective law enforcement services.

2. We believe in high professional standards of integrity, ethics, and behavior—guided by the letter and spirit of the Law and the Law Enforcement Code of Ethics.

3. We believe in a balance between personal and professional life.

4. We believe in attaining and maintaining excellent physical conditioning, current intellectual competence, and optimum mental health.

5. We have a personal and professional commitment to improve our communities and earn their trust, respect, and support through active partnerships, involvement, and service.

6. We believe that we should treat all people with respect, fairness, and compassion.

7. We believe in loyalty and support for each other and the community without compromise of the high ethical standards of law enforcement.

8. We believe in recognition for and valuing of each individual's contribution to the department and the community regardless of position, assignment, or role.

9. We believe in open and honest communications, both internal and external.

10. We believe in an empowering work environment that encourages innovation, input, and participation, and values each member's diversity.

11. We believe in all members working together to achieve department goals through partnership with each other and the community.

12. We believe in initiative and autonomy at all levels with responsibility for our own actions and the actions of those we lead and influence.

13. We believe in an equitable system that evaluates each person on his or her merit and provides for appropriate recognition and just sanctions.

14. We have pride in the Law Enforcement Profession with a productive work ethic and a high level of commitment to the department and the community.

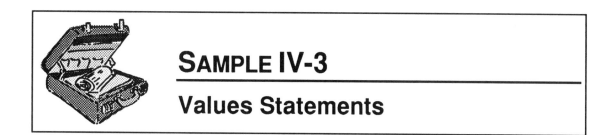

SAMPLE IV-3

Values Statements

From a school system:

VALUES

- We believe that students are our top priority.

- We listen to, respect, and trust all members of the school community.

- Parents are essential to student success.

- Exemplary programs result from expertise, standards, resources, and accountability.

- Effective leadership comes from all members of our school community.

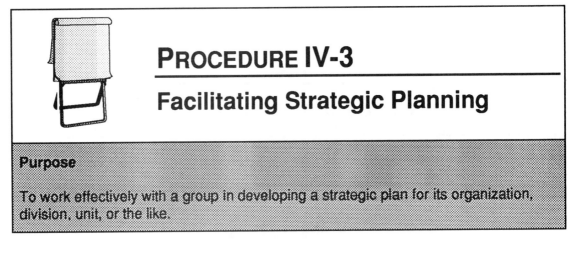

PROCEDURE IV-3

Facilitating Strategic Planning

Purpose

To work effectively with a group in developing a strategic plan for its organization, division, unit, or the like.

Summary Description

A strategic plan outlines what a group or an organization intends to do to successfully accomplish its mission in the environment(s) in which it operates. Strategies are created based on the group's analysis and interpretation of the environments it must operate in and the resources and competencies it possesses. An organization's strategy encompasses its **intent** (macro goal, end state) and **actions** (how it will achieve its intent). The actions are created in more detailed plans for all units in the organization. Strategic planning therefore involves understanding the relevant environment(s), assessing the resource base and core competencies, identifying strategic alternatives, choosing the strategy (or strategies) to pursue, and identifying the actions needed.

A good planning process must include analysis and interpretation of relevant data, development of a consensual view of the environment and the organization, generation of alternative strategic directions, and decisions concerning the strategy to pursue related resource allocations.

There are many books, models, and variations for strategic planning. The model presented here is a composite and represents a basic, generic process that could be used, with slight modifications, with almost any organization. As we have included separate procedures on facilitating mission and vision meetings, this procedure excludes the mission and vision work that generally precedes strategic planning.

When to Use the Procedure

Strategic thinking should be an ongoing responsibility of the whole organization. Strategic planning generally occurs in a cyclical fashion (often yearly), with a rolling multi-year focus (e.g., 3 to 5 years).

Participants

Number: Twelve to 20 group members. (This procedure can be conducted with a larger group).

Type: Senior management or representatives from various organizational levels (a diagonal "slice" of the organization).

Resources *(checkmarks indicate recommended equipment)*

✔ Flip chart and markers

✔ Laptop computer

Facilitator(s)

One facilitator works with the group. The facilitator should be familiar with the work yet still be able to maintain strict neutrality on the content of the mission statement. Separate recorders can also be used.

Time

Generally, two to four days for the planning meetings, culminating in a final planning session. Other preparatory work may take place over many months, before and in between meetings. For the purposes of this procedure, we are breaking the work into four parts, with one day allocated to each part. You can modify according to your needs.

Method

1. Determine who will be included in the planning process directly (at the meetings) or indirectly (through providing input).

2. Send letters to the participants outlining their roles, responsibilities, charter, timeline, and meeting dates. You might also include information on strategic planning and the specific processes to be used.

3. Convene the group for a preliminary meeting. At this meeting:

   - Review the charter, outcomes, roles, and timeline.

   - Review and/or train people in the strategic-planning process to be used.

   - Establish the foundation for the group work (e.g., inclusion, ground rules).

   - Review the organization's mission and its vision and values.

   - Review or create what you intend the end-product to look like (e.g., length, format, elements).

- Have the group identify its relevant external environments, the data it needs, and the sources of that data. See the "Understanding the Environment" information sheet at the end of this procedure.

- Develop a plan and make arrangements to collect and organize the data it needs about the external environments. Again, see "Understanding the Environment" information sheet.

4. Reconvene the group to share, integrate, and interpret the external and internal data it has been collecting and assembling.

First, have the various external data shared. You should work with the participants before this meeting to help them organize their data so it is readily understood by all.

Second, create the summaries discussed in the information sheet, "Understanding the Environment." In this step, you want clear, concise statements about the general, market-specific, and industry/sector environments for the planning horizon you have determined (e.g., 3 to 5 years).

Third, share the various internal data. Have the group summarize this information, for example, strengths, weaknesses (or vulnerabilities), and critical development needs *in relation to the industry/sector* and *the environmental view* created above.

Note: You might continue in this meeting with the next step. Or you might break here with some thinking/reading/researching assignment on strategy, strategic alternatives, what competitors or substitutes are doing, and so forth. In the latter case, the next step becomes the next meeting.

5. In this step, you want to facilitate a strategic discussion. That is, you want the participants to discuss opportunities and threats in *conjunction with* their strengths and weaknesses. Also, participants need to generate strategic alternatives and to discuss their pros and cons in light of the organization's capability and its development needs.

First, have them match their strengths and weaknesses against the opportunities and threats they see. Where are their strengths adequate and where are their weaknesses a problem? What is their distinctive competence (if any)? Are there any bases for competitive advantage?

Second, have them brainstorm and consolidate the strategic alternatives they could pursue.

Third, have participants divide into small groups to further analyze, and to prepare to present, the different strategies. Members can analyze the strategies by relating them to the future and their potential competitive advantage, identifying pros and cons, highlighting adequate and inadequate capabilities, outlining development that would be needed to be successful with a given strategy, and estimating (in ballpark figures) resource needs.

Fourth, have small groups present their various cases. Facilitate discussion. Use consensus-building methods to determine which strategic alternatives will be kept or dropped as strategic alternatives.

Note: At this time, you may need a further round of discussion or analysis on the remaining alternatives. Another option is to assign further outside research on the remaining alternatives and then reconvene for the next step.

6. Now, it's time to select a strategy. The future cannot be predicted with complete accuracy. Your data is always incomplete. Some ambiguity is natural in planning. Subjective factors, intuition, values, politics, and personalities will all come into play in weighing the previous work and committing to a strategic path. To make the selection process as productive and fair as possible, take these steps:

First, allow individuals or groups to advocate for or against any of the alternatives. Conduct a time-limited discussion, if necessary.

Second, use your agreed-upon decision-making method to select a strategy—or, if there are still three or more, narrow them down to two and then make a selection.

Third, either in this meeting or through small-group assignments and report-backs, identify more specifically the implications of the chosen strategy on needed actions, changes, developments, and resources.

With an overall strategy in place, all of the organizational teams, project teams, and other groups can develop their strategic and operational plans (what they're going to do and how) in alignment with the organization's direction.

REFERENCES

Thompson, A., & Strickland, A. (1995). *Crafting and implementing strategy* (6th ed.). Chicago: Irwin.

Worley, C.; Hitchin D.; & Ross, W. (1996). *Integrated strategic change.* Reading, MA: Addison-Wesley.

Barney, J. (1997). *Gaining and sustaining competitive advantage.* Reading, MA: Addison-Wesley.

INFORMATION SHEET

A. Understanding the Environment (External)

In order to understand an organization's outside environment, we need to know what to look at or scan for (i.e., we need information that could make a difference in terms of the organization's mission).

Different types of organizations (profit, nonprofit, governmental, educational) will use some or all of the following ways to look at their environment:

❑ **The General Environment.** It's useful for organizations to scan their general environment, by domains, for events, trends, and occurrences that could lead to opportunities or threats for the organization. They generally include the following domains:

➤ *Social*—including *demographic factors* such as age, gender, education, race, and religion; and *cultural factors* such as life-styles, customs, changing values, ideologies, norms, and social structures.

➤ *Technological*—including new *technologies* that will have an impact on what the organization produces or provides or how the organization will work, *innovations*, and *scientific breakthroughs.*

➤ *Economic*—including *expectations* of growth or decline, critical *economic indicators*, monetary and fiscal *policies*, budget and trade *deficits* and *surpluses.*

➤ *Environmental*—including *policies, laws, regulations*, and *enforcement mechanisms* concerning the physical environment and the use of natural resources.

➤ *Political*—including *in-favor ideology and trends, government regulations*, domestic and foreign policies, *tax and budget policies*, and major *court decisions.*

The data collected from such a scan should then be summarized as events, trends, or anticipated changes and the implications (opportunities or threats) identified for the organization.

❑ **Stakeholders.** It is also helpful for the organizations to analyze their key stakeholders. For most organizations, these include such groups as customers, shareholders, suppliers, elected officials, employees, or the public. With each stakeholder, you can analyze these issues:

➤ What they care about specifically in terms of what you do and how you do it

➤ Their level of influence or power to affect you

➤ What they want (to change or stay the same) or value

The summary for this data is to prioritize stakeholders by their potential impact on your organization, highlighting their wants and what they value.

❏ **Industry Sector.** There are characteristics and trends about sectors of the organizational world (e.g., higher education, nonprofit, city government) and industries (e.g., healthcare, consumer goods, financial institutions) that absolutely must be understood. In general, it's helpful to know about:

➤ Structure, size, and number and types of players in your sector or industry

➤ Stage of development

➤ Economic factors (costs, capacity, margins, etc.)

➤ Key success factors

➤ Forces driving change and the pace of the change

➤ Specific issues or trends

➤ Ease of entry, substitutions, rivalry, and buyer or supplier power

➤ Competitors—number, dominance, strengths, vulnerabilities, strategies

In summarizing this type of information, you want to focus on understanding the current attractiveness of your industry/sector, the optimistic and pessimistic scenarios, the nature of the competition, and your relative position.

❏ **Market-Specific.** Sometimes it helps to get data that identifies important differences among your specific markets or customer segments (e.g., California, Northeast, Hispanic, teenagers). These could include local and regional variations, different buying patterns, relational differences, or population characteristics.

In summarizing, you want to focus on the specific differences and the implications for your endeavors.

To pull together your understanding of the environment (environmental intelligence), you can now integrate the information you've surfaced by:

➤ Stating assumptions about the future that will affect you

➤ Developing various scenarios of what will occur and "so what" for you

➤ Identifying key strategic issues

➤ Highlighting all opportunities and threats

B. Understanding the Environment (Internal)

We also need a second type of data about the organization in its current state—its strengths, weaknesses, competencies, and resources. Again, we have to decide what to look at. There are numerous models used in the organizational diagnosis literature. This procedure, Facilitating Strategic Planning, outlines a composite that should provide a good base of internal information to use in the next phase of planning.

In general, internal analysis is conducted in order to accurately and honestly know the organization's strengths and weaknesses, which are critical in identifying such things as strategic alternatives and potential bases of competitive advantage, or in determining how capable the organization is to carry out various strategies.

Resource Base

A popular approach used today is to assess the organization's resources or "assets" to see what can be used productively in the pursuit of a strategy. In profiling resources, the following are generally considered:

- Financial—budgets, cash flow, equity, etc.
- Physical—plant, equipment, land, natural resources, etc.
- Human—talent, expertise, motivation, labor availability, etc.
- Organizational—leadership, structure, culture, processes, systems, etc.
- Reputational—history, brand identity, perceived quality, etc.

For different kinds of organizations, these resources will have different impacts, yet all are applicable to most organizations.

Understanding the resource base is necessary in assessing the organization's ability to survive (in its business environment), compete, and excel. The resource base also helps in identifying any distinctive competence (better than others) the organization might have as well as any critical development needs.

Performance Outcomes

Another useful way to analyze the organization's capability is to review its performance, both in general and in relation to the key success factors for its industry/sector. Again, this helps us understand the real strengths and weaknesses to take into account when selecting a strategy. In this analysis, we might include such factors as:

- Cost structure
- Productivity
- Quality
- Cycle time
- Customer satisfaction
- Value-adding activities
- Functional evaluation (e.g., marketing, production, human resources)

The combination of the internal and external environmental analyses provides the basis for creating a consensual view of the "business" world the organization needs to operate in and the current capability of the organization. These form the foundation for the rest of the strategic-planning process.

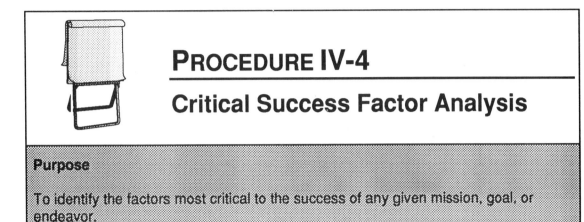

PROCEDURE IV-4

Critical Success Factor Analysis

Purpose

To identify the factors most critical to the success of any given mission, goal, or endeavor.

Summary Description

Critical Success Factor Analysis is one of the most useful planning tools that groups can use to guide their projects. The technique was originally developed to guide new business start-ups. It was described in *The Harvard Business Review* by Maurice Hardaker and Bryan K. Ward in 1987. Since then, it has become increasingly used in a number of planning applications. The practical adaptation that follows stays close to the original "process quality management" process as described by Hardaker and Ward, but includes several adaptations learned from personal experience with implementing the technique.

One possible implication of Critical Success Factor Analysis is that to be successful in anything, you need only identify between four and eight key factors. If you accomplish these things, you will be successful. The secret to success lies in getting the right critical success factors (CSFs).

Critical success factors are those things that you must be or have to be successful in any given endeavor.* The process of identifying CSFs requires that the group first be clear on the specific mission or goal for a given project. Then the group proceeds to identify between five and nine CSFs necessary to accomplish the mission. Every CSF must be absolutely necessary to success, and all of them together must be sufficient to ensure success. The group can stop after having identified the CSFs or can proceed with several other planning steps for a more comprehensive planning session.

To proceed, the group identifies all the things that must be done to accomplish each individual CSF. These tasks—or more often clusters of tasks—are referred to as "processes." Then the group assesses each process to determine the extent to which

---

*Thanks to Ken Olsen of the Mid-South Regional Resource Center in Lexington, Kentucky, for suggesting this "be or have" distinction, which helps to ensure that the CSFs identified are outcomes or objectives rather than tasks.

it will have an influence or an impact on the CSFs and the group's present capability to conduct the process. An "owner" is also identified for each process. The owner is assigned primary (not sole) responsibility for the successful conduct of that process.

Finally, priorities are assigned for each process by multiplying the number of impacts that the process will have on the CSFs by the "grade" that represents the present capability of the group to perform the work. A formula is used where those processes with the highest number of impacts on CSFs and the lowest present-capability grade receive the highest priority.

When to Use the Procedure

- At the beginning of a new project, business, venture, or task force

- At crisis times for the organization, when survival is questionable

- In planning a particularly critical project where the risk of failure is exceptionally high

- Following the revision of a mission statement

Participants

Number: A small group of between five and nine members.

Type: If the technique is used to identify organizational critical success factors, then the top management team becomes the task group. For other applications, task group members should have requisite expertise related to the project and knowledge about the people and the systems within which the processes will be implemented.

Resources *(checkmarks indicate recommended equipment)*

- ✔ Flip chart and markers
- ✔ Overhead projector
- ✔ Storyboards (or tack board) and note cards

Facilitator(s)

A facilitator should definitely be used during the conduct of this activity. A separate group recorder, not involved in the decisions or content, is also highly valuable.

Time

Either 6 hours or one full day to proceed though all the steps

Method

1. The process for critical success factor identification must first be explained as follows:

   (a) Copy the definition of a CSF on a flip chart and show it to the group.

Critical Success Factor

Definition:

A critical success factor (CSF) is one of between four and eight factors that is MOST critical to the success of any given mission, project, or goal. It is what you MUST be or have to be successful.

   (b) Explain the rules for composing or writing critical success factors by copying the information below onto a flip chart and going over it with the group.

Rules for Writing CSFs

1. No verbs
2. Only objects or objective phrases
3. No "ands" or "ors" or slashes
4. Identifies only one subgoal or issue
5. Seven words or less
6. Less is more
7. Absolute (unanimous) consensus is necessary

   (c) Show a sample set of CSFs. Share the examples below. The first is taken from Hardaker and Ward (1987). The other is Northwestern University football coach Gary Bennett's "Winning Formula" of CSFs designed to transform the team from the Big Ten's whipping boys into Rose Bowl champions, a mission he accomplished from 1991 to 1995. Write the example(s) on a flip chart, or make up your own.

Critical Success Factors
Sample 1

Mission: To restore market share and profitability over the next two years, and prepare the company and marketplace for further profitable growth

CSFs

1. Best of breed product quality
2. New products that satisfy marketplace needs
3. Excellent suppliers
4. Motivated, skilled workers
5. Excellent customer satisfaction
6. New business opportunities
7. Lowest delivered cost

—From Hardaker and Ward, 1987, p. 114

Critical Success Factors
Sample 2

Mission: We will foster an environment that teaches young men to relentlessly pursue and win the Big Ten Championship.

CSFs

1. Talent recruitment
2. Physical training
3. A system that works
4. Work ethic and discipline
5. Belief in our vision of winning

2. Have the group practice writing some CSFs. Select a simple task, drawing on your own experience if possible. Here is an example from one of the authors:

Someone once told me there were only two things to remember if a person wanted to make a good omelet. From that cooking tip, I developed this exercise:

    (a)   Challenge the group to come up with the CSFs "for a novice cook to make a good omelet."

    (b)   Have them practice identifying CSFs by completing the phrases "We must be" and "We must have."

    (c)   Have the group brainstorm CSFs following the rules above.

When they are through, I share the cooking tip—that is, the "CSFs":

        1.   [We must have] eggs whipped to death.
        2.   [We must have] low heat.

I explain that my experience proves this to be true: Without knowing anything about cooking, I am always able to make a good omelet if I follow those two "CSFs." This exercise also illustrates the "less is more" rule of writing CSFs.

You may be able to construct a similar example from your experience. Here are a few other ideas you could use for practice.

Missions:

"For the [sports team] to beat the [sports team] on [date of upcoming game]."

"To get the best possible deal on a new car."

"To get a raise within one year."

"To lose 5 pounds in six weeks in a healthy way."

"To write a book within the next year while still employed full-time."

"To get into an exercise routine and stick to it for one year."

3. Explain all the steps in the process. Copy the list below and share it with the group. If you are only identifying the CSFs and do not plan to go further, stop with Step 3. If you are planning to complete all the steps in the process, make an overhead of the sample matrix shown later in Step 14.

Critical Success Factors
Analysis Process

1. Clarify your mission or overall goal.
2. Brainstorm potential critical success factors for reaching the goal.
3. Reduce the list to four to eight CSFs that are each necessary and all sufficient.
4. Identify the tasks or "processes" that will be necessary to achieve the CSFs.
5. Count the number of impacts that each process has on each CSF.
6. Grade each of the processes according to the present capability of the group to execute the process.
7. Assign "owners" for each of the processes.
8. Calculate the priority by multiplying the number of impacts by the capability grade.
9. Delegate further planning on processes to each process owner.

---

4. Clarify the group's mission or goal statement. The statement should be crisp and relatively short—less than 25 words. (For more help, see Procedure IV-1: Developing Mission Statements.)

5. Brainstorm potential critical success factors.

6. Check all the factors for conformance with the rules stated above.

7. Conduct a discussion of the factors nominated, having group members share what they think is most critical without attempting any consensus.

8. Have each group member identify the five CSFs he or she would choose if five could be selected. (For a quick and easy method, see "Self-Adhesive Stickers as Voting Aids.")

9. Using the vote as a guide for discussion only, see how many CSFs group members can unanimously agree on.

10. Review the agreed-on items and see if everyone further agrees that each item is absolutely essential (i.e., you could not be successful if you failed to achieve this). Eliminate CSFs that are not considered essential.

11. Ask the group if all the CSFs combined together are sufficient to ensure success in fulfilling the mission or goal. If the answer is "no," then add more CSFs until the group feels that the "sufficiency" test is passed.

12. Take each CSF in turn and ask, "What must we do to accomplish this?" These processes will become the basic "to do" list. Post the rules for writing the processes, shown below, on a flip chart.

Rules for Generating Key Processes

1. Each is a verb-plus-object simple sequence.
2. Each process must have one owner, who is a member of the group that is present.
3. No one owner should have more than 3 or 4 processes.
4. Each must be necessary.
5. All must be sufficient.

—From Hardaker and Ward, 1987

Use note cards and a storyboard or tack board to generate the processes. Record each process on a note card; this way you will be able to mix them up in a subsequent step.

Try to create groups of tasks that form a process. A process is a set of tasks that forms a sequence leading to an outcome or tasks that are carried out simultaneously to accomplish a common end purpose. For example, "Train new staff" and "Survey target consumers" are preferable to very specific tasks such as "Develop new sales training" and "Construct focus group agenda."

13. Check the processes identified to see that they meet the "Each is necessary" and "All are sufficient criteria" rules, just as you did in the identification of the critical success factors in Steps 10 and 11 above. As you check each process, also assign a "process owner" from the group. Any process not "claimed" by an owner is not included. The owner accepts primary responsibility for following through to ensure that the process is executed. Others may also volunteer to help with specific tasks. Write down one owner for each task. If more than one person is working on the process, the first person listed is considered the "owner."

14. Shuffle all the process note cards; then place them, in random order, along the left-hand side of the board, creating the vertical axis of what will become a matrix. Make cards for each of the critical success factors and place them across the top of the board, creating the horizontal axis of a matrix. Make a card for "Capability Grade," a card for "# of Impacts," a card for "Owner," and a card for "Priority." Place these four cards to the right of the CSFs, creating the matrix shown below:

Matrix of Critical Success Factors and Key Processes								
	CSF 1	CSF 2	CSF 3	CSF 4	CSF 5	Capability Grade	# of Impacts	Owner	Priority
Process 1									
Process 2									
Process 3									
Process 4									
Process 5									
Process 6									
Process 7									
Process 8									
Process 9									

15. Count the number of impacts that the first process has on each CSF, and write that number in the "# of Impacts" column. Then determine the capability grade for each process. Ask everyone to call out what grade they think the process should have. Provide the following choices on a flip chart:

Capability Grades

A = Excellent Performance (1 pt.)

B = Good Performance (2 pts.)

C = Fair Performance (3 pts.)

D = Bad Performance (4 pts.)

E = Not performed, performed only informally, or embryonic performance (5 pts.)

If there is considerable disagreement, discuss the different evaluations. If not, have the "owner" pick a grade. Record the grade in the "Capability Grade" column.

16. Proceed through the remainder of the processes in the same manner.

17. After you have recorded the capability grades and impacts on CSFs, calculate the priorities. To do this, convert each capability grade into points (see chart above); then multiply the points by the number of impacts. Your score acts as a guide for ranking the processes by priority. (The lowest capability grades and highest impacts will equal the highest-priority scores.)

18. Tell the owners to come up with the next steps for developing each of the processes, and assign a date for your next planning session.

REFERENCES

Hardaker, Maurice, & Ward, Bryan K. (1987, November–December). Getting things done: How to make a team work. *The Harvard Business Review,* 112–119.

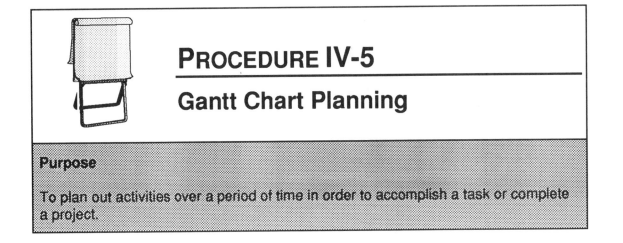

PROCEDURE IV-5

Gantt Chart Planning

Purpose

To plan out activities over a period of time in order to accomplish a task or complete a project.

Summary Description

The facilitator works with the project leader (or previously with the group) to identify the mission of the project and the key outcomes that must be achieved. The group brainstorms the tasks needed to achieve the key outcomes. The tasks are sequenced horizontally on a planning chart that lists the project outcomes on its vertical axis. After the tasks are sequenced, completion dates and persons responsible for each task are identified.

Several different methods can be used to do Gantt chart planning. This procedure describes two different types of Gantt planning.

When to Use the Procedure

- When you need to clarify the activities and responsibilities for conducting any given project

- When you want to give the group a better sense of the entire task with which it is confronted

- When time is limited and you need to make sure that you consciously plan your course of action and manage your time effectively

- When the group has agreed on a broad strategy and you need to plan out its implementation

Participants

Number: Three to nine participants

Type: Preferably everyone who will be responsible for completing tasks on the project

Resources *(checkmarks indicate recommended equipment)*

✔ Flip chart and markers

✔ Laptop computer

✔ Other: Your need for the following will depend on the options you choose for this procedure:

❑ A roll of butcher paper

❑ Different-sized and/or different-colored Post-it notes

❑ Different-sized and different-colored index cards

❑ 4-by-6-inch index cards

❑ Small task cards (with room for task, person responsible, start-finish dates)

❑ Copies of the Gantt chart planning aids attached to this procedure

❑ Copies of the Gantt chart templates attached to this procedure

❑ Bulletin board

❑ Tack board or storyboards

❑ Adhesive spray

❑ Pushpins

❑ Tape

❑ Scissors or paper cutter

Facilitator(s)

One person works as the group facilitator. Two people record data on task cards or Post-it notes.

Time

Approximately 4 to 6 hours for most projects

Method

1. If the project manager has not already been identified, identify this person now.

2. Meet with the project manager to identify the key outcomes that will be accomplished on the project. Use this cue sentence for outcome statements:

   "When we finish the project, we will have [state outcomes]."

3. If possible, identify several definite stages for the project (e.g., "Research and Education," "Alternative Generation," "Alternative Evaluation and Selection," and "Implementation Planning"). Also identify the approximate completion dates for the stages.

4. Decide on the Gantt planning method you will use and the materials you will need (note that you will require ample wall space for the Gantt chart "group memory" regardless of the method chosen). There are several options for doing this planning:

Option A: Tape several flip chart pages together side by side (or use a roll of butcher paper) and mount the paper on a wall surface. Use different-sized and/or -colored Post-it notes to record your outcome statements and to write tasks and milestones.

Option B: Copy the templates attached to this procedure (reproduce as many Project Outcome boxes as needed). Cut out the template copies with scissors or a paper cutter. Then follow these steps:

1. Mount the Project Outcome boxes vertically along the left-hand side of a bulletin board, storyboard set-up, or sheet of butcher paper; use pushpins, adhesive spray, or tape.

2. Mount the first month of your project above and immediately to the right of the Outcome boxes. Lay out the days of the months horizontally below that month.

3. Mount any other planning months to the right of the first month. Put the "Week" squares below each month horizontally.

The photo below shows one example of a GANTT chart using the templates provided with this procedure:

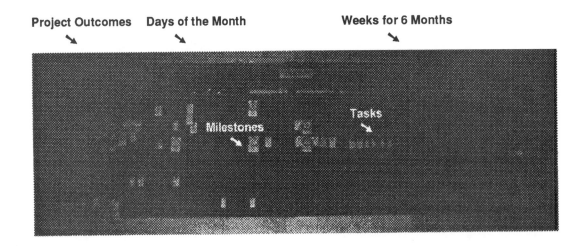

Project Outcomes   Days of the Month   Weeks for 6 Months

Milestones   Tasks

Option C: Use markers and chart paper or butcher paper to make your planning board. You can write tasks directly on the butcher paper. The disadvantage of this method is that you cannot make changes without making a mess.

Option D: To create a planning board, use some form of tack board or commercial storyboards; pushpins; and various sizes and colors of index cards.

Select one of the above options, or create some combination that will work for you. When your planning board is ready, the group can begin identifying tasks that must be accomplished to achieve the outcomes.

5. The project manager convenes a planning meeting with everyone who will be performing tasks related to the project. Conduct a group review of the outcomes that have been developed. Present the outcomes and ask members if they concur that those are the key outcomes to be accomplished. Revise and/or add outcomes as suggested during the group review.

6. Group members now individually generate a list of tasks for each outcome that they see as necessary to accomplish the outcome. Have members record the list, task by task, on index cards or Post-it notes, or on copies of the "Tasks" planning aids attached to this procedure. If you use cards or Post-its, instruct members to leave space at the bottom to fill in persons responsible and the start and finish dates. The "Tasks" aids have cells designed specifically for this purpose (e.g., "PR" for "persons responsible").

7. Ask members for the recorded tasks for the outcomes. Either lay them out on a tabletop or pin/paste them to the wall. The tasks now should be sequenced and put in the most logical order for completion. You can have the group work together on this activity, proceeding outcome by outcome; or you can ask members to pair up and give each pair specific outcomes to work on. The task materials (notes/cards/aids) should be ordered in rows, with the first task first, the second to the right of that, and so on.

8. Next, date each of the cards. You can write both start and finish dates or just record the finish dates.

9. Position each of the tasks underneath the date posted horizontally across the top of the wall chart that corresponds to the date you have written on the task. Also locate the tasks horizontally to the right of the outcome that is posted vertically on the left side of the wall chart.

10. Next, identify the tasks that should be considered "milestones" or particularly critical events. A task should be considered critical if it is a high-priority task that will significantly contribute to the success of the project, or if it has to occur at a given time or you will be in trouble. Either use the "milestone" planning aids that come with this procedure or make up some other symbol that indicates a milestone (e.g., a different-colored index card or a "star" drawn in red on the Post-it note).

11. For each milestone, identify one person who will have primary responsibility for the task and others who will be involved in doing the work. Fill in the planning aid or write the names on a Post-it or card, underlining or circling the name of the person with primary responsibility. Primary responsibility usually refers to the person who (a) initiates work and (b) does a large part of the work.

12. For the remaining tasks, assign a "person responsible" and "others" who will be involved in task completion. You can do this in one of three ways:

    • Make the assignments with the entire group.

    • Assign for each set of tasks (grouped by outcome) a person to be primarily responsible for their completion, and ask that person to further develop tasks for the outcome and to make the assignments.

    • Assign for each task a person responsible for its completion, and ask him or her to submit a plan for the task's accomplishment. In some cases, you may want to have plans include resource allocations, special materials needed, and budgets.

13. For some tasks, the start dates may be as important to remember as the finish dates. In such cases, make out two "Tasks" aids (or notes/cards). Place both on the chart, one below the task's start date, the other below the finish date.

Notes

1. Projects vary a great deal in their complexity, and you will want to tailor your Gantt planning to the complexity of the project.

2. After conducting a Gantt planning session, you will be wise to follow these two standard project management practices:

    1. List deliverables on a weekly basis. You can do this in a half-hour to 1-hour weekly project management meeting, or you can have the project director do it by listing the deliverables and notifying people, in writing, on a weekly basis.

    2. Hold monthly project planning meetings, usually 2 hours in length, in order to track progress and adjust plans.

Variations

1. Software is now available for doing Gantt charting. To do planning in a group, you can use a program such as Microsoft Project with an LCD display device and an overhead projector. Because you can only see one screen at a time, computer programs in group settings do not work out as well as a wall-chart group memory. You can, however, transfer the planning work done on a wall-chart to a Gantt-type software program, make handouts of the Gantt charts, and subsequently work from those.

GANTT CHART PLANNING AIDS
Tasks

Task		Task		Task		Task		Task	
PR	Others:	**PR**	Others:	**PR**	Others:	**PR**	Others:	**PR**	Others:
Start	**Finish**	Start	**Finish**	Start	**Finish**	Start	**Finish**	Start	**Finish**

Task		Task		Task		Task		Task	
PR	Others:	**PR**	Others:	**PR**	Others:	**PR**	Others:	**PR**	Others:
Start	**Finish**	Start	**Finish**	Start	**Finish**	Start	**Finish**	Start	**Finish**

Task		Task		Task		Task		Task	
PR	Others:	**PR**	Others:	**PR**	Others:	**PR**	Others:	**PR**	Others:
Start	**Finish**	Start	**Finish**	Start	**Finish**	Start	**Finish**	Start	**Finish**

GANTT CHART PLANNING TEMPLATES
Milestone Markers

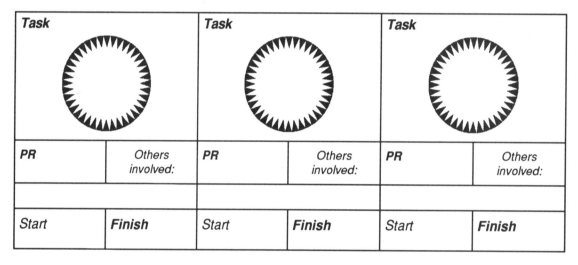

Task		Task		Task	
PR	Others involved:	**PR**	Others involved:	**PR**	Others involved:
Start	**Finish**	Start	**Finish**	Start	**Finish**

Task		Task		Task	
PR	Others involved:	**PR**	Others involved:	**PR**	Others involved:
Start	**Finish**	Start	**Finish**	Start	**Finish**

Task		Task		Task	
PR	Others involved:	**PR**	Others involved:	**PR**	Others involved:
Start	**Finish**	Start	**Finish**	Start	**Finish**

GANTT CHART PLANNING TEMPLATES
Project Outcomes

Project Outcome Number One

Project Outcome Number Two

GANTT CHART PLANNING TEMPLATES
Project Outcomes

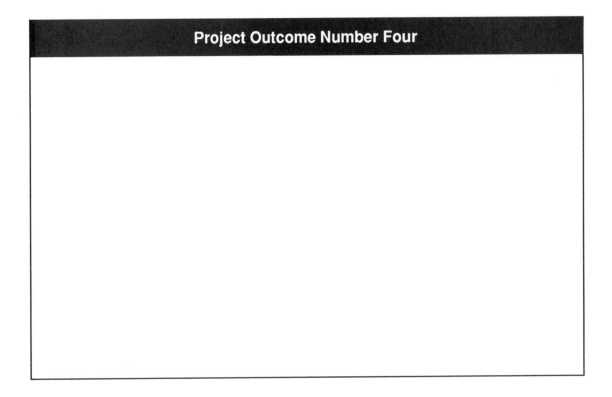

Project Outcome Number Three

Project Outcome Number Four

GANTT CHART PLANNING TEMPLATES
Project Outcomes

Project Outcome Number Five

The template below can be copied for additional outcome statements.

Project Outcome Number

GANTT CHART PLANNING TEMPLATES
Project Coordination

Project Coordination and Management

(This template is placed below the project outcomes. It is used to plan project coordination and management activities that cut across the other outcomes.)

GANTT CHART PLANNING TEMPLATES
Months

January

February

March

April

May

June

GANTT CHART PLANNING TEMPLATES
Months

July

August

September

October

November

December

GANTT CHART PLANNING TEMPLATES
Weeks

Week One	Week Two	Week Three	Week Four	Week Five
Week One	Week Two	Week Three	Week Four	Week Five
Week One	Week Two	Week Three	Week Four	Week Five
Week One	Week Two	Week Three	Week Four	Week Five
Week One	Week Two	Week Three	Week Four	Week Five
Week One	Week Two	Week Three	Week Four	Week Five
Week One	Week Two	Week Three	Week Four	Week Five

GANTT CHART PLANNING TEMPLATES
Days

SECTION V

FACILITATING WITH TECHNOLOGY

➥ Overview
➥ Facilitator Resources

OVERVIEW

By Eric Olson*

Before we begin, consider this:

> A facilitator started work with a group representing the MIS department of a Fortune 500 company and its internal customers. A half hour into the session, the MIS group members were in shock: *They had just discovered that their 10 priorities for service were exactly the opposite of what their internal customers wanted!* The session was still in its early phase! How did they learn so much about themselves and their clients so quickly?

> The facilitator had began the session by entering into a laptop computer a list of services the internal customers had identified through pre-session interviews. Audience response software enabled each individual MIS staff person to rate each service on a 1 to 9 scale of importance. Using hand-held keypads that fed information into the computer, they pushed a number button to give each item a score. Within seconds of their final vote, a bar graph showing the group's results flashed on the screen. With a few clicks of a mouse, the facilitator instantly saw how the MIS group's vote differed from the internal customers' votes.

> This information made quite an impact on the MIS group. Normally, the sessions dragged on and on without much progress; this time everything was different. Members spent the rest of the session listening to the customers and gaining an understanding of the root causes of the mismatch—thereby making genuine progress.

If the main purpose of good facilitation is to make groups work more effectively, then the main purpose of facilitating with technology is to make groups work even more effectively than they could without it. In truth, it doesn't always work out as nicely as it did for the MIS group. Facilitating with the use of technology is still very much in the development stage. Yet through my experience with using technology to facilitate groups (over 300 groups in the past five years), I have learned there are some basic principles—some specific do's and don'ts, some pluses and minuses of various approaches—that can make a notable difference to anyone interested in facilitating with technology.

---

*We invited Eric Olson, President of Transition Resources International (TRI) in Pasadena, California, to present this overview and introduction to "Facilitating With Technology." He and his firm are playing a leading role in bringing technology into organizational development work with groups.

The wonderful thing about technology is that once you learn how to use it as a tool, it can serve you in so many ways. Technology is being used today to help facilitate strategic planning, operational business issues, customer focus, marketing and sales meetings, creativity and brainstorming, conflict resolution, 360-degree feedback, and team building. Its potential uses pose a challenge to both reason and imagination.

This is not to say there is no tension between love of technology and love of facilitation. Some technologies easily become the end, rather than a means to the end, of the group endeavor; they limit the role of the facilitator rather than enhance it. Some even make the role of facilitator irrelevant. Be that as it may, for good or bad, technology is here to stay. And if the advances that have led us into the Information Age are any indication of what is to come, the force of technology will increase, not decrease. We need to be ready for it.

THE FIVE BASIC STEPS OF FACILITATING WITH TECHNOLOGY

If you plan to use technology as a facilitation tool, be prepared to take these steps:

1. Determine if there is a need for facilitating with technology.
2. Select the right technology for the right purpose.
3. Do session pre-work.
4. Take the measures needed to create a successful session.
5. Do follow-up tasks.

The following discussion will give you a good idea of what each step involves and how to approach your group session.

Step 1: Determine if There Is a Need for Facilitating With Technology

You need to assess whether or not the use of technology can add value to the group's work. Here are some common reasons why facilitators might need to use technology:

➤ **To help groups in different locations work together simultaneously.** Geographical separation is a key reason why many groups turn to technology-assisted facilitation. With the right technology, they can simulate a group meeting without the expense of actually bringing people together.

➤ **To build trust with a highly conflicted group.** Some groups have tried many of the traditional approaches to conflict resolution and still remain at odds. Facilitating with technology can be helpful for two reasons:

    1. It changes group dynamics by providing distance (sometimes geographical, sometimes psychological; affording a "safer space"). Technology itself is impersonal, and thus introduces a more objective element into the group. Members focus not just on one another but also on

the technology (which often gives them something to hate besides one another).

2. Most forms of technology create anonymous data. It becomes easier to find areas of agreement when people do not have to identify themselves publicly; thus facilitators skilled at leveraging technology's strengths can find new ways to negotiate differences or find champions to resolve conflicts.

➤ **To increase the creativity of a "stuck" group.** It's ironic that many groups who come together to discover new opportunities get buried under the mountains of flip charts they create. There are limits as to how many flip charts a group can put up on a wall and not feel overwhelmed by them. Technology can allow a group to brainstorm and create in paperless ways that do not bog down the process with a lot of clutter, covered windows, or tape. A few technologies are designed to encourage the creative process through voting techniques that capture multiple scenarios for success.

➤ **To increase group productivity and speed.** Anyone who has facilitated a session in which group members prioritized issues by marking flip charts knows how long the process can take when the group exceeds 12 members. Certain types of audience response systems and groupware technology (see Step 2) can provide you with a variety of instant prioritizations (paired-comparison, Likert scale, etc.) that keep a group moving rapidly. Groups can accomplish in a few hours what normally would take weeks or even months to accomplish.

➤ **To provide real-time documentation of group process and results.** The term *real-time* means seeing the results of your work immediately, not days or weeks later. Real-time work for groups is made possible by the incredibly fast speed of computer microprocessors. A simple laptop can instantly handle audio, visual, and textual information from multiple groups. (It's the facilitator's job to keep up with the speed of the information being processed and then help make it understandable and useful to the group!)

As it becomes increasingly difficult to take people away from work for off-site meetings, it becomes more important for groups to work as efficiently as possible. A number of technologies capture the group's agenda, discussion, ideas, recommendations, decisions, action plans, and conclusions in electronic form—often in real-time, as the group is working. It is now possible to hand participants color printouts of the session's results as they walk out the door—a big improvement over mailing the results to them later. Groups enjoy taking part in a survey and seeing the results immediately. Directly after the session, members can show their outputs to other working groups, who are usually surprised and impressed by the speed of the results. There's an "ooh and aah" factor at play the first few times a group accomplishes this feat.

➤ **To quantify qualitative information.** As business increases its efforts to leverage intellectual capital, it becomes imperative that facilitators measure their contribution to this quest. Certain technologies allow a group to assign a numerical or scaled value to highly subjective information. Software then translates this information into normative data that can statistically reveal group tendencies, standard deviations, and ranges. Even more important, the information can be archived and compared with future group sessions to measure progress (or the lack of it) on difficult to quantify issues such as trust and communication.

➤ **To elicit anonymous feedback.** As more organizations move from hierarchical to team- or networked-based work environments, the use of performance evaluations increases. Technology's ability to generate anonymous feedback makes it a natural for use by groups who still fear retribution for giving a boss critical comments. Also, the feedback's paperless documentation (which can be achieved for future comparisons) means that facilitators can use the results for a variety of purposes, such as coaching, making training recommendations, and developing employee competencies.

➤ **To link disparate organizations.** In the aftermath of downsizing and reengineering many firms are growing again but with fewer personnel to accomplish the work. Often the work involves communicating and coordinating with a collection of teams brought together by merger or acquisition but not much else. Technology can link groups from different parts of an enterprise and create "knowledge management" solutions, which rapidly give groups applied information about various tasks.

When Not to Use Technology

It's equally important to know when not to use technology to facilitate groups. Technology *should not* be used for the following:

— *To cover or substitute for a lack of good facilitation skills.* Facilitators at one global network were drawn to using technology as a way to grow their businesses. Within two years, most of the group had given up the attempt, returning to traditional approaches. Exit interviews revealed that the majority of those quitting did not have flourishing practices as facilitators before the attempt. Even the most razzle-dazzle technology won't cover up poor facilitation skills for long.

— *When the group's decisions are likely to be overruled by an autocratic decision maker.* In the middle of a facilitated, high-level meeting, a CEO got up and left the room, not to return. The problem? An audience response system was being used, and he didn't like its democratic influence on the group. This example highlights the value of ensuring that senior decision makers know what technology can and will do to change groups.

— *To avoid solving problems.* Technology often brings groups together through anonymous means; consequently, it's easy for people to turn to technology when they want to seem hard at work on a problem while avoiding critical issues—such as clarifying roles and expectations or examining a flawed strategy behind the problem.

— *To introduce newly formed groups to working together.* Groups just coming together for the first time need a chance to get acquainted via face-to-face interaction. Technology, misapplied, can easily block the intimacy needed to start the stages of group development.

— *To avoid confrontations or the building of trusting interpersonal relationships.* Sometimes people hide behind the technology—its computers, video cameras, audio equipment—to avoid dealing with the nitty-gritty issues of power, control, and conflict.

Step 2: Select the Right Technology for the Right Purpose

Technology and its forms continue to multiply rapidly, and there are numerous choices available to facilitators. You can find out more about these choices via Internet searches, groupware conferences, and vendors or exhibitors at human performance and learning conferences (organization development, training and development, instruction design, etc.).

To organize a search for the right technology, try this approach. Begin by asking the question "What is the group trying to accomplish?" Then break down the question into two parts: "How simple or complex is the group's task?" and "How cohesive is the group?" Next, apply Olson's Rule for technology selection: The simpler the issues and more unified or cohesive the group, the more virtual (people in different locations connected by telecommunications equipment and computers) the technology can be. A matrix for applying this rule is provided below; but first, let's take a brief look at how we organize group technologies for use in that matrix and at what those technologies involve.

Group technologies can be organized according to five categories:

1. Videoconferencing
2. On-line groupware
3. Audience response systems
4. Audio teleconferencing
5. Fixed location groupware

Videoconferencing links video images of conference participants in different locations, via modems and telephone lines, so that participants can see one another while communicating. Systems vary in complexity: Some require elaborate electronic connections that must be set up and maintained by a technician; other simpler systems can be operated by the participants themselves.

Uses: Primarily used for groups working from different locations; ideal for relatively unified groups with clearly defined, relatively simple problems to solve.

On-line groupware is software that lets people who are connected by a network (either a local area network [LAN] or the Internet) communicate via written data. (At this time, most usage is confined to keyboarded data, though video and graphic images can also be communicated.) The software also allows for the electronic processing of information (e.g., electronic brainstorming and voting).

Uses: Primarily used for groups working from different locations; ideal for relatively unified groups with clearly defined, relatively simple problems to solve.

Audience response systems combine software and interactive keypads (the kind used to facilitate communication in face-to-face meetings). Participants sit separately at computers, each with its own keypad. Questions are posed, with a set of response choices, all of which are projected on a large screen. Using the keypad, participants enter the response that best matches their own opinion. The software processes the data and then feeds it back to the audience in graphic form.

Uses: Primarily used with groups who are located in the same place at the same time in order to solve more complex problems successfully. This technology can be the best solution for new, conflicted, or strategic-level groups; it can also be the best choice when working with cohesive groups.

Audio teleconferencing is the same as the "conference call" method—it connects participants in different locations via telephone lines joined in a single circuit.

Uses: Primarily used with groups in different locations.

Fixed location groupware is a LAN-based system that lets you conduct an electronic meeting using software that presents the meeting steps to the group. Members work at computers, in the same room, while one facilitator (a "chauffeur") operates the software. The computers are usually connected to one another through hardware wires.

Uses: Primarily used with groups who have complex problems to solve.

The Application Matrix and Its Quadrants

The application matrix follows, along with an explanation of its quadrants.

	Complexity of the Group Task	
	Low	High
Low **Cohesion of the Group**	I Audio Teleconference Videoconference On-Line Groupware	II Audience Response Systems Fixed Location Groupware
High	III Audio Teleconference Videoconference On-Line Groupware	IV Fixed Location Groupware Audience Response Systems

Quadrant I—Low Complexity, Low Cohesion

Both audio teleconferences and videoconferences have a limited ability to handle multiple-voice inputs. They are best used for sequential information processes (e.g., people talking in turn, giving their comments in response to a cued question; or a panel talking in a question-and-answer format). Groups work together, though in different locations, and, by necessity, remain fairly cohesive, as the technology does not afford real opportunities to forge a consensus by wrestling with divergent thoughts.

The facilitator brings the groups together in order to build a common knowledge base around a simple issue. Often the group's task is one of listening to an expert or panel of experts deliver content knowledge, while the facilitator's task is to manage question-and-answer activities.

In a like manner on-line groupware can be used for fairly simple problems where the group is not conflicted. The "same time, same place" fixed location groupware can help a divided group to more quickly solve a complex problem.

Quadrant II—High Complexity, Low Cohesion

Audience response systems (ARS) promote the flow of an interactive process while also providing anonymity for a new or conflicted group that needs to build cohesiveness and trust. The unobtrusive nature of most ARS technology keeps the focus on the group task and does not draw attention to the technology.

The facilitator works with the new or conflicted group that needs to build consensus around complex issues, data, or problems.

Quadrant III—Low Complexity, High Cohesion

Audio teleconferences, videoconferences, and on-line groupware allow for only limited interpersonal dynamics during the session. The technologies work best with groups that have already worked through conflicts related to the task at hand and need a minimum of face-to-face contact in order to successfully complete the task or a particular segment of a task.

The purpose of the facilitation is to assist well-operating groups to add to their knowledge or solve problems.

Quadrant IV—High Complexity, High Cohesion

Fixed location groupware and audience response systems are ideal for cohesive groups dealing with relatively complex problems. These technologies provide a combination of interpersonal contact and increased speed and productivity of information processing (e.g., electronic brainstorming or voting).

Facilitation helps the already intact, largely cohesive working group deal with complex data, decisions, and problems.

Taking a Closer Look: Questions and Answers

This section will provide you with a more detailed description of each category.

Videoconferencing

How does it work?

In its simplest form, a videoconference unites groups across a distance by sending an audio-visual picture from the main group site (where the facilitator is located) to one or more remote sites. Each remote site is equipped with a monitor-like device to receive the signal. Two-way communication takes place through a teleconference or computer line. More expensive systems can simultaneously transmit and receive audio-visual information from multiple sites so that several groups can see and hear each other in close to real-time. While some companies own their own systems, a number of them hire specialty firms that produce videoconferences, or they rent time from places like Kinko's that have specially equipped videoconference rooms.

What does the facilitator do?

In addition to filling the standard facilitation roles, a videoconference facilitator becomes a director and "air-traffic controller"—he or she lets group members know who is speaking and when it is OK for them to respond. He or she must explain this role to members at the start of the session, ensuring that they understand they will get a chance to speak when the time comes for it; otherwise, members may get sidetracked by frustration, wondering "Is it my turn to talk?"

Facilitating video sessions becomes complex when multiple sites are involved, because there is often a brief lag time in the audio signal. This audio delay makes it difficult to know whether someone has finished speaking or is merely pausing (or being interrupted) in mid-speech. The effect is similar to watching a stage play and having the mikes go off halfway into an actor's soliloquy.

When working with larger groups, the facilitator must deal with the movement of a camera (which often does not locate a speaker until several sentences have been delivered). The facilitator must be skilled in voice recognition, as the quality of the video image may not always be clear enough to show who is speaking.

On-Line Groupware

How does it work?

Technology such as Lotus Notes and other forms of groupware connects participants through laptops or desktop computers that are networked or otherwise linked together. The greatest growth in this type of technology has been with systems that use on-line software to create electronic meetings via the Internet. Because of its primary reliance on keyboard data entry, this technology is best suited for facilitating text-based issues with small groups who may be working in different locations. However, small inexpensive cameras that capture black-and-white or color pictures and send video through the computer can turn an on-line session into a videoconference as well. Many newer groupware technologies are built for Internet or Intranet application so that the broadest possible combination of participants is possible at the cheapest price.

Groups often take part in some form of electronic brainstorming, which links or threads comments together. More sophisticated forms of groupware allow the group to prioritize issues through a variety of voting technologies. Participants work in a virtual group (meaning they are anywhere in the world but are attending the session "virtually" via telecommunications equipment, computers, and communications software).

What does the facilitator do?

With groups that are virtually linked, the facilitator works to keep the discussion focused on the stated agenda by typing in comments that bring the group back from divergent issues. This can be done either by reminding the group what the main point of discussion is or by asking the group to respond to a particular comment written earlier in the session.

Audience Response Systems

How does it work?

Each participant is given a handheld keypad that is linked (wired or wireless) to a computer. A projection device allows the entire group to see its voting or discussion results. Because keypads are so much more user-friendly than keyboards, groups find this kind of technology easy to use. The proprietary software in each system determines whether the group votes at a fairly simple level (survey types using Likert scales, yes/no, or multiple choice) or at a more strategic level (weighted paired-comparison votes complete with real-time interpretation). Most systems allow collection of demographic data so that the facilitator may examine the group's consensus (or lack of) at a variety of levels. Most companies rent the technology to facilitators or organizations who know how to operate the system rather than sell the technology outright.

What does the facilitator do?

This kind of facilitation is most like traditional facilitation because (a) the group is physically together, and (b) the technology is small enough to minimize interference with group dynamics. As with all group technologies, the facilitator working with an audience response system faces an expanded role. Not all facilitators feel comfortable with this expansion—it can be a bit unnerving to keep one eye on the group and the other on the technology. Yet the power of the technology, which rapidly moves a group to results, makes the effort worthwhile.

While the simpler systems generate results that need little interpretation, more complex strategic systems (like CoNexus®) require skill to link results to a creative process generated by the software. In such cases, the facilitator is simultaneously managing theory, methods, and tools.

Audio Teleconferencing

How does it work?

The audioconference is one form of technology that most facilitators are already familiar with. An audioconference links groups via a telephone line equipped to handle multiple callers. Because it is probably the most frequently used type of group communication technology, and at the same time probably the most poorly utilized, there is a definite need for its effective facilitation.

What does the facilitator do?

The facilitator works with the teleconference leader to ensure that the technology is used effectively. A number of tasks must be completed if the teleconference is to be a productive medium of communication and action. These tasks (see Guide V-2: Facilitating Effective Audio Teleconferences and Guide V-3: Audio Teleconference Participant Tips) can be handled by either the meeting leader, the facilitator, or some combination of the two.

A key role for the facilitator might be to coach the meeting leader on how to facilitate the teleconference. In this coaching scenario, the facilitator can then listen in on the teleconference and provide feedback to the leader after the call is completed. Another approach is for the facilitator and the meeting leader to review the facilitation roles and decide who will do what. For instance, the meeting leader may want to handle most of the conference alone but call on the facilitator to help people work through a particular task. Yet another possibility is for the facilitator to train small groups in how to simultaneously lead and facilitate the conference.

Fixed Location Groupware

How does it work?

Fixed location groupware involves both software and hardware. The software enables information processing, such as electronic brainstorming and voting; the hardware enables the group to work together in one room, usually via devices that link the computers. Members sit alone at a keyboard (or, if computers are limited, share with another member) and enter data in response to cues given by the "chauffeur" or the technical meeting facilitator—the one who operates the software system and leads the group through the various phases of the meeting.

The software in most systems can be used for many purposes, such as planning meetings, brainstorming electronically, prioritizing ideas or group voting, commenting on specific proposals or ideas, and producing a meeting record for distribution immediately following the meeting. The groupware is purchased via a licensing agreement with the vendor; cost varies according to the number of people who will be using the system.

When groups are working on-line in one room, the facilitator's task becomes more complex. The group not only can converse via the keyboard but may discusses ideas face to face. The facilitator needs to keep the rhythm of the session, alternating between data entry and analysis and face-to-face discussions. Members easily become bored and frustrated if the appropriate balance is not maintained.

Because the effective operation of the technology is a significant task in itself, groups using fixed location groupware often benefit from a facilitation team: one person who is the technical facilitator or "chauffeur," and another person who manages the face-to-face group processes.

Step 3: Do Session Pre-Work

It's important to remember that technology can easily double or triple the preparation time needed for a traditional approach. Before facilitating with technology, go through the following checklist of activities to make sure the session goes well:

☐ *Ensure management buy-in for the use of technology.* Do key decision makers understand how technology might change group dynamics? Are they open to the more democratic process that technology brings? Has the system been demonstrated if you're not sure about buy-in or understanding? Buy-in from the top is essential before proceeding further. Remember: Few managers like surprises.

☐ *Rate the group's experience level.* Have members used technology before? What has their experience been like? If they had a bad experience, what went wrong?

☐ *Fit the technology to the group's capabilities.* It's insensitive not to consider the limitations of a technology before trying it with a group. Evaluate the extent to which characteristics of the technology could interfere with people who have various challenges—problems with eyesight, hearing, manual dexterity, language differences, and so forth.

☐ *Set up and test the technology.* Murphy's Law certainly applies to technology—probably doubly so. Make sure you not only have backup technology wherever possible but also can use a low-tech fallback approach to facilitate the group if all systems fail (facilitate long enough and they will).

Do a test session with a group; it's a great way to discover disasters before they reach epic proportions. Solicit feedback on ways to improve the process.

☐ *Coordinate roles and responsibilities between the facilitator and technology operator(s).* Technology adds a level of complexity to the facilitation process. If you're working by yourself, you need to be sure you can do two things at once—run a group and run technology. (A key tip: Don't do it unless you absolutely have to. It creates too many migraine moments.) If you have someone operating the technology, be clear upfront that the technology serves the group, not vice versa. Discuss ahead of time what you'll do in various situations, how you will deal with the inevitable lag times that come up, and when to schedule breaks.

☐ *Coordinate roles and responsibilities with co-facilitators.* Establish who is better at facilitating the technology learning curve, who is better on their feet in dealing with resistance, who can interpret the group's results from technology, and so forth.

Step 4: Take the Measures Needed to Create a Successful Session

The lists below include some of the most important guidelines you can follow in order to create a successful session.

Keys to Success With Videoconferencing

➤ Keep remote-site participants plugged in. Even if they have a great audio and video signal, they will not pick up all the nonverbal cues that the main group will. Explicitly identify the state of the main group's thinking and feeling as time goes on; check with remote groups to see if they are tracking. If there are large groups involved, work with the camerapersons to keep the scene lively. Static shots can kill the visual interest.

➤ Video is the best technology for facilitating a "town-hall" type of meeting, in which groups at different sites are linked but only a few individuals need to be speaking. The limitations of this approach become apparent when multiple individuals from multiple sites attempt to talk with one another.

➤ Combine facilitating groups from various locations that need to see not only each other but also drawings, product samples, and other items. Facilitation can be enhanced if augmented with electronic white boards that document group output in real-time and display at multiple sites.

➤ Design the session with an eye on some typical drawbacks: cost, technical limitations with large groups, and the boredom typical of most video productions.

Keys to Success With On-Line Groupware

➤ Participants need to be keyboard literate. More than this, they need to feel comfortable using the technology. One Fortune 500 firm spent over $250,000 on a groupware program in order to facilitate sessions with senior management. The move proved a disaster when the executives declared that keyboard work was the job of their administrative assistants. Beware of dinosaur mentality!

➤ Stay involved at your keyboard. Jump in with comments to let the group know how it's doing (e.g., "Excellent brainstorming—we need more memory to keep up with you," or "We're seeing a lot of comments on side issues—does anyone remember the main point for discussion?").

➤ Keep the discussion focused. Threaded on-line conversations can become overwhelmingly complex if the facilitator doesn't help the group break the task down into manageable parts. Remember: With distant technology, simple is better.

Keys to Success With Audience Response Systems

➤ Let group members experiment with technology early in the process. Their curiosity is aroused, they want to play with the "toys," so give them some practice upfront. To make them feel comfortable, collect some demographic information about the group and then show them the results; this will give them an idea of the technology's potential to capture the group's thinking in real-time. It's amazing how many people can listen to a facilitator describe the capabilities of the technologies but still not understand it until they have begun to use it.

➤ Go beyond the obvious. Once the group has seen its results, skilled facilitators learn how to exploit the power of the software and discover previously unknown opportunities. For example, the following voting profile shows how individuals in a group voted on the issue of leadership's influence and performance in their company's culture. The group voted the importance of "influence" using a weighted paired-comparison technique. For the performance vote, it rated the issue on a 1-to-9 Likert scale (9 = practically perfect; 1 = not at all). With nearly 100 people in the group, it would be extremely difficult without technology to find the subset of participants who felt that leadership was a highly important but underperforming contributor to company culture. With ARS it was accomplished in less than 15 minutes. The facilitator noted that there were 19 participants who felt the issue of leadership had high potential for influence but was currently not performing very well.

➥ Leverage the technology's strengths—real-time feedback and anonymity. The technology is particularly helpful for groups dealing with significant change, because the anonymity of the voting allows new views to emerge. As a result, the facilitator can play a key role in supporting the champions for change who emerge as a result of the process.

➥ Give participants a chance to catch up to the speed of their actions. I've had numerous groups go into "voting shock" when they've resolved an issue in minutes or hours rather than days or months. Psychologically they need a chance to step back and appreciate the reality of their accomplishments. After viewing voting results, I will often divide the group into small breakout teams. They are asked to share their personal responses to the vote and then answer the question "What do we hope and/or fear will happen as a result of this vote?" When the groups come back together and debrief, they often find similar issues raised by the different groups. This helps to ground the vote in the group's "real-world" business climate and suggests practical next steps for successful implementation.

Keys to Success With Audio Teleconferencing

➥ Identify who is present at the conference by "calling the roll" and asking each person to respond.

➥ Review the purpose of the conference call and the agenda. Before the call, fax agendas to everyone on the call.

➥ Ask participants to identify themselves before speaking and to state to whom they are directing their comments, if not the entire group.

➥ Poll group members as to their opinion on an issue under discussion, or do a round of "turn taking," where each person takes a turn speaking.

➥ If plans call for some type of structured planning or problem-solving activity, lead the group through the steps of the activity.

➥ Don't move from one item to another until you have summarized the discussion and reviewed the agreed-upon actions to be taken.

➥ Moderate disagreements—ask questions that facilitate individuals' resolving their differences. Because of the technology's limits, be prepared to delay activities, to delegate further problem solving, or to table items more often than you would in the face-to-face meeting.

➦ Control the pace of the conference, and ask people to slow down if the pace is too rapid for effective recording of the information.

➦ Take notes and document the conference, paying particular attention to agreed-upon actions and decisions.

➦ Review and summarize the conference call, listing action items, agreements, and next steps.

Keys to Success With Fixed Location Groupware

➦ With groupware that brings people into the same room, mix and match on-line time, face-to-face time, and experiential activities to keep the group energized.

➦ When you are working with groupware technology that combines on-line with face-to-face opportunities, it's crucial to minimize the physical barriers of technology. Groups get poorer results and incur major frustration when they have to peer around PCs to see one another. One solution is to move to a separate part of the room where the group can interact unhindered by computers.

➦ Pre-run your meeting with two or three people to test out how it will work. This will also enable you to clarify roles if you are working with a co-facilitator.

➦ Team up with another person. One person becomes the technical facilitator or "chauffeur," and the other facilitates face-to-face interactions. This is particularly important with some of the fixed location groupware that calls for a significant skill level in order to effectively use the technology.

➦ Use the agenda-building capacity of the groupware to plan the agenda with the meeting leader. Review the agenda with the group prior to initiating the work, and make any necessary adjustments suggested by the group and approved by the meeting leader.

➦ Before the meeting, find out if anyone is "keyboard illiterate" or terminally slow with keyboard entries. You can pair this person with someone who is quick at the keyboard. You can also use the "pairing" strategy for all participants, letting the most keyboard-literate person handle the entries for both people.

Step 5: Do Follow-Up Tasks

As the session draws to a close, wrap up a number of items raised by technology. This is an important step that includes the following:

(a) Capture all group results. It's easy to forget what the technology has documented and what it has not. Double-check for accountability (who does what and when) before losing the technology connection. In one group, after a two-day brainstorming session, members got carried away celebrating their many accomplishments and tore down the flip charts on the wall and shredded them before they remembered that at least half the ideas on the charts hadn't been saved in the computer yet. Oops! The group then had to do an unexpected team-building exercise called "Reconstructing the Charts."

(b) Evaluate the technology's effectiveness. It's always helpful to do a debriefing about lessons learned, changes for next time, and so on, even without technology involved in the facilitation; but it's a must with a group using technology, for it often uncovers significant learning about how to improve technology's role in future sessions. One way to finish up is to use ARS and on-line technology to conduct a real-time evaluation of the session, the technology, and the facilitator. This is a paperless way to fill out an evaluation form, and most participants are grateful for the speed with which the questions can be answered compared to the traditional method. Sometimes a combination of technology and paper is important to capture open-ended comments if the technology does not require a keyboard.

(c) Connect the entire group in the final report. Because technology can automatically create a single conversation, it's easy to think everyone understands what the session accomplished and what was agreed upon. Experience tells otherwise. Whether you are dealing with a video conference, on-line resources, or ARS, it's important to issue at least an executive summary of the major conclusions along with action items needing accountability. Document "parking-lot" issues that have been raised but will not be discussed until a future session.

(d) Follow up to gauge the sense of buy-in for group results. Within two weeks after the session, call several participants to get a post-mortem perspective. Did the sessions live up to expectation? Were the sponsors glad they used technology? Would they do it again? And so forth.

What has been presented here are some definitions of what several technologies can do to help make groups effective, the role(s) of the facilitator in helping groups to use the technology effectively, a series of logical steps to take in using technology to work with groups, and some key success tips on how to make the different types of sessions effective. To go further with learning about how to use the various technologies, you will want to access some of the tools that are presented in the Facilitator Resources and begin using the various technologies. Guide V-1: Getting Started will provide you with further suggestions for getting some hands-on experience.

FACILITATOR RESOURCES

Getting Started: The Electronic Meeting

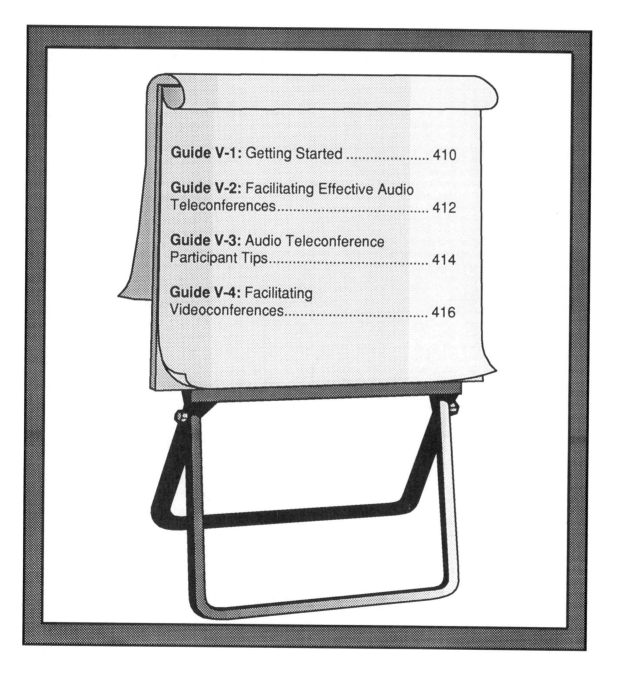

GUIDE V-1

Getting Started

If you're fairly new to using technology with groups, here are some tips on how to get started:

■ **Take it easy.** Trying to do too much too fast will just frustrate you and could turn off prospective users to technology. Take your time and create some safe learning experiences for yourself.

■ **Find a partner.** Find someone else who is interested in pursuing the use of technology with groups. If your techno skills are pretty limited, try to find someone who is further along on the tech side to be a partner.

■ **Find a client "sponsor."** Identify someone with whom you are working who is interested in using technology with groups. Explain that you are "spooling up" to use technology and looking for some groups to work with. Caution the person that it will take some time before you're ready to work with teams.

■ **Order products on a trial basis.** Order groupware on a trial basis. Most of the suppliers have a 30-day trial offer. Or try out an offer such as the Meeting Works policy, which lets you use the groupware for free with eight people or less.

■ **Create an easy, safe way to try things out.** Pick a small group of people to create a safe environment in which to get started.

■ **Use conferences and networking groups to learn.** Find someone in your ASTD or OD network who is working with technology, and ask him or her to observe one of the sessions. At the next large training, facilitation, or OD conference you attend, plan to spend time in demo sessions of groupware. Stop by and talk to vendors. List the things about facilitating with technology that are still a mystery to you, and intend to get those questions answered at the conference. Form or join a groupware user group in your area.

■ **Warm up to videoconferencing.** You might invest in an inexpensive camera for your computer. Do this in coordination with friends or colleagues that already have one or want to have one. (Both you and the person with whom you are visually communicating may need to have the same type of camera.) Find a commercial vendor who produces videoconferences. Tell them you are a facilitator and want to learn more about the technology for your client(s). Ask them if they would allow you to observe a session, interview them at a videoconference site, and so forth. If you have a Kinko's videoconferencing center near you, visit it. For center locations, see Kinko's Website: http://www.kinkos.com.

(Continued)

Getting Started *(Concluded)*

■ **Check out some print resources.**
We have included a bibliography in
this section with several outstanding
resources (see Guide V-9: Technology
Bibliography). You can also learn a lot
about groupware on-line at the groupware
Websites we have listed in Guide V-6:
Groupware Resources.

■ **Get product-specific training.** After
you've checked out the different types of
groupware and made a selection of what
to use, enroll in the training that they
offer. If you have an organizational

sponsor to support your learning, you
may be able to reduce the cost of such
training.

■ **Stay in touch with how you learn
best.** Some people learn best by reading
books or observing sessions. Others do
best by calling tech-support numbers for
groupware and other resources.

GUIDE V-2

Facilitating Effective Audio Teleconferences

The Importance of This Guide
More and more group work is being done over the telephone. The cost savings of such meetings are enormous, and there are actually some advantages to working via the phone, especially if the audio teleconference is conducted using the guidelines below.

EFFECTIVE FACILITATION OF AUDIO TELECONFERENCES

GUIDELINES

1. One person should be responsible for arranging the phone hookups for the conference.

2. One person should be responsible for constructing an agenda and getting it to participants at least one day before the phone conference. The agenda should be limited to a page and include the purpose of the conference, the expected outcomes, the suggested steps for achieving the outcomes, and the names of all participants. Send out well ahead of time any materials that participants should review for the conference. Included on the agenda should be the method people should use to connect to the conference and any call-in numbers needed to connect or reconnect if they should get cut off. Ask participants to call in to one person if they will be at a number other than their regular number.

3. Send out along with the agenda the audio teleconference participant tips provided in Guide V-3, unless you are sure that all the participants are already well aware of the tips.

4. One person should act as a facilitator, moving the group through the suggested steps on the agenda. This same person can serve as a timekeeper, or a separate person can watch the time allocations for each item. It is often wise to have a person who is not the group leader act as the facilitator for the call. When there is a clearly designated group leader and a separate facilitator, the facilitator should run through the agenda with the group leader prior to the call.

(Continued)

Guidelines *(Concluded)*

5. One person should be responsible for taking notes during the conference and getting the notes out to participants within 24 hours. Best practice is to fax notes immediately following the audio teleconference.

6. Remind people of a few conference-calling "ground rules" at the start of the call. Here are some of the most common ground rules:

    *   Always identify yourself.

    *   Speak in the order of your name on the participant list, unless otherwise indicated. You can pass if you have no comment.

    *   Wait for one person to finish before speaking; otherwise, comments will be muddled or cut off on speakerphones.

    *   Stay on the call from start to finish. If you cannot stay on the call, let people know at the start of the call.

    *   No interruptions. Have someone else handle business while you're on the call.

7. "Round robin" speaking should be used at audio teleconferences. The facilitator calls on each participant in turn and asks for comments. Use the participant list and call on each person in the same order each time there is a discussion. This avoids one person being cut off before he or she is finished or more than one person trying to speak at once.

8. Before moving from one agenda item to the next, the facilitator summarizes the discussion, the actions agreed upon, or the next steps for doing agreed-upon actions.

9. Limit audio teleconferences to 90 minutes maximum. Well-organized conference calls should take less than an hour to conduct. Stop at the agreed-upon maximum time for the call, even if you have not completed the agenda.

10. Identify the appropriate next steps before the end of the call. Schedule subsequent calls or meetings before completing the call.

11. At the end of the call, the facilitator should summarize the discussion and clarify the actions agreed upon. Persons responsible for action items should be named and one person designated as "responsible" if more than one person is working on an item.

12. Each person should sign off at the end of the call, letting others know he or she is going off the line. If some people want to talk after the call for any reason, this should be arranged between them while all the other people are still on the line.

GUIDE V-3

Audio Teleconference Participant Tips

MAKING AUDIO TELECONFERENCE CALLS WORK

IDEAS AND TIPS

➤ When using a speakerphone, wait until there is a slight pause before speaking; otherwise, you may cut off the last speaker before he or she is finished.

➤ Arrange for someone else to handle your work while on the call. Don't allow interruptions.

➤ Stay on the line for the whole call. If you must leave before the scheduled ending time, announce your problem at the start of the call. Accept decisions made by others in your absence.

➤ Always state your name before commenting. Also, state the name of the person to whom you are addressing your comments. Research indicates that both practices improve audioconference productivity.

➤ Take notes. Jotting down notes holds your attention in the absence of face-to-face contact. Take the notes according to who says what. For example:

Jack: "We can't get them to come to that many meetings."

Mary: "It wasn't too much last year in Kansas City."

➤ Keep notes about points you want to make. Don't offer your thoughts immediately. Wait until it's your turn, or until you have several things to say. You will be amazed how often others will say what you are thinking, saving you stress on your vocal cords.

➤ If no one is assuming the role of facilitator for the call, suggest that someone do so.

➤ Speak in turn according to your place on the name list for the call.

➤ Acquire a shoulder rest for your phone if you're not using a speakerphone. If you do a lot of audioconferencing, invest in one of the recently improved types of speakerphones, which enhance your voice quality substantially.

(Continued)

Ideas and Tips *(Concluded)*

➡ Lightweight headsets are the best tool to use for audio teleconferencing. The headset should attach to the phone with a long cord so you can move about the room. These will pay off in improved productivity in much of your other work also.

➡ Hold the receiver away from your mouth to avoid breathing noises.

➡ Enunciate clearly, and use concrete examples. Speak at slightly slower than normal speed. Experienced communication observers report that conference participants perform better if they slow down their delivery a bit.

➡ Be especially conscious of your tone and vocal inflections. People interpret vocal cues more accurately than facial expressions or body language. Alliances and factions are more easily recognized, as are resisters and supporters.

➡ Be on time for the call. Calls patching in after the conference has started are even more disruptive than late entrances to face-to-face meetings.

➡ View the conference calls as an opportunity to sharpen your listening skills.

➡ Be conscious of your "air time." Don't overdo and don't hold back. Ask for the thoughts of others who may not be contributing enough.

➡ Look over related materials before the call so that you can keep up with the group.

➡ Get your coffee or beverage, go to the restroom, and so on before the call so that you're not frustrated while on the call.

➡ Do your part to encourage a focused approach to conference calling. If an agenda is not pre-published, ask that one be developed before the call gets in full swing. Check that follow-up notes will be distributed to all members. Clarify decisions and agreements before the group moves from one agenda item to the next. Ask that responsibilities for assignments be clarified between meetings.

➡ If people are sharing a speakerphone, everyone should move close to the microphone so they are clearly audible. Better speakerphones can pick up from a range of 12 to 15 feet. Most are only effective in much shorter ranges.

➡ For an important audio teleconference, you can establish a memory system of the people who are on the call by making name placards out of index cards and placing them on a table. You can even look at the card when addressing your comments. If you are part of a team that audioconferences frequently, make reusable placard cards with each team member's picture.

ACKNOWLEDGMENTS

Thanks to Anita Pierce, Jane Storms, Dick Zeller, and Caroline Moore of the Western Regional Resource Center for sharing audio teleconferencing resources, which greatly contributed to this guide.

GUIDE V-4

Facilitating Videoconferences

About This Guide

In this guide, we will take a quick look at the basics of facilitating with videoconferencing. These basics include being familiar with the different categories of videoconferences, the use of videoconference centers, and technical concerns. Also presented are ideas and tips to consider when setting out to facilitate the videoconference. We suggest that you supplement the material here with Eric Olson's observations on videoconferencing in this section's Overview.

Keep in mind that videoconferencing is the technology with which you're most likely to have a bad experience. Many groups get excited over the prospect of what this technology can do for them and the potential cost benefits of eliminating expensive face-to-face meetings. Consequently, too often people rush into videoconferencing, neglecting to do the necessary planning, preparation, and facilitation work. The result is often a rather drab and confusing interchange, which turns people off to the technology. We hope this guide—its narrative and ideas and tips—helps you avoid that pitfall and others associated with videoconferencing.

Introduction

In one of the best resources available on the effective use of videoconferences, Lynn Diamond (1996) describes videoconferencing this way:

> Videoconferencing adds video images to voice telecommunication among two or more locations. It creates a "virtual reality" of being in the same room with people who may be thousands of miles away. You can do virtually anything in a videoconference that you would do in an in-person meeting—hold discussions, create and display graphics, demonstrate products, and more. (p. 3)

The latter half of Diamond's statement may be something of a stretch at the current time. Videoconferencing is just beginning to come into play in the more traditional processes for working with groups. Because of technology's cost, and the considerable difficulties of making videoconferencing work for many processes, some time may pass before we see it used as extensively as other emergent groupware applications for conferencing. Even so, there is a definite place for videoconferencing in group work, especially for groups separated by a great distance.

Videoconference Categories

There are several types of videoconferences:

- Point-to-point videoconferences enable one site to be hooked up with one other site at any given time.

- Point-to-multipoint videoconferences originate at one site and are received at multiple sites.

- Multipoint-to-multipoint hookups allow for two-way audio and video transmissions between multiple sites, though you can see and hear only one site at a time.

Videoconferences may also be divided into two basic types: active and passive. Burleson (1990) explains the difference between them. In the **passive videoconference**, a presentation is made from one point; then limited responding (such as a question-and-answer session) is done from other sites; in the **active videoconference**, actual face-to-face meetings and discussions take place, as well as many of the group processes normally used in a same-place meeting.

Videoconference Centers

Videoconference centers are specially equipped rooms with video cameras and transmitting equipment. The rooms are soundproofed to improve acoustics and usually can accommodate somewhere between 6 and 20 people. Microphones are used to transmit the audio signals. Videoconference centers vary greatly in how extensively they are equipped to produce videoconferences. Some conference centers have the "basics" of audio and video transmission capabilities, while others resemble full-scale television studios.

Commerical centers for videoconferencing are rapidly growing, as are related specialist services that will help you plan and conduct a videoconference. The largest and most accessible of these efforts is the chain of conference centers recently established by Kinko's. Currently, there are 155 centers in operation. Though most rooms are small and will not accommodate a large group, rates are quite reasonable. (For more information, call 1-800-KINKOS, or check out the company's Website at http://www.kinkos.com.)

Another approach is to use portable videoconferencing equipment, which allows you to conduct conferences in any room. This is not the most preferable option, however, because the acoustics, lighting, and sound quality of most rooms provide less than ideal conditions.

Technical Concerns

The technical aspects of conducting the videoconference are extremely critical. In most cases, you will be working with a technician who sets up the connections and handles other technical needs of the conference. The skill level of the person handling the cameras and controls can make or break the conference, and you will want to check the person out carefully before your conference. It is possible for one individual to handle the technical side and facilitate the group(s) at the same time, but that individual will have to be extremely comfortable with managing the camera, microphones, and switching modes and selections.

Video and audio transmissions can be sent from one site to another in several ways. The simplest transmission is via small cameras that are connected to one person's computer. This enables one computer user to visually conference with one other user, provided that the second person also has a compatible camera and software set-up. The cameras and software have a limited range and limited capabilities but are quite affordable. Using these cameras and a telephone speakerphone, you can conduct a limited type of videoconference.

The major disadvantage to videoconferencing is purely technical: the brief lag time in the transmission of the signals. This delay requires there be a slight pause between speakers or else a part of the transmission will be cut off. (This is also true of the audio teleconference.)

Facilitating the Videoconference: Ideas and Tips

Here are some ideas and tips for you to consider when you set out to facilitate the videoconference. Although it is beyond our scope here to provide an exhaustive list of possibilities, the following deal with some of the most important aspects of the videoconference:

☝ *Set up facilitation roles to make the conference successful.* One person should be selected to serve as videoconference chairperson at the master site for the conference. Another person can act as the videoconference "facilitator," or the chairperson can take on the facilitation role. There also should be one meeting leader and/or facilitator at each additional site.

☝ *Plan, plan, plan.* Start planning early: The videoconference calls for more detailed planning than the traditional meeting and thus more lead time for this step. In addition to planning the typical agenda for a meeting, you need to plan for the various switches to different sites and whether these switches will be voice-activated or director-activated. You will need to take the time to coordinate your meeting designs with the technician who will be handling the mechanics and the switching to make sure your designs will work with the technology. Simple purposes and clear outcomes are called for. Don't expect to be able to do everything in the videoconference that can be done in the face-to-face meeting; include some traditional group processes in your meeting design, to keep the session from becoming tedious, but be selective. The conference agenda or "storyboard" should be faxed to all sites before the meeting and posted in chart form at the master site. Best practice is to check with all the site leaders before the conference to make sure the agenda meets their approval. Changing agendas on the spot can lead to big problems.

👍 ***Think and plan visually.*** Effective videoconferences require visual thinking and thinking visually. This is a different sort of orientation from the standard facilitation for a meeting. The videoconference facilitator or planner needs to think more like a film or video director, attending to camera angles, visualizing a particular scene and thinking of how it can look attractive and hold the interest of the participants. Using a variety of visual media and making use of graphics will guard against the boredom that can occur if the conference becomes a long string of individual dialogues.

👍 ***Plan several shorter sessions rather than one lengthy one.*** Like the audio teleconference, participants seem to have a shorter attention span for the videoconference. In most cases, you are better off planning four separate 1-hour sessions than trying to complete a single 4-hour agenda.

👍 ***Prepare simple and clear questions and activity introductions.*** Activities and questions need to be introduced with exceptional clarity so that confusions are avoided and everyone is kept "on the same page." It is a good idea to write out your questions and activity introductions ahead of time, producing a "script" from which to operate, just as a film or video director would.

👍 ***Set up an audition if you are new to videoconferencing.*** Until you are familiar with the technology, it's a good idea to set up an audition in the studio or conferencing center before the meeting. Don't just visit the center and then show up the day of your conference. If this presents an additional cost, view the additional cost as a training investment. You will be much more confident and relaxed for your actual session if you have had a chance to get familiar with the technology beforehand. You will want to repeat the "audition step" a few times as you conduct more conferences, so that you keep "practicing."

👍 ***If you are using videoconferencing equipment in a room that serves some other purpose, prepare the room for the videoconference.*** Take a portable camera into the room you will be using and "pan" around to see what the room looks like. Take down any distracting paintings. Look for the best area of the room in which to set up the conference. See how the lighting looks to you, and arrange for alternate lighting if needed. Don't forget to think about the seating arrangements—you will want to avoid seating participants opposite each other. Use the portable camera to try out different seating possibilities. If a technician is available, ask him or her to do the room check with you. Discuss camera angles and any visuals that will be used during the conference. Ask the technician to show you how to operate the equipment. Make a personal commitment to learn how to use it on your own; this will make you more confident in your ability to conduct the videoconference.

👍 ***Welcome all sites and participants, and have people identify themselves before starting the meeting.*** Begin the round of personal introductions, having the chairperson and/or facilitator at your site go first; then ask the participants at your site to introduce themselves. Next, switch to the other site(s) and have everyone else do the same. As in the face-to-face meeting, you can use the introductions as an icebreaker activity by asking that each person add some type of data to his or her introduction.

👆 ***Brief people at all sites on videoconference ground rules.*** Meeting leaders can conduct briefings at each site shortly before the conference starts, or the leader or facilitator at the master site can present suggestions during the first few minutes online. Here are several ground rules for you to consider; some are more essential than others, and some apply only in certain cases:

- Always pause before speaking.

- Keep comments brief. (Optional: There will be a _____ minute limit on commenting.)

- Before commenting, announce from which site you are speaking and state your name.

- Speak in a normal tone and at a normal volume.

- Look into the monitor while speaking.

- Refrain from side conversations.

- Don't play with your microphone. Let the technical person make any adjustments.

- Move a little slower than you normally would. Avoid moving around or fidgeting a lot.

- Refrain from shuffling papers or making other distracting noises.

- Avoid making sudden gestures, which can make the video image choppy.

Another alternative is to mail the ground rules to the participants ahead of time and ask them to look over the rules. If you do a mailing, you can also include some tips on how to dress and "look your best" (see Burleson, 1990, or Diamond, 1996).

👆 ***Model looking into the camera when you talk.*** You can help build the norm of looking into the camera when speaking by consistently modeling the behavior yourself.

👆 ***Track participation.*** Because not everyone is in the same room at the same time, it is more difficult for the facilitator to keep track of who is participating and who is not. Keeping written track of participation is one helpful option. You may want to make a list of participants, by site, before the conference; then you can keep this list in front of you during the conference, marking each time a participant speaks. Or you can ask another person at the master site to do this for you, and then refer to the list periodically.

👆 ***Before signing off, summarize the meeting and let everyone know how the meeting record will be distributed.*** Build time into the agenda for a good summary of the meeting, including the actions and decisions agreed on and the next steps of the overall process. Appropriate closure is particularly important in distance communication. Before ending the session, check out your summary with each site and invite participants to clarify its contents and to add anything you may have missed. Give each site the opportunity to say good-bye and sign off. Let everyone know how, and when, the meeting record will be distributed. If the record is being faxed immediately, ask that someone at each site remain there to receive the fax.

REFERENCES

Burleson, Clyde W. (1990). *Effective meetings: The complete guide.* New York: John Wiley & Sons, Inc.

Diamond, Lynn. (1996). *Effective videoconferencing: Techniques for better business meetings.* Menlo Park, CA: Crisp Publications Inc. [For more information, call (800) 442-7477.]

FACILITATOR RESOURCES

Technological Tools and Applications

GUIDE V-5

Tips on Facilitating With Groupware

Introduction

There are several types of groupware applications for facilitating meetings. When groupware is used, meetings are most commonly differentiated in the following way:

- **Same time, same place.** Participants are together in one room, using some form of groupware. They all may be connected to a central computer, controlled by the meeting "chauffeur"; or only one person may have a computer and operate the groupware as the others input data non-electronically.

- **Same time, different place.** Participants are at different locations, connected simultaneously by either LAN-based groupware or Internet-based groupware. (This type of meeting includes audio- and videoconferences.)

- **Different time, same place.** Participants work from the same area but input data at different times for the ongoing meeting. (Some companies set up a "team room" where people can come in and input data on computers configured with the groupware.)

- **Different time, different place.** No one is ever with someone else in the same room at the same time. Participants check in to a system whose software allows them to see the most up-to-date entries and respond to, or comment on, the entries. They can then leave the "site." (Examples of technologies used under these circumstances are voice mail, E-mail, and some forms of on-line groupware; this approach is useful for group documentation production and editing.)

Each type of meeting operates quite differently. Yet we can offer some overall tips on effectively using groupware, as well as give you some suggestions for specific types of meetings. Because the "same time, same place" meeting demands the most facilitation expertise, the suggestions below are skewed toward facilitating that type of meeting.

Facilitating Groupware: Tips and Suggestions

☝ *Plan more time to plan.* The groupware does not cut down on the need for planning. In fact, when initially using the tools, you will need more than the usual amount of time for planning, plus time for checking equipment and test runs. The planning time will decrease dramatically as you become increasingly comfortable with the groupware.

Do your planning so that you can focus on one or two key outcomes. Keeping the outcomes simple and clear is particularly important to the success of technology-supported meetings. Make sure you come up with a good, solid, well-thought-out agenda. If you have a poor design for your meeting, you'll find that the electronics will take all the blame for its failure and people will develop a negative attitude about such meetings. Remember, first impressions cut deep. So don't plan on just playing around with technology your first time out. Instead, plan to plan, do the planning, and work the plan. If you plan with more than one person, keep the group small (two or three members) in order to avoid introducing complexities that can muddy the waters.

☝ *Identify ahead of time what you want your final document report to look like.* Look into getting software that will help you set up your final document format before the meeting. One advantage of groupware is that you can produce the meeting record instantly, thus saving you or someone else the bother of producing a record from notes or flip charts; but first you have to know exactly what you want the final product to look like. If you haven't prepared a format, you'll need to spend time after the meeting putzing with the data before producing a clean, accurate record.

You will also want to be clear about the intended use of the document. Is it just to be an "in-progress" task group record, or is it to be presented as an official recommendation for review by higher authorities? The type of the document you want to produce will also influence how you set up the meeting and which software tools you use.

☝ *Clarify facilitation roles.* If more than one facilitator is involved, spend some time upfront getting clear on who will do what. This doesn't necessarily mean that one person operates the software and hardware and another handles face-to-face interactions with the group. These responsibilities can be shared if that works best for you. Just clarify ahead of time how it will work.

Whenever possible, work with people you know and are comfortable working with. Co-facilitation of the technology-assisted "same time, same place" meeting works best when it is a real collaboration. If you are an external facilitator, you will be wise to contract to help select the internal person with whom you work. If you are internal, you will want to team up with someone you are confident you can work well with.

☝ *Allow for resistance.* If you've been working as a facilitator for a while (or just plain working a while), you probably know that people tend to resist change unless they're the ones suggesting it. Thus, expect varying degrees of resistance. There is also a natural temptation to blame anything that doesn't work on the technology, so be ready for that, too. In most cases, you don't have to do anything about the resistance; in fact, it's better if you don't. You can acknowledge frustrations without defending the technology. When people have success using it and they see productivity increase, their resistance will decrease rapidly.

☝ *Follow good process rules.* A meeting is a meeting, even if it's aided by technology. All the rules about good process still stand. What can happen when you first start to use groupware is that you get so preoccupied with making the technology work, you lose your overall focus on enabling the group to succeed in its task. When technology is used well, it seems as if the groupware is running "in the background," not as if there's an elephant in the room you have to work around. Groupware experts with whom we consulted agree that in effective technology-assisted meetings (at least in "same time, same place" meetings), the participants are engaged in the technology a **maximum** of 20% of the total meeting time. So your overall facilitation success is still reliant on the effective use of the traditional tools described in the first four sections of this book.

☝ *Carefully and accurately craft your probe questions.* Most groupware uses some sort of survey format whereby people select responses to multiple-choice questions. The wording of the questions has to be very specific and exceptionally clear, and any choices or "anchors" on which people will vote or respond need to be clearly distinguished. To achieve this level of clarity, you may have to draft and re-draft the questions, asking others to check them for clarity and distinguishability, or reviewing them with a critical eye yourself. It is surprising how many people will construct confusing questions or not follow simple test-construction basics like making sure all the "anchor" items on a Likert-type scale are positive. So if you are having others draft questions, make sure you review them carefully. Trying to clean them up in the middle of a session is messy and frustrating to everyone.

☝ *Attend to the room set-up.* When working with "same place" technologies, be sure to make the physical space conform to the particular technology you're using. If working with a "same place" meeting, you will probably be using a projector, which means lighting is critical. It's ideal if you can leave all the lights on, but most projection systems require some darkness; therefore, you'll have to play around with the lighting, adjusting it so participants can both see the screen and work at their stations. You may need to set up two screens: one for the regular overhead and one for the computer projection device.

When dealing with a situation where each participant will have his or her own computer, make sure the equipment is set up as needed and operating correctly. Keep in mind that flip charts are still useful in most meetings, especially in larger meetings where small groups will be working on consensus regarding the data to input into the groupware system.

The general-meeting set-up standard for facilitators is to arrive 1 hour before the meeting; the standard for electronic meetings is an hour and a half to 2 hours before the meeting. Even better is to set up the room several hours ahead of time, although this may not always be feasible.

When working on "same time, same place" meetings, work with laptop computers whenever you can. Avoid the temptation to meet in the company "computer training room," which is usually quite cramped and not really set up for effective interactive meetings. Even when the computer room is one of the glitzy spacious showroom-type training rooms, the desktop computers may hinder good face-to-face communication. Laptop computers enable you to arrange the space to meet the needs of the group, instead of the group having to "work around" the fixed position desktop computers.

👍 **Test-drive your meeting design.** It is particularly critical to "test-drive" your meeting design. A private practice session is essential to a smoothly running technology-supported meeting. You will want to check out the tools you have set up, such as the survey questions and the associated anchors, to make sure they are sufficiently clear. You will also want to run through the various technology-assisted processes and try out those with which you are least familiar.

👍 **Arrange coaching support for new participants.** When people are unfamiliar with the tools being used, or not very familiar with computers, they will be much more at ease if they can quickly receive individual coaching at their workstations without having to hold up the group with a question. For smaller meetings, the "chauffeur" or "technical facilitator" can probably provide this support if facilitating with someone else. In larger meetings, you may want a separate person available to play the role of "roving coach." For different-place meetings, it is wise to make sure there is one person available in each place who knows the technology and can provide support as needed.

👍 **Force limited responses.** Because groupware enables participants to input a lot of data in a short period of time, it is quite possible, even probable, that you will end up with "garbage in, garbage out" if you don't limit the volume of people's responses. You want to get the participants to "cut to the chase" and input their most critical, significant data. For example, when using the electronic brainstorming feature of the groupware, ask everyone to jot down their ideas for *x* on a notepad or in a separate window on the computer. Then ask them to give you their top two ideas. If you don't get many ideas, or if the ideas aren't rich enough, you can always try again with another limited response. By following the standard of "less is more," you will increase the chances of your group's success by liberating it from having to deal with a lot of extraneous data.

You also want to be very cautious about assigning data gathering between sessions. When people come back to the meeting with a ton of data they have gathered from others, you are in real danger of increasing the chances of "garbage in, garbage out," unless the data collection has been very carefully thought out and organized into a definite format, such as a survey. Generally speaking, it is best to ask participants to enter their own thoughts, opinions, and votes. They can talk to anyone they want in order to arrive at the conclusions, but it's best to set aside the lists of what other people think during the actual session.

👍 **Mix and match tools.** Most groupware comes with several types of tools for brainstorming, survey analysis, voting and prioritizing, document review, commenting on alternatives, and so on. Many of the tools can be used outside face-to-face or "on-line" meeting time. For instance, a survey might be constructed and sent out to participants before the meeting. The responses are then analyzed and presented at the time of the face-to-face or on-line meeting. A "same time, same place" meeting might be designed to produce the top three strategic alternatives. Following the meeting, participants further "flesh out" the alternatives, adding data "on-line" from different locations to further define the choices, and comment back and forth on the additions, using groupware tools; then a second "same time, same place" meeting is set up to present the newly expanded alternative descriptions and arrive at consensus on one key strategy.

Another example would be to use on-line Internet groupware to construct and analyze the data base related to the group charge. After the data base is analyzed, the group is brought together for a "same time, same place" meeting to generate alternatives and reach consensus. The alternatives for "mixing and matching" group technologies are nearly endless. Employing several different methods may well contribute to producing breakthrough results.

When you design a "same time, same place" session, make sure that you don't overly rely on the groupware tools to "carry" the meeting. Select good non-electronic processes to provide richness and depth to the meeting design. Using electronic groupware exclusively to facilitate processes can make the sessions seem mechanical and thoughtlessly designed.

Kick off the meeting with an "on-task" enjoyable use of the technology. People attracted to using groupware in meetings are, as a general rule, even less enamored with cutesy "icebreaker" activities than the general management meeting populace. But there are some opening activities you can conduct using groupware that are on task, that teach the use of the groupware, and that are fun enough to loosen up the group and get everything off to a good start.

For instance, if ordering out for lunch, you can set up the luncheon-menu items for electronic voting. Everyone inputs what they want to eat for lunch. They can also comment on any of the choices. That way they get to learn the basics, such as how to use the mouse, the send key, and the enter-comments key. Then you can show the results of the voting, and display all the comments, and you have an instant menu selection, illustrating the economies and enriched information that can come from the groupware.

For an Internet "different place, same time" meeting, you could ask everyone to describe the high point and low point of your last session and one key thing that would make this session successful. Display all the data and have people vote on the single most important key for success today; then display the voting results. Again, everyone gets to learn the basics while making a simple yet productive contribution to the meeting. Or you might have everyone input a "psychic prediction" of an event that will occur within the next year. The prediction could be about anything in general (Liz Taylor will publish a book called *Making Marriage Work*, and it will be a bestseller) or something related to your work ("We'll merge with *x* company, and the corporate headquarters will be shut down"). Everybody votes on their favorite—or the one they most believe will come true, or the one that's most clever—then you display the results.

However you decide to start the meeting, have people get right into using the groupware tools. People new to the groupware will get irritated and frustrated staring at the "toolbox" in front of them and not being able to use it right away.

☞ *Close the laptop lids for discussions.* In keeping with good group process standards, you will want to suggest some ground rules for the group session. One good, practical rule for "same time, same place" meetings is that everyone close their laptops during group interactions and discussions that do not require data input. This eliminates annoying visual blocks, keeps people from fooling around with the computer when their attention should be focused on the task at hand, and helps you maintain the equity norm state.

☞ *Don't make a big deal out of the groupware.* You will find that the groupware tools work best if you don't overemphasize their importance or get caught up in magnifying their wondrous attributes. You may remember the heyday of programmed instruction—how it was touted to be the everything tool for training. It came and went in a big splash. Unfortunately, many useful tools fall from favor, and are never allowed to achieve their real potential or lasting utility, in part because they were over-hyped in the first place.

So if you want to keep your costly groupware investment from falling into the "retired flavor-of-the-month" club, be cautious in your promises about groupware and modest in describing its possibilities. It is essentially a computer application. All computers do is count a lot of stuff real fast in a lot of different ways. We know that creative applications of this rather simple concept have forever changed the landscape of the workplace, but when applications take off, they do so because of an increase in productivity, not as a result of marketing. Your taking a low-key approach toward groupware may increase the chances that it will gain real and lasting utility in the organizations with which you work.

☞ *Don't be worried about a lack of keyboarding skills.* Facilitators new to using groupware are typically anxious about participants' keyboarding skills. You will usually find the lack of keyboarding skills in the organization's lower levels (non-clerical line workers) and highest levels (CEOs). There aren't many mid-level employees in today's workplace who don't work on a daily basis with computers. Besides, people who don't have keyboarding skills do fine in the groupware sessions. Most "hunt and peck" and perform splendidly, though some may prefer to team up with a "buddy" who handles keyboard entries for them. And try to follow the guideline that only 20% of any face-to-face meeting should be spent directly using computers and the groupware. It is far more important that you get the right people in the session than it is that they know how to type.

If you have a large number of people who lack keyboarding skills, you will want to consider this when planning the session. For instance, you may want to use the comments feature less. Or if you have access to audience response systems with voting pads, you may want to use these instead of software/hardware that requires the use of individual computers. You can also color-code keys to the entries allowed by the software. Yet another solution is to have one "technographer" who handles data entry for each group of five to nine people.

☝ *Occasionally, simultaneously brainstorm ideas while building the data base.* One creative way to apply groupware is to brainstorm alternatives at the same time you are constructing the group data base. For example, you might have an expert speaker give a presentation on best practices in *x*. During the presentation, you can charge participants to note on computer their comments and brainstormed ideas for applying the practices in their organization. When the speaker has finished, you switch over the screen, take a look at participants' comments, and have the speaker address the comments; then you do the same for the participants' ideas. The group modifies the ideas as needed and votes on alternatives.

Or, when conducting an Internet on-line meeting, you can charge half the group with entering information for group database building and half with interpreting the data and suggesting alternative actions. When these kinds of tactics are well planned and executed, they can produce fast, amazing results.

☝ *Use the groupware to check for levels of agreement and consensus.* You can construct a scale that measures the level of agreement on any given proposal (e.g., a scale from –4 to +4, with –4 equaling "Do this and I'll quit" and +4 equaling "This has my wholehearted support). Participants use electronic voting to anonymously enter their support level for the proposal; then it is determined, by the group and/or meeting leader, whether that level of support is sufficient to adopt the proposal or more work is needed. This method is quicker than others and guarantees the anonymity of the input, yielding a much more reliable gauge of the agreement on a given proposal.

☝ *Keep "different time" or "different place" meetings simple.* We can't stress this point enough. Clarity in the instructions is of paramount important. One purpose for one meeting. The agenda should state precisely what tasks the group will complete; then you must rigorously keep participants on track, ensuring that they maintain focus on those tasks.

☝ *Make sure you all have the proper access tools for on-line meetings.* If your software requires a Java-enabled browser or any other particular features, make sure, before the meeting, that every workstation is equipped with those features.

☝ *Have a "parking-lot" file working all the time.* Create a "parking-lot" file or "bin list" for ideas or issues that come up in the meeting but are not directly relevant to the agenda topic at hand. This is similar to using a flip chart page as a "parking lot," with data more quickly accessible via the groupware. It also allows you to use the "parking-lot" concept when facilitating "different time" or "different place" meetings.

☝ *Adapt for working with large groups.* Groupware can be used nicely in large-group face-to-face meetings provided some key adaptations are made. Small groups, comprising five to nine members, should be seated at tables, each equipped with a flip chart. If your groupware links computers in the same room, set up one computer at each table, making sure all are linked to the technical facilitator's computer. One central facilitator should give the groups an instruction such as "Brainstorm all your ideas for *x*." The groups use their flip charts to work on the problem; then they are instructed to select a limited number of the brainstormed ideas for computer input, and the data are typed in and displayed. Groups perform the next step of working at their tables and determining their small-group choices. These data are entered into the large-group electronic data base. You may want to use small-group facilitators and to assign one person to be responsible for inputting data.

👍 ***Encourage the group to own the process.*** As a facilitator, your goal should always be to have the group take ownership of the process by becoming the master of the groupware tools. Members naturally become excited when they see all their ideas up on the screen. But it's when **they** start moving things around, and making electronic process suggestions, that you see the groupware's real promise put into effect. When they say, "Let's open a new window and put people problems over there," you will feel something that can only be described as magic. People start owning the process as they start using the tools themselves and taking control of the process. Then they take charge of change, and resistance to change virtually evaporates.

ACKNOWLEDGMENTS

We are grateful to Katherine Lamka, co-principal with Enterprise Solutions in Seattle, Washington, for her major contributions to this guide. She kindly shared with us many ideas and practical tips gleaned from her extensive experience facilitating electronic meetings. You can find out more about her company's tool, *Meeting Works for Windows*, and related products and services in Guide V-6: Groupware Resources. For additional tips and techniques, check out the company Website at http://www.entsol.com.

Thanks, too, to Jeff Conklin from Group Decision Support Systems in Washington, D.C. For some excellent and thought-provoking articles on facilitating with groupware, visit the GDSS Website at http://www.gdss.com.

REFERENCES

Johansen, Robert; Sibbet, David; Benson, Suzyn; Martin, Alexia; Mittman, Robert; & Saffo, Paul. (1991). *Leading business teams: How teams can use technology and group process tools to enhance performance* [OD series]. Reading, MA: Addison-Wesley.

Kayser, Thomas, A. (1995). *Mining group gold: How to cash in on the collaborative brain power of a group.* (2nd ed.) El Segundo, CA: Serif Publishing.

GUIDE V-6

Groupware Resources

About This Guide

Groupware products number in the hundreds. Here we present a few alternatives for facilitators to explore. Our selection is based on any of several factors: (a) the product is widely used; (b) we have experience with the product; (c) representatives demonstrated the product at the International Association of Facilitators (IAF); or (d) we found the product through an Internet search.

Many of the descriptions here are taken directly from the suppliers themselves, with some modification to reduce the originals' marketing language. We provide some pricing information* to make the descriptions more complete. Always contact the product supplier for the most current prices before deciding on a purchase.

RESOURCE SELECTIONS

Domino, by Lotus

Lotus Notes is among the most widely used groupware in the business community today. The Notes system is used for communications between computer users, most often users connected by a local area network (LAN).

The **Domino** program is a Web-server technology that allows you to extend the power of the Notes program to anyone with a Web browser. The program allows you to build an interactive Website, which can be used to share information and/or conduct electronic meetings. "Domino.Doc" is part of the Domino family of products by Lotus. It provides a group with a common set of tools to access, manage, and collaborate on a broad range of document types, including text, images, audio, and video files, and other formats. It can also capture the content of other files such as Microsoft Office 97. Essentially, the software facilitates the sharing of information across different computer applications and formats. In one place, you can share content from the Web, Lotus Notes, Word files, and other sources. It enables a group to have a common, collaborative data base.

*Note: Prices quoted in this guide are current at time of printing and are subject to change.

Instant! TEAMROOM™ is a rentable Domino-based application that enables anyone with an Internet-ready PC to set up a secure collaboration site, choose the team members, invite them in, and share ideas and documents. You subscribe to TEAMROOM through selected Internet service providers and use it as long as you need it. To hook up a TEAMROOM meeting, all you need is a PC or Mac with Internet access, a standard Web browser that supports file attachments, and a credit card.

Costs for Lotus Notes will depend on whether you are a current user or not. The Lotus Notes 4.5 Client Full Version is currently list priced from $360 (1-license pack) to $6,940 (20-license pack). Domino 4.5 Full Server versions run from $1,095 (single processor) to $3,395 (multi-processor).

☞ **For more information, contact:**

- For Lotus notes, see Website: **Lotus.com**
- For Domino program, see Website: **Lotus.com/worktheweb**

Meeting Works for Windows, by Enterprise Solutions

Meeting Works for Windows comes in three versions. The original version is a LAN-based system that allows you to conduct an electronic meeting with a group of people who are all working at computers in the same room, with one facilitator, a "chauffeur," who operates the software that leads the participants through the meeting steps. The more recently developed Web version of the software combines the Meeting Works brainstorming and evaluation tools with the global access, cross-platform support of the Internet, enabling meetings to be conducted "anywhere, anytime." A more limited version of the software is contained in the Meeting Kit® version, essentially an "electronic flip chart," which allows the "chauffeur" to utilize the software to enter and manipulate non-electronically received data from meeting participants.

The Meeting Work™ for Windows software supports the electronic facilitation of a face-to-face meeting where all participants are in the same room and seated at linked computers. It is a "same time, same place" type of electronic meeting. Using the "ScriptWriter" in the Meeting Works software, the "chauffeur," working with the client group or group leader, inputs the meeting goals, what to discuss, when to vote, and the decisions to be made. This becomes the meeting's "script," which can be followed in the order it was prepared, or varied as needed. The "chauffeur," following the script, drives the main PC, which is connected to a computer projector or LCD panel and overhead projector. Participants each have access to a computer station, where they can anonymously enter their ideas, votes, comments, and other input. The participant data is collected and displayed at the chauffeur screen, allowing the group to view the data along with other information, such as the level of agreement among the group. The software enables participants to gather data, brainstorm ideas, organize the ideas, prioritize/evaluate the ideas, and vote. Advanced tools show the group the cross-impact of one given action on all other items on the agenda and enable the group to assign different weights to decision criteria. Graphic tools display bar graphs and other representations of data generated. The software can also be used to produce printed reports instantly.

The Meeting Kit for Windows is the basic software package for Meeting Works for Windows, but without support for participants to enter data electronically at computer stations.

Meeting Works InternetEdition allows meeting participants to access a Meeting Works meeting over the global Internet or an organizational Intranet. It is an add-on addition to Meeting Works for Windows and is purchased separately. The Internet Edition of Meeting Works allows participants to use the "Evaluate," "Generate," and "Cross-Impact" tools over the Internet.

The Meeting Works™ InternetEdition™ is a "different place" meeting technology. In a "different place" meeting, the facilitator prepares the meeting in advance and "posts" the meeting to a home page on the Web server. The facilitator then notifies the participants that they can access the meeting. Over a specified period of time (usually several days), the participants can access the meeting at any time, and from any place, and enter their ideas, votes, and other data. At the end of the time period, the facilitator collects the meeting results and prepares the final report.

You can download Meeting Works for Windows™ for a free trial that allows you to use it with up to eight participants. The upgrade to use the product with up to 15 participants is $5,000; each additional 10 participants is $4,000. Current single-user price for Meeting Kit® is $495 plus shipping, including a hard-copy user manual. For the Meeting Works™ InternetEdition™, the initial license fee is $1,000, with additional seat licenses priced the same as Meeting Works™ for Windows.* Training is also available.

> ☞ **For more information, contact:**
>
> Enterprise Solutions, Inc.
> 601 Union Street, Suite 3232
> Seattle, Washington 98101
>
> Phone: (206) 467-1234
> Website: http://www.entol.com

*Prices quoted were current in July 1997, and are subject to change, as are all other prices quoted in this section.

Facilitate.com, by McCall, Szerdy & Associates

This small California-based firm first developed a proprietary client/server-based system and have now switched to providing a fully enabled Web-based application. **Facilitate.com Version 4.01** provides a virtual meeting area over the Internet. It allows you to set up and maintain multiple-structured, focused on-line discussions and meetings. Discussions can be conducted in "real-time" or be ongoing. Group leaders set up meeting agendas that include a series of topics or problem statements. Access can be restricted to team members, a department, or an organization, or the topic can be made available to anyone with Internet access. Participants log into the electronic meeting room to discuss the topics, generate ideas, and prioritize solutions. While adding their own ideas, participants view and respond to contributions from the whole group, creating a dynamic interchange of information and perspectives.

A review in the October 1994 issue of *Meeting Manager* magazine summarizes the capabilities of the system:

> In all, C.A.Facilitator* includes many features, such as flexible agenda preparation; group brainstorming and idea generation; idea organization and categorization; voting and decision-making tools; action plans, responsibility charts, and Gantt charts; process mapping and multimedia graphics; embedded spreadsheet, drawing, and word processing applications; presentation quality documentation; and a relational database for analysis across teams and meetings. (p. 2)

The basic license is priced at $5,995. The license includes access for an unlimited amount of users, 90 days of technical phone support, and 180 days of E-mail support. Training is also available.

☞ **For more information, contact:**

McCall, Szerdy & Associates, Inc.

Phone: (805) 682-6939
Website: http://www.facilitate.com

GroupSystem® for Windows Professional Suite, by Ventana Corporation

The Ventana Corporation is a major pioneer in the groupware business. The **GroupSystem Standard Tools** groupware includes a well-tested mix of five tools that support the planning, problem-solving, and decision-making needs of most groups. The *Categorizer* helps the group generate a list of ideas and supporting comments. Then the ideas and comments can be sorted into categories that you create. *Electronic*

---

*This was apparently an earlier name for facilitate.com.

Brainstorming supports idea creation, and *Group Outliner* allows the group to create and comment on a multi-level list of topics. The *Topic Commenter* allows participants to generate ideas in a way that is more structured than open brainstorming but less structured than the Group Outliner. *Vote* provides a variety of ways to evaluate a list of ideas, displaying the results in statistical and graph formats that helps groups to reach consensus and make decisions.

Ventana also offers other products that can boost the power of the GroupSystems Standard Tools. They have "Survey," "Alternative Analysis," and "Activity Modeler," an aid to process reengineering. A remote accessing system is available that enables participation from a distance through the use of a Web browser. The "GS Remote" works with the Categorizer, Topic Commenter, Vote, Alternative Analysis, and Survey. The GroupSystem product is a mature product that is now being used by an increasingly sophisticated group of mostly internal facilitators. User groups have formed, and the growing network provides peer learning and coaching possibilities that are probably not as well developed in "younger" products. The cost of the product deters many external facilitators from using it.

A 10-user license for the Ventana "Professional Suite," which includes all the group system tools (Electronic Brainstorming, Categorizer, Vote, Topic Commenter, Group Outliner, Alternative Analysis, and Survey), is $17,950. Each additional user is $895. The price includes two training seats for a two-day training. Additional training seats can be purchased at $650 each. Initial price includes one year of maintenance and support (all software updates, a toll-free hot-line number for technical and facilitation support with unlimited incidents, WorldNet electronic bulletin board service, and quarterly newsletters). After one year, annual maintenance price is $3,000. Discounts are available for government and educational organizations.

☞ **For more information, contact:**

Ventana Corporation
1430 East Fort Lowell Rd., Suite 301
Tucson, Arizona 85719

Phone: (800) 368-6338; (520) 325-8228
Website: http://www.ventana.com

QuestMap, by Group Decision Support Systems

QuestMap for Windows is one of the more unique groupware products available to facilitators. The best news is that the product is designed to deal with the many complexities of problem solving that go considerably beyond the electronic brainstorming and simple data-analysis/voting features of most electronic meeting groupware. The bad news is that it takes time and training to be able to use its enhanced capacity correctly.

That's not necessarily bad news if you can make the investment necessary to master the product. QuestMap can take you beyond linear text-limited network conversations and allow you to view the same conversations in a graphical "map" format. It has a colorful interface that presents the data in a "map" form, providing a more comprehensive view of an issue.

The system is designed to be used with "same time, same place" meetings in a meeting room, or "same place, different time" interactions with team members on the desktop. In the "same time, same place" meeting room, one computer is hooked up to the computer display. The facilitator either inputs everything that is said, or works with a person who enters the data as the facilitator concentrates on working with the group. Two skill sets are required for mastery of the system. One is fluency in IBIS, or Issues-Based Information System, a problem-solving model constructed by Horst Riddle. The system is best used for complex and long-standing problems. The second skill set is fluency in the operation of the QuestMap software.

The system's designers assert that among its key advantages is that it produces an easy-to-understand graphic display of the processes and thinking that go into making up a decision, thereby increasing stakeholder acceptance of solutions because stakeholders can see the reasoning process that led to the recommendation.

A single-user pack, which enables you to use the tool in face-to-face meetings, with one person entering data from group members, sells for $895. A 10-user pack is $3,990, and a 25-user pack is $8,750, with further discounts based on volume. One year of unlimited phone and E-mail support is available for between $134 (single user) to $2,494 (25 users). Training is also available (one-day workshops range from $2,000–$4,000).

☞ **For more information, contact:**

Group Decision Support Systems
1000 Thomas Jefferson St., Suite 100
Washington, DC 20007

Phone: (202) 338-2525
Website: **http://www.gdss.com**

Council™, by CoVision Inc.

Council™ is an electronic meeting system that is run on networked PowerBook™ laptop (Apple) computers (any Macintosh computer can also be used). It can be used in small or large groups, from 10 to over 200 participants. The program operates via several different kinds of "moves," which are screen configurations that the Council Guide (facilitator) builds to send around the network to each person's computer. The moves include "IdeaList," a basic brainstorming window; "CommentSet," which allows participants to type in comments related to a specific topic within a list; "CheckVote," a voting system that enables participants to "check" preferred items, which are then re-ordered by the "groupMind," beginning with those items receiving the most checks; "TopRank," which allows you to drag items from the list and rank them relative to one another; and "TheNines," which gives each item on a list a score of between 1 and

9 points. In the groupMind, you can then view the average score for each item, plus a histogram of the distribution scores.

Any participant can create an action item at any time, defining the who, what, why, and when of the action. The groupMind then arranges all suggested actions through a menu arranged by names, steps, objectives, and due dates. Remarks can be entered by any participant at any time and reserved for later discussion.

Guide-Drive utilities available include "Context," which enters the meeting's objectives or agenda; "Powwow," an "electronic flip chart" for real-time recording of a group's discussion; and "Time Manager," enabling users to select a countdown clock for timing the group's activities.

This is an electronic meeting planning and facilitation service only. No software is sold. Charges for Agenda Planning and on-site Council management are $1,500 per day. PowerBooks can be provided for a rental charge that varies from $50 per PowerBook per day to $100, depending on the number of days the computers are used.

> ☞ **For more information, contact:**
>
> CoVision Inc.
> 832 Folsom St., Suite 810
> San Francisco, California 94107
>
> Phone: (415) 563-2020
> Website: http://www.covision.com

Caucas™ 3.1, by Screen Porch LLC

This is an Internet-based electronic conferencing system that can be installed on any UNIX-based Web server and used by anyone with any standards-based browser such as Netscape Navigator or Internet Explorer (copyrights of Netscape and Microsoft, respectively).

The postings in a **Caucas** conference are called "discussion items" or "discussion topics." Comments made about discussion items are called "responses." Caucas keeps track of which items and responses have been seen by each individual; when someone asks to see the "new" items and responses, they are displayed in the sequence in which they were entered. Participants therefore feel they are taking part in multiple conversations, even though these conversations are happening in virtual time and space, not "real-time" and space.

A Caucas™ 3.1 license includes the Caucas server, the Caucas Markup Language, and templates for a complete Caucas conference center. Licenses start at $2,995. Special pricing is available for educational institutions.

> ☞ For more information, contact:
>
> Screen Porch LLC
>
> Phone: (703) 243-6622
>
> Website: http://www.tmn.com

SolvingRight™, by Xerox

SolvingRight™ is based on a proven six-step process that gives users a "road map" for addressing critical business problems. The product is software designed for "same time, same place" meetings and is used by one person at one computer station. It does not have interactive features that enable participants to input data via their own keyboard. It represents an affordable alternative for getting started with electronic meetings. With this software, teams focus on a critical business issue and then use consensus and facts to create a measurable problem statement. It helps teams resist the temptation of jumping to popular (and often faulty) solutions by facilitating in-depth analysis to identify root causes of issues. With SolvingRight™ teams generate effective solutions, document their progress, and complete the implementation of the solution. Includes "MeetingRight" application formerly sold as a separate product.

> ☞ For more information, contact:
>
> Xerox Quality Services
>
> Phone: (800) 438-5077; (716) 423-1049
>
> Website: http://www.xerox.com

Consensus @nyWARE®, by Soft Bicycle Company

Michael Doyle, the co-author of the classic *How to Make Meetings Work,* is the Chairman of Soft Bicycle, a groupware firm based in Washington, D.C. The **Consensus @nyWARE®** software is an Internet- or Intranet-based product with Java-enabled tools that facilitate information exchange and decision making; these tools enable participants to discuss and vote on ideas without the personal inhibitions that normally arise in face-to-face meetings. The software was designed for Windows NT and can be operated on Windows 95. The company also sells "QuestMap" (see above) and a few other groupware products, and is allied with GDSS (Group Decision Support Systems). A 25-user license is $3,995. Unlimited-user license is $9,500. A "Turnkey" package is available for $18,000; it includes a Pentium 166 computer (with the software running on the Windows NT system), one year of technical support, two days of training, and product upgrades.

☞ **For more information, contact:**

> The Soft Bicycle Company
> 1000 Thomas Jefferson St., NW, Suite 608
> Washington, DC 20007
>
> Phone: (888) 565-BIKE; (202) 342-0532
> Website: **http://www.softbicycle.com**

ACT Canoe™ Team Performance Manager, by American Consulting and Training

ACT Canoe™ Team Performance Manager is an organizational performance feedback system with many features that may make it of interest to practicing facilitators and their work groups.

The ACT Canoe™ Team Performance Manager is proprietary software that has among its features the capacity to support teamwork and streamline the meeting process. It stores information regarding team and organizational performance for individuals, departments, and entire organizations in an easy-to-access format.

The software can be used by managers and facilitators to substantially reduce wasted time in regular meetings, while increasing the speed at which issues are addressed up, down, and across the organization. It can also help to manage the many teams that form, evolve, and end as they meet the organization's need for speed.

The software helps to develop team agendas, decisions, and follow-up assignments. It can keep track of deliverables done or not done by teams or individual contributors.

☞ **For more information, contact:**

> American Consulting and Training
> 655 Redwood Hwy., Suite 395
> Mill Valley, CA 94941
>
> Phone: (415) 388-6651
> Fax: (415) 388-6672

GUIDE V-7

Audience Response System Resources

About This Guide

You will find listed below three suppliers for audience response systems. The product descriptions are adapted from information available on their Websites or based on personal conversations with representatives.

The systems are quite similar in technical capabilities; we suggest you contact company representatives and see which company you prefer to purchase from. Also check with systems users to determine their satisfaction with service and their assessment of the quality of training provided. Always contact a representative to find out the most current prices before deciding on a purchase.

ARS RESOURCES

The Option Finder System, by Option Technologies, Inc.

The **Option Finder System**, like the other resources discussed in this guide, is a combination of software and interactive keypads that are used to facilitate communication in face-to-face meetings. Each participant sits at a computer with his or her own keypad. Questions are posed to group members with a set of response choices, all of which are projected onto a large screen. Participants enter on the keypad the response that best matches their own opinion. The software processes the data and presents it back to the audience in graphic form. Up to 500 people can be accommodated in a session.

For $16,530, you can get the standard system: 20 keypads, the software, a user guide, a transceiver box, and a case for transporting the system. Included in the price is one year of maintenance, software upgrades, and two consecutive days of training for up to five people (you pay travel for trainers to come to you or for your people to go to them). Additional pads are $285 each, with a 5% discount for purchase of more than 50. There is a maintenance fee of $400 per year if you want continued technical support, free software upgrades, and reduced rental prices.

☞ **For more information, contact:**

Option Technologies, Inc.
389 West Second St., Suite B
Ogden, Utah 84404

Phone: (801) 621-2500
Fax: (801) 621-4677
Website: http://www.OptionFinder.com

The Innovator, by Wilson Learning Corporation

The **Innovator** is a group decision support system utilizing group-polling software, audience response keypads, and distinctive group process facilitation to provide immediate and anonymous feedback involving all members of the audience. The Innovator gives participants the ability to see their level of consensus, quickly prioritize issues, and anonymously generate feedback toward proposed options. Ideal group size is recommended at 12 to 18, but the system can accommodate 500. Works in same way as the Option Finder described earlier. First, strategic questions are posed to the group. Next, the participants may engage in a series of group or individual exercises, while the facilitator records the results of these exercises. Finally, the participants anonymously and individually vote on the central factors or issues involved in the session.

Prices vary according to the distributor. We got these prices from Wilson. The license for the software is $8,500, including a technical manual and one day of training (you pay travel). The transceiver, including a case, is $1,500. Keypads are $300 each. For 20 keypads, the transceiver, and the software/license, you will pay $16,000. Wilson offers more in-depth facilitator training for $5,000, including four facilitator manuals. Additional manuals are $295. There is also a yearly renewal fee.

☞ **For more information, contact:**

Wilson Learning Corporation
7500 Flying Cloud Dr.
Eden Prairie, Minnesota 55344

Phone: (800) 328-7937
Direct: (612) 944-2880
Website: http://www.wilsonlearning.com

Meeting CoNexion, by Leadership 2000

Meeting CoNexion is a general-purpose tool for group polling, gathering data, and prioritizing important information for groups. It is designed to facilitate data collection through the computer's keyboard or through the CoNexus® Network® keypads, simultaneously handling up to 127 people. You can use it to construct and analyze responses for simple surveys, to prioritize items, and to construct multiple-choice questions. Profile diagrams can be constructed from any combination of prioritizations and surveys to provide a multi-dimensional view of complex issues and situations. Display options include bar charts (2D or 3D), scatter diagrams, Cartesian plots, pie charts, and more. You can classify participants according to demographic categories to allow for post-session analysis of subgroups.

Both a "wired" and wireless system are offered. In the wired system, you connect all the keypads with wires. Both systems include 20 keypads, the CoNexus meeting software, (Meeting CoNexion), and one other CoNexus software product (Customer CoNexion or Strategist [for group strategic planning, reengineering, re-design, and decision making]). The wired system is $12,500; the wireless system, $17,500. Additional wired keypads are $200; wireless, $285. No charge for continuing usage.

☞ **For more information, contact:**

Leadership 2000, Inc.
3333 N. 44th St.
Phoenix, Arizona 85018

Phone: (602) 852-0223
Fax: (602) 852-0232
Website: **http://www.L2000.com**

GUIDE V-8

Computer Projectors and Facilitation

Introduction

Computer projectors are becoming increasingly prevalent in training and facilitation settings. For those still unfamiliar with the tool, it is a projector that connects to a computer and projects whatever image is in the computer file onto a screen. An LCD (liquid crystal display) panel can also be connected to a computer and perform the same function, though the newer computer projectors provide distinct advantages, such as remote-control devices that allow you to forward slides from anywhere in the room. The technology has been available for several years, but it is just coming into more frequent use as advances are made in the quality of the projectors and prices drop as more companies enter the market. Usage has also increased with the development of presentation software, such as PowerPoint, Corel Presentations, and Harvard Graphics, all of which produce high-quality graphic presentations in color. The projectors pose both interesting possibilities and real dangers to the effective facilitation of groups. This guide is intended to present some of these possibilities and caution against some of the dangers.

When Not to Use the Projector With Groups

The computer projector is still essentially a *training* tool, not a facilitation tool. It is designed to present information and concepts more effectively. In most cases the introduction of the projector changes the group dynamic. The session moves into a "presentation" mode, and the facilitator is no longer a facilitator but a trainer. When information is presented, there is essentially one or more teachers and several learners. The teacher is put in the superior setting, while the learner becomes subservient to the teacher. This is not the group dynamic that best enables groups to solve problems or plan. The dynamic of equity required for effective participatory group work is automatically disturbed with the introduction of the projector. Even when it is used solely as a memory device, the technological expertise is usually placed in the hands of one person, thus modifying the equity norm state.

Also, most presentation software does not allow you to easily move around in a given computer file and re-present an image once you have initially presented it. Your group memory thus becomes restricted to a single visual image, which reduces the information immediately available to all group members.

For these reasons, the facilitator needs to be particularly careful not to become so enamored of the possibilities and attractiveness of the computer projector that the group becomes handicapped rather than enabled by the introduction of technology.

Of course, sometimes when facilitating groups you will find the computer projector not only helpful but even essential. Let's now look at the effective use of the projector as an aid to facilitation.

Using Projectors in Facilitating "Same Time, Same Place" Meetings

Software developers have produced several programs that will enable groups to electronically support the performance of some of the key tasks of the group. Many of these groupware alternatives can be used with groups who are meeting in one place at the same time, as opposed to programs that facilitate data entry and processing between computer users at different times or different places. With "same time, same place" electronically facilitated meetings, the computer projector (or an LCD device with an overhead projector) is used to display the data generated and analyzed by the group.

A key tip is that the projector should be bright enough to allow the group to work comfortably. If the room is not well lighted, it will be more difficult for participants to see their keyboards (if computers are linked together for data entry). Low light also inhibits group interaction and the ability to read or do paper-and-pencil work at workstations. Most manufacturers claim that their projectors can be used in lighted rooms, but few of the ones we have seen actually do provide enough light to allow you to keep all the lights in the room on and still see the screen image clearly. So check out projectors carefully prior to purchase, and test them in the rooms in which you intend to work.

Plan for increased preparation and set-up time when you are facilitating with groupware, a computer, and a computer projector. Make sure that the computer you are using is compatible with the projector. Many projectors are incompatible with certain computers. This problem will probably be remedied as their use becomes more commonplace, but numerous horror stories have been reported to date. The time horizon for room set-up and equipment tryouts needs to be increased. A good practice is to set up the room several hours—or even a day—before the scheduled meeting to give yourself time to deal with any technical roadblocks that you may encounter.

Finally, make sure that you have sufficient technical expertise available so that technological snafus with the hardware or software don't become the focus of your meeting. If you aren't much of a technophile, get a partner to handle operating the software/hardware while you deal with the group. Many people who are fluent in the necessary computer applications still prefer to split responsibilities with a partner who attends solely to the operation of the hardware/software.

Appropriate Uses of the Computer Projector With Groups

There are times when training activities can be combined with group work to enhance the quality of the group's decisions. Here is an example that illustrates how training and facilitation functions can be appropriately mixed. Recently, one of the authors was working with a change design team that was charged with the conduct of an organizational change project that would produce a new organizational design. The team had little experience with large-scale complex change projects. Several different models of approaches to such projects were presented, using presentations software and a computer projector. The group received handout copies of the slides presented. Then the group established its own goals for the change project, generating these on flip charts. Using the goals as criteria, group members then weight the pros and cons of the different models and built their own design for the project.

Sometimes the group falls into a rut and needs to be given new data to come up with fresh solutions and strategies. At this time, high-quality attractive presentations can help to create the data base needed to generate new alternatives. When using presentations with groups, it is important for the facilitator to be aware of the changes in the dynamics that result when information is presented and to be able to "switch" back quickly, from being "the teacher" to being a facilitator, following the presentation of data. Two ways to avoid mixing these roles is to present data in a part of the room separate from the small-group working area and to use a different seating arrangement.

You can also use the computer projector with large groups to present the instructions for small-group work. Many training rooms are now equipped with a large screen that makes information clearly visible from all parts of the room. When facilitating several small groups working independently, the facilitator can project the instructions on the large screen and thus help groups follow specific steps for an exercise.

You can also use the projector to signal passing from one activity to another on the meeting agenda. Slides can be created for announcing each of the agenda items and the steps for the group work. You can also use the projector in combination with the flip charts. A slide can be presented with an instruction for an activity. The data associated with the instruction is then generated on flip charts, achieving resolution and consensus "one step at a time." The slides become a type of pacing device that keeps the group moving in a systematic way toward quality solutions.

GUIDE V-9

Technology Bibliography

Most of the resources listed below were gathered from David Coleman's Website at **http://www.collaborate.com.** Coleman is the author of *Groupware: Technology and Applications*, the most complete and up-to-date discussion of the technological applications available to facilitators that we have seen.

Becker, Franklin, and Fritz Steele, *Workplace by Design: Mapping the High-Performance Workscape,* Jossey-Bass, San Francisco, 1995.

Bock, Geoffrey E., and Dave A. Marca, *Designing Groupware,* McGraw-Hill, New York, 1995.

Bostrom, Robert P., Richard T. Watson, and Susan T. Kinney, *Computer Augmented Teamwork: A Guided Tour,* Van Nostrand Reinhold, New York, 1992.

Coleman, David, *Groupware: Technology and Applications,* Prentice Hall, Englewood Cliffs, New Jersey, 1995.

Davidow, William H., and Michael S. Malone, *The Virtual Corporation: Structuring and Revitalizing the Corporation for the 21st Century,* HarperBusiness, New York, 1992.

Diamond, Lynn, *Effective Videoconferencing,* Crisp Publications, Menlo Park, CA, 1996.

Fraase, Michael, *Groupware for the Macintosh: A Complete Guide to Collaborative Computing,* Business One Irwin, Homewood, IL, 1991.

Galegher, J., R. E. Kraut, and C. Egido, *Intellectual Teamwork: Social and Technological Foundations of Cooperative Work,* Lawrence Earlbaum Associates, 1990.

Goldstein, Jeremy, *Videoconferencing and Money, Money, Money,* Boca Press, Boca Raton, FL, 1995.

Grantham, Charles E., and Larry D. Nichols, *The Digital Workplace: Designing Groupware Platforms,* Van Nostrand Reinhold, New York, 1993.

Grief, Irene, *Computer-Supported Cooperative Work: A Book of Readings,* Morgan Kaufman Publishers, 1988.

Holtzman, Steven R., *Digital Mantras: The Languages of Abstract and Virtual World,* MIT Press, Cambridge, MA, 1994.

Jessup, Leonard M., and Joseph Valacick, *Group Support Systems: New Perspectives,* Macmillan Publishing—now Simon & Schuster, Riverside, NJ, 1993.

Johansen, Robert, *Groupware: Computer Support for Business Teams,* Macmillan Publishing—now Simon & Schuster, Riverside, NJ, 1988.

Johansen, Robert, David Sibbet, Suzyn Benson, Alexia Martin, Robert Mittman, and Paul Saffo, *Leading Business Teams: How Teams Can Use Technology and Group Process Tools to Enhance Performance,* Addison-Wesley, Reading, MA, 1991.

Johansen, Robert, and Rob Swigart, *Upsizing the Individual in the Downsized Organization,* Addison-Wesley, Reading, MA, 1994.

Kaye, Anthony R., *Collaborative Learning Through Computer Conferencing, The Najaden Papers,* Institute of Educational Technology, Open University, UK.

Keen, Peter G. W., *Every Manager's Guide to Information Technology: A Glossary of Key Terms & Concepts for Today's Business Leader,* Harvard Business School Press, Boston, MA, 1995.

Keen, Peter G. W., *Shaping the Future: Business Design Through Information Technology.*

Keen, Peter G. W., and J. Michael Cummins, *Networks in Action: Business Choices and Telecommunications Decisions,* Wadsworth Publishing, Belmont, CA, 1994.

Keen, Peter G. W., and Ellen M. Knapp, *Process Payoffs: Building Value Through Business Process Investment,* Harvard Business School Press, Boston, MA, 1995.

Keen, Peter G. W., and Ellen M. Knapp, *Every Manager's Guide to Business Processes: A Glossary of Key Terms & Concepts for Today's Business Leader,* Harvard Business School Press, Boston, MA, 1996.

Khoshafian, Setrag, and Marek Buckiewicz, *Introduction to Groupware, Workflow, and Workgroup Computing,* John Wiley & Sons, Inc., New York, 1995.

Kostner, Jaclyn, *Knights of the Tele-Round Table,* Warner Books, New York, 1994.

Lloyd, Peter, *Groupware in the 21st Century: Computer Supported Co-operative Working Toward the Millennium,* Adamantine Press Ltd., London, 1994.

Mallach, Efrem G., *Understanding Decision Support Systems and Expert Systems,* Dow/Irwin, Houston, TX, 1993.

Marca, David, and Geoffrey Bock, *Groupware: Software for Computer Supported Cooperative Work,* IEEE Computer Press, 1992.

Morton, Michael S. Scott, *The Corporation of the 1990s: Information Technology and Organizational Transformation,* Oxford University Press, Oxford, England, 1991.

Olson, G. M., J. S. Olson, L. A. Mack, P. Cornell, and R. Luchetti, *Computer Augmented Teamwork Flexible Facilities for Electronic Meetings,* Van Nostrand Reinhold, New York, 1993.

Olson, M. H., *Technological Support for Work Group Collaboration,* Lawrence Earlbaum and Associates, 1989.

Opper, Susanna, and Henry Fersko-Weiss, *Technology for Teams: Enhancing Productivity in Networked Organizations,* Van Nostrand Reinhold, New York, 1992.

Penzias, Arno, *Harmony: Business, Technology & Life After Paperwork,* HarperBusiness, New York, 1995.

Sakiaya, Taichi, *The Knowledge Value Revolution, or A History of the Future,* Kodansha International, New York, 1991.

Schrage, Michael, *Shared Minds: The New Technologies of Collaboration,* Random House, New York, 1990.

Schrage, Michael, *No More Teams! Mastering the Dynamics of Creative Collaboration.* Doubleday, New York, 1995.

Semler, Ricardo, *Maverick: The Success Story Behind the World's Most Unusual Workplace,* Warner Books, New York, 1993.

Sproull, Lee, and Sara Kiesler, *Connections: New Ways of Working in the Networked Organization,* MIT Press, Cambridge, MA, 1991.

Tapscott, Don, and Art Caston, *Paradigm Shift: The New Promise of Information Technology,* McGraw-Hill, New York, 1993.

Weatherall, Alan, and Jay Nunamaker, *Introduction to Electronic Meetings,* Electronic Meetings Services Ltd., Hampshire, England, 1995.

White, Thomas, and Layna Fischer, *The Workflow Paradigm: The Impact of Information Technology on Business Process Re-Engineering,* Future Strategies, Inc., 1994.

Wilson, Paul, *Computer Supported Cooperative Work,* Intellect Books, 1991.

Product Catalogues

Coleman, David, *The Groupware Product and Services Catalog, Collaborative Strategies and Creative Networks,* Published annually, San Francisco, CA, 1994.

Lotus Development Corporation. *The Lotus Notes Guide,* Affinity Publishing Co., Seattle, WA, 1994.

Technical/Trade Publications

Business Communications Review, http://www.bcr.com

Byte, http://www.byte.com

Communications of the ACM, http://www.acm.org/

CommunicationsWeek, http://techweb.cmp.com/techweb/default.html

Computer: Innovative Technology for Computer Professionals, http://www.computer.org

ComputerWorld, (800) 669-1002, http://www.computerworld.com

Connections: Journal of Macintosh Connectivity, http://www.informactivity.com

Datamation, http://www.datamation.com

DBMS Client-Server Computing, (800) 334-8152

Enterprise Reengineering, http://www.reengineering.com

Fast Company, loop~fastcompany.com

Forbes, (800) 888-9896

Fortune, Fortune~cis.compuserve.com

Harvard Business Review, (800) 274-3214

Info World, http://www.infoworld.com

InformationWeek, http://techweb.cmp.com/techweb/default.html

Inform, http://www.aiim.org

Internet World, http://www.internetworld.com

Knowledge Inc.: The Executive Report on Knowledge, Technology & Performance,
    http://www.webcom.com/quantera/welcome.html

MacWeek, http://www.zdnet.com/~macweek/

Network World, (508) 875-6400

Open Computing, http://www.wcmh.com/oc/index.html

PC Computing, http://www.zdnet.com/~pccomp

PC Magazine, http://www.pcmag.com

PC Week, http://www.pcweek.com

PC World, http://www.pcworld.com

Scientific American, info~sciam.com

Software Magazine, softwaremagazine~mcimail.com

Upside, http://www.upside.com

Virtual Workgroups, http://www.bcr.com

Wired, http://www.hotwired.com

World-Wide Web Week, http://www.webweek.com

GUIDE V-10

Knowing the Lingo—A Glossary

As facilitators, we know that one of the most powerful means of bringing a group together is to make sure everyone speaks the same language. This guide will help you do just that.

We found the following definitions at the Lotus Notes Website (**http://www.lotus.com**). They provide a useful glossary of the basic technological terms.

ADN (advanced digital network)—Usually refers to a 56-Kbps (kilobytes per second) leased line.

ANS—The American National Standards Institute disseminates basic standards like ASCII and acts as the United States' delegate to the ISO (International Standards Organization).

ASCII (American Standard Character for Information Interchange)—A standard code, consisting of 128 seven-bit combinations (0000000 through 1111111) for characters stored in a computer or to be transmitted between computers. This is the de facto worldwide standard for the code numbers used by computers to represent all the upper- and lower-case letters, numbers, punctuation, and so forth.

Bandwidth—The capacity of a medium to transmit a signal. Usually measured in bits per second. More informally, the mythical "size" of the Net, relating to its ability to carry the files and messages between sites. Some view certain kinds of traffic (FTPing hundreds of graphics images, for example) as a waste of bandwidth and look down upon them. The higher the bandwidth, the more data can pass through.

Bit—The smallest unit of data processing information. A bit (or binary digit) assumes a value of either 1 or 0. There are eight bits per character.

Chat or chat session—A live on-line conference or meeting. People participating in the chat type in comments that others in the chat "room" can see on their computers. Some of these meetings are structured by topic and are led by hosts/monitors while others are informal by-chance meetings.

Chat room—A place in the on-line service where people may go to talk with others who are also in the room.

Cyberspace—A term coined by William Gibson in his fantasy novel *Neuromancer* to describe the "world" of computers, and the society that gathers around them. Currently used to describe the whole range of information resources available through computer networks.

DNS (Domain Name Server)—The method used to convert Internet names to their corresponding Internet numbers.

Domain—A part of the naming hierarchy. Syntactically, a domain name consists of a sequence of names or other words separated by dots.

Domain name—The unique name that identifies an Internet site. Domain names always have two or more parts, separated by dots (.). The part on the left is the most specific, and the part on the right is most general. For example: col.k12.me.us

Download—To transfer, from somewhere else on the network, a file or document to your computer. When you download a file, you are making a copy of it and loading that copy onto your computer's hard drive. (In some cases when using the Internet, you need to save the file/document onto the server through which you are connected to the Internet and then transfer it to your computer later.)

Electronic mail—A method of sending messages, files, and multi-media electronically from one computer to another. Using the Internet as a gateway, you can send E-mail from anywhere to the political science department at the University of Iowa, researcher at Stanford University, America Online, Genie, Prodigy, CompuServe, and a host of other on-line services or Internet sites.

E-mail—The vernacular abbreviation for electronic mail.

Gateway—An entrance/exit from one computer system/network to another. For example, most BBSs and commercial on-line services provide a gateway to the Internet, allowing users to send and receive information through the Internet from the BBS or service. Also a special-purpose-dedicated computer that attaches to two or more networks and routes packets from one network to the other. In particular, an Internet gateway routes IP (Internet Protocol) datagrams among the network it connects. Gateways route packets to other gateways until they can be delivered to the final destination directly across the physical network.

Gopher—Gopher is an Internet tool which uses a menu system to enable you to browse Internet resources. Typically, you can navigate the Internet using Gopher by selecting the desired item from a series of lists. You can then continue in a series of lists until you locate the information you are seeking.

Home page—The primary document for a World Wide Web site. Many contain links to other documents within that site as well as elsewhere.

HTML (hypertext markup language)—The coding language used to create hypertext documents for use on the World Wide Web. HTML files are meant to be viewed using a WWW program such as Netscape.

http (hypertext transport protocol)—Makes hypertextual browsing through the World Wide Web possible. The user clicks on links that are established in a Web document and moves to that document, even though it may be located on a different computer.

Hypertext—Data which provides links between key elements, allowing users to move through information non-sequentially.

Interface—The software go-between that makes computing easy to use. An interface can have type commands, a choice of numbers or letters from a menu, or icons to click on.

Internet—A giant network composed of numerous other networks. Started by the U.S. government for defense purposes and now used by businesses, universities, K–12 schools, and individuals. The concatenation of many individual TCP/IP campus, state, regional, and national networks (such as NSFnet, ARPAnet, and Milnet) into one single logical network all sharing a common addressing scheme.

Internet provider—A business or organization that provides users with access to the Internet through its connections.

Kilobyte—A thousand bytes. Actually, usually 1024 bytes.

Local area network (LAN)—Any physical network technology that operates at a high speed over short distances (up to a few thousand meters).

Logon—To connect with an on-line service or network.

Megabyte (MB)—A million bytes. A thousand kilobytes.

Mosaic—Software that provides a graphical browser interface to the Internet, similar to Macintosh or Windows interfaces. Other browsers include Netscape Navigator and Microsoft Explorer.

Network—A group of computers connected together so they can transmit information to one another.

On-line—Connected to a telecommunications service or network. While on-line you can send messages, read and receive mail, find information, download information, and so forth.

Off-line—Not connected to a telecommunications service or network. You can compose messages and prepare files to send while off-line and then go on-line and send your work.

Operating system—The underlying software that manages the internal functions of the computer. DOS is the Disk Operating System on which IBM computers run, System 8.0 is the current Macintosh operating system. Other examples are OS/2 and UNIX.

POP—Two commonly used meanings: "Point of Presence" and "Post Office Protocol." A point of presence usually means a city or location where a network can be connected to, often with dialup phone lines, so if an Internet provider says they will soon have a POP in Bath, it means that they will soon have a local phone number in Bath and/or a place where leased lines can connect to their network. The second meaning of POP refers to the way E-mail software gets mail from a mail server. When you obtain a SLIP, PPP, or shell account you almost always get a POP account with it, and it is this POP account that you tell your E-mail software to use to get your mail.

RAM (random access memory)—Refers to the amount of memory a computer has installed. Usually measured in megabytes, for example, 8 MB of RAM.

RFD (request for discussion)—Usually a two- to three-week period in which the particulars of newsgroup creation are battled out.

Route—The path that network traffic takes from its source to its destination.

Router—A dedicated computer (or other hardware device) that sends packets from one place to another, paying attention to the current state of the network and the destination address on the packet.

Server—A computer that shares its resources, such as printers and files, with other computers on the network. An example of this is NFS server, which shares its disk space with other computers.

Telnet—Telnet is an Internet tool that allows you to log onto remote computers, access public files and databases, and even run applications on the remote host. Allows users to log onto distant computers without long-distance charges and interact with a remote timesharing system at another site as if the user's terminal were connected directly to the remote computer.

UNIX—A multi-tasking, multi-user computer operating system developed by AT&T with built in TCP/IP. It is the most common operating system for servers on the Internet.

URL (uniform resource locator)—The standard way to give the address of any resource on the Internet that is part of the World Wide Web. A URL looks like this: http://www.enc.org. The most common way to use a URL is to enter it into a WWW browser program, such as Netscape or Lynx.

WAN (wide area network)—A network spanning hundreds or thousands of miles. The Internet is the "ultimate" WAN.

World Wide Web (WWW)—While Gopher is a menu-based approach to browsing the Internet, the World Wide Web offers an innovative alternative. WWW is an Internet tool that makes traveling through and finding resources on the Internet easier with its use of sound and graphics and its ability to link to other WWW files and sites. WWW enables you to browse the Internet by using a hypertext series of links (like a Windows Help file). When you a select a hypertext link, you activate a program running in the background, which may move you to another place within the same location or to another computer thousands of miles away to browse that information.